The Path to Genocide in Rwanda

Rwanda's genocide in 1994 was a tragic and world-changing event that has indelibly etched itself on the global conscience. *The Path to Genocide in Rwanda* combines extensive, original field data with some of the best existing evidence to offer a rigorous and comprehensive explanation of how and why the genocide occurred, and how and why so many Rwandans participated in it.

Drawing on interviews with over three hundred Rwandans, Omar Shahabudin McDoom systematically compares those who participated in the violence against those who did not. He contrasts communities that experienced violence early with communities where violence began late, as well as communities where violence was limited with communities where it was massive. His findings offer new perspectives on some of the most troubling questions concerning the genocide, while also providing a broader engagement with key theoretical debates in the study of genocides and ethnic conflict.

OMAR SHAHABUDIN MCDOOM is Assistant Professor of Comparative Politics in the Department of Government at the London School of Economics. A political scientist and lawyer by training, he has been researching Rwanda's genocide since he first visited the country in 2003. He has previously held research fellowships at Harvard University and Oxford University and, prior to academia, he worked as a Policy Officer for the World Bank, where his interest in the genocide originated.

African Studies Series

The African Studies series, founded in 1968, is a prestigious series of monographs, general surveys, and textbooks on Africa covering history, political science, anthropology, economics, and ecological and environmental issues. The series seeks to publish work by senior scholars as well as the best new research.

Editorial Board:
David Anderson, *The University of Warwick*
Catherine Boone, *The London School of Economics and Political Science*
Carolyn Brown, *Rutgers University, New Jersey*
Christopher Clapham, *University of Cambridge*
Michael Gomez, *New York University*
Richard Roberts, *Stanford University, California*
David Robinson, *Michigan State University*
Leonardo A. Villalón, *University of Florida*

Other titles in the series are listed at the back of the book.

The Path to Genocide in Rwanda

Security, Opportunity, and Authority in an Ethnocratic State

OMAR SHAHABUDIN MCDOOM
London School of Economics, University of London

CAMBRIDGE
UNIVERSITY PRESS

University Printing House, Cambridge CB2 8BS, United Kingdom

One Liberty Plaza, 20th Floor, New York, NY 10006, USA

477 Williamstown Road, Port Melbourne, VIC 3207, Australia

314–321, 3rd Floor, Plot 3, Splendor Forum, Jasola District Centre, New Delhi – 110025, India

79 Anson Road, #06–04/06, Singapore 079906

Cambridge University Press is part of the University of Cambridge.

It furthers the University's mission by disseminating knowledge in the pursuit of education, learning, and research at the highest international levels of excellence.

www.cambridge.org
Information on this title: www.cambridge.org/9781108491464
DOI: 10.1017/9781108868839

© Omar Shahabudin McDoom 2021

This publication is in copyright. Subject to statutory exception and to the provisions of relevant collective licensing agreements, no reproduction of any part may take place without the written permission of Cambridge University Press.

First published 2021

A catalogue record for this publication is available from the British Library.

Library of Congress Cataloging-in-Publication Data
Names: McDoom, Omar Shahabudin, 1973– author.
Title: The path to genocide in Rwanda : security, opportunity, and authority in an ethnocratic state / Omar Shahabudin McDoom, London School of Economics.
Other titles: Security, opportunity, and authority in an ethnocratic state
Description: New York : Cambridge University Press, [2020] | Series: African studies series | Includes bibliographical references and index.
Identifiers: LCCN 2020022153 (print) | LCCN 2020022154 (ebook) | ISBN 9781108491464 (hardback) | ISBN 9781108798327 (paperback) | ISBN 9781108868839 (ebook)
Subjects: LCSH: Genocide–Rwanda. | Rwanda–Ethnic relations. | Hutu (African people)–Rwanda–Politics and government. | Tutsi (African people)–Crimes against–Rwanda.
Classification: LCC DT450.435 .M383 2020 (print) | LCC DT450.435 (ebook) | DDC 967.57104/31–dc23
LC record available at https://lccn.loc.gov/2020022153
LC ebook record available at https://lccn.loc.gov/2020022154

ISBN 978-1-108-49146-4 Hardback

Cambridge University Press has no responsibility for the persistence or accuracy of URLs for external or third-party internet websites referred to in this publication and does not guarantee that any content on such websites is, or will remain, accurate or appropriate.

Contents

List of Figures	page x
List of Tables	xi
Acknowledgements	xiv
List of Abbreviations	xvii

1 What We Do and Do Not Know   1
   A Synopsis of the Genocide   3
   What Is Distinctive and Puzzling about Rwanda   5
   What We Know Already   6
   Why Consensus on the Genocide Is Limited   8
   The Questions That Remain   12
   Theories and Hypotheses   13
      Wars, Insecurity, Threats and Fear-Based Explanations   14
      Demographic and Environmental Explanations   16
      Deprivation-Related Explanations   17
      Identity/Ethnicity and Racism/Prejudice-Based Explanations   18
      Ideologies, Myths, and Narratives   20
      Political and Material Opportunism   21
      Group Behaviour and Collective Action   22
      The State, Elite, and Obedience-Related Explanations   23
      Dispositional and Situational Explanations   25
      Bystander, Inaction, and Impunity Effects   26
      External and International Factors   27
   The Argument Sketched   28
   Research Design: The Evidence and Methods   35
      The Research Design   36
      The Evidence   37
      A Critical Note on the Methods Used in the Project   40
   Organization of the Book   43

2 An Extraordinary Baseline   45
   Tracing Rwanda's Historical Evolution   46
      Precolonial History (c. Fourteenth–Seventeenth Century to 1897)   46

v

	The Colonial Epoch (1897–1962)	53
	Rwanda's Revolution and the Postcolonial Era (1959–1990)	56
	Rwanda's Unusual Society, Demography, and Geography	61
	A Highly Agrarian Society	63
	Exceptional Population Density	64
	Ethnic Bipolarity	65
	Cultural Homogeneity	66
	Ethnic Dominance	67
	Small Territory, Road Network, and Centralized Capital	68
	Ethnic Settlement	69
	Rwanda's Ecological Homogeneity	70
3	**Security: War-Time Threat**	73
	Introduction	73
	Synopsis of Rwanda's Civil War	75
	The Links between War and Genocide	79
	The Media and Civilian Radicalization	84
	Establishing the Baseline: Life before the War	92
	The Psychological Impact of War	93
	Radicalization Mechanism I: Ethnicization	95
	Radicalization Mechanism II: Outgroup Homogenization	104
	Radicalization Mechanism III: Ingroup Loyalty	106
	Radicalization Mechanism IV: Violence Legitimization	111
	Rwanda's Extraordinary Amplifiers	114
	Limitations of War as an Explanation of Genocide	116
	Rethinking Radicalization and the Radio	117
	Radicalization as Consequence and Cause of Violence	118
	Rwanda's Hate Radio's Limited Impact	120
4	**Threat and Opportunity: The Dangers of Freedom**	123
	Introduction	123
	The Context for Liberalization	125
	Rwanda's Unusual Baseline Characteristics	126
	The Impact of Liberalization on Rwanda	127
	Liberalization at the National Level	127
	Liberalization at the Local Level	134
	Southern Rwanda: War Distant, Party Politics Intense	134
	Mwendo Cell, Maraba Commune, Butare Prefecture	134
	Tamba Cell, Shyanda Commune, Butare Prefecture	137
	Northern Rwanda: War Close, Party Politics Weak	138
	Mutovu Cell, Nkuli Commune, Ruhengeri Prefecture	138
	Ruginga Cell, Kinigi Commune, Ruhengeri Prefecture	140

	The Mechanisms of Liberalization	141
	Political Pluralization	145
	Against Ideological Singularity	146
	Ideological Pluralism in Rwanda	147
	Kayibanda's Ideology	147
	Habyarimana's Ideology	150
	The Catholic Church's Ideology	152
	The Primacy of Moderation	155
	Ideological Beliefs 'From Below'	157
	Political Competition	162
	Theorizing Contestation	162
	Moderate-Extremist Contestation in Rwanda	165
	Escalation and De-escalation in Rwanda	167
	Inter-group contestation	169
	Inter- to Intra-group contestation	171
	Intra to Inter-group contestation	171
	Explaining Escalation: Weak Constraints and High Impunity	172
	Political Participation	173
5	**Opportunity II: Death of the Nation's Father**	178
	Introduction	178
	The Window of Opportunity	184
	Macro-level Analysis	184
	Within-Group Contestation	184
	Between-Group Contestation	191
	Dynamics at the International Level	193
	Anti-Tutsi Violence	194
	What Was Known Outside Rwanda?	196
	Could the International Community Have Done Anything?	198
	Who Killed Habyarimana?	201
	Meso-level Analysis	205
	Early Violence Onset: Mukingo Commune	205
	Late Violence Onset: Taba Commune	207
	Explaining Variation in Violence Onset	209
	Micro-level Analysis	215
	Mwendo Cell: Low Violence	215
	Tamba Cell: High Violence	223
	Mutovu Cell: High Violence	227
	Ruginga Cell: Low Violence	230
	The Micro-mechanics of Mobilization	234
	The Emergence of Ethnic and Political Entrepreneurs	235

Critical Masses: The Importance of Small Groups	240
Harnessing Group Forces: Ingroup Policing and Peer Pressure	241
Mobilization Amplifiers	244

6 Authority: Rwanda's Privatized and Powerful State 248

Introduction	248
Dimension I: Weak State Autonomy	253
Continuity in Clientelist Governance	253
The Party-State	254
The Weakness of Civil Society	255
Dimension II: High State Legitimacy and Symbolic Authority	258
A Post-Revolutionary State	258
Institutional Continuity	262
Boundary Continuity	263
Demographic Particularities	265
Dimension III: High Material Capacities	266
Evidence of the State's Compliance and Coordination Capabilities	267
Amplifier I: Favourable Geography and Demography	272
Amplifier II: Institutional Configuration	275
State Power and Perpetrator Heterogeneity	278

7 Why Some Killed and Others Did Not 281

Introduction	281
Counting the Killers and Victims	284
The Perpetrators	284
Methods and Evidence	285
Findings	286
What the Data Tell Us	288
The Victims	289
Methods and Evidence	291
Findings	293
Establishing the Number of Hutu Victims	295
Comparing Perpetrators and Non-perpetrators Systematically	297
Demographic Profiles	300
Cluster I: Masculinity and Youth-related Theories	302
Cluster II: Deprivation-Related Theories	305
Cluster III: Ethnicity-Related Theories	311
Cluster IV: Threat-Related Theories	316
Cluster V: Influence-related Theories	320
Perpetrator Heterogeneity	322
Motives and Rationales	331
Quantifying the Many Rationales	333

Contents

	Delving Deeper into the Rationales	336
	The 'Opportunity' Rationale	336
	The 'Security' Rationale	338
	The 'Authority' Rationale	339
	Motivations and the Passage of Time	340
	Why Some Killed and Others Not	342
	It's Where You Live	343
	It's Who You Know	349
	Sociological or Ecological? Explaining Extraordinary Mobilization	356
	Modelling Participation	357
8	**Conclusion: Rwanda in Retrospect**	362
	Tracing the Causal Pathway to Genocide	363
	Toward a New Consensus on Rwanda's Genocide	371
	Contributions to Rwanda and Genocides Generally	377
	Broader Implications for Theories of Genocide	384
References		389
Index		407

Figures

3.1	Speed of the violence in Kibuye prefecture	*page* 119
3.2	Comparison of speed of violence against speed of radio radicalization	121
4.1	Pre-genocide timeline of escalatory and de-escalatory events	168
5.1	Genocide timeline of escalatory and de-escalatory events	189
5.2	Burgomasters' party affiliations by commune in April 1994	211
5.3	Onset of genocidal violence by commune	212
5.4	Spatial integration of Hutu and Tutsi by commune	214
6.1	The structure of the party-state	256
7.1	Relationship between numbers of perpetrators and targets	289
7.2	Settlement pattern in Tare sector	345
7.3	Modelling mobilization	358
8.1	Tracing the causal pathway to genocide	364

Tables

2.1	Rwanda's extraordinary baseline characteristics in comparative perspective	page 47
2.2	Linkages to unusual characteristics of the genocide and violence	62
2.3	Numerically dominant ethnic groups in sub-Saharan Africa	67
3.1	Perceptions of war's impact and significance	81
3.2	Fearmongering: misinformation and disinformation during the war	85
3.3	Radio audiences in Rwanda	89
3.4	Collective memory of Hutu-Tutsi relations	94
3.5	Psycho-social mechanisms of civilian radicalization in RTLM radio broadcasts	96
3.6	Perceptions of decline in Hutu-Tutsi relations	99
3.7	Historical narrative of Tutsi privilege and oppression of Hutu	101
3.8	Perceptions of Rwanda's Revolution	103
3.9	Awareness of Burundian president's assassination	103
3.10	Identification of the enemy as the Tutsi	107
3.11	Identification of enemy collaborators	110
3.12	Perceptions of the legitimacy of the violence	115
3.13	Pre-genocide violence in ten northern communities heavily exposed to the war	117
4.1	Impact of multipartyism at local level	143
4.2	Political participation at the local level	144
4.3	Beliefs concerning ethnic consciousness and Tutsi indigeneity and privilege	158
5.1	Assassinations of African (sub-Saharan) heads of state in context	181

5.2	Number of communes that experienced genocidal onset in each time period	210
5.3	Genocide profile of four selected cells	218
5.4	Power of local state authority figures during the genocide	237
5.5	Profiles of 160 grassroots leaders of Rwanda's genocide	238
5.6	Identifying committed killers or 'critical masses'	241
5.7	Importance of ingroup policing and peer pressure during the genocide	242
5.8	Contagion effects of the violence	246
6.1	Dimensions of Rwandan state power across time	252
6.2	Measuring the Rwandan state's social control and mobilizational power	269
6.3	Perceptions of the state's provision of public goods in Rwanda	274
7.1	Perpetrator estimates by category of crime and prefecture	287
7.2	Demographic profiles of killers and non-killers	301
7.3	Occupations of killers and non-killers compared	303
7.4	Age groups of killers and non-killers compared	305
7.5	Deprivation profiles for killers and non-killers	307
7.6	Ethnicity-related indicators for participation in violence	313
7.7	Threat-related indicators for participation in violence	318
7.8	Influence-related indicators for participation in violence	323
7.9	Corroborated 'kill rates' for 69 sampled perpetrators	325
7.10	Dispositional differences among perpetrators	327
7.11	Quantifying rationales for violence (Hutu respondents only)	335
7.12	Most common rationale for violence by type of question asked	336
7.13	Samaritans in Rwanda's genocide	342
7.14	Comparative profile of Tare sector, Rwanda	344

7.15 Neighbourhood as a predictor of participation in
  Rwanda's genocide 346
7.16 Descriptive statistics on social connections of killers
  and non-killers 351
7.17 Social connections as predictors of participation 352

Acknowledgements

At the time that I write, it has been twenty-five years since the genocide and sixteen years since I first arrived in Rwanda and began to ask the questions that would ultimately lead to this book. It has taken me longer than I thought to document my answers to them. And in this time, I have incurred many debts.

I owe intellectual debts to five individuals who have generously provided scholarly advice and guidance over the years that have deeply shaped my thinking and greatly improved the ideas in this book. The time they committed went beyond what professional responsibility and academic collegiality would demand. I thank Stuart Kaufman, David Keen, René Lemarchand, Scott Straus, and Peter Uvin. A number of individuals deserve mention for having taken the time to listen or else to give feedback on my work at various stages in its evolution. Whether they realized the value of their contributions or not, I am grateful to Tim Allen, David Anderson, William Ayers, Marie Besançon, Nikoloas Biziouras, Catherine Boone, Stephanie Brancaforte, Alison Des Forges, Helen Fein, David Gisselquist, André Guichaoua, Lee Ann Fujii, Kelly Greenhill, Thomas Homer-Dixon, Michael Horowitz, Jean-Paul Kimonyo, Victor Levine, Timothy Longman, Neophytos Loizides, Jonathan Monten, Catherine Newbury, Thi Minh Ngo, Roger Petersen, James Putzel, Marie Des Rosières, John Sidel, Sherrill Stroschein, and Lars Waldorf. I would also like to acknowledge the generosity of those who have responded to my many requests for information over the years. In some cases, fulfilling my requests involved quite some effort on their part. I thank Dan Clay, Barbara Harff, Francois Nsanzuwera, Filip Reyntjens, Benjamin Valentino, Philip Verwimp, and Marijke Verpoorten. I would like also to thank the two editors with whom I have worked, Maria Marsh and Daniel Brown, at Cambridge University Press. Research assistants do not always get a mention but Malak Azer, Phoebe Cole, Ella Hutchinson, and Roxana Legezynska each had a genuine intellectual interest in this research and took much of the toil out of writing this book.

In my time spent in Rwanda I racked up further debts. Moses Kayihura was my interpreter, research assistant, and travel companion who lived with me during my first visit to Rwanda. Moses showed patience and determination in what were at times stressful circumstances. Rwanda was a difficult place to do fieldwork, and there were several lonely and demoralizing moments when I doubted my ability to complete this research. I would like to thank a number of individuals who provided practical assistance, advice, or moral support at these times: Spencer Bugingo, Philibert Gakwenzire, Véronique Geoffroy, Petra van Haren, Klaas de Jonge, Charles Kayitana, Jean-Paul Kimonyo, Edison Mpyisi, Elizabeth Muchamba, Déo Musabyimana, Francois Xavier Nduhira, Evariste Ntakirutimana, Godie van de Paal, Déo Rutamu, Emmanuel Shingiro, Anastase Shyaka, Maaike Smit, Marco de Swart, Jean-Marie Vianney, Lars Waldorf, and my teams of research assistants who conducted various surveys and other research tasks.

The Rwandans about whom I have written must also be acknowledged: those who lost their lives, and those who carry with them the physical and emotional scars of what they survived – and of what they did – in 1994. At the end of my fieldwork I knew I would leave Rwanda, along with the many challenges posed by living in a postgenocide society, for the relative ease of life elsewhere. However, most of those who shared with me their stories cannot leave. They gave me the chance to understand and to convey a little of what they lived through in 1994. In the end, I will receive professional recognition as the author of this book. But I do not forget that they continue to live a difficult reality.

I thank my family who have supported me in what must have seemed my quixotic quest for knowledge. I dedicate the book to my father who passed away before he could see it completed. Finally, I would like to thank my wife, Rachel Gisselquist, who in the final, tumultuous mile of writing has done everything from ensuring I ate well to thinking through some of the more complex ideas in the book with me.

My research has been supported through fellowships provided by the Economic and Social Science Research Council in the UK, the

Belfer Center for Science and International Affairs at Harvard's Kennedy School, and the British Academy in conjunction with the Leverhulme Trust. The United Nations University World Institute for Development Economics Research kindly hosted me in Helsinki as I finished the manuscript.

Abbreviations

AFDL	Alliance des Forces Démocratiques pour la Libération du Congo
APROSOMA	Association pour la Promotion Sociale de la Masse
ARD	Alliance pour le Renforcement de la Démocratie
BBTG	Broad-Based Transitional Government
CDR	Coalition pour la Défense de la République
CND	Conseil National Démocratique
DPKO	Department of Peacekeeping Operations
DRC	Democratic Republic of Congo
DMZ	Demilitarized Zone
FAR	Forces Armées Rwandaises
FDC	Forces Démocratiques du Changement
GOR	Government of Rwanda
ICTR	International Criminal Tribunal for Rwanda
IG	Interim Government
MCC	Military Crisis Committee
MDR	Mouvement Démocratique Républicain
MRND(D)	Mouvement Révolutionnaire National pour le Développement (et la Démocratie)
OAU	Organisation of African Unity
ORINFOR	Office Rwandais de l'Information
PARMEHUTU	Parti du Mouvement de l'Emancipation Hutu
PDC	Parti Démocrate Chrétien
PSD	Parti Social Démocrate
PL	Parti Libéral

RADER	Rassemblement Démocratique Rwandais
RANU	Rwandese Alliance for National Unity
RPA	Rwandan Patriotic Army
RPF	Rwandan Patriotic Front
RTLM	Radio Télévision Libre des Mille Collines
TNA	Transitional National Assembly
UN	United Nations
UNAMIR	United Nations Assistance Mission in Rwanda
UNAR	Union Nationale Rwandaise
UNDP	United Nations Development Programme
UNHCR	United Nations High Commission for Refugees

1 | *What We Do and Do Not Know*

I wish I could say that I would not have done this.

Foreign visitor

We did it because it was the Law. The authorities told us we had to do it.

Perpetrator

It was because people believed they [the Tutsi] were the enemy. It was war.

Bystander

They killed us because they were greedy. Those people just had big stomachs.

Survivor

The words of the foreign visitor reproduced above appear in the guestbook of a former church belonging to the rural community of Nyamata, located in the small central African state of Rwanda. In April 1994, some 5,000 people sought refuge here for the same reason. They were members of Rwanda's Tutsi ethnic minority. Over three days, 14, 15, and 16 April 1994, the men, women, and children crammed inside of the building's brick walls were killed without distinction. Their killers comprised many of their neighbours as well as a smaller number of militia men and soldiers alongside whom they worked. Overwhelmingly, the assailants were drawn from Rwanda's Hutu ethnic majority. Their objective was clear: to kill them all.

The visitor, however, did not give in to the impulse to revile and distance himself from the killers. He asks a deeper, perplexing question. Would he have acted differently if confronted with the same circumstances with which many Rwandans were faced in 1994? It is with these circumstances that this book is concerned. How and why did they arise and culminate in such extraordinary violence in Rwanda, and how and why did they motivate many – but not all – ordinary

Rwandans to participate in this violence? The contrasting statements of the three Rwandans whose words follow those of the foreigner above offer some insight into the difficulty of answering these two questions. Rwandans themselves disagree – often depending on their role in the violence. Although I heard many reasons and motivations, I present these three perspectives because I encountered them often while in Rwanda. They also reflect the three ideas central to the explanation of the violence that emerged from my research. Authority, security, and opportunity are each, I will show, a part of the answer to these two questions.

At only forty-five minutes by car from the capital Kigali, Nyamata is one of the more commonly visited massacre sites in Rwanda. Yet the events that took place there were replicated in many locales across the country in 1994. In churches, schools, government buildings, hilltops, and even hospitals, Tutsi gathered and were killed. For others who hid or fled alone, they often met their end in much lonelier places: in swamps, amid planted fields, in their own homes, or at the side of a road. Their stories may never be known. Together, however, these many hundreds of thousands of individual dramas would come to shock the world, etching themselves indelibly into global public consciousness as it became clear that they were part of an organized attempt to eliminate an entire ethnic group. By my estimate, the killing – recognized belatedly as genocide – would claim the lives of between 491,000 and 522,000 Tutsi – as well as thousands of Hutu.[1] Rwanda became the high water-mark for violence in Africa, and also for international indifference toward it.

The failure to prevent and stop the killing would change the world in several important ways. The genocide would help inspire the articulation of an international 'responsibility to protect' and lend impetus to the movement to establish an International Criminal Court.[2] It drew

---

[1] The number of Hutu killed in the years following the genocide's end in July 1994, mainly in the Democratic Republic of Congo (DRC), is likely to be much higher. Estimates range from the tens of thousands to the low hundreds of thousands. The evidence on which to base a reliable estimate, however, is limited. See Chapter 7 for more on estimating the number of Hutu and Tutsi killed.

[2] The International Commission on Intervention and State Sovereignty referred to Rwanda's genocide twenty-four times in its 2001 report that first articulated the 'responsibility to protect'. It also reproduced Kofi Annan's words as UN Secretary-General: 'If humanitarian intervention is, indeed, an unacceptable assault on sovereignty, how should we respond to a Rwanda, to a Srebrenica – to

attention to the scourge of sexual violence in war when it was recognized that rape could qualify as an act of genocide.[3] And it continues to serve as an ominous reminder of inaction, having been invoked in an effort to mobilize international attention in the Sudan, Ivory Coast, Central African Republic, Kenya, and other African contexts where violence had been framed in ethnic or religious terms. Rwanda's genocide was a world-historical event whose lessons continue to resonate and whose origins deserve to be explained.

1.1 A Synopsis of the Genocide

Mindful of the distortionary role that emotions and politics often play in accounts of violent conflict, I begin by presenting a summary of the background and events leading up to the genocide using facts around which contestation is minimal. In 1994, and still today, Rwanda comprised a large Hutu majority, a Tutsi minority, and an even smaller minority of Twa.[4] A Tutsi monarchy had governed the area as a kingdom for at least two centuries before European colonization. Both Germany from 1897, and then Belgium from 1916 permitted the native king, the *Mwami*, to remain in place but ruled indirectly through him. The Belgians saw the Tutsi as racially superior, privileged them, and reified the differences between them and Hutu. They also propagated the idea the Tutsi originated outside of Rwanda. Then, shortly before Rwanda's independence in 1962, a 'Hutu revolution' overthrew the monarchy. The revolutionaries, led by Grégoire Kayibanda, proclaimed Rwanda's first Republic, dominated by a new Hutu elite from the south of the country. This historic event also triggered the exodus of tens of thousands of Tutsi civilians. Despite several armed attempts over the next few years, the exiles failed to return, and the attacks provoked retaliatory violence against the Tutsi population that had remained within Rwanda. This minority would live under an

---

gross and systematic violations of human rights that offend every precept of our common humanity?'.

[3] In Prosecutor vs. Jean-Paul Akayesu (1998), the Tribunal found that rape and sexual violence '...constitute genocide in the same way as any other act as long as they were committed with the specific intent to destroy, in whole or in part, a particular group, targeted as such'. See ICTR-96-4-T, paragraph 731.

[4] The exact demographic balance before the genocide is contested but most estimates for Hutu range between 85 per cent and 91 per cent, Tutsi between 8 per cent and 14 per cent, and Twa almost always 1 per cent or less.

authoritarian and highly exclusionary regime. Then, in 1973, in a coup d'état, a small group of northern Hutu wrested power from Kayibanda. A young Juvénal Habyarimana became President of Rwanda's Second Republic. He ruled autocratically until October 1990 when the Rwandan Patriotic Front (RPF), composed primarily of the descendants of the Tutsi exiles from the revolution, invaded from across the Ugandan border to the north. This began Rwanda's civil war. At the same time, Habyarimana faced both internal and international pressure to democratize. In August 1993, he finally accepted an internationally brokered power-sharing deal with the RPF and the main, newly established domestic opposition parties. A peacekeeping mission, the United Nations Assistance Mission in Rwanda (UNAMIR), was fielded to monitor the agreement. However, there was intense opposition to the peace agreement from hardliners at home, and Rwandan politics grew increasingly tense.

Eight days before the events in Nyamata's church climaxed, on 6 April 1994 a plane coming in to land at Rwanda's main airport was shot down killing all aboard. Its most well-known victim was Rwanda's Hutu president, Juvénal Habyarimana. Almost immediately, a small group of extremists manoeuvred to seize control of the state, to physically eliminate or co-opt more moderate senior political figures who had previously supported power-sharing with the RPF, and to install a new government composed of Hutu hardliners. Once they had captured the state, they then used its considerable resources and authority to implement a genocidal program. They deployed the state's civilian and military apparatus, and mobilized ordinary Rwandans against the Tutsi civilian population. At the same time, government forces and the rebel RPF army also re-engaged in combat. The international community, instead of intervening to stop the slaughter, moved to evacuate foreign nationals and to draw down the 2,700-strong UN peacekeeping force on the ground. In the end, only 450 blue helmets remained. Some hundred days later, the rebels emerged victorious. They had defeated the Rwandan army and militia, who escaped mainly across the north-west border into neighbouring Zaire. About two million Hutu civilians followed them into Zaire through a humanitarian corridor established by French forces in the south-west of the country. The international community finally responded with a new UN mission, UNAMIR II, as well as massive humanitarian assistance for the refugees. However, it was too little too late for those trapped inside Nyamata's church, as well as for the hundreds of thousands of other civilians who perished in many other places.

1.2 What Is Distinctive and Puzzling about Rwanda

Rwanda's genocide both shocks and intrigues at once. While mass violence is a rare phenomenon, the characteristics of the killing in Rwanda still stand out and capture the imagination for reasons that are worth articulating. First, the intensity of the violence and the targeting of women and children leave little doubt as to whether the intent was genocidal. The aim was to eliminate an ethnic group in entirety. If my estimate is correct, then nearly two-thirds of Rwanda's Tutsi population were exterminated. Second, there is the sheer speed of the violence. These people were killed in little over one hundred days, and, as we shall see in Chapter 3, there is evidence to suggest that the majority of the victims perished in the first two to three weeks. Third, there is the remarkable geographic scope of the violence. It was nationwide. There are very few places in Rwanda where violence did *not* occur. Tutsi were targeted wherever they resided or wherever they fled. Fourth, one of the most controversial and distinctive aspects of the violence was the scale of civilian participation. In practically every community where the Tutsi 'enemy' lived, there were Hutu, and also Twa, who mobilized against them. By my estimate, one in five Hutu men committed an act of violence during the genocide. Their targets were often people known to them personally. Lastly, although less distinctive, the nature of the violence is still distressing to learn. It was collective, crude, intimate, and cruel. Killers often wielded agricultural implements – machetes, forks, and hoes – as well as traditional weapons – nail-studded clubs, knives, bows and arrows, and spears. They confronted their victims face-to-face and overwhelmingly in groups. Sexual violence against women was commonplace and the infliction of gratuitous pain and suffering on victims features prominently in witness accounts (Human Rights Watch, 1996).

It is these extraordinary characteristics of Rwanda's genocide – the scale, speed, and scope of both the violence and the civilian mobilization – that impress themselves upon the mind and that have helped to inscribe it as an event of enduring significance in world history. They also represent an empirical puzzle – distinct from the overall question of why genocide occurred – for which we still do not have a good explanation. How and why did so many Rwandans mobilize, so quickly, kill so many, and in so many places? The urge to explain these disturbing and distinctive aspects of the violence is one of several still-puzzling questions about the genocide to which this book responds.

1.3 What We Know Already

Rwanda has become a paradigmatic case of genocide and as such it has stimulated an abundant literature. We know much already. Three subject areas have emerged and attracted much attention. First, there is the question of responsibility and accountability for the genocide. The forensic investigations into what western governments knew, the meticulous reports of human rights organizations, the many moving first-hand accounts by Rwandans and foreigners on the ground at the time, the various stories told by journalists, and the extensive records of the International Criminal Tribunal for Rwanda (ICTR) may all be found here.[5] The identities of the politicians, military figures, state employees, clergy members, businessmen, professionals, journalists, academics, as well as even some ordinary Rwandans, who each participated in the genocide, have all become public knowledge in this way. Second, there is the aftermath of the genocide and Rwanda's trajectory following it. This area has generated the most writing, some of which has been deeply polarized in assessments of the post-genocide regime's record. The main themes here are justice and reconciliation, development and democracy, and human rights and civil liberties, as well as the regional repercussions of the genocide.[6] Third, there is

---

[5] On the international community's responsibility, see for example Barnett (2002); Cohen (2007); Melvern (2006); Power (2002); Verschave (1994). On the responsibility of Rwandan actors, see for example Des Forges (1999); Guichaoua (2005); Guichaoua (2015); Longman (2010); Rever (2018); Ruzibiza and Vidal (2005); Thompson (2007). The reports of human rights organizations include those by African Rights (1994); Des Forges (1999). First-hand accounts include, by non-Rwandans, Booh-Booh (2005); Dallaire and Beardsley (2004); Khan (2000); Marchal (2001), and by Rwandans, Gasana (2002a); Hatzfeld (2005a, 2005b); Kabagema (2001); Mukagasana and May (1997); Nduwayo (2002); Rusatira (2005); Sibomana et al. (1999). Journalistic accounts include Gourevitch (2004); Keane (1995). The public records database of the International Criminal Tribunal for Rwanda, now closed, can still be accessed online at http://jrad.unmict.org/.

[6] On wide-spectrum assessments of Rwanda's trajectory after the genocide, see Campioni and Noack (2012); McDoom (2011); Straus and Waldorf (2011) On justice and reconciliation in post-genocide Rwanda, see for example Buckley-Zistel (2006); Burnet (2012); Clark (2005); Clark and Kaufman (2009); Ingelaere (2017); Thomson (2013); Waldorf (2006). On democracy and development, see

1.3 What We Know Already

research on the history and causes of the genocide itself and the motivations of the individuals who participated in it. This book belongs to this last category. Although much has been written here also, there remain important gaps in our understanding and highly contentious debates on several aspects of the genocide that persist.

There have already been several excellent reviews of the considerable literature on the genocide's origins, and I recommend them to readers interested in tracing the remarkable evolution in our knowledge and understanding.[7] The consensus on what did – and what did not – contribute to the genocide continues to evolve. Early ideas – media reports of an uncontrollable explosion of immutable tribal passions and the suggestion of state failure – no longer have much scholarly support.[8] Similarly, the claims that Rwandans committed violence out of a cultural predisposition for unthinking obedience – or out of a base desire to acquire the land of their victims in the face of a Malthusian resource crisis – are rarely repeated. However, I believe these perspectives need to be softened and refined. I find there was *some* 'pressure from below' and *some* Rwandans did participate in the genocide out of respect for the state's symbolic authority legitimizing the violence.

Nonetheless, a scholarly consensus has crystallized on several issues in explanations of the genocide. First, the violence was not spontaneous, but highly organized; not a reaction of the masses but the strategy of a small elite (Des Forges, 1999); and not driven by emotions or passions but by power and politics. As mentioned, however, I believe that this top-down perspective overstates elite agency and rationality and underestimates pressures from below. There were individuals at the local level, outside of the state structure and within society, who also pushed for violence. Second, the identities – Hutu and Tutsi and in whose names the violence was framed – were constructed and instrumentalized. In particular, colonial-era racial science embraced by the Belgians magnified and rigidified group differences

---

for example Ansoms (2009); Beswick (2011); Booth and Golooba-Mutebi (2012); Gready (2010); Hayman (2009); Ingelaere (2010); Pottier (2002); Reyntjens (2004, 2013). On the genocide's regional implications, see for example Prunier (2005); Reyntjens (2009); Turner (2007).

[7] Four of the most insightful reviews of the extensive literature on Rwanda's genocide are Kimonyo (2000); Lemarchand (2007); Longman (2004); Uvin (2001).

[8] For a deconstruction of the *New York Times'* framing of the genocide as 'tribal hatred' see Chari (2010). On state collapse, see Zartman (1995).

and the identities became associated with political power (Mamdani, 2001). This equation persisted to deadly effect into post-independence Rwanda. Third, the perpetrators were largely 'ordinary' and their motives heterogeneous (Straus, 2006). It would be difficult to argue that the killers were all extraordinary or deviant in some way given the scale of civilian participation in Rwanda. However, I contend that this implicit view of the perpetrators as an undifferentiated mass overlooks important intra-group differences that matter for understanding the mechanics of mass mobilization. Patterns in motivation were discernible. Fourth, the media, in particular radio broadcasts, framed and propagated messages to stoke fear, resentment, and hostility among the Hutu population toward the Tutsi as an ethnic group, which in turn motivated and mobilized individuals to kill (Thompson, 2007). As we shall see, however, the radio's role was also *ex post* justificatory. Its content radicalized and provided an ideological rationale for the killing primarily *after* much of the violence had been committed. Lastly, few disagree that the genocide was the culmination of a process in which three short-to-medium term factors – Rwanda's civil war, move to multiparty politics, and ongoing peace negotiations - were all consequential in the elite decision-making that pushed Rwanda closer to genocide. Their impact 'below' – how they affected and were interpreted by ordinary Rwandans – however, is less well-documented and the significance of these effects implicitly underestimated.

1.4 Why Consensus on the Genocide Is Limited

Yet the number of issues on which there is a clear consensus is still surprisingly small given the remarkable amount of data and writing that research on the genocide has generated. Numerous theories still circulate and debates persist. Emotions and politics play a part in generating the diversity in explanations. Another reason, already noted, is the uneven quality of the evidence used to support the explanations offered (Straus, 2006, p. 3). Some scholars rely on primary evidence, both archival and oral, collected specifically to build or test theories. Others draw more heavily on secondary sources and their theoretical imagination in making their claims. A final reason for proliferation is methodological. The choices in respect of comparison and level of analysis matter. Comparisons help strengthen causal inferences by pinpointing similarities and differences between cases. While

1.4 Why Consensus on the Genocide Is Limited

cross-case comparisons are often contentious given the persistent debate over how to define genocide, within-case comparisons – between time periods, places, and persons for instance – still offer an opportunity to narrow down explanations. What were Hutu–Tutsi relations like before and after the war started? Why did some regions experience violence early on, but others later? Why did some people kill and others not? There is value in leveraging the considerable and complex variation within the genocide. While we do have studies that make such intra-case comparisons, most commonly between places, rarely do the methodological rationales, when given, align and allow for broader theorization.

The level at which the genocide is analysed – macro, meso, or micro – also affects the explanatory factors identified. The vantage-point matters. Research on perpetrators at the micro-level has yielded fascinating insights into how and why individuals killed. Studies of events at the macro-level have deepened our understanding of how and why the genocide occurred. But how generalizable are findings at lower levels of analysis? And what are the links between individual-level behaviours and national-level processes?

The different levels of analysis that scholars have chosen also represent a useful way to summarize and classify the multitude of theories generated since the genocide. Macro-level explanations are plentiful. The story of Rwanda's genocide has been well-told from the 'top'. These accounts focus on individuals, events, and processes at the national and international levels. Yet they have suggested a very diverse set of structural, conjunctural, and historical factors behind the genocide. Structural processes suggested include growing demographic pressure, increasing ecological scarcity, an acute economic decline, and 'structural violence' and inequality.[9] Conjunctural events emphasized include the start of the civil war, the move to democratize, the failure of the peace process, the rise of hate media, the impact of a structural adjustment program, the assassination of the president, the role of the Church, and the indifference if not complicity of

---

[9] On demographic pressure, see for example Bonneux (1994); Ford (1995). On ecological scarcity, see for example André & Platteau (1998); Newbury (1994); Peter Uvin (1996). On economic decline and structural adjustment, see Chossudovsky (1996); Verwimp (2003a). On structural violence, see Uvin (1998). On inequality, see Gasana (2002a).

international actors.[10] Historical factors raised include Rwanda's history of identity-based politics, an exclusionary founding myth or narrative, a racist ideology, the legacy of a deeply inscribed racial or ethnic cleavage, the memory of one group's inferiority and oppression by another group, as well as a materially strong state.[11] Scholars often weave some combination of these factors together into convincing narratives. Some compare Rwanda to other cases of genocide – and in two instances to cases where genocide could have but did not occur – to make more causally credible claims.[12]

Micro-level explanations, by which I mean how and why individuals came to commit violence, have also grown in number.[13] Numerous theories exist for how and why individuals participated: deprivation, opportunism, peer pressure and coercion, prejudice and racism, threat and fear, conformity and obedience, ideological commitment, displaced frustration, desensitization and habituation, and social ties and interaction are among the many explanations suggested.[14] Some scholars have built sophisticated models, often drawing on psycho-social theory, to explain how individuals become perpetrators.[15] However, we lack a strong empirical basis – a systematic comparison of

---

[10] On the importance of the civil war, see Straus (2006, pp. 224–226). On democratization and also the rise of exclusionary ideology, see Mann (2005, pp. 428–448); Snyder (2000, pp. 296–304). On the failure of the peace process, see Jones (2001); Kuperman (1996). On the complicity of international actors, notably France, see Verschave (1994). On racist ideology, see Uvin (1998). On myths and narratives, see Kaufman (2011); Straus (2015).

[11] On the history of identity politics, see Newbury (1998). On the importance of Rwanda's racial and ethnic cleavage, see Mamdani (2001). On the importance of state power, see Straus (2006).

[12] Comparative analyses that include Rwanda can be found in Chirot & McCauley (2010); Kiernan (2009); Mann (2005); Powell (2011); Sémelin (2005). Straus (2015) and Midlarsky (2005) also compare Rwanda against negative cases – where genocide did not happen.

[13] Uvin (2001, p. 98) first made this observation on the deficit of micro-level studies.

[14] On deprivation, frustration, prejudice, and racism, among other explanatory constructs, see Uvin (1998, pp. 107–139). On opportunism, see Uvin (2001, pp. 98–99). On peer pressure and coercion, see Straus (2006, p. 139). On the role of obedience, see Gérard Prunier (1998, p. 248). On ideological commitments, see Mann (2005, pp. 469–470). On social ties, see Fujii (2006, pp. 149–179). On desensitization, see Scull, Mbonyingabo, and Kotb et al. (2016). On social interaction, see Smeulers & Hoex (2010).

[15] See for example Adler et al. (2008); Baum (2008); Luft (2015); Staub (2003); Tanner (2011); Waller (2002); Williams (2017); Zimbardo (2007).

1.4 Why Consensus on the Genocide Is Limited

perpetrators against non-perpetrators for instance – to confirm or falsify these various ideas.

Meso-level explanations are less common. Yet resistance or cooperation from local authorities and local communities mediated the effect of genocidal directives from the centre. The decisions and actions of subnational actors can profoundly shape local patterns of violence as they often have valuable local information and intelligence as well as local power and influence on which the centre depends for successful implementation of the killing. They represent the link between centre and periphery. In Rwanda, the choices of civilian authority figures – prefects and burgomasters – as well as communal police officers, local opposition parties, and church leaders have each mattered for mobilization and violence.[16] It is worth noting that while local cooperation with the centre typically accelerated the genocide, resistance never prevented it altogether. The resources available to local actors were never a match for the means at the disposal of those who centrally controlled the state.

Although there are points of overlap across these levels of explanation, what is often missing are, first, explicit causal connections between the macro, meso, and micro and, second, attempts at structured comparisons.[17] What are the mechanisms through which the events and processes at the macro-level affected communities and individuals at the meso- and micro-levels? How, for instance, did war alter relations between neighbouring Hutu and Tutsi and lead members of the former to kill members of the latter? How did multipartyism impact the lives of ordinary Rwandans and contribute to their mobilization during the genocide? How exactly did the Rwandan state's authority operate to mobilize citizens to help implement genocide? There is a need for explanation that draws on evidence across levels and synthesizes it into a causally coherent whole. Furthermore, we have too few explanations that rely on comparisons between periods, places, and persons purposely selected to test or build hypotheses. By examining the genocide at differing levels of analysis and through more systematic comparisons, we may better be able to distinguish between the myriad theories that circulate.

---

[16] Excellent meso-level analyses include Boersema (2009); Brehm (2017); Guichaoua (2005); Longman (1995); Straus (2006); Wagner (1998).

[17] Three good exceptions are the work of Fujii (2006); Longman (2010); and Straus (2006).

1.5 The Questions That Remain

The two central questions running throughout this book are (i) what are the circumstances that gave rise to the genocide; and (ii) how did these affect individuals and motivate some, but not others, to kill? These two primary questions raise a number of smaller but important ones. Answers to these secondary questions may help us choose between the myriad explanations that still circulate. I list these questions here to highlight the gaps in our knowledge and understanding and distinguish between those for which the answers we presently have are incomplete and those for which the answers remain contested.

First, we have, in my view, unsatisfying explanations of the four unusual and shocking characteristics of Rwanda's genocide. Why did *so many* people participate in the violence? Why did they *mobilize so quickly*? Why did the violence *spread so rapidly*? And why did it happen in *so many places* across Rwanda? The specific and distinctive form the mobilization and violence took merits a separate explanation from their onset more generally. As we shall see, I believe that these extraordinary characteristics are related to a number of extraordinary features of Rwanda's socio-demography and geography that have not all yet been fully explicated. These unusual characteristics also invite questions relating to local variation across the country in their expression. Why did mobilization and violence occur in some places sooner than others, for instance? And why were more people killed in some locales than in others?

We also have only partial answers – the evidence base is limited – to a number of other important questions. Why did some people kill, but others not? How different were the attitudes and beliefs – that is, how large was the distance or gap – between the perpetrators and the non-perpetrators? Who were the mobilizers at the local level and what were the practical mechanics of mass mobilization? How exactly did fundamental changes in the macro-political environment – the war, multi-partyism, peace process, for instance – affect ordinary Rwandans below and contribute to their mobilization during the genocide? Was there resistance to the killing at either the top or bottom – contestation between pro-and anti-violence elements? If so, why did extremists often prevail over moderates?

Second, a number of questions remain the subject of ongoing debate. How many people participated in the genocide and how many people were killed? What role did emotions, ideology, and ethnicity play among ordinary Rwandans and elite decision-makers? Was the population radicalized and ready to kill before the genocide began? Were there differences among the killers and what more can we say about their motives? Was the genocide intended long in advance? Could early international intervention have prevented it?

I do not pretend to have definitive answers that will resolve these questions or settle these debates once and for all. But I have drawn conclusions and made inferences, supported by evidence I collected, whose merits readers can evaluate for themselves. There remain also a number of highly politicized questions for which I have little new evidence of my own. Who was responsible for shooting down the president's plane that triggered the genocide? And how many Hutu civilians were killed during and after the genocide by the Rwandan Patriotic Army? I will address these questions but rely primarily on interpreting existing sources to do so.

1.6 Theories and Hypotheses

There is no shortage of explanations then about what caused Rwanda's genocide and why Rwandans killed. One of the goals of this book is to test existing theories as well as to develop new hypotheses in relation to both questions. In addition to the voluminous literature specific to Rwanda's genocide then, I also review here theories that have emerged from empirical and theoretical studies of: (i) collective violence; (ii) civil wars; (iii) ethnic conflicts; and (iv) other genocides. All of these literatures have potential implications for Rwanda. In setting these theories out, I have paid close attention to the underlying causal logic behind them in order to bring related macro and micro explanations together into similar analytical categories. For example, 'war', a country-level variable, could be translated at the individual level as 'fear'. The causal logic or mechanism linking the two factors is essentially 'threat' and for this reason I classify them together. Similarly, a cultural propensity to obey authority may well be related to a regime's type as authoritarian or to a state's strong material capacities. I group these together as well.

One of the main reasons for why the range of theories is so broad is the lack of consensus on the concept of genocide. The 1948 United Nations Convention on Genocide defines genocide as 'acts committed with intent to destroy, in whole or in part, a national, ethnical, racial or religious group'. Almost every element in the juridical definition has been the subject of intense scholarly debate: the victim groups protected, the perpetrating agents recognized, the modes of extermination permitted, and the intention required. These debates have been well-covered already (Straus, 2001) and I do not attempt a new general definition of genocide here. Instead, I offer a description of what I believe are the defining characteristics of the violence in Rwanda. The aim is to help evaluate the validity of the comparisons that will inevitably be made with violence elsewhere.

I believe then that Rwanda's genocide may be characterized as action organized by individuals who control the apparatus of the state, in collaboration with members of the general population, that deliberately but not exclusively targets a group whom these individuals perceive as innately distinct, using violence whose purpose is to eliminate the targeted group physically. The involvement of ordinary, private citizens in both the organization and implementation of the violence was a shocking and defining feature of Rwanda's violence. Popular participation in war-time violence, on the side of the state, is not unusual. However, such participation varies in its scale, organization, and relationship to the state. In Rwanda, this participation was massive, organized, and closely coordinated with the state. In contrast, pro-government militias, such as the Janjaweed in the Sudan's Darfur region, while also organized and aligned with the regime, typically involve a much smaller number of individuals. The massive scale of societal involvement in the physical act of killing sets Rwanda apart from many other cases.

Wars, Insecurity, Threats and Fear-Based Explanations

It is widely recognized that wars and genocides have a strong relationship (Sémelin, 2005; Shaw, 2015; Straus, 2015). But the questions of how and why exactly a macro-level variable such as war facilitates genocides have produced some quite different answers. First, it has been argued that wars provide a 'cover' for genocide (Winter, 2003). In the 'fog of war' it is often difficult to obtain reliable information on who is killing whom. Victims can sometimes be mistaken for aggressors, and civilians can be mistaken for combatants. In Rwanda, poor information flow meant that by the time the violence was recognized as

1.6 Theories and Hypotheses

genocide, tens of thousands of Tutsi and moderate Hutus had already been killed. Second, it is argued that wars help genocides because they can create political opportunities or political upheavals that challenge and weaken regimes.[18] Following Habyarimana's assassination, the civil war immediately re-ignited and an extremist minority seized the opportunity to eliminate or co-opt the moderate opposition. It then established itself as the new regime and unleashed its genocidal program. Third, it is argued that wars brutalize people. Through repeated involvement in and exposure to war-time violence, individuals become desensitized to its effects, and become capable of cruel violence themselves. This argument has been made to explain atrocities committed by ordinary American GIs in Vietnam (Faludi, 1999, pp. 291–358). It may also explain the actions of ordinary Rwandans in 1994.

Last, and perhaps the most common explanation, however, is that wars create threats. Threat is a central theme in explanations of genocides that seek to identify the motivation for violence.[19] Security dilemmas, a threat-based concept from international relations theory, can arise *within* countries as well as between them. A domestic security dilemma occurs when one group takes defensive action that is interpreted as offensive by the other side. In such situations 'the drive for security in one group is so great that it produces near-genocidal behaviour towards neighbouring groups' (Posen, 1993, p. 106). Related to this, at the individual-level, war-time threats create *fears*. Fear amplifies the need for security and the 'target for ethnic violence will be the group that is the biggest threat' (Petersen, 2002, p. 68). Threat-driven fear can be strategically framed in collective terms to mobilize communities (Shesterinina, 2016). In the case of Rwanda, it has been argued that Hutu civilians either feared the rebel RPF would kill them, or that it would reverse the revolution and reinstate the Tutsi monarchy that had oppressed them historically. They killed in self-defence. But how widespread were these fears among ordinary Rwandans? Through what mechanisms did they divide communities? We lack answers to these questions.

---

[18] On political opportunities, see Krain (1997, p. 355). On political upheavals, see Harff (2003, p. 62)
[19] See for instance Chirot & McCauley (2010); Sémelin (2005); Straus (2006).

Demographic and Environmental Explanations

Civil wars, or violent conflict more generally, have a long history with both demography and ecology. At the macro-level, one of the more enduring demographic hypotheses has been the 'youth bulge'. Bulges arise when an unusually high proportion of a population is 'young', often defined as those in the 15–24-year-old age bracket. Cross-national research has suggested that this demographic particularity makes countries more vulnerable to domestic armed conflicts, rebellions, and even revolutions.[20] The closest micro-level equivalent is the perceived threat posed by *male youth*. Described as 'loose molecules in an unstable fluid' (Kaplan, 1994), young men, it is argued, are particularly vulnerable to mobilization and recruitment into rebel groups, militia, and gangs. Some argue that it is because their opportunity cost is low: unemployed young men do not have livelihoods or income to lose (Collier & Hoeffler, 2004, p. 569). Others argue that it is about responsibility: young men can afford to engage in risky activity such as violence because they do not have families or established careers to worry about (Goldstone, 2002). Yet others say it has to do with young people's attraction to change and ideas: they are susceptible to ideological appeals for action (Huntington, 2002). In the context of Rwanda, its newly formed political parties did have 'youth wings' that competed and even fought each other before the genocide. Many of these young men allegedly formed the backbone of the attack groups during the genocide. The most infamous of these groups, the *Interahamwe*, were in fact more than a youth wing. They were a militia that had been trained to kill. The role of young men in Rwanda's genocide is a hypothesis that bears investigation.

Ecological explanations of group conflict have at their root a scarcity of natural resources on which the population depends. Arable land, water, and forests, it is argued, are most likely to create tensions within communities when they are in short supply (Homer-Dixon, 1999). The original Malthusian argument has largely fallen out of favour: war, disease, famine, or other disasters do not *inevitably* occur because the population grows faster than the food supply. They are often mediated, usually by human ingenuity to mitigate the underlying resource

---

[20] On youth bulges and armed conflicts, see Urdal (2006). On rebellions, see Moller (1968). On revolutions, see Goldstone (1991).

scarcity. Instead, a softer, neo-Malthusian claim argues that environmental scarcity simply creates conditions in which conflict is more likely to occur.[21] Diamond (2008, p. 23), most popularly associated with the modern Malthusian argument, writes 'Rwanda represents a Malthusian catastrophe happening under our eyes, an over-populated land that collapsed in bloodshed.' When scarcity coincides with other factors such as group inequality, weak conflict-mediating institutions, and demographic pressure, then conflict is even more probable. The causal pathways are varied and complex. In explaining Rwanda's genocide, its land and people are often cited. Rwanda's population growth was high, averaging 3.3 per cent per annum between 1985 and 1991. On average, 422 Rwandans lived in every square kilometre of its farmable land. This made it the highest density in Africa in 1991. There has in addition been evidence to support the importance of a resource crunch at the micro-level and its role in the collapse of Rwandan society (André & Platteau, 1998; Ohlsson, 1999; Verpoorten, 2012b). The importance of land scarcity, then, remains an important hypothesis to investigate in the context of Rwanda.

Deprivation-Related Explanations

The notion of deprivation lies at the root of a wide variety of related concepts used to explain conflict, violence, and also genocide. These include vertical and horizontal inequality, structural violence, relative deprivation, and difficult life conditions among many others.[22] At the heart of some of these ideas is a grievance-centric mechanism. Relative deprivation, for example, occurs when there is a discrepancy between an individual's aspirations and his/her capabilities. The result, it is argued, is frustrated energy that can be displaced and expressed as aggression. Structural violence, a broader term encompassing deprivation, prejudice, and inequality, focuses on a different set of emotions: despair, anger, and cynicism it argues are the antecedents of actual violence. Despite the sophistication of many of these concepts, it is difficult to evaluate their explanatory value across cases. In part, this is

---

[21] See Ishiyama and Pechenina (2012); Uvin (2001, p. 83).
[22] On vertical inequality, see for example Besancon (2005). On horizontal inequality, see Stewart (2002). On structural violence, see Uvin (1998). On relative deprivation, see Gurr (1970). On difficult life conditions, see Staub (1989, p. 44).

because they are not always consistently defined and, in part, it is because they are difficult to measure. Nonetheless, deprivation-related arguments seem to resonate more with Rwanda than in other genocides. As with the demographic and environmental arguments, this is likely to be because of another of Rwanda's particularities: it was a poverty-stricken country in sub-Saharan Africa. Many of its perpetrators were themselves poor. While it is relatively easy to make macro-level generalizations from these facts, individual-level evidence to support deprivation-related claims is in shorter supply.[23] Deprivation-related explanations deserve further investigation at the micro-level.

Identity/Ethnicity and Racism/Prejudice-Based Explanations

Identity – both personal and social – is a powerful motivational force in individuals and groups. It has been studied intensively by social psychologists, who have built numerous competing theories of intergroup relations based on it. Social identity theory, for example, argues that *self-esteem* motivates individuals (Tajfel, 1982). Social dominance theory in contrast assumes a socio-biological *instinct for superiority*: societies are inherently hierarchical and dominant and subordinate groups will always arise (Waller, 2002). Realistic group conflict theory is premised on individual *rationality* (Sherif, 1988). Individuals will exhibit ingroup solidarity when there is competition for scarce resources.

Ethnicity – a particular type of social identity – has captured the imagination of scholars of wars and violence. It has special properties, it is argued, that makes it particularly easy to mobilize groups. 'Ethnic conflict' and 'ethnic violence' have now become distinct phenomena. They continue to command scholarly attention even though they have been shown to be quite rare when compared against the universe of all ethnic groups (Fearon & Laitin, 1996). Several other related concepts have identity or ethnicity at their root: 'primordial attachment', 'ancient tribal hatreds', and 'inter-ethnic enmity' implicitly emphasize the importance of ethnicity.[24] The scholarly consensus now is that ethnic identity is both constructed and relational. Identity is not the

---

[23] An exception is Philip Verwimp (2005) who finds those with something to gain and those with something to lose were more likely to be drawn into the violence.

[24] On primordial attachment, see Geertz (1975). On inter-ethnic enmity, see Straus (2006).

1.6 Theories and Hypotheses

product of essentialist or immutable differences between groups. Instead, its salience varies over time and space as a consequence of both structural and strategic forces. Genocide scholars have also recognized that identity can be instrumentalized by ethnic entrepreneurs to mobilize groups. The consensus among Rwanda specialists is that the meaning of Hutu and Tutsi evolved over the course of its history, i.e., the identities are constructed and malleable (Des Forges, 1999, pp. 31–33; Mamdani, 2001, pp. 73–75; Newbury, 1988). However, under Belgian colonial rule these identities were institutionalized and reified as racially distinct. At the time of the genocide, it is argued, ordinary Hutu assimilated messages that emphasized the distinct racial origin of the Tutsi. They were alien, did not belong in Rwanda, and thus deserved to be removed. However, the extent to which ordinary Rwandans actually believed these statements is largely unknown. The effectiveness of these intentional efforts to increase the salience of these identities needs to be investigated at the individual-level.

At the micro-level, ethnic prejudice and racism are closely related to ingroup and outgroup identities. While *positive* sentiments towards one's ingroup can be expressed as pride, loyalty, and superiority, *negative* feelings towards the outgroup subsume contempt, hostility, and prejudice (Brewer, 1999). A considerable amount of research has focused on this last expression: the causes and measures of prejudice. However, much less is known about the impact of prejudice on actual individual *behaviour*. Would prejudice motivate an individual to commit violence? What exactly is the relationship between prejudice and ethnic conflict?[25] It certainly seems a question that would also be germane to genocide. Anti-Semitism, or rather a particularly pernicious form of it, has been suggested as an explanation of the Holocaust (Goldhagen, 1997, pp. 392–393). Dehumanization of the outgroup, an extreme form of prejudice, is seen as a stage along the path to genocide. Rwanda's history contains many examples of precolonial, colonial, and modern state policies that have discriminated against one or other ethnic groups. Racism, it is argued, is deeply embedded in Rwandan society and was activated during the genocide (Uvin, 1998, pp. 216–217). Both theory and evidence suggest that the role of prejudice needs to be investigated in Rwanda's genocide.

---

[25] For a good review of the literature on the relationship between ethnic prejudice and conflict, see Green and Seher (2003).

Ideologies, Myths, and Narratives

Ideologies, myths, and narratives feature prominently in explanations of wars and genocides.[26] Linking them is the role that each plays in shaping individual and collective beliefs about the targeted group. A diverse set of ideas underlie the ideologies identified by scholars as conducive to the exclusion of a group: notions of purity and contamination; future utopias built on a racial identity; the idea that groups may be considered either civilized or barbarous; the belief that a nation-state was founded for a particular core ethnic group.[27] Nationalism, particularly ethno-nationalist ideology, has a strong association with violence. It emerges in contexts of democratic transition and weak conflict-mediating institutions when 'ethnos' and 'demos' become readily conflated (Mann, 2005, p. 4) or when elites instrumentalize nationalism to rally popular support (Snyder, 2000). As with ideologies, the content of historical myths and narratives embedded in societies about 'other' groups also ranges widely. It includes beliefs that one group has been the victim of injustice by the 'other' group; that this group cannot be trusted and represents a potential threat; and that the group does not belong and originates outside of the society. These myths and narratives cue the emotional reactions – resentment, fear, and hostility for instance – that emerge in intergroup relations (Kaufman, 2001).

Yet the causal role of ideology, myths, and narratives in mass violence is complex and contested. Ideology proponents point to the power of ideas to unify and mobilize a group, and to motivate members to take action (Leader Maynard, 2014). Ideology also justifies this action – including violence – taken against another group (Costalli & Ruggeri, 2015). Others argue that ideologies, such as the founding narrative of the state (Straus, 2015), shape the decisions of the ruling elite to include or exclude particular groups (Chirot, 2010). Perpetrators are 'killers by conviction'.[28] In contrast, others have argued that ideological commitments do not really motivate

---

[26] See for example Harff (2003, p. 62); Kaufman (2015); Snyder (2000, pp. 37–39); Straus (2015).

[27] See Chirot & McCauley (2010); Melson (1992); Sémelin (2005) on purity; Weitz (2005) on utopias; Powell (2011) on barbarism and civilization; and Levene (2005) on the nation-state.

[28] Mann (2005, p. 239), for example, has argued this about Nazi perpetrators.

individuals. They merely provide a rationale, often *ex post*, for otherwise self-interested behaviour (Mildt, 1996, p. 311). For rationalist proponents of ethnic conflict, myths and narratives are merely cultural raw material that political entrepreneurs use to magnify fears and mobilize populations (Lake & Rothchild, 1998, p. 20). They are simply 'amplifiers'. For culturalist advocates, however, these myths are in fact one of the necessary conditions for violence (Kaufman, 2001, p. 30; Ross, 2007). Ethnic conflict is not possible without them.

Group myths were certainly presently in Rwanda. The narrative, common among Hutu, was that Tutsi had arrived in Rwanda as pastoralists after the Hutu. They were strangers in a new land that they colonized. They also pressed into servitude the Hutu settlers, and ruled over them until the revolution toppled the Tutsi monarchy. It has been argued that many of Rwanda's Hutu leaders and population feared that the RPF, comprised principally of Tutsi, would reinstate this pre-revolutionary order. Similarly, it has been argued Rwanda had a *racist* ideology emphasizing past Tutsi oppression and distinct racial origins deeply embedded in its society (Uvin, 1998, pp. 34–39). It was reawakened through extremist media such as the newspaper *Kangura* and the radio station *Radio-Télévision Libre des Mille Collines,* and used to mobilize the civilian population. Appeals to Hutu nationalism were at the core of the 'Hutu Power' movement, it is argued. The movement brought extremists from Rwanda's different political parties under one ideological umbrella. However, the extent to which such an ideology had been internalized by ordinary Rwandans is largely unknown. Those who claim that Rwandans were ideologically radicalized at the time of the presidential plane crash have mainly assumed that what is disseminated from above will be believed below. But how much credibility did ordinary Rwandans give to the radio? Or to the politicians who preached ethnic division? These questions need to be more carefully examined in the Rwandan context.

Political and Material Opportunism

This set of explanations argues that actors take advantage of opportunities and that violence is the outcome of action pursued in their self-interest.[29] The benefits to themselves can be diverse. Political

---

[29] Mitchell (2004) advocates that self-interest is a very important motive.

opportunists seek power by exploiting gaps in the political structure. At the macro-level, democratic transitions, for instance, can create instability and several explanations have focused on the potential for violence in such moments. Competitive politics create incentives for both ruling and 'challenger' elites to mobilize constituents, sometimes along ethno-nationalist lines.[30] Violence becomes politics by other means. Rwanda's move to multipartyism in 1991 is widely recognized as a critical juncture in its trajectory toward genocide but how exactly did party politics push the country closer to ethnic confrontation? Was there a conflation of 'ethnos' and 'demos' (Mann, 2005) in which democracy was equated with Hutu majority rule? Political opportunities may also arise from other types of structural transitions. Wars, revolutions, and other political upheavals can create the necessary break in the opportunity structure for extremists to seize control of the state (Harff, 2003; Krain, 1997). Democratization is only one example of political opportunity creation.

At a more micro-level, opportunity-centred explanations claim that individuals commit violence because it can be a form of upward social mobility. Perpetrators of the Holocaust took advantage of the opportunity to further their careers by showing their willingness to do their 'jobs'.[31] Others argue that the opportunity for self-enrichment is an important motivation. Rwandan *génocidaires* frequently looted the property of their victims. Rape and sexual violence were also prominent features of the genocide and there is evidence that the land of victims was redistributed in some places. How important were the spoils of the genocide and in what ways did they work to motivate individuals in Rwanda?

Group Behaviour and Collective Action

This collection of theories is based on the observation that individuals behave differently in groups to when they are alone. One field of research has been crowd psychology.[32] What turns peaceable crowds into violent mobs? De-individuation – the sense that you are not personally responsible for your actions – is central to these arguments

---

[30] On the risks posed by democratization in Rwanda, see Kimonyo (2016); Roessler (2005); Silva-Leander (2008); Snyder (2000).
[31] See for example Mildt (1996).
[32] See for example Canetti (2000); Le Bon (1896); Tambiah (1996).

(Festinger et al. 1952). Other research has instead focused on riots (Horowitz, 2002), that is to say episodic, seemingly spontaneous outbursts of group violence, or else pogroms (Brass, 1996), which imply greater organization and often the acquiescence of the state. Do these follow predictable patterns? Yet other work argues against a general theory of collective violence and instead highlights multiple, different mechanisms at work (Tilly, 2003). A different and promising avenue of inquiry for Rwanda has been the exploration of the effects of conformity and peer pressure on individual behaviour. As Milgram's (1964) experiments famously suggested, these forces can even cause individuals to inflict harm on others. Others point to coercion or ingroup policing, that is the threat or use of physical penalties, to mobilize a group (Brubaker & Laitin, 1998, p. 433; Pfaffenberger, 1994). In Rwanda, the violence was collective. Rwandans assembled into attack groups to hunt for and kill their targets. What importance should be attached to this fact? Were individuals mostly coerced into the violence or did they participate willingly? Are the forces that initiated individuals to violence different from those that sustained them? These questions bear further investigation in Rwanda.

The State, Elite, and Obedience-Related Explanations

At the country-level of analysis, the connection between the state and genocide is a very strong one. But what aspect of the state is important in explaining genocide? One debate centres on the type of *regime* in control of the state. Authoritarian regimes, it is argued, are more likely to commit genocide than democracies (Rummel, 1995). Institutionalist and normative logics have been proposed as explanations. If power is highly concentrated in a single or a few institutions – as it is in dictatorships – checks and balances are weak and it becomes difficult to organize opposition to state-enforced policies such as genocide. The normative logic points to the respect of human rights and values such as tolerance and pluralism that prevail in democracies as a source of restraint. Another set of arguments focuses on the state's *material capacity* instead. Strong states, particularly those with modern bureaucratic, military, and financial systems, have the means to organize and implement mass violence and have nurtured the argument that genocide is a by-product of modernity (Bauman, 2000). Rwanda has been described as an atypical state in sub-Saharan Africa (Straus, 2006,

p. 202). Its machinery of state was visible and effective outside of urban centres. How did this fact affect the violence? A third set of arguments relate to the state's *authority*. The state can lend its symbolic authority to legitimize its actions. It enjoys the Weberian monopoly on the legitimate use of violence in the enforcement of its order. It is the authority of the state that distinguishes criminal from justified use of force.

At the individual-level, the state authority-oriented argument neatly dovetails with obedience-centred explanations. In countries where the state's authority is strong, it is tempting to infer a 'culture of obedience'. This argument has been put forward to explain participation in Rwanda's genocide and in the Holocaust.[33] Ordinary Rwandans killed because the authorities told them to do so. In reality, it is difficult to know whether the absence of overt civil disobedience indicates a reverence for authority or instead a recognition of the state's capacity to punish dissent: obedience or compliance? Alternatively, perhaps we assume obedience because we do not 'see' dissent even though it is present. Resistance can be covert and subtle. The 'weapons of the weak' are rarely public and confrontational (Scott, 1985). But did Rwandans robotically obey orders to kill or was their action the result of a strategic calculation of what was in their self-interest to do?

The importance of individual agency is more common in explanations that focus on the role of *elites*. The image of the obedient masses also neatly dovetails with the image of a manipulative leadership. The malleability of ordinary citizens is matched by the ability of elites to exploit and mobilize them. This instrumentalist paradigm is popular in accounts of Rwanda. It was a small group of individuals in positions of power and influence who organized and are thus responsible for the genocide in Rwanda. Many of them occupied positions of authority within the state apparatus. The notion that genocide is the product of elite calculation and logic has considerable support among scholars wedded to rationalist explanations of conflict. Ruling elites choose genocide to attain strategic military and political objectives (de Figueiredo & Weingast, 1999; Valentino, 2004) or because it the most 'convenient' solution to a problematic population (Chirot, 2010). However, the emphasis on both the state and elites in these arguments

---

[33] For obedience in Rwanda, see Gérard Prunier (1998, p. 248). For the Holocaust, see Staub (1989, pp. 108–111)

1.6 Theories and Hypotheses

tends to eclipse the extent – if any – to which pressure for the violence originated from below – from within Rwandan society itself. In a challenge to such top-down explanations, it has been argued that mass violence usually also has social roots and popular involvement is commonplace. Social groups of varying agendas either coalesce or compete to redistribute power within society (Gerlach, 2006). The role of ordinary individuals in initiating and sustaining the violence – pressure from below – needs more careful scrutiny in the context of Rwanda.

Dispositional and Situational Explanations

According to the dispositional perspective, individuals commit extraordinary crimes because they possess extraordinary characteristics that predispose them to violence. The list of traits that distinguish such individuals is long and the root causes complex: perpetrators might be especially authoritarian, anti-social, sadistic, or narcissistic for example.[34] However, these explanations do not resonate as strongly in cases of *mass* violence. Could so many Rwandans, for example, have had 'abnormal' personalities? If we do accept that there was something extraordinary about so many Rwandans, the argument almost approaches a culturalist explanation. It suggests that there was something peculiar about Rwandan culture that made so many Rwandans susceptible to genocidal violence. These types of arguments are difficult to prove, especially without comparison to another culture. The hostility to the claim that only Germans could have eliminated the Jews in the Holocaust because of a particular German cultural predisposition reflects the dangers of such an argument.[35]

'Deviancy'-type explanations then give way to 'ordinary men' arguments in the context of mass participation. Ordinary individuals become capable of atrocity only in extraordinary situations. The now-famous psycho-social experiments of Milgram (1963) on authority, Asch (1951) on conformity, and Zimbardo (1973) on situational roles and perceived power underpin a scholarly consensus in favour of situationalist explanations of atrocity commission. This early work has

---

[34] On authoritarian personalities and perpetrators, see Suedfeld and Schaller in Newman and Erber (2002). On anti-social personalities, see Staub (1989, pp. 70–73). On sadism and narcissism, see Baumeister and Campbell (1999).
[35] Goldhagen (1997) had advanced this culturalist argument.

led to sophisticated models of how individuals become capable of evil (Waller, 2002). There is a 'Lucifer effect' (Zimbardo, 2007). Yet more recent research has begun to challenge the methods and conclusions of the first-generation work on the willingness of ordinary individuals to inflict harm on others. Scholars have begun to argue that individual motivations are heterogeneous (Hinton, 2004; Straus, 2006) and that that there are important distinctions between participants, bystanders, and rescuers that require explanation (Baum, 2008). But what evidence do we have of the distribution of the different motivations within society? Do these motives change over time? If so, what causes them to change?

Bystander, Inaction, and Impunity Effects

At the individual-level, 'bystanders' can exert a very powerful influence over perpetrators. Their inaction can legitimize the actions of perpetrators, it has been argued (Staub, 1989, pp. 86–88). This is most apparent in group situations. Passivity is seen as acquiescence and it contributes to group 'norming'. Those who pursue violence – even if they are in a minority – feel that they enjoy the support of the majority that looks on. Their faith in their chosen course of action is affirmed. What were the many Rwandans who did not participate in the genocide thinking and feeling at the time? Did they approve? Were they indifferent? Or did they object but were afraid to voice their objections? The role of the non-participants in the violence deserves a closer look in Rwanda's genocide. This micro-level mechanism has an equivalent at the meso- and macro-levels. The Catholic Church, the civil society actor best-placed to counterbalance the power of the state in Rwanda, was at best equivocal in its condemnation of anti-Tutsi violence before and during the genocide (Longman, 2010). Similarly, it has been argued that the absence of protest or opposition from other governments emboldened the extremist government. The absence of external constraint meant that it felt it could act with impunity. According to this view, the failure of the international community to recognize a genocide in Rwanda, to condemn the actions of the extremists, and to intervene were encouragements to the extremists. The moderates found themselves without outside support to strengthen their position (Des Forges, 1999, p. 2).

External and International Factors

In contrast with the many theories that focus on the domestic determinants of genocide, these explanations highlight forces that operate beyond the confines of state boundaries. Midlarsky (2005) argues that genocide is the product of realpolitik between states and stresses state insecurity created by territorial loss. The RPF, which invaded Rwanda with Ugandan support, eventually made territorial gains that threatened the state controlled by a Hutu elite. More broadly, the role of foreign sponsorship is often highlighted in cases of internal war where an external sponsor provides diplomatic and material support that, if given to challengers, alters the balance of power and intensifies the threat to incumbents. The Habyarimana regime clearly felt it had been attacked by Museveni's Uganda (Gasana, 2002b). A similar logic is used to explain the role of diasporas. Their support, often financial, provides the means for challengers to initiate and sustain rebellions (Collier & Hoeffler, 2004). The RPF owed its capability to wage a war to the efforts to mobilize the Rwandan refugee population by its predecessor organization, the Rwandese Alliance for National Unity (RANU). Insofar as war and genocide are causally related, external actors such as states and diasporas may have contributory roles.

A second set of arguments points to the extra-territorial impact of domestic politics in neighbouring states. Bhavnani and Lavery (2011) argue that transnational ethnic ties mean threats to ethnic kin abroad may affect perceptions of threats at home. The assassination of Burundi's first elected Hutu president by Tutsi soldiers profoundly impacted the trust in Rwanda towards the RPF. Similarly, the unwelcoming politics facing Banyarwanda communities in Uganda and Zaire shaped the decision to seek armed return to Rwanda (Mamdani, 2001, pp. 159–185). Lastly, as mentioned in relation to bystanders, international inaction – the failure to condemn and stop atrocities – may embolden extremists to continue coercion. However, it has also been argued that international action can even increase the risk of genocide. Mediators facilitating the Arusha negotiations underestimated the extent to which Hutu hardliners were willing to go to protect their position and pushed too hard for an agreement that hardliners within the government could not accept (A.J. Kuperman, 1996).

1.7 The Argument Sketched

To answer the two central questions posed in this book – how and why the genocide occurred and how and why ordinary Rwandans came to participate in the ensuing violence – I consider the many theories in circulation against the evidence I collected and present an argument that first identifies the conditions that increased the risk of genocidal violence in Rwanda and then traces the steps in the causal process that ultimately culminated in it. My ontological approach to causal explanation then explicitly recognizes that phenomena such as genocide are the product of complex sequences of events and of strategic interactions between actors that unfold over time.

My argument begins then by recognizing several socio-demographic and historical peculiarities that set this otherwise little-known country apart from others in Africa. These unusual features did not mean that genocide was inevitable in Rwanda. But they did portend that societal division and political contestation would be more likely to occur along ethnic rather than non-ethnic lines in this tiny African state.

To start with, Rwanda's ethnic structure was distinctive. It comprised only three groups, unusual in a continent with the world's highest levels of ethnic diversity, of which one group, the Hutu, constituted an overwhelming numerical majority relative to the Tutsi and Twa minority groups. No state on the continent had an ethnic imbalance as large as that in Rwanda. The asymmetry would lend credence to the claim that Tutsi minority rule was particularly unjust. The relationship between these three groups was also distinctive. They were not tribes or even clearly 'ethnic' groups in the popular or conventional sense. They did *not* inhabit separate regions, they did *not* possess distinct cultures, and they did *not* have different political systems. Hutu, Tutsi, and Twa had instead been ruled together as one people, the Banyarwanda, since the late precolonial era. Moreover, their relationship was *ranked*. Tutsi came to signify higher, and Hutu lower, status. Mobility had once been possible within the social hierarchy. Despite all these particularities, Belgian colonial policy unfortunately failed to recognize the unusual structure, nature, and relationship between Rwanda's 'ethnic' groups. It instead reified the differences and reinforced the ranking between them by favouring Tutsi in the allocation of state offices and by recording ethnicity on compulsory registration cards.

1.7 The Argument Sketched

The institutionalization of ethnicity and of its ranked structure would represent a structural vulnerability for Rwanda.

Rwanda also experienced an idiosyncratic trajectory to independence. Its social revolution, which abolished the Tutsi monarchy and ushered in an independent Hutu-controlled republic, was, along with the Afro-Shirazi revolution in Zanzibar, an exceptional event in the history of African decolonization. It was also a critical juncture in Rwanda's political history. By reversing the Tutsi political monopoly that Belgium had established and creating instead a Hutu ethnocracy, it challenged the ethnic ranking of Tutsi ascendance and Hutu subordination. It also gave rise to an ideology that framed the revolution as the moment of Hutu emancipation and equated democracy with Hutu majority rule. The revolution powerfully reinforced the Hutu–Tutsi boundary. It also triggered an exodus of several hundred thousand Tutsi out of Rwanda. The refugees would always look to return. In short, Rwanda represented a highly unusual baseline. A distinctive ethnic demography, a history of institutionalized ethnic favouritism, and a revolutionary shift in an ethnically ranked order were among the features that distinguished this small central African country. These unusual characteristics magnified the risk that political contestation would follow ethnic rather than non-ethnic boundaries in Rwanda.

This risk was realized in 1994 by the conjunction, against this unusual baseline, of two macro-political events: a civil war and political liberalization. Their coincidence was historical accident. The rebel invasion happened to occur with the democratic wave that swept across Africa following the end of the Cold War. Their origins, however, were causally distinct. Together, they constituted an acute threat: an external military threat and an internal political threat. They induced both mass and elite insecurity. At the outset, however, the war radicalized some, but not many, ordinary Rwandans. In contrast, among the ruling elite, the dual threat instilled an acute sense of vulnerability. It portended the redistribution or complete loss of political power.

Liberalization represented not only a threat to the incumbent political class. It also presented an opportunity for their challengers. Its most immediate impact was to pluralize Rwanda's political landscape. Importantly, moderate rather than extremist ideologies dominated initially. The political competition created by liberalization divided the country primarily along partisan, not ethnic lines. In fact, several of the new opposition parties enjoyed cross-ethnic support at the outset. However, as the war progressed, this changed. It was not simply that the war radicalized Rwanda's politics. Liberalization also drove the war. The two processes interacted. Most fatefully, liberalization resulted in a serious design flaw in the peace process. It produced a multiparty coalition government *before* the conclusion of a peace agreement and power-sharing settlement. The opposition parties participated in the negotiations as part of the Rwandan government delegation. Yet their interests were more aligned with the rebels than with the ruling party. The terms ultimately agreed then conceded too much military and political advantage to the enemy in the view of regime hardliners. The result was the escalation of elite contestation and the rise of ethnic extremism.

This contestation was complex. It took place both between and within actors. The contestation created by the *war* was between the rebel RPF, composed primarily of Tutsi exiles who attacked from Uganda, and the Government of Rwanda, dominated in the initial phase of the war by a northern Hutu elite. This military contestation interacted with and escalated the political contestation created by liberalization. Initially, this political contestation was between conservatives and reformers. Within the ruling party, it took place between loyalists and reformers: individuals committed and opposed to the president. It also took place between the ruling party and the main opposition parties: individuals who sought to preserve or to change the distribution of political power. However, as the war escalated, the contestation between conservatives and reformers evolved into contestation between moderates and hardliners: individuals open or opposed to using force to avoid power-sharing across ethnic lines. Each escalatory action committed by the rebels bolstered the credibility of hawks and undermined the influence of doves within the ruling and opposition parties. In turn, escalatory actions committed by hardliners in these parties strengthened the determination of the RPF to resolve the external contestation on the battlefield. In short, the contestation created by the war and the contestation created by liberalization strategically interacted and drove each other in a mutually reinforcing cycle.

Escalation and extremism, however, were not inevitable in Rwanda. I argue that it was the weakness of domestic and international constraints on the actions taken by each side that enabled the threat to

1.7 The Argument Sketched

intensify and ethnic extremism to rise. At the domestic level, key state institutions and civil society actors failed to respond to extremist rhetoric and violence. Extremists acted with impunity. At the international level, the absence of an intervention force capable of enforcing peace preserved the military threat, and external pressure for democratic reform and participation in power-sharing talks reinforced the political threat. As these dual threats escalated, so too did the inter-elite contestation.

This contestation intensified in the space of opportunity created by Habyarimana's death. His assassination, of by far the longest-serving head of state in sub-Saharan Africa to be killed in office, created an unprecedented political opportunity. In theoretical terms, it marked a sudden rupture in the political opportunity structure. No other country in sub-Saharan Africa had experienced this 'perfect storm' of a civil war, political liberalization, and assassination of head of state. Together, they represented the coincidence of a security threat with a political opportunity. In the power vacuum and uncertainty that ensued, hardliners within the regime manoeuvred for control of the state. Regime moderates responded and were initially successful in rebuffing extremist efforts to seize power. Simultaneously, the civil war resumed as the Presidential Guard engaged the RPF in Kigali, and extremist violence commenced, targeting Tutsi civilians and Hutu political moderates. Both the rebels, whose high command was not divided in how to respond to Habyarimana's death, and the regime's extremists refused to de-escalate.

Yet, I argue, genocide was still not the inevitable outcome of this intensified contestation. The regime's extremists were not destined to prevail over moderates and to capture the state. The power struggle could have resolved in either side's favour. Contestation escalated in favour of violence and extremists, however, because the domestic and international constraints on escalatory actions were, again, weak in Rwanda. At the domestic level, Rwanda's state institutions not only failed to stop the extremist violence targeting civilians, they also failed to mediate the conflict over the president's succession and the continuation of government. Extremists argued that the 1991 constitution while moderates claimed that the 1993 Arusha peace agreement governed the succession. In contrast, it was clear that there was no legal basis for the installation of a new cabinet. Nonetheless, Rwanda's Constitutional Court, the legally mandated institution, was not called upon to resolve either issue. It was viewed as partisan, not independent. Its president, who would be among the first to be assassinated on 7 April 1994, had publicly declared his support for an opposition party. At the international level, the erroneous characterization of the violence as only a civil war rather than also as a genocide, and belated attribution of responsibility to the extremists, along with the decision not to reinforce but to draw down the UN peacekeeping force, played out in favour of those committed to war and violence on both sides. International inaction emboldened extremists and reinforced their sense of impunity.

In the face of weak domestic and international constraints, I argue that the contestation simply resolved according to the relative material capabilities of the parties. At the domestic level, inside the regime, there was no clear advantage in terms of relative *coordination* power. Extremists and moderates both controlled important positions in the civilian and military apparatus of state. Extremists, however, had a clearer advantage in terms of *coercive* power. They had at their command superior military forces in Kigali. This enabled them ultimately to prevail at the national level and to capture the civilian and military apparatus of state. They installed their candidate for president, their candidates for an interim government, and, eventually, their candidate for army chief-of-staff. At the international level, as we now know, between the government and rebels, the RPF ultimately proved to be stronger on the battlefield.

The political opportunity created by the president's assassination also triggered contestation at the local level. Capture of the state locally was crucial for the mobilization of the population and the implementation of the killing. Importantly, these power struggles did not *follow* extremist capture of the centre. They happened concurrently with the contestation at the national level. Across Rwanda's 11 prefectures and 145 communes, some prefects and burgomasters, in particular party loyalists who subscribed to the hardliner position on the war or who had strong personal or kinship ties to hardliners at the centre, took the initiative themselves to use their official power to immediately target their Tutsi populations. In some of these localities, the violence began even *before* the fall of the centre. Violence, then, did not simply radiate from centre-to-periphery or from top-to-bottom. It moved in both directions.

1.7 The Argument Sketched

Other state officials at the local level, particularly those who belonged to opposition parties or who were otherwise not part of the informal network of personal ties linking the centre and periphery, were uncertain what to do or else refused to target Tutsi. However, once extremists captured the centre, officials able to face down local challenges initially were quickly neutralized. The centre had considerably more powerful resources at its disposal to co-opt, coerce, or cast out the recalcitrant. This is why extremism ultimately prevailed everywhere in Rwanda once the centre fell. In addition to pressures from the centre, some local officials also faced challengers – both extremists and opportunists – from within their own communities who sought to replace them. These ethnic and political entrepreneurs were not all tied to the state. Some were private citizens. There was resistance, then, to violence from *within* the state apparatus and also pressure for violence from *outside* of it.

These differences in extremist control at the local level resulted in variation in how quickly violence broke out across Rwanda's communes. Violence was delayed where it took time for local power struggles to resolve. However, it was not only elite resistance from above that mattered. Resistance from below in communities with strong inter-ethnic ties also slowed down the genocide's onset. In some localities, Hutu and Tutsi residents collaborated to prevent violence from entering their communities. It took time to break these social bonds and to divide cohesive communities. This resistance never prevented violence altogether. It merely delayed it. Communities that resisted found themselves subject to extra-local pressures. Individuals and groups from neighbouring communes infiltrated and helped divide and mobilize those communities that wavered. Contagion effects were strong in a small, densely populated country.

Extremists, once in control of the state at either the national or local levels, used the state's considerable power to implement the genocide. This power did not comprise simply the Rwandan state's unusually strong material capabilities to coerce its citizens and to coordinate across its agents. Its power also derived from its unusually high symbolic authority for a postcolonial African state. This authority legitimized, for some Rwandans, the directives of state officials and, consequently, also the violence when framed as national defence. The Rwandan state's low autonomy vis-à-vis society was also important. Low autonomy enabled the capture of the state by private social and political forces. The ruling party had penetrated the state down to the lowest administrative level in Rwanda. Its machinery, even more so than that of the state apparatus, was remarkable. Party extremists instrumentalized the state, which became a weapon of mass destruction *par excellence* vis-à-vis society. Together, these three distinct dimensions of the state's power – its capacity, legitimacy, and autonomy – were each consequential for the genocide and each would matter for mobilizing Rwandans.

Popular mobilization typically followed state capture. In communities across Rwanda, local political and ethnic entrepreneurs – opportunists and racists – emerged and drew on their social networks to establish small groups of supporters to mobilize the wider population. Importantly, these mobilizing agents were not all state office-holders. They were also not all local elites. Many were unconnected to the state and a large number were also ordinary farmers. Pressure for violence existed below within Rwandan *society* too. Once these 'critical masses' had been formed, they jump-started the violence through ingroup policing. Residents were threatened with and suffered social, financial, and physical sanctions if they did not join the attack groups. Yet not everyone participated in the killing. A majority in fact did not. This was, in part, due to differences in individual disposition toward the violence. Contrary to the consensus, killers were not all 'ordinary'. They were also not all 'coerced' into killing. There was heterogeneity among perpetrators and a multiplicity of motivations. Mobilization was in fact a continuum. I found that 'extremists' – often minorities in their communities – moved first, followed by 'opportunists', and lastly 'conformists', typically the largest group. There were also pacifists who resisted participation.

Dispositional differences alone, however, do not explain why some participated and others not. Selection into the violence was also mediated by micro-situational opportunities and relational ties. Settlement patterns and social networks were consequential. Where you lived and who you knew also mattered for whether you would join in the killing. Counter-intuitively, it was not social isolates but rather the most socially connected individuals in communities who were the ones most likely to be drawn into the violence. Social capital had a dark side. Once engaged in violence, individual motivations also changed. Radicalization occurred through the act of killing. Well-known psycho-social mechanisms – desensitization, habituation, and dehumanization – explain how the reluctant could become the zealous. It is also how the coerced could become the cruel. The shocking pain and suffering inflicted gratuitously on some victims, including the sexual torture of women, was also the product of repeated killing and continuing impunity.

Such macabre behaviour is in fact not unusual in cases of ethnic violence and mass killings. However, the violence and mobilization that occurred in Rwanda were unusual in another way. They were extraordinary in their scale, speed, and scope. One in five Hutu men participated in killing nearly two-thirds of Rwanda's Tutsi population in just over 100 days and in almost every community across Rwanda. The reasons for this, I argue, may be traced to Rwanda's highly unusual socio-demography and geography. Rwanda comprised a small territory with a highly agrarian society, an exceptionally high population density, and an unusual pattern of spatially integrated ethnic settlement. This meant that the distances between communities were small, magnifying contagion effects; the social ties among individuals were dense and multiplex, amplifying the social forces of coercion and co-optation; and anonymity and privacy were low, making it difficult for neighbours to escape detection.

In sum, I argue that security (civil war and democratization), opportunity (democratization and assassination), and authority (the state) – the three themes of the book's title – each mattered. To borrow a popular idiom from criminal law, they represent the means (a powerful and privatized state), the motive (a war-time and liberalization threat), and the opportunity (multipartyism and the president's assassination) for genocide.

1.8 Research Design: The Evidence and Methods

Genocide is an empirically complex phenomenon. No single study can account for all aspects of its violence. It is also a highly politicized and deeply emotional subject. On certain issues, the findings may always be disputed and some people may never be persuaded. Researchers may find that they themselves, rather than their research, are the object of scrutiny and criticism. Accusations of revisionism, minimalism, and denialism are among the risks that genocide scholars, including those working on Rwanda, face. Given this, I take the time in this section to explain, in more detail than is customary, the methodological choices made and the evidentiary base relied on in this book to help readers decide how much credibility my findings merit. Transparency will not protect researchers from personal criticisms intended to discredit their character and motivation. However, it may help demonstrate whether their conclusions have a scientifically defensible basis or not.

The Research Design

I made a number of deliberate choices in the book's approach to explaining the genocide and individual participation in it. First, I emphasize mechanisms. The particular structural vulnerabilities and exceptional conjunction of events that gave rise to genocide in Rwanda are unlikely to exist or arise in exactly the same manner in other places. However, I believe some of the underlying mechanisms at work are observable elsewhere. Persistent definitional debates over what constitutes genocide makes grand theorization on genocide and direct comparisons difficult. The mechanisms-focused approach allows more contingent comparisons to be made to other cases.

Second, as already noted, I examine the genocide at several levels of analysis. I synthesize processes and events at the macro-, meso-, and micro-levels in an attempt to identify the forces at work across them and to understand how agenda and actions at the international, national, and local levels interacted.

Third, the approach is explicitly interdisciplinary. I draw on theoretical insights primarily from political science on the nature of the state and state-society relations, civil wars and counter-insurgencies, political communication and framing, and democratic transitions; but also from sociology on social movement mobilization, social networks and recruitment, and collective action and critical masses; and lastly from social psychology looking at, *inter alia*, obedience and conformity, intergroup contact and relations, and social identity theories.

Fourth, the approach relies heavily on comparisons. While this is a study of one genocide in one country, it makes a number of cross-national and sub-national comparisons. It points to Rwanda's exceptionalism by ranking it against other sub-Saharan countries on a range of dimensions relating primarily to its demography and geography. It also compares how the genocide unfolded at multiple levels of Rwanda's territorial administration. Rwanda comprised 11 prefectures, 145 communes, 1545 sectors, and about 9,000 cells in 1994. The book makes structured comparisons between two prefectures, Ruhengeri and Butare, to capture a historically and politically important north-south divide in the country; two communes, Mukingo and Taba, chosen because the genocide began early and late in them respectively; and four cells, selected because two (Tamba and Mutovu) experienced high levels and two (Ruginga and Mwendo) low levels of violence during the genocide. The book also systematically compares individuals who mobilized during the genocide against those who did not. Most studies of perpetrators – primarily from the Holocaust and Rwanda – neglect to study those who did *not* commit violence. Yet studying non-perpetrators is important for understanding how 'ordinary' the killers really were and for helping to explain why some persons participated but others not.

Lastly, the book makes an inter-temporal comparison looking at life before and during the genocide in order to trace the evolution of events that led up to the genocide in these communities. An important question that still needs to be answered is to what extent the violence marked an unexpected rupture in inter-ethnic relations. Were communities widely radicalized before the violence began?

The Evidence

The project collected a diverse set of data types to test its hypotheses. Ultimately the argument presented in this book was constructed from thirteen main sources of information. First, I conducted a survey of 294 Rwandans. The survey questionnaire comprised 223 questions relating to their attitudes, opinions, memories, and beliefs.[36] It also collected information on their demographic and socio-economic characteristics. The sample was stratified two ways. It was divided between perpetrators (104 individuals) and non-perpetrators (190 individuals). This latter group included a small number of genocide survivors (34 individuals).[37] A perpetrator was defined as any individual who joined an attack group that killed at least one individual. The perpetrator then need not have

---

[36] One hundred and sixty of these questions were pre-coded. The remaining sixty-three were open-ended.

[37] In Rwanda, the term 'survivor' refers not only to Tutsi but also to the Hutu wives of Tutsi men who were sometimes also targeted. From among the thirty-four 'survivors', twenty-one were Tutsi, and thirteen were Hutu women formerly married to Tutsi men.

struck a physical blow himself.[38] It was also stratified by region, Ruhengeri prefecture in the north, and Butare prefecture in the south. The sample was designed to be statistically representative of each region.

Second, I talked to forty-two Rwandans in more detailed, open-ended interviews about life before and during the genocide in their communities. I interviewed 21 in depth and on several occasions using a semi-structured interview questionnaire, and 21 who were a subset of the 294 survey respondents, I interviewed in less detail, asking more targeted questions. All forty-two were individuals resident in the four chosen cells at the time of the genocide. Where possible, in each community I talked with survivors, perpetrators, bystanders, figures of state and social authority, and older residents with historical knowledge of the community. The goal was to interview a cross-section of these communities.

Third, I asked literate Rwandan prison inmates – who had been accused of genocide-related crimes – to write histories of the genocide in their communities from their own perspectives. The goal was not to obtain a reliable record of events – which would have been highly unlikely – but to gain an insight into how and what these individuals were thinking beyond what they might choose to reveal in an oral interview.

Turning to the quantitative data presented in the book, I relied on several datasets drawing either on data I had collected myself or on information in other existing datasets. First, I assembled data profiling Rwanda's 145 administrative communes to test hypotheses on why violence began early in some places, but later in others. I drew on several sources but relied primarily on Rwanda's 1991 population census – the last time that information on ethnicity was collected in a Rwandan census. Its credibility on this issue has been questioned, but the raw micro-data, which had until recently been missing, have reappeared and allow the census to be more deeply probed for reliability.

Second, I undertook a census of the population of one administrative sector – about 3,400 individuals – as it existed in 1994, collected data on the spatial location of all 647 households, and mapped the social networks of 116 residents to help explain differential selection into the

---

[38] It became apparent through the interviews that in attack groups that encountered small numbers of Tutsi, only a few individuals were required to carry out the actual act of killing.

1.8 Research Design: The Evidence and Methods 39

violence. Third, I analysed the content of broadcasts from *Radio Télévision Libre des Mille Collines* (RTLM) – infamously known as Radio Machete – from before and during the genocide. I obtained transcripts for 55 of the 360 days that RTLM was on the air. The broadcasts provide a fascinating insight into the evolution of extremist thinking over time, and into the issues to which radio listeners were exposed during this period.

Fourth, I compiled demographic data on 160 individuals identified in a survey as organizers and leaders during the genocide in two prefectures to construct profiles of local mobilizing agents. Fifth, I collected data on the assassinations of African heads of state and on the contexts in which they were killed to situate the significance of Habyarimana's assassination. Lastly, I drew directly from several datasets compiled by others to compare Rwanda with other countries. As I argue, Rwanda was an exceptional country in Africa – an extraordinary baseline for genocide – and these data provide the support for this claim. Too numerous to list here, I acknowledge them in the text when I draw on them.

In terms of other sources of information, I also drew on data from *gacaca*, a traditional institution adapted by the Rwandan government to establish truth, justice, and reconciliation in local communities in the aftermath of the genocide. It was conceived primarily to expedite the processing of the large number of suspected perpetrators by assigning local communities this responsibility. While reliance on *gacaca* data requires caution for a number of reasons, the *gacaca* produced enormous amounts of important information concerning the genocide at the local level. In particular, communities collectively compiled lists of the accused, categorized by the type of crime they had committed, as well as lists of the victims. I also relied on evidence from the ICTR in Arusha, Tanzania. Its public records database contains a wealth of information concerning individuals and events during the genocide. Witness testimony is weighed and evaluated against a high standard of proof before a 'fact' is established. Lastly, I also drew extensively on several archival sources. I am particularly indebted to those researchers who compiled databases of: (i) Rwandan presidential speeches from 1962–1994, whose content I analysed for the evolution in ideological messaging in Rwanda; (ii) declassified UN Security Council documents, including cables from UNAMIR to the UN Secretariat, for the period leading up to and during the genocide, which informed my analysis of what was known and what more could have been done to minimize the killing; and (iii) the minutes of closed meetings held and public statements issued by Rwanda's Military Crisis Committee (MCC) and then its Interim Government (IG) during the genocide. These documents were invaluable for my analysis of how extremists outmanoeuvred moderates to capture the state and implement the genocide.

A Critical Note on the Methods Used in the Project

As with the evidence, the level of transparency in the methods and approach followed should be high enough to allow readers to evaluate their suitability given the deeply contested nature of research on the genocide. Methodological choices often involve trade-offs and taking the time to explain the risks, and the steps taken to mitigate these risks, is particularly valuable in such contexts.

First, the time at which the research was conducted mattered. The evidence I draw on in this book was collected over the course of three main field trips: the first between November 2002 and August 2003; the second in summer 2009; and lastly in spring 2017. I was asking Rwandans questions about events that took place first nine years, then fifteen years, and eventually twenty-three years previously. There was a very strong likelihood that individuals would have constructed narratives of events subsequently, as well of course as the possibility of memory loss.

Second, also related to the timing of the research, the social and political climate in Rwanda almost certainly influenced some individuals' responses. Rwanda's post-genocide government was composed heavily of the rebel group that had won the war ending the genocide. It was widely seen as pro-Tutsi and authoritarian within Hutu circles. Moreover, its policy of national reconciliation made discussion of ethnicity taboo. I anticipated self-censorship or else socially and politically favourable answers on certain issues.

Third, working with perpetrators of violence presented particular problems. In the Rwandan context, it was already a challenge to identify a perpetrator reliably. Many individuals had not confessed to their crimes, even though some had been in prison for nearly fifteen years when I spoke with them. Some were still at large in their communities. Those who had confessed had an incentive to minimize their

1.8 Research Design: The Evidence and Methods 41

personal responsibility, especially as the *gacaca* local courts were in effect when I interviewed them. There were clearly risks in relying on perpetrator testimony. Moreover, there is evidently an ethical dimension to working with perpetrators of violence. One of the greatest risks lies in re-traumatizing individuals when asking them to remember horrific events. It needed to be done with care and sensitivity.

Fourth, there was the risk of using intermediaries when conducting interviews. Unless my interviewees spoke French, I had to rely on the aid of a Kinyarwandaphone interpreter. His identity might well influence responses. In addition, there is bound to have been some loss of the linguistic and cultural nuances in translation. Similarly, all the respondents who were surveyed outside of the prison (190 individuals) were interviewed by enumerators I had hired and trained. Their identity might also have shaped responses.

I tried to devise solutions to all of these challenges. None was a panacea. I attempted then to mitigate self-serving bias and self-censorship, which were at the heart of the first three problems mentioned above, through three techniques. First, I used triangulation. I verified 'facts' by comparing Tutsi survivor testimony against Hutu perpetrator and non-perpetrator statements. As will be evident in the following chapters, I always report answers from both groups. Second, I gave more credibility to 'statements-against-interest'. A Hutu who told me that he holds the current government responsible for the genocide was likely to be sincere in his belief. He faced a strong disincentive to make this view public. Third, I sometimes asked the same question but made a grammatical switch from the second to third person. Instead of asking an individual 'What did you do?' or 'What did you think?', I would ask 'What did others do?' or 'What did others think?' While far from fool-proof, each of these techniques went some way to helping me establish with some more reliability what happened in Rwanda.

Gacaca made differentiating between perpetrators and non-perpetrators somewhat easier. Each community participating in *gacaca* was required to compile a list of the accused, and ultimately to categorize individuals by the crimes they had committed in their communities. However, the lists were not infallible. It was not unknown for false accusations to be made. To minimize this risk, I verified the names against a second list of the accused established by a lesser-known and informal *gacaca* process involving self-confessed perpetrators within the prison system. Only if a name appeared on *both* lists was it included for selection in the perpetrator stratum of the survey. Conversely, non-perpetrators were identified by checking that his/her name did not appear on *either* list.

Intermediary effects were unavoidable given my limited Kinyarwanda. Moreover, my research assistant, Moses, was Tutsi. It quickly became apparent that it was not possible to keep this fact from interviewees. However, to my surprise, when in the prisons talking to Hutu perpetrators, his ethnicity proved to be less of an obstacle to trust than I initially feared. To be clear, trust was not immediate and it was not universal. However, after my first few interviews, word quickly circulated within the prison that there was a 'mazungu' ('white' foreigner) doing research who wanted to understand the genocide from their perspective. We spent several weeks in each prison we visited and at the end of our time in one of them, I was surprised when Moses brought a gift of a portable radio to some of the inmates. The ethnic distance I had worried about was not reflected in the relationship my interpreter had established with the prisoners. In the case of the non-perpetrator survey outside of the prison, I hired enumerators who were Hutu and who were already known in the communities in which they operated. I found this prior acquaintance with the community made a big difference. People naturally found it difficult to trust outsiders. Many of those I ultimately chose were the local primary school teacher trainers. They were well educated and understood the sensitivity of the research, and they were well-respected in the communities. I also verified that they themselves had not been implicated in the genocide.

Lastly, I do not have a simple answer to the ethical dilemma posed by interviewing perpetrators and survivors of genocide. It is a difficult balance to strike between the desire to understand and explain the genocide, and the welfare and privacy of the individuals affected by it. In the chapters that follow, while the names of places are real, the names of most of my respondents have been altered to protect their privacy. However, I did keep the true names of respondents who held public office in Rwanda, as well as the true names of well-known perpetrators. Many of my respondents talked willingly and openly. Others spoke without remorse, and even without emotion. Nonetheless, there were still a few who had difficulty. Informed consent procedures, though used here, did not prevent two individuals with whom I spoke from becoming visibly distraught as they told me their stories.

I ended these interviews quickly, and did not revisit these people. Ultimately, tact, sensitivity, and a respect for the limits of the person are the best advice I can give to others contemplating similar research.

1.9 Organization of the Book

Chapter 2 contextualizes Rwanda for the reader and sets the baseline for the genocide. It shows that Rwanda was a highly unusual country in sub-Saharan Africa by highlighting a set of societal, demographic, and geographic characteristics that set it apart from others on the continent. It explains how – in ways that are sometimes surprising – Rwanda's exceptional population density, spatial settlement pattern, limited urbanization/highly agrarian society, low ecological variability, small territory, cultural homogeneity, ranked ethnic structure, and numerical ethnic imbalance would each amplify the forces that led to the genocide. The extraordinary scale, speed, and scope of the violence and mobilization in Rwanda can also be traced to these extraordinary baseline characteristics.

Chapter 3 then turns to the first of the three conjunctural factors: Rwanda's civil war or 'security'. The chapter focuses its lens on the psycho-social impact of the war on ordinary Rwandans and identifies the mechanisms linking the security threat to civilian radicalization. The chapter makes clear, however, that a war-time security threat alone does not explain the genocide. The opportunity for extremism to emerge from the periphery was also needed and this is the subject of Chapters 4 and 5. Chapter 4 examines the opportunity created by Rwanda's political liberalization, the second conjunctural factor. It analyses the impact of multipartyism at the national and local levels and shows that it initially had an ethnically integrative effect as new parties built cross-ethnic support bases. However, it also shows how liberalization and the war interacted to gradually radicalize Rwandan politics. The internal contestation between moderates and hardliners that evolved within Rwanda drove the external contestation between the government and the RPF. It was through these strategic interactions within and between actors that the war escalated and extremism gained ground.

Chapter 5 considers the impact of the third and final conjunctural factor: the assassination of Rwanda's president – another 'opportunity'. It examines how the unexpected death of Habyarimana created a power vacuum and triggered intense power struggles between moderates and hardliners for control of the state at both the national and local levels. These struggles resolved in favour of extremists because external constraints were weak and because extremists controlled superior coercive forces that allowed them to capture the centre. Chapter 6 then examines the role of Rwanda's state or 'authority'. The state was the means through which the genocide was implemented. The chapter traces the historical origins of the Rwandan state's strong capabilities, low autonomy, and high legitimacy and explains how each of the three dimensions mattered for the state's power over its citizens. Chapter 7 then turns to the question of why and how ordinary Rwandans came to kill. It focuses on the puzzle of why certain individuals were drawn into the violence but others not. It shows that differential selection into the violence was a function of dispositional, situational, and relational factors. The chapter also explains the micro-mechanics of Rwanda's massive civilian mobilization. Finally, Chapter 8 concludes with a stocktaking. It considers what has been cumulatively learned about Rwanda's genocide over the last twenty-five years and explores the implications of the book's findings for theories of genocide more generally.

2 | An Extraordinary Baseline

Genocide is an exceptional event. Yet the violence that ensued in Rwanda was exceptional, even for a genocide. By my estimate, nearly two-thirds of Rwanda's Tutsi population were eliminated; one in five Hutu men participated in their deaths; the carnage was accomplished in just over 100 days; and it took place in almost every community in Rwanda where Tutsi lived.[1] The scale, speed, and scope of the violence have helped establish the genocide as a world-historical event and have deeply inscribed Rwanda into global popular consciousness. But what accounts for this extraordinary mobilization and violence? How did so many Rwandans come to kill so many of their fellow citizens so quickly and in so many places? The answer, I argue, is to be found in the extraordinary baseline upon which the forces that led to the genocide acted. In this chapter I introduce Rwanda by casting a spotlight on a set of historical, socio-demographic, and geographic characteristics that set the country apart from others on the continent.

I focus on these features for four reasons. First, these characteristics amplified the forces behind, and the risks posed by, the three macro-political factors – civil war, democratization, and assassination of an autocrat – that I argue created the threat and opportunity leading to the genocide. Second, they account for the extraordinary characteristics of Rwanda's violence that not only shock but have yet to be fully explained. The intensity of the violence, the speed of the killing, the geographic ambit of the bloodshed, and the genocide's most unusual feature – the scale of civilian mobilization – can all be traced to these distinctive characteristics. Third, several of these characteristics also help explain the remarkable power of the Rwandan state. The state was the instrument that extremists captured and weaponized to deadly effect against Rwanda's Tutsi minority. These characteristics help

---

[1] See Chapter 7 for detail on the method and evidence on which my estimates of the number of victims and perpetrators are based.

explain the state's unusually high symbolic authority and capacity to coerce its citizens and coordinate across its officials. Lastly, several of these features explain why Rwandan politics and society were most likely to fracture along ethnic rather than non-ethnic lines when placed under stress. Other fault-lines existed: clan, region, class, lineage, religion, party, and ideology, among others. However, the divisibility risk was highest for Rwanda's ethnic cleavage because of these characteristics.

I begin by tracing Rwanda's historical evolution, highlighting its more remarkable aspects and how they mattered for the genocide. I then identify and explain how a set of unusual societal, demographic, and geographic characteristics also contributed both to the genocide and to the violence that resulted. Table 2.1 collates and quantifies these features for the reader to digest more succinctly and ranks Rwanda against forty-two other sub-Saharan countries on each characteristic. As can be seen, Rwanda scores first or second on almost every single measure. It was, in objective terms, an extraordinary baseline for a genocide to unfold against.

2.1 Tracing Rwanda's Historical Evolution

Rwanda's history is complex and contested. In part, the reason is evidentiary. Much of its precolonial history is unwritten and relies heavily on oral, linguistic, and archaeological evidence. But, in larger part, it is because its history has been politicized. Hutu and Tutsi, and indeed foreign scholars, have advocated competing narratives of Rwanda's past. I focus here on presenting those aspects of its history I believe are pertinent to understanding the genocide's origins. Wherever possible, I reproduce the consensus and highlight the disagreements.

Precolonial History (c. Fourteenth–Seventeenth Century to 1897)

Both the antiquity and continuity of the Rwandan state are often cited as unusual on a continent where most modern-day African states trace their formation and territorial borders to the colonial era and independence.[2] They are believed to be a source of the modern state's natural authority and to account, partly, for its power to mobilize

---

[2] Straus (2006, p. 207), for instance, emphasizes the institutional continuity in Rwanda's borders from the precolonial to postcolonial periods.

Table 2.1 Rwanda's extraordinary baseline characteristics in comparative perspective

Category	Historical	Socio-demographic					Geographic		
Indicator	Boundary Continuity[a]	Population density[b]	Urban population	Ethnic diversity[c]	Ethnic dominance	Territorial size	Ethnic settlement pattern[d]	Road density	Ecological variability[e]
Units (rank)	Scale from 0 to 1.0	pop./sq.km	Percentage of total population	Scale from 0 to 1.0	Percentage of largest group	sq.km	NA	km/sq.km	Std. deviations
Rwanda	0.99 (2)	242.6 (1)	7.1 (2)	0.18 (1)	0.90 (1)	24,670 (4)	Nationwide	0.57 (1)	0.0002 (4)
Angola	0.53 (22)	9.1 (33)	41.3 (34)	0.76 (20)	0.38 (23)	1,246,700 (38)	Regional	0.06 (28)	0.1932 (31)
Benin	0.67 (13)	46.9 (13)	35.8 (25)	0.62 (8)	0.56 (7)	110,620 (14)	Regional/ urban	0.17 (11)	0.0947 (23)
Botswana	0.90 (6)	2.7 (40)	46.2 (38)	0.35 (5)	0.80 (4)	566,730 (25)	Regional/ urban †	0.03 (35)	0.1564 (30)
Burkina Faso	0.57 (19)	37.0 (18)	14.6 (6)	0.70 (14)	0.50 (10)	273,600 (20)	Regional/ urban	0.34 (4)	0.3062 (35)
Burundi	0.98 (4)	231.0 (2)	6.8 (1)	0.33 (4)	0.80 (4)	25,680 (5)	Nationwide	0.56 (2)	0.0008 (6)
Cameroon	0.86 (7)	28.0 (23)	41.4 (35)	0.89 (39)	0.18 (40)	465,400 (24)	Regional	0.07 (26)	0.1465 (28)
Central Afr. Rep.	0.19 (34)	5.1 (38)	37.1 (26)	0.79 (27)	0.31 (27)	622,980 (27)	Regional/ urban	0.04 (30)	0.0589 (18)
Chad	0.48 (24)	5.2 (37)	21.2 (12)	0.77 (25)	0.34 (26)	1,259,200 (39)	Regional	0.02 (38)	0.3292 (38)
Congo	0.25 (32)	18.1 (28)	28.0 (16)	0.88 (36)	0.21 (38)	341,500 (22)	Regional	0.07 (27)	0.0056 (8)
Congo, D.R.	0.37 (28)	7.6 (35)	55.6 (40)	0.93 (42)	0.16 (41)	2,267,050 (41)	Regional	0.04 (32)	0.0002 (3)
Djibouti	0.11 (37)	26.0 (25)	76.0 (42)	0.61 (7)	0.50 (10)	23,180 (3)	Regional/ urban	0.12 (18)	0.0271 (11)
Equatorial Guinea	0.15 (35)	14.7 (29)	37.2 (27)	n/a	n/a	28,050 (6)	Regional/ urban	0.10 (23)	0.0000 (1)

Table 2.1 (*cont.*)

Category	Historical	Socio-demographic				Geographic			
Indicator	Boundary Continuity[a]	Population density[b]	Urban population	Ethnic diversity[c]	Ethnic dominance	Territorial size	Ethnic settlement pattern[d]	Road density	Ecological variability[e]
Units (rank)	Scale from 0 to 1.0	pop./sq.km	Percentage of total population	Scale from 0 to 1.0	Percentage of largest group	sq.km	NA	km/sq.km	Std. deviations
Eritrea	n/a	31.5 (20)	16.3 (9)	0.65 (12)	0.50 (10)	101,000 (13)	Regional/urban	0.04 (31)	0.1062 (25)
Ethiopia	0.95 (5)	53.5 (12)	13.3 (5)	0.76 (21)	0.40 (20)	1,000,000 (34)	Regional/urban	0.03 (37)	0.3926 (41)
Gabon	0.33 (30)	4.0 (39)	72.9 (41)	0.86 (34)	0.30 (28)	257,670 (19)	Regional/urban	0.03 (36)	0.0000 (2)
Gambia	0.83 (8)	105.2 (4)	41.6 (36)	0.76 (23)	0.41 (19)	10,000 (1)	Regional/urban	0.25 (7)	0.0608 (19)
Ghana	0.66 (14)	70.8 (8)	38.7 (30)	0.85 (32)	0.28 (30)	227,540 (17)	Regional/urban	0.16 (12)	0.0300 (12)
Guinea	0.09 (38)	28.0 (24)	28.9 (17)	0.67 (13)	0.48 (14)	245,720 (18)	Regional/urban	0.12 (19)	0.0339 (14)
Guinea-Bissau	0.56 (21)	38.4 (17)	30.6 (21)	0.82 (30)	0.27 (33)	28,120 (7)	Regional/urban	0.15 (15)	0.0495 (17)
Ivory Coast	0.76 (10)	43.5 (15)	40.5 (33)	0.78 (26)	0.36 (24)	318,000 (21)	Regional/urban	0.25 (6)	0.0078 (9)
Kenya	0.64 (15)	45.4 (14)	17.7 (10)	0.85 (33)	0.28 (30)	569,140 (26)	Regional/urban	0.11 (20)	0.3215 (36)
Lesotho	0.99 (2)	57.0 (9)	15.8 (8)	0.25 (2)	0.85 (2)	30,350 (8)	Regional/urban	0.18 (10)	0.0659 (21)

Liberia	0.56 (20)	21.1 (26)	41.9 (37)	0.90 (40)	0.21 (38)	96,320 (12)	Regional/ urban †	0.10 (21)	0.0002 (5)
Malawi	0.34 (29)	103.1 (5)	12.6 (4)	0.83 (31)	0.28 (30)	94,080 (11)	Regional	0.15 (16)	0.0209 (10)
Mali	0.13 (36)	7.6 (34)	24.6 (15)	0.75 (19)	0.43 (15)	1,220,190 (36)	Regional/ urban	0.01 (39)	0.3479 (39)
Mauritania	0.04 (39)	2.1 (41)	39.8 (32)	0.62 (9)	0.43 (15)	1,025,220 (35)	Regional	0.01 (41)	0.0475 (16)
Mozambique	0.80 (9)	18.9 (27)	24.2 (14)	0.77 (24)	0.38 (22)	784,090 (30)	Regional	0.04 (33)	0.1499 (29)
Namibia	0.38 (27)	1.9 (42)	29.0 (18)	0.72 (16)	0.50 (13)	823,290 (31)	Regional/ urban †	0.08 (24)	0.2081 (32)
Niger	0.29 (31)	6.8 (36)	15.6 (7)	0.64 (11)	0.54 (8)	1,266,700 (40)	Regional/ urban	0.01 (40)	0.1231 (26)
Nigeria	0.49 (23)	115.2 (3)	37.4 (28)	0.80 (28)	0.29 (29)	910,770 (33)	Regional/ urban	0.18 (9)	0.2787 (34)
Senegal	0.20 (33)	41.1 (16)	39.3 (31)	0.73 (18)	0.43 (15)	192,530 (15)	Regional/ urban	0.07 (25)	0.3280 (37)
Sierra Leone	0.64 (16)	55.1 (10)	33.9 (24)	0.76 (22)	0.36 (24)	71,620 (10)	Regional/ urban	0.16 (13)	0.0024 (7)
Somalia	0.03 (40)	10.4 (31)	30.7 (22)	0.81 (29)	0.25 (35)	627,340 (28)	Regional/ urban	0.04 (34)	0.1280 (27)
South Africa	n/a	30.9 (21)	53.5 (39)	0.88 (37)	0.22 (36)	1,221,040 (37)	Regional/ urban †	0.27 (5)	0.3598 (40)
Sudan	0.42 (26)	9.7 (32)	30.8 (23)	0.71 (15)	0.40 (20)	2,376,000 (42)	Regional†	0.00 (42)	0.4311 (42)
Swaziland	1.00 (1)	53.9 (11)	23.0 (13)	0.28 (3)	0.84 (3)	17,200 (2)	Regional/ urban	0.16 (14)	0.0957 (24)
Tanzania	0.74 (12)	31.8 (19)	19.9 (11)	0.95 (43)	0.12 (43)	883,590 (32)	Regional/ urban	0.10 (22)	0.0400 (15)
Togo	0.59 (18)	71.7 (7)	29.9 (19)	0.88 (38)	0.22 (36)	54,390 (9)	Regional	0.14 (17)	0.0304 (13)

Table 2.1 (*cont.*)

Category	Historical	Socio-demographic				Geographic			
Indicator	Boundary Continuity[a]	Population density[b]	Urban population	Ethnic diversity[c]	Ethnic dominance	Territorial size	Ethnic settlement pattern[d]	Road density	Ecological variability[e]
Units (rank)	Scale from 0 to 1.0	pop./sq.km	Percentage of total population	Scale from 0 to 1.0	Percentage of largest group	sq.km		km/sq.km	Std. deviations
Uganda	0.63 (17)	97.9 (6)	11.4 (3)	0.93 (41)	0.16 (41)	197,100 (16)	NA	0.35 (3)	0.0761 (22)
Zambia	0.44 (25)	11.4 (30)	38.0 (29)	0.73 (17)	0.43 (15)	743,390 (29)	Regional/urban †	0.05 (29)	0.0654 (20)
Zimbabwe	0.75 (11)	29.1 (22)	30.6 (20)	0.37 (6)	0.77 (6)	386,850 (23)	Regional/urban	0.24 (8)	0.2470 (33)
							Regional/urban †		

[a] Boundary continuity is defined as 'one minus the percentage of a country's population whose ethnic groups are split across colonial borders'. Source: Englebert (2000).
[b] Country size, road density, population density and urban population are taken from the World Bank (2003) African Development Indicators.
[c] Ethnic diversity is defined as the probability that any two randomly selected nationals would be from two different ethnic groups. Ethnic dominance is defined as the percentage of the total population the largest ethnic group represents. Source: J. D. Fearon (2003)
[d] 'Nationwide' indicates all ethnic groups are found in virtually all inhabitable areas of the country; 'regional' signifies the predominant share of every ethnic group is located within a particular locality; 'regional/urban' indicates the existence of ethnic groups that are either region and/or urban-based. † Indicates the existence of at least one ethnic group that is dispersed but only in some parts of the country. Source: GeoEPR dataset by Vogt et al. (2015).
Note: Liberia's 'indigenous peoples' are settled 'nationwide'.
[e] Ecological variability is the standard deviation in the combined values for temperature, precipitation, and sunshine hours across 0.5 × 0.5 decimal degrees cells within the country. *Source:* Michalopoulos (2012).

2.1 Tracing Rwanda's Historical Evolution

the population during the genocide. The historical reality, however, is more complex.

The modern Rwandan state has its roots in the Nyinginya kingdom. The kingdom's exact age is disputed. Rwanda's pre-eminent and Tutsi historian, Alexis Kagame, dates it foundation to AD 1312 (Kagame, 1972–1975). If true, this would distinguish Nyinginya as the oldest polity in the Great Lakes. However, it is likely that Kagame, who also authored a controversial nationalistic defence of the Tutsi feudal system, purposely exaggerated the monarchy's antiquity. Belgian historian Jan Vansina puts its foundation date as sometime in the mid-to-late 1600s. Vansina identifies the kingdom's first head – known as the *Mwami*, a Tutsi who claimed a divine right to rule – as Ndori. Previous *Mwamis*, he claims, were mythical, '...cobbled together from a collection of fictitious tales in order to legitimize the Nyiginya dynasty and to exalt its majesty...' (Vansina, 2004, p. 44). If true, this would mean the kingdom appeared at about the same time as other polities in the region. Its antiquity would not distinguish it. Notwithstanding the disagreement, we can say that the modern Rwandan state, as the successor to Nyinginya, was at least 260 years old when the country became independent.

The continuity in the territory encompassed by both the precolonial and postcolonial polities is another often-cited particularity of the Rwandan state. After Swaziland, Rwanda's ethnic groups had the smallest percentage of their overall population separated by colonially imposed borders in sub-Saharan Africa.[3] Yet the precolonial boundaries were not constant. The kingdom's original nucleus of power was the Nduga region, in what is present-day central Rwanda. The tiny polity expanded – and occasionally contracted – through military conquests and alliances to become eventually most of the modern-day Rwandan state. However, it was not until the end of the nineteenth century, following a remarkable period of state-building under *Mwami* Kigeri Rwabugiri (1860–1895), that the modern-day borders were largely finalized. The exception was a number of Hutu-led principalities in the north and north-west that resisted annexation up until European colonization in the early twentieth century.

---

[3] Englebert (2000) constructed an index of state legitimacy for modern African states based on his estimation of the percentage of ethnic groups separated by colonial borders.

Concomitant with this state expansion was the cultural homogenization of the people who became the kingdom's subjects. Kinyarwanda, spoken by all Rwandans today, was not spoken throughout the kingdom from its establishment. Rwanda did not achieve linguistic and cultural unity until the end of the eighteenth century (Vansina, 2004, p. 198).

The centralization of power in the precolonial kingdom, while also often cited, was also not a constant.[4] The *Mwami*'s authority was not supreme across the territory from the outset. Over the course of the eighteenth century the kingdom gradually evolved from a mere 'coalition' into a 'unified, centralized, and aggressive entity' (Vansina, 2004, p. 122). The most remarkable period of centralization also occurred under *Mwami* Rwabugiri (1860–1895). The Royal Court exercised its power across the kingdom's territory through a network of local chiefs. The system was originally a delicate equilibrium of power. In each unit of territory, a triumvirate of chiefs was usually established, comprising an army chief, land chief, and cattle chief. Power ebbed and flowed between the centre and this periphery. However, at the peak of Rwabugiri's power at the end of the nineteenth century, these chiefs and the sub-chiefs beneath them were reduced to mere 'bureaucrats'. The *Mwami* became the 'source and symbol of all authority' and 'how much power the Chiefs and sub-chiefs claimed for themselves, and for how long, was entirely dependent upon the *Mwami*'s grace' (Lemarchand, 1970, p. 27). In short, it was only from the end of the nineteenth century that power in the polity came to be highly personalized and concentrated in a single individual: the *Mwami*.

No analysis of the precolonial period would be complete without also discussing the origins and significance of the terms Hutu and Tutsi. These two issues have been the subject of enduring and intense debate.[5] The differences between Hutu and Tutsi, whether real or perceived, lie at the heart of the genocide. Were the Tutsi a distinct people who migrated to and settled in Rwanda after the Hutu? And did Hutu and Tutsi originally signify a biological, racial distinction or something else? Scholars have variously suggested that Hutu and Tutsi represented class, feudal, caste, occupational, political, racial, and

---

[4] See again Straus (2006, p. 206)

[5] For a critical survey of the evidence on the origins of Hutu and Tutsi, see Mamdani (2001, pp. 41–75). For a good critique of the competing meanings of Hutu and Tutsi, see Kimonyo (2000).

ethnic identities. A powerful idea revitalized before and during the violence was the belief that the Hutu, stereotyped as short, squat, and flat-nosed farmers, settled in Rwanda early (after the Twa) and most likely originated from the Chad-Cameroon region; while the Tutsi, typecast as tall, thin, and straight-nosed cattle-breeders, arrived later from somewhere in the area of the Upper Nile, probably Ethiopia.[6] No conclusive proof has been adduced to enable a clear scholarly agreement on the issue of whether the ancestors of modern-day Tutsi had a separate geographic origin to those of modern-day Hutu. However, a consensus has formed that there was no single, fixed meaning of Hutu and Tutsi historically. Initially, in the early precolonial period, their meaning differed between regions and could signify not only occupation, but also financial wealth, physical characteristics, culture, place of origin, and marital ties.[7] However, over time Hutu and Tutsi evolved into general signifiers of low and high status. These status differences would become the basis of a deeply ranked social system. In short, the significance of Hutu and Tutsi has varied over time, and across space. They were constructed identities.

We can, then, summarize the consensus on Rwanda's precolonial epoch as follows: (i) there existed an identifiable polity, the Nyiginya kingdom; (ii) whose boundaries from at least the end of the nineteenth century closely resembled Rwanda's current borders; (iii) whose people, beginning from at least the eighteenth century enjoyed a linguistic and cultural unity; (iv) whose head was a Tutsi monarch in whom political power became highly centralized and personally vested from the end of the nineteenth century; and (v) whose three constituent groups developed over time a ranked relationship that would become the basis of a stratified social system.

The Colonial Epoch (1897–1962)

Although much has been written on how colonial rule laid the foundations for the genocide, there is in fact little that is historically remarkable in how Rwanda's colonial rulers, briefly Germany (1897–1916) and then Belgium (1916–1962), governed the country. Both ruled indirectly through the existing native institutions, the *Mwami* and

---

[6] See Maquet (1961, pp. 10–11) and Prunier (1998, p. 16).
[7] See in particular Newbury (1988, pp. 10–16, 51).

chieftaincies, and the Belgians would favour one 'racial' group, the Tutsi, over the others. Neither practice – indirect rule or group favouritism – was unusual among colonial powers. The animosity generated by discrimination against the excluded groups, and the tribalism this resentment fuelled, was a common colonial legacy (Mamdani, 1996).

After Belgium replaced Germany in Rwanda in 1916, it strengthened the indigenous institutions of the Tutsi *Mwami* and the local chiefs and continued to rule indirectly through them. Between 1926 and 1931, *les réformes Voisin* concentrated power in the centre and, crucially, increasingly in the person of the *Mwami*. Belgian administrators also reorganized the territory into a smaller number of administrative units to make the periphery easier to control by the centre from where the *Mwami* ruled. They also abolished the triumvirate of chiefs in favour of a single appointee, thereby disrupting the balance-of-power that characterized local governance before. And in 1931, they engineered the replacement of the unruly *Mwami* Musinga with the more compliant *Mwami* Rudahigwa to complete the subordination of the indigenous authorities to the colonial administration.

Belgium colonial policy also favoured Tutsi over Hutu. Its administrators privileged Tutsi in allocating state positions and in awarding educational places. Hutu were passed over and Tutsi overwhelmingly appointed as chiefs and sub-chiefs. By 1959, 43 of 45 chiefs as well as 549 of 559 sub-chiefs were Tutsi (Prunier, 1998, p. 27). The Catholic Church, which controlled educational opportunities, also strongly favoured Tutsi enrolment over Hutu. The Tutsi increasingly resembled a 'hegemonic caste' (Lemarchand, 1970, p. 472). Belgium also redesigned precolonial economic institutions that resulted in further Hutu subordination to Tutsi. *Ubuhake*, a cattle-based form of clientship, evolved from being mutually advantageous to both patron (*shebuja*) and client (*mugaragu*) into an intrinsically inequitable relationship between Hutu and Tutsi. *Ubeletwa*, a compulsory labour tax imposed on Hutu alone, also became considerably more onerous in the colonial era. Tutsi favouritism and Hutu oppression would become an increasingly common refrain during the civil war and genocide. Yet Belgium was hardly alone in aggravating tribalism through its colonial policies. Mamdani (1996, p. xviii), an observant scholar of colonial Africa, went so far as to say that tribalism was 'the inevitable consequence of indirect rule' in which a native authority was chosen to rule, often despotically, over other tribes. Colonial favouritism then did not by itself make genocide inevitable in Rwanda.

Belgian colonial rule was, however, more unusual in at least two regards. First, the Belgians propagated the idea the Tutsi were *racially* distinct and, in origin, *alien* to Rwanda. They drew on both racial science and religious scripture to justify these beliefs. Purportedly scientific criteria – measuring crania and noses for instance – underpinned the claim of racial distinctiveness and also supported the Hamitic hypothesis that the Tutsi, as the Biblical descendants of Ham, originated in Abyssinia. The idea that the Tutsi were allochthonous – they did not belong in Rwanda – would become an important theme during the genocide. Second, the Belgians also introduced compulsory registration cards with which to record Rwandans' racial identity. This decision reified group identities and effectively froze social mobility across group boundaries. While Belgium also implemented this policy in Burundi and Congo, its two other African colonies, no other colonial power in sub-Saharan Africa ever issued identity cards on which its subjects' ethnicity, race, or religion were recorded.[8] Group-denoting identity cards were a distinctive and consequential Belgian colonial institution.

Yet the significance of even the more distinctive aspects of the Belgian colonial experience requires qualification. Rwanda's *precolonial* socio-demography was already distinctive. It comprised only three groups who, unusually, did not live in distinct territories, did not have distinct cultures, and did not have distinct political systems. Instead, Hutu, Tutsi, and Twa lived side-by-side and were governed collectively as one people, the Banyarwanda. They did so in a social system that was *already* ethnically stratified. It is true that mobility across group boundaries had once been possible. The decision, then, to use identity cards denoting ethnicity ended this possibility. Moreover, the difference in size between the Hutu majority and Tutsi minority, which pre-dates Belgian colonial rule, constituted the largest demographic imbalance on the continent. It made the Belgian preference for Tutsi minority rule then particularly pernicious. The consequences of these

---

[8] Only in South Africa, Namibia, Ethiopia, and Kenya has group classification featured on mandatory identity cards. In these cases, however, the measures were not introduced by colonial rulers. Note South Africa deposed the German colonial administration in Namibia during World War I and the territory remained annexed to South Africa until its independence in March 1990.

colonial-era choices were, unfortunately, more pronounced against Rwanda's unusual socio-demographic baseline. Furthermore, whereas Burundi and Congo ended the practice of recording ethnicity on identity cards upon independence, Rwanda's two post-independence leaders, Kayibanda and Habyarimana, chose to retain it. The postcolonial state, then, must share some of the responsibility for the institutionalization and reification of ethnicity. The continued political and social salience of these identities did not lie solely with misguided Belgian colonial policy.

Rwanda's Revolution and the Postcolonial Era (1959–1990)

In contrast with the somewhat unremarkable colonial epoch, Rwanda's revolution, which ushered in the country's independence in 1962, was an exceptional event in the history of African decolonization. By ending oppressive Tutsi rule, it legitimized the two Hutu ethnocracies that succeeded it; and by abolishing the monarchy and chieftaincies, it weakened the bases of traditional power within Rwandan society. I take the time here to explain the origins of the revolution and to explicate its consequences for the civil war and genocide.

The scholarly literature on the revolution's origins is extensive, but three main factors are discernible. First, the international political context mattered. The revolution occurred in the context of the Cold War and decolonization across Africa and Asia. Independence was coming. A series of UN assessment missions had been despatched to Rwanda between 1949–1957 and Belgium, like other colonial powers at the time, sought to engineer a post-independence outcome favourable to itself. This led to the second important factor for the revolution: the birth of a Hutu counter-elite. Until then, Belgian administrators had favoured and had ruled Rwanda through a Tutsi elite. However, fearful that this elite would align itself with the communist bloc, and resentful of their anti-colonial stance, they sponsored the emergence of a Hutu counter-elite, aggrieved at Tutsi socio-political dominance. The Church was complicit in this task. It was concerned that the Tutsi clerical elite it had trained would take over control of the Church in Rwanda. Thus, reforms began in the 1950s that would alter the balance of power between Tutsi and Hutu. A decree in 1952 created new institutions for native representation of which the most important was the Conseil Supérieur du Pays. However, local elections in

1953 and national elections in 1956 resulted in only a slight increase in Hutu representation as direct, universal suffrage was not permitted at all levels. Frustrated, in 1957 the Hutu counter-elite published the *Bahutu* Manifesto. In unambiguous language it stated: 'The problem is above all a political monopoly which is held by one race: the Tutsi.' The manifesto articulated a grievance that had grown during colonial rule and that would provide the motivational force for the revolution. The turning point, however, was the decision by Belgium in 1959 to allow the creation of political parties. The four most important were: (i) the militant, pro-Hutu Parti du Mouvement de l'Emancipation Hutu (PARMEHUTU) party; (ii) the populist, pro-Hutu Association pour la Promotion Sociale de la Masse (APROSOMA) party; (iii) the progressive, pro-Tutsi Rassemblement Démocratique Rwandais (RADER) party and (iv) the conservative, pro-monarchy Union Nationale Rwandaise (UNAR) party. The momentum for change had now reached a critical level and the parties became the instruments through which these forces were expressed.

The third important factor for the revolution also came from within Rwanda but this time from below. Prolonged Tutsi subjugation and exploitation, beginning under *Mwami* Rwabuguri (c. 1860–1895) but intensified in the colonial era, had fostered a collective Hutu consciousness. Newbury (1988) describes it aptly as the 'cohesion of oppression'. It was to provide the popular impetus for the revolution. Scholars have debated the relative contributions of elite agency and mass participation to this historic watershed. Newbury (1988, p. 209) stresses the importance of the latter:

Yet Hutu leaders did not 'create' Hutu ethnic consciousness. The grievances that formed the basis of this consciousness and provided the motivating force of its political effectiveness were already there, products of the realities of everyday for non-Tuutsi.

Lemarchand (1970, p. 484) in contrast emphasizes the Hutu counter-elite:

Although the revolutionary elites were by definition of rural background, the revolution can hardly be said to have been instigated by the peasantry *per se*. The initial push came not from the bush peasants but from the educated Hutu elites and rural politicians; only at a later stage, partly through the manipulation of latent grievances [...] did the peasant masses become active participants in the revolutionary process.

This disagreement over the origins of Rwanda's revolution merits mention because it mirrors a similar debate over Rwanda's genocide. Where does elite responsibility end and popular accountability for the violence begin? Was it an outcome engineered by a Hutu counter-elite or the expression of an aggrieved Hutu populace? As we shall see, I show that the impetus for the genocide may be traced not only to elite decisions made 'at the top', as is widely argued, but also to societal forces operating 'from below'.

The spark that eventually ignited the revolution was an attack on PARMEHUTU party activist and Hutu sub-chief, Dominique Mbonuyumutwa, on 1 November 1959.[9] Two days later, the false rumour of his death triggered spontaneous violence against Tutsi chiefs and, significantly, Tutsi civilians. The monarchist UNAR party quickly responded with an organized counter-attack that targeted Hutu party leadership. As with the genocide in 1994, the anti-Tutsi violence spread with astonishing speed and extended across much of the country, though it was far less deadly. Within two weeks, by 14 November and after the Belgian authorities finally intervened to restore order, at least two hundred civilians had been killed, several thousand Tutsi homes had been either burned or looted, and an exodus of Tutsi had begun. Guy Logiest, the new Belgian military officer on the ground, did not disguise his pro-Hutu partisanship. He summarily appointed over three hundred interim Hutu chiefs and sub-chiefs in response to what he interpreted as a popular verdict on Tutsi rule. Belgian authorities subsequently organized local elections in July 1960. These were to contest the new position of burgomaster in each of the newly created communes. Rwanda's new territorial structure was modelled on the Belgian administrative system. The PARMEHUTU came away with a handsome majority and repeated its success in national, legislative elections in September 1961. In fact, the Republic had been declared by the head of the PARMEHUTU party, Grégoire Kayibanda, on 28 January 1961. The elections had the effect of legitimizing the extra-legal process that had effectively reversed Rwanda's socio-political order. Thus, the First Republic was established, with Kayibanda as its first elected president, following a referendum in which 80 per cent of Rwandans voted against the monarchy. Rwanda

---

[9] For one of the best accounts of the events of the revolution, see Lemarchand (1970, pp. 159–196).

officially became independent on 1 July 1962. However, the government was already in place by virtue of a revolutionary coup.

The revolution had important consequences not only for the new Rwandan state, but also for the genocide. It contributed five pieces to the puzzle of the genocide. First, it created a massive Tutsi refugee community. Between 1959 and 1973 several hundred thousand Rwandan Tutsi (mainly) went into exile in Tanzania, Uganda, Burundi, and eastern Congo following the revolution and persecution at home.[10] Their descendants formed the backbone of the rebel Rwanda Patriotic Front (RPF) that initiated the civil war in 1990 culminating in the genocide. Second, it strengthened an ethnic identity and consciousness among Hutu. Group solidarity was both a cause and consequence of the revolution. Third, it created a revolutionary, ideological discourse that persisted up until the genocide. The revolution had democratized Rwanda and emancipated the Hutu majority from domination and exploitation by the Tutsi minority. In this founding narrative, ethnocracy and democracy were synonymous. Fourth, it established a relationship between external threat and anti-Tutsi violence. Between 1962 and 1967, Tutsi exiled by the revolution would launch ten attacks on Rwanda in an attempt to force their return home. Whenever Tutsi outside of Rwanda threatened, Tutsi inside the country faced reprisals. The most threatening of these attacks, from Burundi in 1963, resulted in the deaths of an estimated 10,000 Tutsi civilians in Rwanda. Last, and perhaps most consequentially, the revolution ended the socio-political dominance of a Tutsi ruling class. It marked the shift from a ranked ethnic system in which a Tutsi elite had been ascendant in terms of political power, economic resources, and social prestige to a new ranked system in which a Hutu elite displaced the Tutsi elite in their monopoly over political power.

Following the revolution and Rwanda's independence, Kayibanda would rule Rwanda autocratically for the next eleven years. As under monarchic rule, power was again centrally concentrated and again highly personalized. With the advent of independence and formal, modern state institutions, patrimonialism became neo-patrimonialism. Rwanda's First Republic became a *de facto* single party state and Rwanda's new Big Man governed through a party apparatus

[10] Gérard Prunier (1998, p. 63) estimates the number of refugees as between 600,000–700,000. However, a 1964 UNHCR census put the figure at 336,000 refugees in Burundi, Tanzania, Uganda, and Zaire. Cited in Guichaoua (1992, p. 20).

composed overwhelmingly of individuals bound together through a complex network of ethnic, regional, kinship, and other personal ties. Political power, having been concentrated in the hands of a Tutsi elite in the colonial era, had simply shifted into the hands of a Hutu elite in the postcolonial epoch.

Tutsi were excluded almost entirely from political life, and faced considerable harassment and discrimination. In 1972, massacres of Hutu, described by some as selective genocide, by the Tutsi army in neighbouring Burundi fuelled popular resentment against Tutsi inside Rwanda. Angry Hutu organized 'public safety committees' to expel Tutsi – sometimes violently – from schools, para-statals, and private businesses where Tutsi were believed to be over-represented. The instability created an opportunity to overthrow Kayibanda. Northern Hutu elites resented the favouritism that Kayibanda had shown towards his southern Hutu brethren in the allocation of jobs and other privileges of power. In July 1973, a thirty-six-year-old General Juvénal Habyarimana, a northerner from Gisenyi prefecture, seized control and established Rwanda's Second Republic.

Habyarimana would perpetuate the political culture of his predecessor. In 1975 his Mouvement Révolutionnaire National pour le Développement (MRND), became by law the only permitted party, and every Rwandan automatically a member. As under Kayibanda, the party apparatus would be practically indistinguishable from the state apparatus. The state continued to be subordinated to and instrumentalized by private interests. Power was exercised through a network of individuals, variously connected to Habyarimana through regional, ethnic, and kinship ties, whom he placed in influential government and parastatal positions. Within this, an inner circle of power emerged, known as the *akazu* or 'little house', in which his own wife and her family's clan were extremely influential. As a military man, Habyarimana also commanded the loyalty of the Rwandan army, and ensured that its officer corps remained exclusively Hutu, and mostly northern Hutu like himself. He enjoyed particular loyalty from the Presidential Guard, the elite unit that would play a particularly deadly role during the genocide. He also secured the support of the Catholic Church, which would help assure his influence at the grassroots level of Rwandan society. He introduced *umuganda*, a form of compulsory community service under which Rwandans contributed some portion of their labour every week to provide local public goods such as digging anti-erosion ditches or building roadways. It would become a powerful state institution of popular mobilization. However, while Habyarimana ensured that the main levers of state remained firmly within the hands of his northern Hutu network, in a departure from his predecessor he introduced ethnic (and regional) quotas, albeit contested ones. He was also ultimately less repressive of the country's Tutsi minority than Kayibanda. Until the outbreak of the civil war in 1990, there would be no major incidents of state-sponsored violence against Tutsi civilians.

All in all, Rwanda's revolution was arguably the most unusual and noteworthy feature in the country's history before the genocide. It sowed the seeds of Rwanda's civil war by putting the exiled Tutsi on a collision course with the Hutu elite who had seized power and, as we shall see later, it would also imbue the new republican state with unusual authority and legitimacy. Both the security threat created by the civil war and the remarkable power enjoyed by the postcolonial state would prove to be important factors in the onset of the genocide and the scale of the violence.

2.2 Rwanda's Unusual Society, Demography, and Geography

Yet it was not only the historical peculiarity of a social revolution on the eve of its colonial emancipation that set this small African nation apart from others on the continent. Rwanda possessed several unusual societal, demographic, and geographic features that would also prove consequential for the genocide and the violence it produced. I enumerate these characteristics here. In so doing, I draw an important analytical distinction between the *genocide* and the characteristics of the *violence* that ensued.[11] I do so because the reasons for the decision to eliminate Rwanda's Tutsi population were, I believe, different to the reasons for why the violence was as intense, rapid, and widespread as it was. The election and expression of violence had distinct roots. So, the genocide and the form of the violence that resulted deserve separate consideration. These societal, demographic and geographic features amplified both (i) the forces leading up to the genocide and (ii) the mobilization and violence that resulted. My focus here is on explicating the causal logic linking these unusual characteristics to both phenomena. Table 2.2 summarizes these linkages. As we shall see in the

---

[11] Kalyvas (2006, p. 6) has similarly recognized the importance of analytically decoupling the onset of civil war from the violence that ensued.

Table 2.2 Linkages to unusual characteristics of the genocide and violence

	High boundary continuity	High population density	Low urban population	Low ethnic diversity	High ethnic dominance	Small territorial size	Highly integrated settlement	High road density	Low ecological variability
Forces producing the genocide									
Civil war (security)									
Political liberalization (threat and opportunity)		✓			✓	✓	✓	✓	
Assassination (opportunity)						✓		✓	
State (authority)	✓	✓		✓	✓	✓		✓	
Characteristics of the violence									
Scale of violence		✓	✓			✓	✓	✓	✓
Speed of violence		✓				✓	✓	✓	
Scope of violence			✓	✓		✓	✓		
Scale of mobilization	✓	✓						✓	
Speed of mobilization		✓						✓	
Scope of mobilization						✓	✓		

2.2 Rwanda's Unusual Society, Demography, and Geography

chapters to come, there was a set of core mechanisms in operation. Identification, influence, contagion, coordination, contact, mobility, communication, and surveillance were all logics at work both before and during the genocide that can be traced to these unusual features.

A Highly Agrarian Society

Rwanda was the second most rural and agrarian society, after Burundi, in all of sub-Saharan Africa on the eve of the genocide. In 1993, just over 7 per cent of its population lived in urban areas compared with a mean urban population of 31 per cent for the rest of sub-Saharan Africa (World Bank, 2003). The 93 per cent resident in rural areas, on Rwanda's thousands of hills, were practically all involved in some form of sedentary agriculture. Much, though not all, of this was the result of a state policy of keeping Rwandans on their farms. Rwanda's ruling elite depended on receipts from the country's two largest export-earners, coffee and tea, for their wealth. Both crops required intense rural labour, and the government had at times forced Rwandans to plant them over subsistence crops. The highly rural character of Rwandan society would be consequential for the remarkable scale of the civilian mobilization and violence observed during the genocide.

The reason has to do with the nature of rural social networks. The ties linking individuals in agrarian *communities* evidently differ significantly from those in more urban *societies* (Tönnies, 1940). Durkheim (1960) would likely have characterized Rwandan society in 1994 as based more on *mechanical* than *organic* solidarity as social cohesion was achieved more through homogeneity in values and beliefs than through interdependence and a complex division of labour. Moreover, in agrarian societies families have strong ties to the land, particularly if this is the principal livelihood opportunity available, and individuals consequently often stay within their communities their entire lives. So, the ties between community members are enduring and multiplex. The transiency and anonymity that characterize urban societies are less pronounced (Simmel, 1971). In Rwanda, this would make identification of Tutsi as targets much easier. You could not be unknown. It would also amplify social influences. Mass mobilization during the genocide, we shall see, would depend in part on the intensity of coercion, co-optation, and peer pressures operating among community members.

Exceptional Population Density

Rwanda was also the most densely populated country in sub-Saharan Africa. In 1993, it had an average of 243 persons per square kilometre (World Bank, 2003). This fact has given rise to a series of Malthusian-related explanations for the genocide that essentially argue ecological scarcity exacerbated social tensions within communities.[12] I show the limits of this logic in Chapter 7. I argue that Rwanda's extreme population density did matter, but in a number of other ways. It has already been noted that it strengthened the *vertical* accountability of Rwandans by making the monitoring and enforcement capacities of the state more effective.[13] Rwandans could not readily escape state-imposed obligations. It would also, however, reinforce *horizontal* accountability through the same mechanisms as Rwanda's unusually high rurality. Living in such close proximity created dense social networks that made privacy and anonymity difficult (the identification logic) and also amplified peer pressures (the influence logic). It also reinforced Rwanda's clientelist culture. Frequent face-to-face interaction meant that neither patrons nor clients could easily evade their obligations to each other.

High population density would not only affect the scale, but also the speed of the violence and mobilization. Information diffused quickly through these close-knit networks both within and between communities. Behaviours also spread rapidly. The logic of contagion was strong. These forces in fact mattered *before* the genocide too. As we shall see, the political liberalization initiated in 1991, one of the three macro-political forces that pushed Rwanda closer to genocide, engaged a surprisingly large number of ordinary Rwandans in the tumult of party politics. The high level of political participation resulted in deep divisions in many communities long before the genocide began.

[12] For a solid critique of the Malthusian arguments made in relation to Rwanda, see Uvin (1998, pp. 180–202). For pro-Malthusian claims, see Ford (1995); Diamond (2008); Newbury (1994); Olson (1995); and Verpoorten (2012b).
[13] A similar point on the surveillance capacity of the state is made by Straus (2006, p. 215).

Ethnic Bipolarity

Rwanda was also, by one measure, the least ethnically diverse society in sub-Saharan Africa and by other measures it ranks consistently within the bottom six.[14] It was effectively bi-ethnic. Hutu and Tutsi were the two numerically dominant ethnic groups. The Twa represented less than 1 per cent of the population and had been historically marginalized. Bi-ethnic societies are rare. In sub-Saharan Africa, only Burundi, Zanzibar, Lesotho, and Swaziland share this demographic particularity.[15] The first two also have histories of violent inter-group conflict. Bi-ethnicity carries then the risk of producing ethnically *bi-polar* societies in which rivalry between the two principal groups engenders deep societal divisions and interposes high ethnic distance. The risk of polarization is particularly acute when the position or rank of each group is not stable but in fact shifts over time as the groups vie for ascendancy. Movement in the relative status of groups is the core logic behind one prominent theory of ethnic conflict.[16] The rise of a previously subordinate group threatens the position of the superordinate group and anxiety for their status motivates the conflict.

Rwanda did experience such shifts in rank between Hutu and Tutsi. Moreover, ethnic bi-polarity did ensue. The ethnic ranking that had emerged in the precolonial era and deepened in the colonial era saw Tutsi at the apex of Rwanda's socio-political hierarchy. In Weberian terms, Tutsi had historically been ascendant in terms of political

---

[14] Fearon's (2003) index of ethnic fractionalization ranks Rwanda as the least diverse country in sub-Saharan Africa. Fractionalization is defined as the probability that any two individuals randomly selected from within a country would come from different ethnic groups. The original ethno-linguistic fractionalization index based on the Soviet *Atlas Naradov Mira* (1964) ranks Rwanda fifth of forty-three; Alesina et al. (2003) rank it sixth of forty-five; Roeder (2003) ranks it fourth of forty-four; Scarritt and Mozaffar (1999) rank it joint third of forty-two; and Mitchell et al. (1989) rank it third of forty-one.

[15] At the time of writing, estimates for each country's ethnic make-up are: Burundi: Tutsi (15 per cent) and Hutu (85 per cent); Zanzibar (if distinguished from mainland Tanzania): Arabs (22.7 per cent) and Africans and mixed Arab-Africans (72.3 per cent); Lesotho: Zulu (15 per cent) and Sotho (85 per cent); Swaziland: Zulu (9.9 per cent) and Swazi (85 per cent).

[16] For more theorization on the relationship between group status and ethnic conflict, see Horowitz (1985, pp. 22–36).

power, economic resources, and social prestige (Weber, 1978). However, Rwanda's social revolution weakened this hierarchy in the postcolonial era and heralded a historically rare shift to a new ranked system in which the formerly subordinate group replaced the superordinate group in its monopoly of political power. Hutu and Tutsi alternated in their control of the state across the colonial and postcolonial eras: a Tutsi elite dominated before independence, and a Hutu elite thereafter. The development of political competition along ethnic boundaries meant political liberalization in Rwanda carried particular risks. While liberalization was not an unusual event in sub-Saharan African in the 1990s, in Rwanda it provided the space of opportunity to re-ignite the historic ethnic competition. Ethnic bipolarity then was a structural vulnerability.

Cultural Homogeneity

Another distinguishing characteristic of Rwandan society, related to its low ethnic diversity, was its cultural homogeneity. Rwanda's 'ethnic' groups, unusually, spoke the same language, worshipped the same God and shared the same culture. Equally unusually, Hutu, Tutsi, and Twa were governed together as subjects of the same kingdom. Although they identified as three distinct groups, they did not develop separate political systems. Ethnically autonomous rule would have presented a practical challenge given another unusual demographic particularity: Hutu, Tutsi, and Twa did not inhabit distinct territories but lived side-by-side in the same areas. A single, ranked social system emerged instead to bind them together.

These similarities presented both communication and coordination advantages. Having a common language, Kinyarwanda, made it easier for authorities to communicate with the population either directly in face-to-face meetings or else indirectly, as for example over the radio. Moreover, Kinyarwanda was not a second or third language that Rwandans shared, but was the mother tongue of Hutu, Tutsi, and Twa, and its subtleties and ambiguities were understood by all. In addition, having a common culture provided a repertoire of symbols, myths, and sayings that leaders could draw on that were interpretable by all Rwandans. Homogeneity in both language and culture were important advantages for governing and ultimately for mobilizing the population.

Table 2.3 *Numerically dominant ethnic groups in sub-Saharan Africa*

Country	Ethnic Group	Percentage of Population
Rwanda	Hutu	85%–91%
Burundi	Hutu	85.0%
Lesotho	Sotho	85.0%
Swaziland	Swazi	84.3%
Botswana	Tswana	80.0%
Zimbabwe	Shona	77.0%
Benin	Fon	55.5%
Niger	Hausa	54.0%
Mauritius	Hindu	51.8%
Burkina Faso	Mossi	50.0%

Source: J. D. Fearon (2003)

Ethnic Dominance

The final distinguishing characteristic of Rwanda's demography was the numerical dominance of the Hutu ethnic group. Rwanda ranks first among sub-Saharan states in a measure of ethnic dominance.[17] For a bi-ethnic society, the percentage gap between the majority Hutu and minority Tutsi was considerable. Although there are competing estimates, the range in the scholarly consensus is between 85 per cent and 91 per cent Hutu and between 10 per cent and 15 per cent Tutsi.[18] Table 2.3 ranks the top ten countries in Africa that were home to the most ethnically dominant groups. As can be seen, only five countries have ethnic majorities of 80 per cent and greater and the decline is steep with the tenth-most dominant group being the Mossi of Burkina Faso who represent only 50 per cent of the population. Such an overwhelming numerical superiority of Hutu had two effects. First, it reinforced the claim of legitimacy for the two Republics that were

---

[17] Ethnic dominance is measured by calculating the percentage of the overall population that the largest ethnic group represents.
[18] Extrapolating the 1991 Rwandan Population Census data would put the Hutu population at 90.6 per cent of the overall population. The 1978 Census data would place it at 89.2 per cent and a 1983 Administrative Census would make it 89.0 per cent. However, other scholars have claimed that the Tutsi population was either deliberately underestimated or else Tutsi declared themselves Hutu to avoid harassment. See Chapter 7 for more details.

Hutu-controlled. In this narrative, Hutu majority-rule became synonymous with democracy and Tutsi minority-rule equated with dictatorship. Second, it made mobilization of the population during the genocide easier. There was only a single interest or identity group to which ethnic entrepreneurs needed to appeal. This made the choice of mobilizational frame more straightforward. As we shall see in Chapter 3, the shared history of Hutu subjugation and exploitation by a Tutsi minority became an important ideological refrain from above and resonated strongly against Hutu collective memory below.

Small Territory, Dense Road Network, and Centralized Capital

With a surface area of 24,670 sq.km, Rwanda is the fourth smallest country in continental sub-Saharan Africa. Only Swaziland, Lesotho, and Djibouti are smaller. It also had, along with Burundi, by far the most dense road network of all sub-Saharan countries, with 0.57 km of road per square kilometre (World Bank, 2003). Its capital, Kigali, was situated at the geographic centre of the country, and being at least three times more populous than the next largest town, it had no rival urban centres.[19] One evident implication, already recognized for Rwanda, is that in a territory so small and so accessible – I could drive from the capital Kigali in the centre and reach any of Rwanda's four border countries within three hours – the state could project its power, that is, 'broadcast its authority' everywhere.[20] There were physical outposts of the state in all of Rwanda's 145 communes, and in most of its 1,545 administrative sectors.

The small distances and high accessibility had other less obvious implications, however. Before the genocide, the move to multipartyism in 1991, the key feature of Rwanda's political liberalization, generated intense political rivalries between party elites in the capital, Kigali. The political dramas that rocked the centre would also reverberate strongly

---

[19] Rwanda's 1991 census puts the population of Kigali-ville at 235,664. Although the census does not distinguish the population of Rwanda's other towns, it does specify the population of the communes in which they were located. Gitarama town, located in Nyamabuye commune, had a population of 79,952; Gisenyi town, Nyamyumba commune, 58,107; Ruhengeri town, Kigombe commune, 53,467; and Butare town, Ngoma commune, 32,930.

[20] For the strongest case on the relationship between state power and state size and shape, see Herbst (2000, pp. 139–172). Straus (2006, p. 215) recognized its relevance to Rwanda.

at the periphery. The ties between party leaders and their bases were strengthened by the high mobility that leaders enjoyed between the capital and their local constituencies. You could travel to almost any rural community in Rwanda and return the same day to Kigali. Party meetings, rallies, and protests would become a common sight throughout Rwanda before the genocide. The rural population was highly engaged politically and readily mobilizable long before the genocide began. Political parties were well-represented and organized at the local level. Information also travelled fast and local reactions to national-level events were swift. The response to Habyarimana's assassination on 6 April 1994, for instance, was immediate in much of Rwanda. Violence began the next day in a number of communes and in less than a week in the majority of communes across Rwanda.

The small distances implied also meant that the violence had 'contagion effects' during the genocide. As we shall see, what happened in one community quickly became known and occurred in other communities. Local extremists, operating usually with a small hardcore of supporters, either moved rapidly to other places to commit and incite violence there or else inspired political and ethnic entrepreneurs to do the same in their own communities. Contagion explains much of why the mobilization and violence happened so quickly and why they happened almost everywhere in the country. There were few places so isolated or inaccessible that communities were insulated from what was happening elsewhere. The role of simple physical geography is easily missed but it was consequential in Rwanda.

Ethnic Settlement

Unusually for sub-Saharan Africa, Rwanda's three ethnic groups did not live in geographically distinct areas. There was no separate Hutuland, Tutsiland, or Twaland. Instead, these groups commonly lived side-by-side in ethnically mixed communities. To put this fact into comparative perspective, no country other than Burundi has all of its ethnic groups dispersed throughout almost all inhabitable areas of the land. It is much more common for ethnic groups to be concentrated in a particular region or to be found in urban areas. For the few ethnic groups in other countries whose settlement pattern was not localized in this way, their dispersion was limited to a small number of areas within the country.[21] No ethnic groups in sub-Saharan Africa other than the Hutu and Tutsi of Rwanda and Burundi enjoyed *nationwide* intermixing.

This unusual settlement pattern would again matter both before and during the genocide. Allport (1958) famously first theorized that contact between groups may reduce prejudice under conditions of equal status, common goals, inter-group cooperation, and support from authority. As we shall see, communities with high rates of inter-ethnic marriage in Rwanda were more resistant to attempts to divide them. Neighbourly ties did matter. However, Rwanda's civil war, framed in ethnic terms, contravened several of contact theory's conditions. Threat nullified the benefits of inter-group contact that psycho-social theory has long advocated. The close proximity and contact within communities between the two main ethnic groups instead amplified the distrust some Hutu felt toward their Tutsi neighbours during the war. They suspected the Tutsi of secretly supporting the rebel RPF. This ethnic interspersion would also amplify the threat of a Tutsi fifth column, the enemy within, following the president's assassination and the renewal of the fighting in the war. Some Hutu feared that their Tutsi neighbours planned to assist the RPF or else even to kill them. Finally, close proximity would also make the killing much easier once the genocide began. Hutu knew exactly where their Tutsi neighbours lived, and usually where they could hide. They could locate them quickly. As Tutsi were settled throughout the country, violence also occurred in almost every community in Rwanda.

Rwanda's Ecological Homogeneity

Why then does Rwanda have so many distinctive socio-demographic features? The root cause for several of these characteristics, notably its high population density, low ethnic diversity, cultural similarity, and ethnic interspersion, can all ultimately be traced in large part to Rwanda's relative ecological homogeneity. Rwanda is, first, one of

---

[21] Ethnic groups in sub-Saharan Africa that are dispersed but not nationally distributed are the Kru of Liberia, the Masalit and Zaghawa of South Sudan, the Herero, San, and Whites of Botswana, the Coloureds of South Africa and Namibia, the Europeans of Zimbabwe, and the Asians of Uganda. Only the Hutu and Tutsi of Rwanda and Burundi are dispersed nationwide today. See the GeoEPR dataset by Wucherpfennig et al. (2011).

2.2 Rwanda's Unusual Society, Demography, and Geography

the most suitable locations on the continent for sedentary agriculture. Both its climatic variables and its soil conditions made it particularly attractive for arable and pastoral farming. A global dataset measuring soil nutrient and organic content, as well as average temperature, sunshine, and precipitation levels, ranks Rwanda's overall land quality eighth on the continent.[22] As a temperate tropical country located within the highly fertile inter-lacustrine region, Rwanda unsurprisingly attracted and sustained a dense level of human settlement.

Second, and more consequentially, Rwanda has very low ecological *variability*. It has no coastlines or deserts, limited mountainous areas, and today little rainforest or savannah. More precisely, variation in temperature, precipitation, and sunshine hours is low in Rwanda. Much of this is can be attributed to its small territorial size. Nonetheless, Rwanda's is the fourth least ecologically diverse country, after Gabon, Equatorial Guinea, and Congo-Brazzaville, in sub-Saharan Africa. This enabled the diffusion of similar farming practices throughout the land. Recent research correlates ecological diversity with ethnolinguistic diversity and suggests that the reason has to do with the tendency of ethnic groups to form when the land supports particular occupations and skills (Michalopoulos, 2012). Rwanda's ecology supported the co-existence of both herders, historically Tutsi, and farmers, historically Hutu. The ecological opportunity for other specializations and thus other ethnic groups was limited. The close proximity in which these two groups lived and interacted then facilitated their mutual acculturation.

***

I have taken the time to enumerate and explain the unusual baseline that Rwanda represented because several of its distinctive historical and socio-demographic features constituted vulnerabilities that made

---

[22] I draw on the dataset established by Michalopoulos (2012) that in turn draws on a dataset constructed by Ramankutty et al. (2002). Both datasets divide the earth's surface into grid cells 0.5 × 0.5 decimal degrees in size and estimate, first, the mean pH (nutrient availability) and carbon density (organic content) to determine average soil conditions in each cell; and, second, the mean-monthly values (1961–1990) for precipitation, temperature, and potential sunshine hours to determine average climatic conditions in each cell. Both the soil and climatic variables are then combined to calculate the probability that the land is suitable for agriculture. Rwanda comprised sixteen such grid cells in the dataset.

the risk of any stress-induced fracture in Rwandan society and politics more likely to follow ethnic rather than non-ethnic lines. To be clear, none made genocide inevitable or otherwise explains the genocide. They simply increased Rwanda's ethnic divisibility risk. Ethnicity was the premise of a ranked social system that emerged in the precolonial era out of an unusual ethnic demography. It was unusual to have three distinct but culturally homogenous ethnic groups who lived side-by-side in a single polity and where one group constituted an overwhelming numerical majority. In the colonial era, the institutionalization and reification of this ethnic ranking were reinforced when it became the basis for state-instituted discrimination and exclusion. Then in the postcolonial era a social revolution weakened this ethnic ranking through the emergence of a Hutu elite who developed an aspiration for political power to challenge the dominant position of the Tutsi elite class. In short, ethnicity was not destined *ab initio*, but rather evolved over time to become the dominant fracture line in Rwandan society and politics. It was never inevitable that social and political conflict would be framed in ethnic terms in the face of stress such as that posed by a security threat. However, it was more likely than framing in non-ethnic terms given Rwanda's particular socio-demographic characteristics and historical trajectory.

This chapter marked also the importance of separating analytically the explanation for the genocide's onset from the explanation of the violence and mobilization that ensued. The forces that ultimately led to Rwanda's genocide – the civil war, the democratization attempt, and the president's assassination – are, when considered individually, commonplace in Africa. The violence and mobilization that followed, however, were not. Rwanda's unusual characteristics magnified the impact of these commonplace forces and made the consequences of their unusual coincidence particularly devastating. In the next three chapters, I move to explain how and why I believe the genocide occurred. I focus on identifying the mechanisms behind the three macro-political forces that led to the genocide and describe how Rwanda's unusual characteristics amplified their effects.

3 Security: War-Time Threat

3.1 Introduction

Rwanda's civil war was the first of the three macro-political events whose conjunction – against the unusual baseline described in the previous chapter – I argue led to the genocide. The war began in 1990 as an unremarkable, low-intensity campaign, but ended dramatically nearly four years later in genocide. In fact, between 1955 and 2016, thirty-four of forty-five cases of genocide and politicide occurred in the course of civil wars.[1] A clear consensus, based on comparative research, has formed that a strong relationship exists between war and genocide.[2] Rwanda's genocide appears to be no exception. Most scholarly explanations highlight the war's role. But what is less well-established is *how and why* civil wars matter. How exactly did Rwanda's civil war escalate and push this tiny African nation closer to genocide? Even less well-evidenced are how civilian attitudes and behaviours change during war-time. How exactly did Rwanda's civil war – if at all – lead some Rwandans to support and to commit violence against other Rwandans? Were many Hutu radicalized by the war or was it just a few? And what role did the media play in this radicalization and in war-time propaganda? The micro-level impact of the war and the media on the attitudes and actions of ordinary Rwandans remains under-explored.

---

[1] The thirty-four cases of genocide and politicide that occurred within the context of an internal war (and the eleven cases in which they did *not* occur in the context of an internal war) are identified using the Political Instability Task Force's (PITF) datasets on ethnic wars, revolutionary wars, and genocides and politicides (Marshall et al., 2017).

[2] Krain (1997, p. 346), drawing on quantitative analysis of thirty-five cases of genocides and politicides between 1945 and 1982, finds '[...]civil war involvement is the most consistent predictor of the onset of state-sponsored mass murder.' Barbara Harff (2003) finds 'political upheaval' a necessary condition for genocide and politicide, and that internal wars are such an example.

I will show that Rwanda's civil war created a security threat that would have an important psychological impact on the civilian population. Using psycho-social theory, I identify four mechanisms through which this threat contributed to what I term the 'radicalization' of Rwandans. First, I show how the war ethnicized Rwandan politics and society: the stronger the threat, the greater this ethnicization became. The war amplified the salience of ethnic boundaries and increased the distrust and distance between the two main ethnic groups. More and more Hutu suspected Tutsi of supporting and collaborating with the rebels and saw the war in historical terms. Second, the war homogenized perceptions of the outgroup: the stronger the threat, the more indistinguishable members of the target outgroup became. As the threat peaked, not only rebel combatants but eventually all Tutsi civilians would become identified as the enemy. Intra-group distinctions weakened. Third, the war strengthened ethnic solidarity: the greater the threat, the stronger the demand for ingroup unity became. Accusations of Hutu disloyalty increased in response to the growing threat and were used to enforce cohesion among Hutu. Lastly, the war justified outgroup targeting: the greater the threat, the stronger the justification of self-defence grew. Some Hutu came to accuse Tutsi in fact of plotting to exterminate them in order to legitimize their own genocidal action against the Tutsi. These four effects, I argue, are together a measure of civilian radicalization in war-time.

At the same time, I argue that we should not overstate the importance of wars in genocides. While many genocides have occurred during civil wars, most civil wars have not led to genocides. Rwanda's civil war contributed to, but did not determine, the genocide alone. Two other events coincided with it to push the country to genocide: its move to democratize and the assassination of its longstanding head of state. To return to the criminal law metaphor, the war provided the motive (a security threat) while the assassination supplied the opportunity (a power struggle). Democratization, as we shall see, would amplify both the threat and the opportunity. Moreover, Rwanda's civil war was also quite an ordinary war when compared with other African conflicts. By itself, it cannot account for the extraordinary outcome and characteristics of its genocide.

I demonstrate these four psycho-social effects of the civil war through two comparisons. The first, over time, is between the pre-genocide and genocidal phases of the war. In the initial phase

(1 October 1990–5 April 1994), the threat was moderate and the population, as we shall see, was not widely radicalized. In the second, terminal phase (6 April 1994–17 July 1994), however, the threat intensified and broadened and ordinary Rwandans radicalized significantly. The second comparison, across space, is between the north and the south of the country. In the north, located on the war's front lines, the threat was present and clear and we will see that Rwandans were widely radicalized. In the south, where the war by contrast was distant, the population remained relatively unaffected and there is little evidence of prior radicalization.

The chapter is structured as follows. In Section 3.2, I begin by briefly summarizing the main events in Rwanda's civil war. Section 3.3 then evaluates the theoretical links between wars and genocides. Section 3.4 considers Rwanda's media, in particular radio broadcasts, and their role in war-time propaganda and in radicalizing Rwandans. Section 3.5 presents baseline data on the state of inter-ethnic relations in Rwanda before the war. Section 3.6 then presents the evidence of the war's impact on inter-ethnic relations and each of the four mechanisms through which I believe the war led to radicalization. Section 3.7 then explains the limitations of war as a factor in genocide. Finally, in Section 3.8, I suggest two implications of these findings for our current understanding of Rwanda's genocide.

3.2 Synopsis of Rwanda's Civil War

As noted in the last chapter, the roots of Rwanda's civil war lie in events three decades earlier. Rwanda's Hutu revolution (1959–1962) had triggered an exodus of hundreds of thousands of (mainly) Tutsi civilians, many of whom fled over Rwanda's borders into Uganda, Burundi, Tanzania, and Zaire. Between 1962 and 1967, these exiles made ten armed attempts to return, each ending in failure. It was not until their descendants established the Rwandan Patriotic Front (RPF) in 1987, along with dissidents from Habyarimana's Rwanda, that the next attempt was made.[3] On the afternoon of 1 October 1990, a force

---

[3] The Rwandan Alliance for National Unity (RANU), established in 1980 in Uganda, was the precursor to the RPF. The RPF first nominated Colonel Alexis Kanyarengwe, a Hutu who had fled Rwanda following a failed coup attempt against Habyarimana. Many interpreted his appointment as a politically symbolic act to broaden the support base of the movement across ethnic lines.

of RPF soldiers launched a lightning strike on a Rwandan border-post from Uganda. This attack, rapidly repulsed with French and Zairean support, marked the start of Rwanda's civil war.[4] The war's ostensible objective was refugee return. The RPF also set out, in an eight-point programme, aspirations for democratic reform and ethnic unity inside Rwanda. Yet for regime hardliners the rebels' officially promulgated aims were not to be trusted. This was a war of conquest. The RPF had ambitions to capture the state, reverse the revolution, and perhaps even reinstate the monarchy.[5]

The context for the war was important. It began at a time of rising elite discontent within Rwanda. Resentment of presidential power and privilege animated calls for political reform from senior figures within the Mouvement Révolutionnaire National pour le Développement (MRND) who lacked the regional, clan, and kinship ties to be included in Habyarimana's innermost circle of power. At the same time, Rwanda's refugees faced an increasingly hostile political environment inside Uganda. Although indebted to the many Banyarwanda who fought alongside him to topple Milton Obote, Uganda's president, Yoweri Museveni found it increasingly difficult to support them openly. The refugees' future prospects were dim in Uganda. At the international level, the recent end of the Cold War had emboldened the desire to expand the liberal international order. This aspiration expressed itself in the promotion of democracy on the continent. Habyarimana would come under pressure from western states – the US, Germany, and Belgium in particular – to reform Rwanda politically.

The war's trajectory followed two distinguishable periods: a pre-genocide and a genocidal phase. The pre-genocide phase, lasting 1,285 days, was unremarkable. The RPF, having lost its military commander, Fred Rwigyema, in the initial attack in October 1990, reorganized under Paul Kagame. Its strategy quickly changed. By April 1991, it was pursuing a war of attrition. It no longer sought to capture and hold territory and instead engaged in a low-intensity guerrilla campaign. Its military strikes were often followed or preceded by Tutsi massacres organized by local authorities. These atrocities, while

---

[4] For more detailed accounts of the war, I recommend Guichaoua (2015); Prunier (1998).

[5] These fears were articulated in the infamous Forces Armées Rwandaises (FAR) report published in September 1992 entitled *The Definition and Identification of the Enemy*.

3.2 Synopsis of Rwanda's Civil War

sometimes described as early warning signs of a genocide, were also unremarkable. Indiscriminate civilian targeting is not an unusual counterinsurgency strategy (Downes, 2007). Massacres have strategic as well as retributive value.

With little prospect of an outright military victory for either side in sight, in June 1992 the peace process formally commenced. The government began negotiations with the RPF under the auspices of the Organisation of African Unity (OAU) with several regional and western states participating as observers.[6] Over thirteen months of meetings, a settlement crystallized that, for regime loyalists at least, signified a surrender to the RPF. The power-sharing protocol, finalized in January 1993, granted the MRNDD and RPF each five ministerial portfolios, with the newly created Mouvement Démocratique Républicain (MDR), Parti Social Démocrate (PSD), Parti Libéral (PL), and Parti Démocrate Chrétien (PDC) parties sharing the remaining eleven. In the Transitional National Assembly (TNA), the RPF, MRNDD, the MDR, the PSD, and PL would each receive eleven seats, the smaller PDC four seats, and one seat was reserved for other agreed parties – which potentially included the radically pro-Hutu Coalition pour la Défense de la République (CDR). The armed forces protocol, agreed in August 1993, foresaw an integrated national army in which the RPF contributed 40 per cent of the rank-and-file and 50 per cent of the officer corps. In short, the MRNDD became a minority player politically and the RPF secured a veto militarily, and potentially politically, if it could maintain an alliance with the main opposition parties. Opposition to the Arusha Accords was understandably strong among regime hardliners.

Why did the peace process yield such an unbalanced outcome? One key reason was because the military balance-of-power had in fact shifted in favour of the RPF in the two years following the rebel group's doubtful beginning. The war was not a stalemate. In part, this was because the RPF had stepped up its recruitment and financing; but in part it was because the FAR suffered a decline in discipline and

---

[6] The regional powers comprised Zaire (supportive of the Government of Rwanda (GOR)), Uganda (supportive of the RPF), Burundi, Tanzania, Senegal, and Nigeria. The western states represented were France (supportive of the GOR), the United States, and also Belgium and Germany (as the former colonial rulers). Tanzanian president, Ali Hassan Mwinyi, was appointed as the facilitator but delegated his function mainly to his Ambassador, Ami Mpungwe.

morale as the regime struggled financially. The RPF grew from 2,500 in 1990 to a force of 25,000 by 1994 through the enrolment of volunteers not only from neighbouring Uganda, Burundi, Zaire, and Tanzania but also from within Rwanda itself. Uganda covertly resupplied the RPF militarily, and the Tutsi diaspora, particularly those in Belgium, Canada, and the US, donated important sums to the cause. In contrast, the regime found itself strapped financially and unable to meet the cost of buying munitions and paying what would become an army of 50,000 – overwhelmingly conscripts – without incurring unsustainable public debt. A World Bank structural adjustment programme had devalued the Rwandan franc by 40 per cent at the outset of the war, and a second devaluation, by a further 15 per cent, occurred in 1991. At the same time, following the US-led effort to end the production quotas in the International Coffee Agreement, the price of coffee – Rwanda's main foreign exchange earner – crashed.[7] The regime's inferior military position was brought painfully home in February 1993 when the RPF launched a major offensive that would bring it within 30 km of the capital. Were it not for French military reinforcements, Kigali would have fallen.

A second reason for the skewed outcome of the peace process lay in the fact that the peace negotiations occurred at the same time as a broader democratization effort. In this respect, the pre-genocide phase of the war was distinctive. The unusual coincidence of these two processes, as we shall see in the next chapter, accelerated the rise of ethnic extremism in Rwanda. The introduction of multipartyism in June 1991 turned the two-sided civil war into a three-way contest between the RPF, the government, and the newly created opposition political parties. In a reversal of the liberal international model, this unusual coincidence resulted in a coalition government involving the main opposition parties *before* the peace agreement was finalized. This would prove calamitous. The regime found itself represented for much of the peace process by a foreign minister chosen from the largest opposition party, the MDR. Regime loyalists believed that Ngulinzira deliberately conceded too much to the RPF.

---

[7] In June 1989, the price of coffee stood at 1.80USD per pound. By July, in the newly deregulated market, it traded at 0.60USD per pound. The regime depended on coffee for over 70 per cent of its foreign exchange earnings at the time.

The peace agreement, then, was deeply unpopular with loyalists at home. Its implementation nonetheless began following its signature on 4 August 1993. Politics inside Rwanda grew tenser and events climaxed on 6 April 1994 with Habyarimana's assassination. His death re-ignited the civil war. The war then entered its second, genocidal phase that lasted a further 102 days. I examine the dramatic trajectory of this second phase in Chapter 5.

3.3 The Links between War and Genocide

What does theory tell us about how wars contribute to genocides? Two main mechanisms emerge from the literature: first, wars create *threats*; second, wars make *political opportunities*.[8] This latter mechanism is behind a broader group of crisis-driven explanations that includes revolutions, acute economic upheaval, as well as wars.[9] I examine political opportunity separately in the next two chapters. However, I argue that Rwanda's civil war contributed to the genocide primarily through the *threat* it created. I focus here on explaining the psychology of this threat and its impact on Rwandans.

Broadly, threat-centric theories of ethnic warfare divide into rationalist and emotion-centric explanations. Proponents of the former emphasize strategy, interests, logic, and manipulation.[10] Elite agency is central to these theories. In contrast, advocates of the latter highlight identities, loyalties, symbols, and myths.[11] Mass sentiment is at the heart of these explanations. Despite their different emphases, both

---

[8] Melson (1992) suggests a third link: war serves as a 'cover' for genocide. I provide a more a detailed theoretical critique of the role of threat in existing explanations of wars and genocide in McDoom (2012).

[9] In explaining why genocides, politicides, and mass violence happen, Krain (1997) points to 'breaks in the political opportunity structure'; Barbara Harff (2003, p. 62) argues that 'the greater the extent of political disruption, the greater the opportunities for authorities to seek a 'final solution' to present and potential future challenges; and Stuart J. Kaufman (2011, p. 32) writes 'ethnic groups must have enough freedom to mobilize politically without being stopped by state coercion'.

[10] Proponents of rationalist approaches include de Figueiredo and Weingast (1999); Lake and Rothchild (1998); Posen (1993); Valentino et al. (2004).

[11] Proponents of emotionalist approaches include Costalli and Ruggeri (2015); Horowitz (1985); Kaufman (2001); Petersen (2002); Ross (2007); and Shesterinina (2016).

approaches share a recognition of *fear* as a powerful motivational force in war. Yet two fundamental questions remain unresolved in theorization on the role of fear. What is the *object* of this fear? Is it a fear of physical extinction or a fear of losing power? These motives are not the same and we should specify which one matters. And what is the *outcome* of this fear? Is it simply public support for war, or does it refer to actual participation in violence? The distinction between sentiment and action is not trivial. How ethnic groups move from supporting to committing violence deserves separate explanation.

First, theories are unclear on whether it is the 'fear from above' – usually elite concerns with power – or the 'fear from below' – typically mass concerns for security – that is consequential. Generally, rationalist theories have dominated and have emphasized the threat to elite power. Existing explanations of Rwanda's civil war have embraced this approach and focused on elite concerns for the threat posed by the war. According to these explanations, Rwanda's ruling elite did not trust the rebels' promulgated agenda. The rebels' stated goals of democratization, national unity, and the return of Tutsi refugees were merely a pretext. The true intention of the RPF, the Rwandan government announced, was 'to re-conquer Rwanda by force and to place power in the hands of a minority outside of the country that was nostalgic for a return to the feudal and monarchical regime that the Rwandan people had rejected thirty years ago'.[12] It was this fear, these explanations argue, that ultimately motivated known extremists, and that radicalized other members of Rwanda's ruling elite.

Less well-known, however, is whether and how ordinary Rwandans experienced this fear. Yet it was ordinary Rwandans who mobilized and who committed much of the violence. I asked Rwandans, in open-ended questions, to describe the changes in their communities following (i) the outbreak of the war in 1990 and (ii) the president's assassination in 1994. Table 3.1 summarizes the three principal

[12] In January 1991, just three months after the start of the war, Rwanda's Ministry of Foreign Affairs published a 'White Book' in which Rwanda's government exposed what it saw as the rebels' unstated agenda. The document also reproduces the RPF's *stated* political goals. In order, these were: 'consolidating national unity; strengthening democratic institutions; building national economic independence; eliminating all forms of corruption and abuse of power; resettling the refugees living in neighbouring countries; improving basic social services; guaranteeing the security of persons and property; reshaping foreign policy and consolidating national independence'. Copy on file with author.

Table 3.1 Perceptions of war's impact and significance

	Ethnicity		Perpetrator Status		Region	
	Hutu	Tutsi	Non-perp.	Perp.	South	North
	(N=268)	(N=21)	(N=166)	(N=102)	(N=131)	(N=137)

Question: Did life in your community change in any way after the war started in October 1990?

Yes, life did change	79.0%	95.1%	80.8%	46.7%	79.9%	81.5%
Unable/unwilling to answer	5.7%	0%	4.8%	22.3%	4.1%	6.1%

Question: If so, in what ways did life change in your community after the war started? (open-ended, multiple answers permitted)

	(N=268)	(N=21)	(N=166)	(N=102)	(N=131)	(N=137)
Deterioration in inter-ethnic relations	53.4%	71.5%	54.4%	30.5%	60.6%	46.4%
Deterioration in sense of security	32.1%	28.3%	32.3%	27.8%	20.7%	43.2%
Deterioration in economic conditions	31.4%	23.5%	31.8%	20.0%	14.6%	48.4%

Question: Describe what happened in your community after President Habyarimana died? (open-ended, multiple answers permitted)

	(N=264)	(N=21)	(N=167)	(N=97)	(N=137)	(N=148)
Deterioration in sense of security	62.5%	61.4%	62.8%	57.0%	58.0%	67.0%
Deterioration in inter-ethnic relations	66.5%	90.7%	65.9%	78.5%	96.6%	36.6%

Table 3.1 (cont.)

Question: During the war what were people thinking would happen if the rebel RPF were to win? (open-ended)

	Ethnicity		Perpetrator Status		Region	
	Hutu	Tutsi	Non-perp.	Perp.	South	North
	(N=267)	(N=21)	(N=164)	(N=103)	(N=128)	(N=139)
The Hutu would be killed	71.8%	67.8%	69.1%	46.6%	62.8%	72.6%
The Hutu would be oppressed and/or the Tutsi monarchy restored	14.2%	16.9%	16.7%	21.2%	16.7%	17.1%
The Tutsi would govern well	9.3%	6.6%	6.1%	15.3%	5.3%	7.9%
They did not think the RPF could win	4.7%	5.4%	5.0%	12.1%	9.8%	1.2%
Unable/unwilling to say	0%	3.2%	3.1%	4.8%	5.4%	1.1%

3.3 The Links between War and Genocide

impacts that emerged from their responses. Insecurity[13] was the second most common type of response, preceded by ethnic distancing,[14] and followed by economic hardship.[15] Moreover, the survey also shows that this insecurity increased dramatically in the second, genocidal phase. While only 32.1 per cent of Rwandans reported a sense of insecurity following the outbreak of war in 1990, 62.4 per cent in contrast felt unsafe following the president's assassination in 1994. The relationship between threat and security fears was visible in the inter-regional comparison as well. The survey data also show that northern Rwanda, located on the war's frontlines, was more adversely affected in all three respects than southern Rwanda, where the war was distant.[16] 43.2 per cent of northerners were fearful for their safety compared with only 20.7 per cent of southerners.

The war then did instil fear among ordinary Rwandans. But was it fear for the implications of the loss of political power or was it fear for their physical safety? I asked Rwandans in an open-ended question what they thought would happen if the rebels won the war. Nearly 72 per cent reported that they feared they would be killed. The threat 'below' then was primarily existential. Ordinary Rwandans feared for their lives. In contrast, only 14.2 per cent of ordinary Rwandans stated that they feared occupation or subjugation by the RPF. Fear that power would transfer from a Hutu to a Tutsi ethnic elite did not affect ordinary Rwandans as much as it did Rwanda's ruling elite.

---

[13] References to insecurity in the south typically meant a fear that the war might eventually reach them there. However, in the north insecurity was more concrete and dramatic. It included references to the deployment of soldiers and the machinery of war, immobility resulting from roadblocks, compulsory participation in night-time security patrols, the arrival of refugees fleeing the war, personal stories of flight from rebel attacks, as well as the killing of civilians.

[14] Within the 'ethnic distancing' category, I most frequently encountered general references to distrust (*agasuzuguro* in Kinyarwanda), and to lesser extents misunderstandings, disagreements, lower cooperation, and occasionally hate between ethnic groups as a result of the war. Northern respondents additionally mentioned arrests, harassment, and sometimes violence that targeted Tutsi.

[15] Economic hardship during the war usually referred to the inability to farm one's land in safety, the theft of food crops by war-refugees, price increases, the closure of local markets, and more generally hunger, poverty, and an unwillingness to work with an uncertain future ahead.

[16] Although a greater proportion of southerners (60.6 per cent) than northerners (46.4 per cent) reported a deterioration in inter-ethnic relations, this was because in several of the northern communes there were few if no Tutsi resident.

The second aspect of war-induced fear for which theories are also unclear concerns its *effect*. Does fear explain merely increased public support for war or does it also explain popular participation in violence? The distinction between attitude and behaviour is important and I distinguish analytically civilian radicalization – support for war – from civilian mobilization – participation in war. In this chapter, I focus on civilian radicalization as we lack direct evidence of the effects of war-time threat on individual attitudes and beliefs. The macro-to-micro linkages are under-specified and under-theorized. We also lack direct evidence tying fear to an individual's willingness to kill. I examine the question of civilian mobilization in Chapter 7 where I find that perpetrators and non-perpetrators alike felt threatened by the war. Fear alone did not explain why some killed and others not, but it was an important background condition for the violence.[17]

3.4 The Media and Civilian Radicalization

In times of war, the media often exerts one of the strongest influences on a society's perception of threat. It has the ability to magnify fears and to polarize societies through its power over the quantity and quality of information made available to the public. It is through misinformation and disinformation that wars can also act as covers for genocides. It is easy to misrepresent the number and identity of the victims, as well as the actions of your enemy. About three-quarters of Rwandans depended on the media for news of its civil war. Only the minority who lived in the north near the war's frontlines experienced the sights and sounds of the war first-hand before the genocide.[18] The Rwandan government employed its influence over the country's media to scaremonger its citizens. It manufactured rumours and events and attributed the insecurity to the enemy. Table 3.2 documents the

---

[17] Fujii (2009) argues that ethnic fears had no causal role in the violence and claims they were merely part of a 'script for violence' that Rwandans 'performed'. It is possible that she draws this conclusion because she implicitly equates the question of why the genocide occurred with the question of why Rwandans committed violence. I treat them as analytically distinct. Fear could be a necessary background condition for the genocide. However, it need not explain why some Rwandans killed and others not.

[18] The two prefectures on whose territory the war was mostly fought were Ruhengeri and Byumba. They contained just 11.4 per cent and 11.0 per cent of the entire population respectively.

Table 3.2 *Fearmongering: misinformation and disinformation during the war*

Start Date	Actual insecurity	Manufactured insecurity	Outcome
I. Nationwide Repression			
4 October 1990	Initial RPF attack, 1 October 1990	Rwandan army fakes attack on the capital Kigali, 4 October 1990	Arrest and detention of over 13,000 Tutsi. Dozens tortured and killed
II. Kibilira Massacres: Gisenyi Prefecture (Kibilira and Satinsyi communes)			
1 October 1990	Initial RPF attack, 1 October 1990	(i) Population shown bodies of two dead Hutu. (ii) Rumours that (a) that Hutu school children had been killed (b) that two Hutu army colonels had been killed and (c) that an armed RPF infiltrator was at large	367 Tutsi killed. 550 homes destroyed
Early March 1992	None	Rumour broadcast on Radio Rwanda that Tutsi planned to attack important Hutu leaders	5 Tutsi killed. 74 homes destroyed
Late December 1992	None	Infamous inflammatory speech by Leon Mugesera, November 22 1992 in nearby commune, Kabaya. Warns of Hutu extermination and describes Tutsi and Hutu opposition parties as accomplices of the enemy	Tutsi and Hutu opposition party members attacked. One person killed, dozens injured.

Table 3.2 (*cont.*)

Start Date	Actual insecurity	Manufactured insecurity	Outcome
III. Bagogwe massacres: Ruhengeri Prefecture (Mukingo and Kinigi communes) and Gisenyi prefecture (Giseke, Karage, Giciye, and Mutura communes)			
Late January to March 1991	RPF attack on Ruhengeri town, 23 January 1991	Faked assault on Bigogwe military base in the region	500–1,000 Bagogwe Tutsi killed
November and December 1992	None	Four Hutu dead bodies allegedly found in Gishwati forest	Burned and looted Bagogwe Tutsi homes. No-one killed
IV: Bugesera Massacres: Kigali-rural prefecture (Kanzenze, Gashora, and Ngenda communes)			
4 March 1992	None	(i) Series of landmine explosions by unidentified authors. (ii) Rumour broadcast on Radio Rwanda that (a) Tutsi planned to attack important Hutu leaders and (b) that Tutsi militants had infiltrated.	277 Tutsi killed

Source: Report of the International Commission of Investigation on Human Rights Violations in Rwanda since October 1990

3.4 The Media and Civilian Radicalization

rumours the government propagated. They comprise stories that Hutu civilians had been killed, that the enemy was about to attack, or that the enemy had already infiltrated and was at-hand. The media also propagated events the government fabricated: faked attacks on particular locales, the discovery of dead bodies, and explosions from landmines or grenades.

Rwandans had access to two forms of media during the war: print publications and the radio. Its print media was remarkably diverse during the war, but it had only a marginal and indirect impact on the majority of Rwandans' lives. There were at least eighty different newspapers, magazines, journals, and other publications in print during the war. Twenty have been classified as extremist or pro-Hutu in character.[19] However, in 1991 only 56.2 per cent of the population aged over seven years old knew how to read and write and only 6.5 per cent of the population aged between fifteen and twenty-four years old had had more than a primary-school education.[20] So the overall reading level of even most 'literate' Rwandans was below what was needed to understand what was published in the print media. Moreover, twenty-nine of the eighty publications were written in French, yet only 5.1 per cent of Rwandans spoke this language.

The radio instead was the most effective tool for direct mass communication in Rwanda. 29.9 per cent of all Rwandan households, that is nearly one in three, owned a radio in 1991.[21] During the war Rwandans, reception permitting, had a choice of three radio stations. The first was Radio Rwanda, the national radio station that had been broadcasting from before the start of the war. Up until early 1992, it was effectively the voice of the government. However, following a Tutsi massacre in the Bugesera region in which the radio was implicated, opposition parties successfully demanded less partisanship and more moderation.[22] The second was Radio-Télévision Libre des Mille

---

[19] This is based on an analysis of Chrétien's impressive work (1995, pp. 383–386). One of the most infamous publications during the war was *Kangura* whose founder, owner, and editor, Hasan Ngeze was convicted of incitement to genocide, among other crimes, in December 2003.

[20] See Government of Rwanda, Commission Nationale de Récensement (1994, pp. 131–148).

[21] *Idem*, p. 350.

[22] The radio falsely broadcast that Tutsi planned to kill important Hutu leaders, especially in Bugesera, which then triggered anti-Tutsi violence there. As a result,

Collines (RTLM), a private radio station that began its transmissions on 8 July 1993 and stopped reporting 360 days later on 3 July 1994 when the RPF captured Kigali.[23] Infamously known as Radio Machete during the genocide, RTLM was largely under the control of a well-known Hutu ideologue, Ferdinand Nahimana, who was convicted in 2003 of using the radio station to incite the Hutu population directly into violence during the genocide. A third radio station, Radio Muhubura, based in Uganda, broadcast on behalf of the Rwandan Patriotic Front (RPF) from July 1992. Although its discourse emphasized national unity over ethnic differences, its signal reportedly did not extend far into Rwanda.[24]

The radio whose content was most likely to radicalize its listeners then was RTLM. But did people tune into this radio station for news of the war? In spite of the political climate, a surprisingly high number of Rwandans, 61.3 per cent of my survey respondents, admitted that they listened to RTLM. These high numbers on listenership in the north and south in the country are challenged by the claim that RTLM reception was unlikely to be nationwide because of Rwanda's hilly topography and the limited power of its transmitters (Straus, 2007, p. 617). However, they are consistent with a technical assessment of the range of RTLM's two transmitters, located in Kigali (a 100-watt transmitter) and atop Mount Muhe in the north (a 1,000-watt transmitter) (Yanagizawa-Drott, 2014, p. 1962). It is also possible RTLM employed relay stations that would have extended the reach of the transmitters (Des Forges, 1999, p. 520). Table 3.3 confirms that northerners listened to RTLM more than southerners. It shows also that perpetrators and non-perpetrators were equally likely to listen to RTLM. Exposure to the radio's message alone then did not determine who participated in

---

Ferdinand Nahimana, a staunch MRND supporter and Radio Rwanda's supervisor at Office Rwandais de l'Information (ORINFOR), the government news regulatory agency, was replaced by Jean-Marie Vianney Higiro, a member of the opposition.

[23] Although RTLM was privately-owned, it had strong ties to elements of both Rwanda's ruling elite and hardliners. Of its fifty shareholders: forty came from the north, the region of president Habyarimana's birth; thirty-nine belonged to the ruling MRND party; and two belonged to the extremist CDR party. See Gulseth (2004). In addition, RTLM benefited from the appearance of a close association with the national radio station, Radio Rwanda, on whose frequencies it was permitted to broadcast between the hours of 8.00 and 11.00am before the genocide began.

[24] See Des Forges (1999, p. 68).

Table 3.3 Radio audiences in Rwanda

	Ethnicity		Perpetrator Status		Region	
	Hutu	Tutsi	Non-perp.	Perp.	South	North
Question: Did you ever listen to RTLM during the war?						
	(N=271)	(N=21)	(N=168)	(N=103)	(N=131)	(N=140)
Yes, I listened to it	61.3%	47.4%	61.4%	59.4%	38.4%	84.1%
Question: Did you mostly believe what you heard on RTLM?						
	(N=271)	(N=21)	(N=168)	(N=103)	(N=131)	(N=140)
Yes, I believed it or some of it	18.6%	4.7%	18.8%	14.7%	11.4%	25.6%
Question: Why did you/did you not believe what you heard on RTLM?						
	(N=161)	(N=12)	(N=94)	(N=67)	(N=55)	(N=106)
Disbelieved because it divided Hutu and Tutsi	23.9%	50.2%	23.6%	28.2%	39.6%	16.4%
Disbelieved because it preached bad ideas	12.9%	16.7%	12.8%	14.9%	15.2%	11.8%
Disbelieved because it did not tell the whole truth	39.0%	33.1%	40.4%	14.4%	33.2%	41.7%
Believed because I thought it told the truth	9.2%	0.0%	9.5%	5.4%	0.0%	13.6%
Question: Did you ever listen to Radio Muhubura during the war?						
	(N=265)	(N=21)	(N=168)	(N=97)	(N=125)	(N=140)
Yes, I listened to it	60.3%	61.7%	60.4%	57.6%	46.5%	73.6%
Question: Did you mostly believe what you heard on Radio Muhubura?						
	(N=263)	(N=21)	(N=166)	(N=97)	(N=124)	(N=139)
Yes, I believed it or some of it	32.2%	56.9%	32.6%	25.3%	33.8%	30.6%

the violence and who did not. Less surprisingly, given the sensitivity of the question, only 18.6 per cent of Rwandans claimed to *believe* what they heard on RTLM. In post-genocide Rwanda, supporting RTLM would be seen as having supported the genocide.

How popular was Radio Muhubura, the rebel radio, in contrast? While just over 60 per cent also claimed to *listen* to it, a higher percentage, 32.2 per cent, claimed to *believe* the RPF broadcasts. However, there is good reason to doubt the statistic. The majority of the population distrusted the RPF during the war. Both before and during the genocide, Rwanda's Hutu had fled in front of rebel advances. Many respondents were instead likely giving politically favourable responses because the RPF dominated Rwanda's post-genocide government. If true, it is possible that more Rwandans also listened to and believed RTLM than the survey suggests. Whether the true number was higher or not, we can at least say that RTLM had the power to communicate widely with Rwanda's civilian population.

What impact – if any – did RTLM have on the violence? The causal role of the radio in the genocide remains the subject of debate. It has been claimed that RTLM contributed to civilian radicalization, as well as to civilian mobilization through its calls-for-action (Yanagizawa-Drott, 2014). The radio station stands accused of instilling both anti-Tutsi hate and fear in Rwanda and also of directly inciting listeners to violence. However, there remain two major gaps in our knowledge. First, we have largely assumed that RTLM rhetoric influenced or reflected popular sentiment. We have little rigorous micro-evidence to support this assumption.[25] Were individual Rwandans in fact thinking and feeling what RTLM was broadcasting? Second, there has been little analysis of the evolution in the content of RTLM broadcasts over time. Did the radio transmit a consistent stream of extremist invective or did it gradually radicalize? If it did radicalize over time, did the violence coincide with the radio's radicalization?

I address these gaps in our knowledge in two ways in this chapter. First, I juxtapose the main messages 'from above' (distilled from a quantitative analysis of RTLM broadcasts) against statements of beliefs 'from below' (evidenced in survey data and unstructured

---

[25] Of the many content analyses of RTLM broadcasts that have emerged since the genocide, to my knowledge only two have also involved research into the views of Rwandans exposed to the broadcasts: Li (2004) and Straus (2007).

3.4 The Media and Civilian Radicalization

interviews with ordinary Rwandans). The goal was to see how closely RTLM's content reflected popular sentiment. As we shall see, most RTLM messages were similar to the beliefs of many ordinary Rwandans. Second, I present the analysis of the broadcasts in two timeframes: before and during the genocide. We shall see that RTLM took a significant radical turn only *after* the president's assassination. It is unlikely that it deeply radicalized the population *before* the genocide. Moreover, as we shall also see, it is even possible that the population had mobilized and was committing violence even *before* the radio began its own calls for violence.

In analysing a voluminous amount of data such as radio transcripts it is difficult to achieve balance, and it is all too easy to 'cherry-pick' sections that support the contention of the analyst. I chose to conduct a comprehensive quantitative analysis of the radio's content to minimize these risks. Such an approach of course is not without its own risks, and so I take a little time to explain the data used and method followed to help the reader to judge the results.

The radio transcripts came from the International Monitor Institute, a non-profit organization commissioned by the International Criminal Tribunal for Rwanda (ICTR) to translate a selection of RTLM broadcasts into English and French for use as evidence in trials. The selected transcripts I received covered 55 of RTLM's 360 days of broadcasting: 16 days from before the genocide and 39 days from during the genocide. So the overall sample size, if measured in days of broadcasting, was 15.3 per cent. Altogether, eight journalists reported on RTLM and all were represented in the sample.[26] The selection of transcripts was intended to be representative, but it was not random. The ICTR was most interested in broadcasts that touched on ethnicity or that incited the population into action. Following expert guidance, it purposively selected transcripts to achieve a balance between the most incriminating and the most exculpatory broadcasts.

The content analysis was conducted in two stages. In stage one, I compiled a list of words that I believed would indicate radical content for each of the four indicators of radicalization I was testing. I then listed *all* the words used in the broadcasts in order of their frequency. Altogether, there were 410,067 words in the database. I compared the

---

[26] All eight RTLM journalists had previously worked with either pro-MRND newspapers or with government media.

two lists to establish a 'dictionary' of radical terms. I then counted the occurrence of each of these terms in each day's broadcast. Stage two involved more intensive human judgement. I checked that the context in which each occurrence of these words was embedded was consistent with what I was aiming to test. Those words used in a different context were rejected. Finally, I calculated the occurrences of each of the remaining words as a *proportion* of all words used in each day's broadcast. This allowed me to compare the relative concentration of radical content across time.

3.5 Establishing the Baseline: Life before the War

Before examining the media's framing of the war and its impact on Rwandans, we need to establish what life was like for Rwandans before the war began. Before October 1990, while there was a palpable ethnic division within society, inter-ethnic relations had been stable for some time. Since Habyarimana's seizure of power in July 1973, there had been seventeen years of non-violent co-existence. An entire generation of Rwandan children had grown up having experienced neither an internal nor external security threat. The last attack on Rwanda had been in 1967, when Tutsi exiles made the last in a series of armed attempts to return home. The war in 1990 came as a shock.

This historical record of an inter-ethnic peace is consistent with ordinary Rwandans' memories of the pre-war years. Here is how Willene, a Tutsi survivor from the northern community of Ruginga, remembered life before the war.

Did you ever have any problems in Ruginga before the war started because you were Tutsi? No one was being hunted in Ruginga before the *Inkotanyi* [term to describe Tutsi rebels] invaded. *Were there no tensions at all?* When I was in school they would teach the history of Rwanda. This might have caused suspicions among the students. They taught that the Tutsi used to rule with an iron fist. The students would tease me about being Tutsi. After classes you would have to hide to avoid the other students. *Were you ever or anyone else ever attacked?* I was never beaten. No one was ever beaten. It was just teasing. After classes you would feel afraid and so you did not linger in case they [the students] got hungry for you. So you would rush straight home. They would say things like the 'Tutsi ruled with an iron fist'. But really, I do not know of any serious problems between Hutu and Tutsi. Before the war things were normal. (*Willene, Tutsi survivor, aged 36, author-led interview in Kinyarwanda with interpreter, Ruhengeri town, northern Rwanda, June 2003*)

Clearly, as the history lessons and schoolyard teasing suggest, there was a real ethnic consciousness and pervasive discrimination in Rwanda before the war. The north, in fact, was a region where anti-Tutsi sentiment was arguably high even before the war. Historically, it had been the site of several autonomous Hutu principalities that had resisted Tutsi monarchic rule. Demographically, it was overwhelmingly Hutu, following an exodus of Tutsi in the wake of Rwanda's Hutu revolution on the eve of independence in 1962. Politically, it was loyal to the incumbent party and to the president, who was himself a northerner. Despite this, even Willene felt that pre-war relations between Hutu and Tutsi were not so poor when compared with those during the war.

Broader survey data confirm Willene's favourable recollection of pre-war cohabitation. Table 3.4 shows that when asked when relations were last poor between Hutu and Tutsi, most Rwandans felt this was *over three decades earlier*. The incident that had impressed itself most deeply in collective memory was the Hutu Revolution. A total of 88.7 per cent of all Hutu cited this as the last time they remember that Hutu-Tutsi relations were poor. And 87.4 percent of northerners shared this recollection. Willene's impression of Hutu–Tutsi relations was not atypical. Despite an already high anti-Tutsi baseline in the north, the war would cause ethnic sentiment to radicalize even further.

3.6 The Psychological Impact of War

How then did RTLM frame the war and what impact did it have on the attitudes and beliefs of ordinary Rwandans? In the following subsections I present the theory and evidence behind each of the four psychological mechanisms that I argue drove civilian radicalization in Rwanda.[27] I draw on three main kinds of evidence to illustrate the impact of threat. First, I present the analysis of RTLM radio broadcasts from before and during the genocide. It points to the radicalization of extremist elite sentiment over time. Second, I draw on survey questions

---

[27] More detail on the findings of the war-time civilian radicalization documented here may be found in McDoom (2012).

Table 3.4 Collective memory of Hutu–Tutsi relations

Question: Before the war were there other times in Rwanda's history when relations between Hutu and Tutsi had been bad? (open-ended, multiple answers allowed)

	Ethnicity		Perpetrator Status		Region	
	Hutu	Tutsi	Non-perp.	Perp.	South	North
	(N=270)	(N=21)	(N=167)	(N=103)	(N=131)	(N=139)
The time of the Hutu Revolution (1959)	88.7%	95.3%	89.3%	78.7%	90.0%	87.4%
During the first Hutu Republic (1961–1973)	11.2%	19.2%	11.6%	5.5%	18.9%	3.7%
The coup that started the second Republic (1973)	18.3%	38.3	18.0%	24.3%	29.5%	7.3%
Unable/unwilling to answer	5.4%	0%	5.4%	6.6%	4.7%	5%

3.6 The Psychological Impact of War

relating to the war asked of ordinary Rwandans. The survey corroborates that radicalization above was matched by radicalization below. Lastly, I enrich these findings with insights from two northern and two southern communities on the impact of the war.

Radicalization Mechanism I: The Stronger the Threat, the Greater the Ethnicization

The ethnicization of society and politics is the first indicator of civilian radicalization. Extensive psycho-social research on intergroup relations identifies threat as a moderator of both positive bias in favour of ingroups and negative bias against outgroups.[28] Ingroup favouritism may be expressed as pride, loyalty, and perceived superiority; outgroup negativity may manifest as stereotyping, discrimination, and prejudice. In the context of inter-ethnic relations, threat then activates latent ethnic boundaries and raises the salience of ethnic identities. As the threat intensifies, ethnic distance increases and ingroup hostility toward the ethnic outgroup escalates. This distance and hostility can be amplified when the threat is framed as having historical and contemporary parallels. The threat then resonates against the collective memory and shared perceptions – the myths and narratives – that the threatened ingroup has of the threatening outgroup.

In Rwanda, RTLM broadcasts illustrate the activation and heightened salience of ethnic boundaries in the framing of the conflict in increasingly ethnic terms as the war escalated. In the pre-genocide stage of the war, when the threat was minor, RTLM broadcasters used the non-ethnic identifiers 'RPF' or 'rebels' to describe the enemy. In the genocidal phase, however, when the threat was more acute, the use of these neutral descriptors declined and ethnic identifiers instead increased. Table 3.5 shows that the use of the terms *Inkotanyi* and *Inyenzi* increased two-fold and ten-fold respectively in the genocidal phase of the war. *Inkotanyi*, or 'fierce warriors' is a historical reference to a regiment in the Tutsi king's army of old; *inyenzi*, or cockroaches, refers to Tutsi invaders of the 1960s, so named because they often attacked at night. Rwandans understood both terms to refer to Tutsi.

---

[28] For a review of the literature on threat perception and identity theory, see Sears, Huddy, and Jervis (2003, pp. 539–542).

Table 3.5 *Psycho-social mechanisms of civilian radicalization in RTLM radio broadcasts*

	Pre-genocide (100ths of %)	Genocide (100ths of %)
Mechanism I: Ethnicization and intergroup distancing		
Enemy outgroup identified non-ethnically as "rebels" or "RPF"[†]	39.29	29.57***
Enemy outgroup identified ethnically as *Inkotanyi*[††]	29.60	57.68***
Enemy outgroup identified ethnically as *Inyenzi*[†††]	2.99	33.06***
Negative references to Tutsi outgroup oppression of Hutu	2.17	5.46***
References to Ndadaye's assassination in Burundi	10.73	6.26***
Mechanism II: Outgroup homogenization		
Inyenzi distinguished from all Tutsi outgroup members	2.89	13.73***
Inyenzi equated with all Tutsi outgroup members	0.0	2.01***
Inyenzi-Tutsi outgroup distinction ambiguous	0.10	17.09***
Mechanism III: Ingroup cohesion		
Use of term "Hutu"	19.70	14.92***
Use of term "Tutsi"	23.62	16.96***
Use of term "Rwandan"	144.39	308.20***
References to Tutsi outgroup disloyalty	0.52	0.70
References to Hutu ingroup disloyalty	1.65	3.03***
Ethnically ambiguous references to disloyalty	2.78	0.83***
Mechanism IV: Justification of outgroup targeting		
References to legitimate self-defense	3.40	7.28***
References to extermination of Hutu	1.86	2.11
References to extermination of Tutsi	0.41	3.83***

[†] *Rwandan Patriotic Front, mainly Tutsi rebel group;*
[††] *Kinyarwanda term for fierce warriors identified with Tutsi;*
[†††] *Kinyarwanda term for cockroaches, again identified with Tutsi.*
*/**/*** *Proportions compared using a Wald test of significance at 10%, 5% and 1% thresholds respectively.*
Source: McDoom (2012)

3.6 The Psychological Impact of War

Once ethnic boundaries had been activated, ethnic distance grew as the war escalated. This distance was most evident in the mounting distrust between the two groups. Members of the ethnic ingroup increasingly suspected members of the ethnic outgroup of supporting the enemy. In the northern community of Ruginga, located within the zone of combat, immediately following the initial rebel attack in 1990, villagers from a neighbouring community took three of Ruginga's thirty-five Tutsi to the local government office where they were interrogated and beaten before being released. Following a major RPF attack on Ruhengeri town four months later, the same group of villagers attacked and killed the head of the same family targeted previously. The following juxtaposition from a Tutsi and Hutu in the second northern community researched, Mutovu, exemplifies this mutual distrust.

What happened in your community after the RPF attacked in 1990? There was distrust between the Tutsi and the Hutu. Almost everyone was demoralized as it was the first time for many people that they heard of an attack or a war against Rwanda. In the evenings and in the mornings the Tutsi liked to stick together in groups. We were always afraid of these groups as it was being said that they were making a plan to kill us. We were afraid of each other. Then when Habyarimana died the fear became generalized. We did not do anything and we did not go anywhere. We stayed in our homes as was ordered. The killers led by the councillor started their work to kill the Tutsi on the same day we heard of the president's death. (*Donatelle, Hutu farmer, aged 35, Mutovu cell, northern Rwanda, July 2003*)

What happened in your community after the RPF attacked in 1990? When the RPF attacked the country the trust between us and the Hutu was broken. They [Hutu] began to say that it was us [Tutsi] who had started the war against Rwanda and that we were making them suffer for it. The Hutu began to control all our activities. They said that we were sending our children to fight at the front but it was not true. It was just an excuse to threaten and to attack us. It is thanks to God that before 1994 we did not suffer any human losses, if I remember rightly. But when the plane came down it was another thing. We were hunted like wild animals. My wife and children were killed in these operations. I had fled and hid myself in the bushes. It was by the grace of God they did not find me. (*Constantin, Tutsi farmer, aged 44, Mutovu cell, northern Rwanda, July 2003*)

In contrast, in the south where the war was more distant, the distrust was less pronounced following the start of the war. There were no arrests, harassment, or other highly visible forms of ethnic distancing within these communities. The suspicions, if any, were latent as Véronique, a genocide survivor describes:

What happened in your community after the war started in 1990? For those who had radios, they were afraid but for those who did not, they were not concerned. It was everyone who was afraid – not just the Hutu but also the Tutsi as they had both heard there was war. But there were no problems between Hutu and Tutsi as a result here. There was nothing bad said about the Tutsi at the time. Perhaps people said it in their huts but they did not say it to me. (*Véronique, Hutu woman married to Tutsi farmer, aged 31, Tamba cell, southern Rwanda*)

Survey data corroborate the war's effect of ethnic distance. As Table 3.6 shows, 40.1 per cent of the surveyed Hutu identified the start of the war in October 1990 as a turning point in inter-ethnic relations. An even higher proportion of Tutsi (61.3 per cent), who as a minority were more sensitive to changes in ethnic tensions, also viewed the war as a cause of ethnic distance. Again, where the threat was greater, the ethnic distance was more widely felt. Thus, twice as many northerners (56.5 per cent), who lived within proximity of the war, as southerners (25.9 per cent) felt that it created distance between the two groups.

Ethnic distance was also evident in increasing negative associations made with Tutsi as the conflict intensified. This hostility was manifest in the foregrounding of an anti-Tutsi narrative that permeated Rwandan society. It comprised two core historical beliefs. First, the Tutsi were alien invaders. According to this belief, Hutu had arrived first as farmers, and Tutsi settled subsequently as herders. By implication, Tutsi had a weaker claim to the land than Hutu. Second, Tutsi had historically oppressed Hutu. The Tutsi king and his mainly Tutsi chiefs had controlled a feudal system that had subjugated Hutu until the Revolution of 1959–1962 toppled this oppressive order. RTLM broadcasts strategically framed the civil war increasingly in these historical terms. As Table 3.5 indicates, references to this historical oppression more than doubled following the president's assassination. RTLM emphasized two points in propagating this frame. First, the RPF rebels were the descendants of the generation of Tutsi exiled following the Hutu Revolution. Here is how Ferdinand Nahimana, a renowned Hutu ideologue, described the relationship on RTLM.

There is no difference between the RPF and the *Inyenzi* [lit. cockroaches] because the *Inyenzi* are refugees who fled Rwanda after the mass majority Revolution of 1959, the fall of the monarchy and the establishment of a democratic Republic. Those who denied the Republic and democracy went

Table 3.6 Perceptions of decline in Hutu-Tutsi relations

Question: When did relations between Hutu and Tutsi first begin to worsen in your community? (open-ended)

	Ethnicity		Perpetrator Status		Region	
	Hutu	Tutsi	Non-perp.	Perp.	South	North
	(N=265)	(N=21)	(N=162)	(N=103)	(N=132)	(N=133)
With the war in October 1990	40.1%	61.3%	41.3%	24.2%	25.9%	56.5%
With multipartyism in 1991	12.4%	14.6%	12.5%	10.3%	20.6%	3.7%
With the genocide in April 1994	43.3%	24.1%	42.2%	62.3%	53.5%	32.9%
Some other time between 1990–1994	1.3%	0.0%	1.0%	3.2%	0.0%	1.0%
Unable/unwilling to say	2.9%	0.0%	3.0%	0.0%	0.0%	5.9%

into self-imposed exile. Not long after, between 1962 and 1967, those refugees tried to replace the new Republic with the former monarchy. They launched attacks that killed people. However, Rwanda had then a national army, the National Guard. Those sons of the nation did their best and drove those attackers out and in 1967, the *Inyenzi* stopped their attacks. (*Interview with Ferdinand Nahimana, RTLM broadcast, 20 November 1993*)

RTLM's second point was that these Tutsi exiles did not just want to come home. They wanted to reverse the gains or '*les acquis*' of the Revolution and to reinstate the former socio-political order in which a Tutsi elite had monopolized power and had subjugated Hutu. Here is how Froduald Karamira, a leader of an extremist Power faction of the MDR, responded to the question of what the difference is between the political contests of 1959 and the 1990s.

Froduald Karamira [originally in Kinyarwanda]: This is an important and long question... At the beginning of the war we thought it was a matter of refugees who wanted to come back to their country. Is it now still the case? Before the RPF said it wanted Habyarimana. We wonder what they are fighting for now that have they killed him. They are fighting for the power they had in 1959 and think they can get it back. War has clearly shown their intentions and Rwandans have realized it. That is why if they hope that the people and political parties will go on quarrelling, they are wrong because it is no longer possible. Now they are aware of the hidden meaning of the war. Tito Rutaremara [one of the founding fathers of the RPF] has pointed it out on Radio Rwanda. He asked: 'Who do you think the refugees are? Do you confuse them with those who are hidden in the rivers? The refugees are those who fled the country in 1959 and 1973. These are the only refugees we know and we are fighting for.' (*Interview on RTLM radio station with Vice-President of MDR Party, Froduald Karimira, 22 April 1994, eighteen days into the genocide*)

Did this strategic framing of the conflict resonate below with Rwanda's Hutu population? Ethnic distance amplifies if the threat is framed to resonate against the collective memory and shared perceptions – myths or narratives – that the threatened group has of the other group. Rwanda's civil war was framed, first, as having a historical parallel with the 1959 Hutu Revolution, and second as having a contemporary parallel with events in neighbouring Burundi.

I found that Rwanda's Hutu population possessed a very strong collective memory – that is they were aware of myths or narratives – of past Tutsi oppression against which these broadcast messages resonated. I asked a series of questions to probe Hutu attitudes towards Rwanda's pre-revolutionary history. As Table 3.7 shows, the majority

Table 3.7 Historical narrative of Tutsi privilege and oppression of Hutu

	Ethnicity		Perpetrator Status		Region	
	Hutu	Tutsi	Non-perp.	Perp.	South	North

Question: When he ruled, did the Mwami (Tutsi monarch) favour any ethnic group?

	(N=270)	(N=21)	(N=167)	(N=103)	(N=132)	(N=138)
The Mwami favoured the Tutsi	70.3%	52.8%	70.1%	74.8%	72.1%	64.7%
Unable/unwilling to answer	12.2%	9.5%	12.5%	6.7%	9.8%	14.1%

Question: Under ubuhake (an outlawed form of feudal clientship), who was usually the shebuja (master) and who was usually the mugaragu (servant)?

	(N=269)	(N=21)	(N=167)	(N=102)	(N=130)	(N=139)
Tutsi was master and Hutu was servant	80.4%	67.0%	79.7%	92.1%	84.7%	73.2%
Unable/unwilling to answer	9.2%	0.0%	9.4%	4.8%	2.5%	13.9%

Question: Do you think that ubuhake (an outlawed form of feudal clientship) was fair?

	(N=271)	(N=21)	(N=169)	(N=102)	(N=131)	(N=140)
No, it was not fair	75.4%	61.9%	74.7%	88.5%	81.5%	66.5%
Unable/unwilling to answer	5.7%	0.0%	5.9%	3.2%	2.3%	7.9%

remembered it as a period of subjugation and injustice: 70.3 per cent believed the Tutsi monarch had favoured Tutsi over Hutu; 75.4 per cent saw *ubuhake*, an institution associated with monarchic rule, as unfair. *Ubuhake*, an outlawed form of feudal clientship, involved the exchange of a cow from a patron or master (*shebuja*) against a life-time of service from the client or servant (*mugaragu*). A total of 80.4 per cent believed that Tutsi were usually the masters, and Hutu usually the servants. Abuses by some Tutsi patrons had created the popular perception of *ubuhake* as a form of Hutu slavery. All respondents also knew of the Hutu Revolution. I asked them what they thought of it – a very sensitive question in the post-genocide climate. Unsurprisingly then, as Table 3.8 indicates, the majority (64 per cent) said the Revolution was 'bad', and a high proportion (13 per cent) said they could not or would not tell me. However, the minority (23 per cent) of Hutu respondents who admitted to seeing the Revolution positively, associated it with democracy, freedom, and independence for their brethren. These were the gains that many feared to lose in the war. The second, often-cited parallel that amplified ethnic distance was with the situation in Burundi. Burundi is Rwanda's neighbouring cousin. It too is a small, densely populated, former Belgian colony in central Africa. Demographically, it too is composed of Hutu, Tutsi, and Twa in similar proportions to Rwanda. The Barundi of Burundi share a common language and culture, as do the Banyarwanda of Rwanda. However, unlike in Rwanda, it was a Tutsi, not Hutu elite that controlled the post-independence state. In the early 1990s, Burundi took steps towards democracy just as Rwanda did. Elections on 29 June 1993 saw the victory of Burundi's first Hutu president, Melchior Ndadaye. A mere 114 days later, however, on 21 October 1993, he would be assassinated by low-ranking Tutsi soldiers. Another 167 days after this, on 6 April 1994, Rwanda's own Hutu President suffered what seemed a parallel assassination. Most Hutu believed that the RPF was behind it. The assassination confirmed, at least for elite thinking in Rwanda, that ethnic power-sharing was not possible: the RPF sought to monopolize, not share power.

However, the assassination in Burundi did not reverberate quite as strongly as the historical parallel with the Revolution. As Table 3.5 shows, RTLM references to the situation in Burundi in fact diminished in the second, genocidal phase. In addition, as Table 3.9 shows, while knowledge of the revolution was universal among Hutu survey

Table 3.8 Perceptions of Rwanda's Revolution

	Ethnicity		Perpetrator Status		Region	
	Hutu	Tutsi	Non-perp.	Perp.	South	North
	(N=271)	(N=21)	(N=168)	(N=103)	(N=132)	(N=139)

Question: On the whole did you think Rwanda's 1959 Revolution was a good or bad thing?

It was a good thing	23.2%	4.9%	21.3%	56.6%	16.6%	25.9%
It was a bad thing	64.0%	90.2%	65.5%	38.7%	66.6%	67.1%
Unable/unwilling to answer	12.8%	4.9%	13.2%	4.7%	16.8%	7.0%

Question: Why in your view was the 1959 Revolution good or bad? (open-ended)

	(N=249)	(N=19)	(N=149)	(N=100)	(N=118)	(N=131)
Bad, as it divided Hutu and Tutsi	19.2%	26.2%	19.5%	14.7%	18.7%	19.7%
Bad, as it led to violence and war	44.8%	63.1%	46.3%	20.2%	44.7%	45.0%
Bad, as it exiled Tutsi	6.1%	5.4%	6.1%	5.6%	9.9%	2.5%
Good, as it brought freedom and/or democracy	22.5%	5.4%	20.7%	52.5%	20.7%	24.3%
Some other reason	7.3%	0.0%	7.3%	6.9%	6.1%	8.5%

Table 3.9 Awareness of Burundian president's assassination

	Ethnicity		Perpetrator Status		Region	
	Hutu	Tutsi	Non-perp.	Perp.	South	North
	(N=269)	(N=21)	(N=169)	(N=100)	(N=130)	(N=139)

Question: Did you know what had happened to President Ndadaye of Burundi by the time the genocide began?

Yes, I knew Ndadaye had been killed	63.2%	43.1%	63.5%	58.0%	70.9%	55.7%

respondents, only 63.2 per cent admitted to even remembering Ndadaye's assassination

The Burundian assassination, however, would affect Rwanda in two other ways. First, as we shall see in Chapter 5, it marked the birth of the 'Hutu Power' movement. The assassination precipitated an internal split into extremist and moderate factions of Rwanda's two main opposition parties, the MDR and the PL. Second, the assassination triggered a wave of Burundian Hutu refugees into southern Rwanda. Many of these refugees would also participate in the violence there (Des Forges, 1999, p. 283).

Threat then ethnicized social and political relations in Rwanda. Consistent with psycho-social theory, the evidence presented here suggests that ethnicity was instrumental, variable in salience, and the meta-rationale for group mobilization, However, as we shall see in Chapter 7, ethnicity, does not by itself explain why some committed violence in Rwanda's genocide and others did not.

Radicalization Mechanism II: The Stronger the Threat, the More Broadly Defined the Enemy Outgroup

The second indicator of civilian radicalization is outgroup homogenization. In psycho-social theory, outgroup homogenization is an expression of threat-driven ingroup bias (Messick & Mackie, 1989). As the threat increases, the definition of the enemy outgroup enlarges. The enemy is no longer only rebel combatants, but also encompasses civilians. The boundaries of the outgroup expand. When the threat is most acute, the enemy outgroup is ultimately de-individualized to form a single homogenous group, all of whose members represent a threat to be eliminated.[29]

RTLM journalists played on the ambiguity in the distinction between Tutsi civilians and rebel combatants during the war. The ambiguity can be seen in the evolution in their use of the pejorative ethnic identifier *inyenzi* to define the enemy. Table 3.5 shows that across the pre-genocide and genocide periods, there was a significant increase in references to the *inyenzi* enemy in contexts that signified unequivocally *all* Tutsi – civilian men, women, and children. At the

---

[29] Straus (2006, p. 162) identifies a similar effect in his research on Rwanda and termed it 'collective ethnic categorization'.

3.6 The Psychological Impact of War

same time, there was also an increase in references in contexts that clearly distinguished between Tutsi combatants and civilians. However, there was also an increase in statements in contexts that left it unclear in listeners' minds whether *inyenzi* referred to Tutsi civilians or combatants. The uptick in these conflicting statements amplified uncertainty as to who the enemy was. This increased uncertainty was integral to the process of homogenizing the outgroup.

The plasticity in outgroup boundaries can also be seen through an inter-regional comparison. For northerners, the Tutsi were identified with the enemy from early on in the war – even before its genocidal phase. In the two northern communities of Ruginga and Mutovu, Tutsi faced intimidation, arrest, detention, and violence, especially when the rebels advanced. They were seen as enemy collaborators. One northerner explains the mental equation between the rebel RPF and his Tutsi neighbours thus:

What happened in your community after the war broke out in October 1990? In October 1990 when we learned on the radio that the country had been attacked by the RPF, who were mostly Tutsi and the brothers of our neighbours, we told ourselves that if they [our neighbours] were not accomplices they would have told us that the country was going to be attacked. If they did not inform us of the danger then they must be the enemy. Some Tutsi families secretly began to send their own sons to the front to fight for the RPF, saying that their children were going to study. This aggravated the distrust between the two ethnic groups because a neighbour was now becoming the enemy. (*Jean-Marie, Hutu shopkeeper, aged 39, Mutovu cell, northern Rwanda*)

In contrast, the story in the two southern communities was quite different. In the pre-genocide phase, Tutsi were not targeted as collaborators as they were in the north. Even in the genocidal phase, Hutu and Tutsi initially cooperated following the president's assassination, manning roadblocks and participating in night patrols together. The expanded definition of the enemy outgroup was realized late in the south. Here is one young man's description of how Mwendo's residents came to realize that the Tutsi were the target.

Tell me what happened in your community right after Habyarimana died: In a few days we started to see smoke of burning houses coming from Gigonkoro [a neighbouring prefecture]. Then everyone was afraid – both Hutu and Tutsi. We wondered who was burning the houses? People said those who were doing the burning had covered themselves in banana leaves so you could not see who it was. But when we found out that it was Tutsi houses burning, the fear of Hutu decreased while the fear of the Tutsi increased as they now knew who was the enemy. After a few days it was evident that there were two groups – those being hunted and those who hunted. Then people became greedy and started killing and eating people's cows. After it was clear that there were some people [Tutsi] who were the enemy, some people said that 'we are used to this because of history'. Then those hiding people told the people to flee rather than dying where they were hiding. (*Leopold, secretary of the Gacaca committee, aged 32, April 2003, Mwendo cell, southern Rwanda*)

What happened in these four communities was not unusual. Table 3.10 shows that in most southern communities Hutu and Tutsi participated together in night patrols even *after* the president's assassination. Tutsi respondents (80 per cent) corroborated this. Southern Hutu then did not identify Tutsi with the enemy even on the eve of the genocide. However, as we know, this changed during the violence. When asked whom people thought were the enemy during the genocide, 70.5 per cent responded that it was *all Tutsi*. An additional 20.6 per cent concurred but went on to say that the enemy also included others such as Hutu collaborators.

Radicalization Mechanism III: The Greater the Threat, the Stronger the Demand for Ingroup Loyalty

The third indicator of civilian radicalization is ingroup cohesion. At the heart of this mechanism is group loyalty. In psycho-social theory, group solidarity is a natural consequence of group threat (Sumner, 2007). Pressure for ingroup solidarity is expressed both in ever-more demands for loyalty, and also in ever-more accusations of disloyalty. The stricter conditions for membership lead to ingroup contraction, the converse of outgroup expansion seen in the previous mechanism. War-time threats reduce societies into binary groups of 'them and us'. Identities polarize but not simply along ethnic lines.[30] The identities become friend and foe or patriots and traitors. As the threat intensifies, the space separating these two poles diminishes, forcing individuals to

---

[30] Wood (2008) also finds identity polarization is one of a number of social processes that occur during wars.

Table 3.10 Identification of the enemy as the Tutsi

	Ethnicity		Perpetrator Status		Region	
	Hutu	Tutsi	Non-perp.	Perp.	South	North

Question: When did the night patrols to look for the enemy first start in your community?

	(N=257)	(N=20)	(N=160)	(N=97)	(N=131)	(N=146)
Before the President's death	67.0%	69.6%	67.6%	56.1%	42.3%	89.8%

Question: When the night patrols first started, did the Tutsi also participate in them to look for the enemy?

	(N=260)	(N=20)	(N=163)	(N=97)	(N=126)	(N=134)
Yes, the Tutsi participated	64.0%	80.0%	63.1%	80.5%	91.9%	36.7%

Question: During the genocide who did people think was the enemy? (open-ended)

	(N=268)	(N=21)	(N=166)	(N=102)	(N=129)	(N=139)
All and only Tutsi	70.5%	90.5%	71.2%	57.4%	76.5%	64.5%
All Tutsi and others	20.6%	9.5%	19.8%	34.4%	18.1%	23.0%
RPF rebels only	1.9%	0.0%	1.8%	3.4%	2.5%	1.3%
Other response	1.1%	0.0%	1.2%	0.0%	1.2%	1.1%
Unable/unwilling to say	5.9%	0.0%	5.9%	4.8%	1.7%	10.0%

choose between them, leaving less room for exit and less tolerance for voice. The zero-sum mindset of 'either you are with us or you are against us' eventually prevails. As we shall see, the negative accusation of disloyalty proved more powerful in strengthening ingroup cohesion than positive appeals to patriotism or nationalism.

RTLM broadcasts reflected the evolution in the ingroup definition in Rwanda. The drive for ingroup solidarity was visible first of all in greater appeals to nationalist sentiment. Table 3.5 shows that the usage of the ethnic identifiers Hutu and Tutsi *declined* during the genocide, while the nationalist term 'Rwandans' more than doubled. RTLM relied heavily on the ambiguous term 'Rwandan' to mean 'Hutu'. The following passage typifies this ambiguity (my emboldened italics).

When **people** unite, they always attain their objective. So **we** should keep on being united to win this war, to vanquish the *Inyenzi Inkotanyi*, to make them understand that **we**, the **Rwandans**, really stood up together, united, worked together. And that **we** will vanquish them no matter what, as it is now obvious. So, those who hear the term *Interahamwe* should understand that it means all of **us Rwandans** who became united. *Interahamwe* does not mean the youth of a particular party as most of the **people** who are waging this war are obviously the youth member of all the parties of this country. (*Habimana Kantano, RTLM journalist, 21 May 1994, RTLM*)

The terms 'Rwandan' and 'interahamwe' implicitly excluded Tutsi, who – as we shall see – were popularly perceived as an alien group that had migrated to the country centuries previously. However, RTLM employed accusations of *disloyalty* more than appeals for nationalist *loyalty* to enforce group solidarity. In the pre-genocide phase, charges of complicity with the enemy were relatively limited in number. When made, RTLM levelled these accusations mainly at Tutsi and at moderate Hutu politicians who favoured peace through negotiation with the RPF. Thus, the opposition politicians Faustin Twigaramungu, leader of the MDR, and Agathe Uwilingiyimana, the prime minister in the coalition government, were frequent targets. In this passage just before the president's assassination, the RTLM journalist defends Rwanda's most extremist party, the CDR, by attacking the prime minister, who had accused the CDR of recent massacres.

Madame is a Hutu accomplice [*ibyitso*]. She is the accomplice responsible for the massacre of these people. How could these people be murdered and the authors of the crimes not be arrested whilst she was the prime minister? She

3.6 The Psychological Impact of War

states that these people [members of the extremist CDR party] are Hutu. She accuses Hutu while she is herself a Hutu? (*Noel Hitimana, RTLM journalist, 3 April 1994*)

In the genocidal phase, however, as Table 3.5 illustrates, RTLM allegations of Hutu complicity with the enemy nearly doubled, compared with a minor and statistically insignificant increase in allegations of Tutsi collaboration. Now, not only Hutu opposition politicians, but any Hutu was vulnerable to the charge of collaborator [*ibyitso*] through their action or inaction. RTLM's list of activities deemed disloyal was extensive: advocating dialogue with the rebels, desertion from the Rwandan army, civilian looting or engaging in other opportunistic crime, and fleeing the capital instead of staying to confront the rebels. Disloyalty spelt exclusion from the ingroup, and reclassification as a member of the outgroup. In this passage, Valerie Bemiriki uses the infamous enemy label of 'cockroach' [*inyenzi*] to describe Hutu who fled instead of fighting.

The worst kind of *Inyenzi*, I don't mean just Tutsi who are all *Inyenzi*, for me the worst kind of *Inyenzi* is a Hutu *Inyenzi*. A Hutu who plots with other Hutu telling them: 'Get up, run away' when the *Inyenzi* are not even there yet. (*Valerie Bemeriki, RTLM journalist, RTLM broadcast, 14 June 1994*)

Ordinary Rwandans also reported that the charge of enemy collaboration was used to enforce group cohesion in their communities. Table 3.11 shows that when respondents were asked in an open-ended question who was called an enemy accomplice or *ibyitso*, the answer was not just the Tutsi.[31] Many Hutu were also accused of disloyalty. Moreover, the accusation was more common in the north than in the south, again reflecting the differential impact of the war on these regions. Thus, twice as many Hutu who belonged to the opposition parties were seen as enemy collaborators in the north (45.7 per cent) than in the south (24.8 per cent). As we shall see in more detail in Chapter 5, the label 'accomplice' [*ibyitso*] was a powerful weapon of

---

[31] Although about two-thirds of respondents in both the south and north indicated that Tutsi were called '*ibyitso*', I suspect that the figure was in reality lower for the south before the genocide. The survey question did not clearly distinguish between the pre-genocide and genocide periods of the war and instead used the ambiguous phrase 'during the war'.

Table 3.11 Identification of enemy collaborators

Question: During the war, who were people calling 'ibyitso' (enemy collaborators) in your community? (open-ended, multiple answers allowed)

	Ethnicity		Perpetrator Status			Region	
	Hutu	Tutsi	Non-perp.	Perp.		South	North
	(N=261)	(N=20)	(N=160)	(N=101)		(N=126)	(N=135)
All Tutsi	66.1%	95.1%	68.1%	30.0%		65.6%	66.6%
Tutsi in the opposition parties	12.8%	0.0%	12.3%	22.2%		4.5%	21.1%
Tutsi who supported the rebel RPF	8.0%	0.0%	6.8%	28.4%		4.7%	11.2%
Hutu in the opposition parties	35.3%	19.8%	35.4%	33.8%		24.8%	45.7%
Hutu who supported the Tutsi	25.5%	25.1%	25.7%	22.1%		31.4%	19.7%
Hutu who supported the rebel RPF	10.4%	15.1%	9.3%	30.9%		5.9%	14.9%

social coercion used at the local level to peer pressure ordinary Hutu into participating in the violence.

As the threat intensified then, we see that group boundaries shifted, but not strictly along ethnic lines. Rwanda was not simplistically reduced to a Hutu ingroup and Tutsi outgroup. At the peak of the genocide, it was not enough just to be Hutu to belong to the ingroup. Ingroup membership demanded demonstrations of loyalty. Failure to act exposed you to classification with the enemy outgroup.[32]

Radicalization Mechanism IV: The Greater the Threat, the Greater the Violence Justified to Counter It

In this final indicator of radicalization, we will see how wars facilitate genocide by legitimizing measures – including violence – against the identified enemy target. The mechanism at work here is a self-defence logic. The Hutu majority were framed as the victims, and the Tutsi minority as the aggressor. The greater the threat, the stronger the measures that may be used to counter it. In cases of extreme threat – existential menaces that may destroy a community or civilization – these measures may even include violence even against civilians. This logic has normative resonance even in western political philosophy. 'Supreme emergencies' permit derogations from the principle of civilian immunity in the conduct of war (Rawls, 1993; Walzer, 2006). The security of the majority in effect overrides the liberty of the minority.

RTLM broadcasts stressed self-defence in two ways. The first frame emphasized Hutu victimhood and involved three central ideas. Rwandans were (i) victims; (ii) innocent; and (iii) defending themselves. Table 3.5 shows that these references more than doubled in concentration after the president's assassination, when the rebel threat was renewed and was felt even more acutely. This RTLM excerpt, from half-way through the genocide, illustrates the framing of Hutu as innocent victims.

I would like to add that it has been revealed that they have discovered about 50,000 bodies in Uganda, near Lake Victoria; these bodies are coming from

---

[32] At the height of the genocide, the accusations of complicity with the RPF extended to not only ordinary Hutu, but included Ugandans, Belgians, and even the United Nations Assistance Mission in Rwanda (UNAMIR) and its force commander Roméo Dallaire.

Rwanda. There can be no doubt that these are people who were thrown into the Akagera river by the RPF after they killed them. These people were trying to flee to Tanzania. I think the information unmasks the murderer. The news also tells us that the RPF soldiers massacred children in the schools with their rifles and with grenades. Who is the murderer? The murderer is the RPF. Who must stop the massacres? It is the RPF-*Inkotanyi* who must stop massacring. These massacres have their roots in the war. Whoever wants to stop the massacres must first stop fighting a war. However, the RPF is not killing our soldiers. It is clear that they are killing innocent civilians. So the RPF must stop the massacres. From our perspective you cannot attribute these massacres to us because we have been attacked and our soldiers have been compelled to make war against the RPF-Inkotanyi. It is the RPF who must stop the massacres. (*Gaspard Gahigi, RTLM journalist, RTLM broadcast, 31 May 1994*)

Even at the very end of the genocide, when one-sided massacres had undeniably occurred, RTLM continued to justify and to encourage violence against the Tutsi as self-defence.

If people said that we avenged His Excellency the President of the Republic, we were really just defending ourselves against the enemy. It was self-defence. According to me, the revenge has not yet come, but I feel that it will. (*Valerie Bemeriki, RTLM journalist, RTLM broadcast, 28 June 1994, eighty-three days into the genocide.*)

The second frame emphasized Tutsi aggression. RTLM repeatedly warned of a plot to exterminate the Hutu: not merely to kill, but to eliminate. Table 3.5 shows that RTLM accusations of a plan to exterminate the Hutu featured prominently in broadcasts before and during the genocide. In response, in the second phase calls to exterminate the Tutsi increased more than nine-fold. Confronted with a greater threat, a greater level of violence was justified. In this case, extermination justified extermination. It also reinforced the rationale for *pre-emptive action*: attack them, before they attack us.

The more the Inkotanyi refuse to negotiate, the more the anger of the people will increase. The more the Inkotanyi are everywhere, the more the anger of the people will grow. You the Inkotanyi, you think that you are going to exterminate us but it is we who are going to exterminate you. (*Habimana Kantano, RTLM journalist, RTLM broadcast, 3 July 1994*)

The brutal logic at work here is that Hutu massacre Tutsi because they believe Tutsi intend to massacre Hutu. The logic is self-reinforcing and

3.6 The Psychological Impact of War

pre-emptive. Rwanda's extremist government also reinforced the self-defence rationale by requiring the population to participate in the nation's security. It issued official orders to local authorities to implement a civilian self-defence program, and to mobilize the population.

As our country has been attacked, every Rwandan is duty-bound to protect it to the best of his ability and using all the means at his disposal. Each Rwandan ought to contribute to the defence of the Rwandan people, his family, and his property [...] it is imperative that we marshal our most effective weapon which is the Rwandan people who have relentlessly given their unflinching support to the current government in order to defend our fatherland in peril. (*Written directive from prime minister to all prefects on the organization of civilian self-defence, 25 May 1994*)

Ordinary Rwandans also drew on the self-defence frame when accounting for their actions, but to a lesser extent than RTLM and the extremist government. Thus, I encountered for example the refrain of doing exactly what is feared will be done to oneself.

What did people in your community say about the RPF during the war? There were those who had political interests and who would say that the *Inyenzi* objective was to exterminate the Hutu to the point that the children of the Tutsi will ask what the image of a Hutu would look like. It was intended to stimulate hatred between the ethnicities. They said they [the RPF] would bring back *la chicotte* [the whip]. This brought back the fear and the hatred. *How did the fear and hate express themselves?* There were ethnic tensions before Habyarimana died. They could be seen in a Tutsi man from Gashikiri. He was turbulent and had worked in Gigonkoro in a development project. He would come to Tabagwe and say that 'when we win the war, we will take wooden sticks and impale them in the vaginas of Hutu women'. (*Oriel, Hutu accused of genocide-related crimes, aged 45, primary school teacher, author-led interview in French, Butare central prison, southern Rwanda, April 2003*)

Oriel's image of a woman impaled with a pointed stick was in fact a form of sexual mutilation that Tutsi women suffered during the genocide. Similarly, his allusion to the extermination of the Hutu mirrored what was attempted against the Tutsi population. Oriel was implying that these things happened in his own community because it is exactly what the Tutsi extremist had threatened to do to Hutu.

Yet we should not overstate the importance of self-defence as a motive for ordinary Rwandans. I asked Hutu respondents whether they thought other people felt their actions during the genocide were legitimate. Surprisingly, nine years later, a very high proportion (54.2 per cent) still reported yes, as Table 3.12 shows. When asked *why* they thought people felt justified, the most common explanation was indeed self-defence. However, at only 21.9 per cent of respondents, self-defence was not the unique motive. The next two most common motives were, first, personal profit and, second, the orders of the authorities. People felt justified because it benefited them individually, and because the state had legitimized the action. Their answers reinforce the importance of opportunity and authority, the two other themes of this book.

Rwanda's Extraordinary Amplifiers

The war's psychological impact on ordinary Rwandans was amplified by one of the several unusual socio-demographic features that characterized Rwanda: the country's unusual ethnic settlement pattern. Hutu and Tutsi lived not in distinct territories, but side-by-side as neighbours. This fact would amplify the mutual fear and distrust that the war-time threat generated between more and more individuals across the ethnic divide. While this may appear to run counter to contact theory's prediction that inter-ethnic contact would – through increased information about the other – improve inter-ethnic relations, the converse outcome is explicable by the particular conditions under which this contact occurred. Contact theory assumes that groups have – at least – equal status, shared goals, and contact supported by authority (Allport, 1958; Paluck et al., 2018). Yet the survey data indicate that many Hutu believed Tutsi had been historically privileged and saw the war as an ethnic conflict. And instead of supporting cross-ethnic cohesion, the Rwandan government's reaction to the war had been to view its Tutsi population as a fifth column, and arrested and detained them *en masse*. Under these circumstances, proximity did not increase actual contact but instead led to withdrawal or hunkering down within communities. As Donatelle and Constantin's earlier accounts of how Hutu and Tutsi behaviour changed in Mutovu with the war, this disengagement exacerbated distrust because individuals interpreted the decreased quotidian interaction as proof that their suspicions of the other were grounded.

Table 3.12 Perceptions of the legitimacy of the violence

	Ethnicity		Perpetrator Status		Region	
	Hutu	Tutsi	Non-perp.	Perp.	South	North

Question: During the genocide did people think that what they were doing was right at the time?

	(N=267)	(N=20)	(N=168)	(N=99)	(N=128)	(N=139)
Yes, they thought it was right at the time	54.2%	100.0%	54.1%	55.9%	71.0%	46.8%
Unable/unwilling to answer	12.8%	0.0%	12.6%	15.2%	20.1%	3.0%

Question: Why did people think it was right? (open-ended, multiple answers permitted)

	(N=265)	(N=19)	(N=166)	(N=99)	(N=127)	(N=138)
It was self-defence against the enemy	21.9%	25.1%	21.9%	22.0%	20.6%	23.1%
They profited materially	16.4%	37.3%	17.2%	2.0%	32.6%	1.1%
The authorities ordered it	10.9%	10.7%	10.4%	19.5%	20.1%	2.2
No one stopped them	10.2%	21.0%	9.7%	19.5%	12.5%	8.0%
They had believed in a bad ideology	5.4%	15.7	5.5%	3.3%	7.5%	3.3%
They were avenging the President's death	4.0%	0.0%	4.1%	1.1%	0.0%	7.8%
Hutu hated Tutsi	1.8%	15.5%	1.8%	1.6%	0.2%	3.3%
They just did as everyone else did	0.2%	0.0%	0.0%	3.3%	0.3%	0.0%

3.7 Limitations of War as an Explanation of Genocide

While I have argued that Rwanda's civil war facilitated the genocide through these four mechanisms, genocide was not the inevitable outcome of the civil war. There are two reasons for the limited explanatory power of the war. First, although genocides have often occurred in the context of wars, very few wars have led to genocides. A total of 134 of the 164 internal wars waged between 1955 and 2016 did not do so.[33] Less than one fifth of all internal wars resulted in such extreme forms of violence. War, then, is not enough. As we shall see, I argue that in the context of Rwanda, political opportunity – in the form of the transition to more democratic rule and the assassination of the Head of State – was important too. There had to be an opportunity for extremist challengers to capture the state and for incumbent moderates to radicalize.

Sub-national analysis of the violence in Rwanda reinforces the point that a security threat is not enough. Extremist capture of the state at the sub-national level was also necessary. Data on violence in the pre-genocide phase of the war, collected in fifty-five cells from ten northern sectors – where much of the population did live in insecurity and fear – show that violence only occurred in very specific areas. Certain areas did not experience anti-Tutsi violence at all even though Tutsi were resident in them. Table 3.13 shows that in the sectors within Nyamugali and Ndusu communes where there were important Tutsi communities, no violence occurred at all before the genocide. In contrast, communes such as Kinigi and Nkuli – with comparable Tutsi populations and exposure to the war – experienced several episodes of anti-Tutsi violence. The decisive factor, we will see, was the commitment of the local state authorities in these areas to extremist action.

The second limitation of the war's explanatory power has to do with the character of Rwanda's civil war itself. It was not an unusual African civil war. In its pre-genocide phase, the war was not especially brutal in its civilian casualty count, intensive in its use of military resources, extensive in its territorial coverage, long in its duration, or

---

[33] The 134 internal wars in the context of which neither genocide nor politicide occurred were identified using the Political Instability Task Force datasets on ethnic wars, revolutionary wars, and genocides and politicides. See Marshall et al. (2017).

Table 3.13 *Pre-genocide violence in ten northern communities heavily exposed to the war*

Commune (Sector)	Tutsi Population (%)	Pre-genocide violence?	Number killed *in situ*
Butaro (Kayange)	2 (0)	No	0
Cyabingo (Muramba)	7 (0.2)	No	0
Cyeru (Rugendabare)	0 (0)	No	0
Kinigi (Bisate)	111 (1.7)	Yes	13
Mukingo (Busogo)	248 (3.4)	Yes	5
Ndusu (Mataba)	93 (1.8)	No	0
Nkuli (Mukamira)	368 (5.2)	Yes	7
Nkumba (Nyanga)	0 (0.0)	No	0
Nyamugali (Muvumo)	55 (1.1)	No	0
Nyarutovu (Kiriba)	13 (0.2)	Yes	1

Source: Author-collected data corroborated against Rwandan Government *gacaca* data

unusual in its motivation.[34] Its ordinariness cannot account for the extraordinariness of its genocide. Rwanda's civil war was a necessary but insufficient factor behind the genocide. I argue in the next two chapters that the shift to democracy and the assassination of the president, were the additional macro-factors that tipped Rwanda into genocide.

3.8 Rethinking Radicalization and the Radio

I now consider two implications of these findings for our understanding of prior radicalization as a cause of civilian participation in the violence and the radio's role in mobilizing Rwandans to kill.

---

[34] On casualties, in the pre-genocide phase the estimate is between 2,500-3,000 Tutsi civilian dead. We have no reliable estimate of RPF killings of Hutu in this period. On military intensity, RPF forces in early 1991 totalled about 5,000 and swelled to an estimated 25,000. Government's forces rose from approximately 5,000 in 1990 to 50,000 by mid-1992. On geographic scope, for most of the war the fighting was concentrated along Rwanda's northern borders with Uganda and the then Zaire, mostly affecting only two of its eleven prefectures: Ruhengeri and Byumba. On duration, the war lasted 1,386 days, shorter than the average ten-year lifespan of post-World War II civil wars. On motivation, the rebel objective was either to topple the government or else force it into a power-sharing arrangement: essentially a contest over territory and power.

Radicalization May Be a Consequence as well as Cause of Violence

The evidence presented here leaves us with a puzzle. I have shown that ordinary Rwandans, with the exception of northerners, were not widely radicalized before the genocide. Yet Rwandans mobilized extremely quickly following the president's assassination, and the violence also occurred extremely rapidly. How was this possible if most Rwandans were not widely radicalized beforehand? One explanation, I argue, is that radicalization was not only a cause of mobilization, but also a consequence. Rwandans also radicalized *because* they participated in violence. It is not only that radicalization can lead to violence. Violence can also lead to radicalization. The causation runs in both directions.

Let us consider the evidence that suggests this implication. Starting with the speed of mobilization, research on the onset date of violence following the president's assassination shows considerable variation in when genocidal violence across Rwanda's 145 communes began (Straus, 2006, p. 56). Nonetheless, as we shall see in Chapter 4, in 85 of 145 communes, that is, in nearly 60 per cent of them, genocidal violence began within the *first five days* following the president's assassination. The exceptions were Butare and Gitarama in the centre and south of the country where genocidal violence began nearly a full two weeks after the assassination. The delay, as we shall see, was the result of the time it took extremists to win a power struggle and capture the state there. Nonetheless, assuming that civilians were involved in much of this violence, in most of the country mobilization then was indeed extremely rapid.

Second, let's consider the exceptional speed of the killing. The main evidence here is based on a database of genocide victims in Kibuye prefecture compiled by *Ibuka*, a Rwandan organization for survivors of the genocide. Its survey identified, by name, 59,050 genocide victims, that is just over 79 per cent of Kibuye's resident Tutsi population in 1994.[35] For 43.2 per cent of these victims the project also

---

[35] The survey employed roughly two hundred enumerators who went from cell to cell and interviewed both Tutsi survivors and Hutu who did not participate in the genocide in order to identify Tutsi victims by name. The enumerators were themselves Tutsi who were familiar with the commune in which they worked. The data collection started in 1996 and the dictionary was published in December 1999. Note that it did not collect data on Hutu victims. For more information, see Verwimp (2004).

3.8 Rethinking Radicalization and the Radio

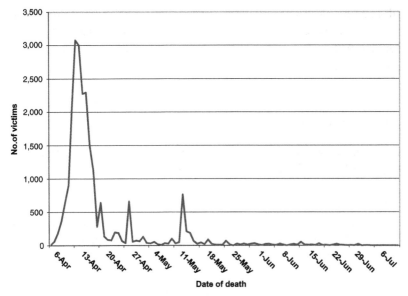

Figure 3.1 Speed of the violence in Kibuye prefecture

identified the date on which they were killed. Figure 3.1 charts the number killed on each day throughout the genocide. The main finding is that *within a period of only nine days, between 10–18 April 1994, just over two-thirds (67.2 per cent) of all Kibuye's genocide victims were killed.* If this pattern is similar to other prefectures, the two implications are that: (i) much of the violence was concentrated early on – in the first two weeks; and (ii) the violence did indeed occur very quickly.

Yet the data in this chapter suggest that the population was only moderately radicalized *before* the president's plane crash. The extraordinary speed of the mobilization, and the extraordinary speed of the killing following the plane crash would logically suggest that some Rwandans must also have radicalized in the course of the killing. There was no other time that this could have happened. I provide more qualitative evidence to support this claim in Chapter 7. Many Rwandans claim that they were initially coerced into participating. However, I show that over time some Rwandans rapidly adapted to the violence. They would come to participate willingly and self-interestedly. It was through their participation in the violence that they would come to see all Tutsi as the enemy, non-participating Hutu as disloyal, and their own actions as self-defence and so on, that is, to radicalize in the way defined in this chapter. It is, then, in this way that radicalization was both cause and consequence of the violence.

Rwanda's Hate Radio Broadcasts May Have Had a Limited Impact

The genocide's remarkable speed points to a second implication: the role of RTLM radio in mobilizing (that is, inciting the population to commit actual violence), may well have been overstated. RTLM, as we now know, took a significant radical turn only after the president's assassination. However, I find that much of the killing had been completed *before* it broadcast most of its inciteful and incendiary language. To illustrate this, I examined references to (i) Hutu disloyalty; and (ii) Tutsi extermination across two time periods: early genocide – when much of the violence occurred (6–21 April 1994); and late genocide – when violence continued but at a lower intensity (22 April–3 July 1994). As before, I looked at relative frequencies given the uneven length of daily broadcasts, and corroborated the context of each individual reference.

The results show that the radio's inciteful language was very muted in the early phase of the genocide, but spiked in the later phase, when much of the killing – at least in Kibuye prefecture – was over. References to Tutsi extermination doubled, and to Hutu disloyalty quadrupled between the early and late genocide periods. I also charted the evolution in the use of the term *'inyenzi'* [lit. cockroach] over the course of the genocide. The term was a useful indicator of radio radicalization because it was used with an unambiguously derogatory intent, it came to be popularly understood to refer to all Tutsi, and it occurred with great frequency. When plotted against the speed of the violence in Kibuye prefecture seen earlier, Figure 3.2 shows that the radio reached its peak in radical intensity, indicated by the frequency of the Kinyarwanda term *Inyenzi*, only after much of the killing had occurred. While we must be cautious because there are gaps in the broadcast data – notably for a twenty-one day period between 23 April and 14 May 1994 – we do have the data for much of the critical first two weeks following the president's plane crash when most of the violence

3.8 Rethinking Radicalization and the Radio

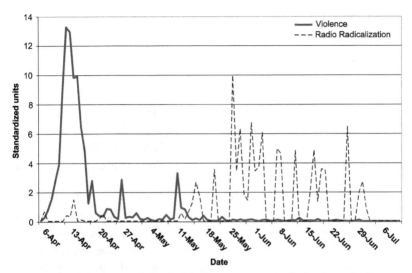

Figure 3.2 Comparison of speed of violence against speed of radio radicalization

took place.[36] Both Figures 3.1 and 3.2 clearly show that the inciteful and inflammatory language escalated and peaked only *after* most Tutsi in Kibuye had been killed.[37]

Having said this, while we may need to reconsider RTLM's role in *directly inciting* violence, the radio did have other important impacts on civilian attitudes and beliefs as already described in this chapter. Actual mobilization, as we'll see in Chapter 5, often resulted from more local forces within communities. It was often the immediate product of a direct encounter between a violence entrepreneur and his supporters. But RTLM, as we have already seen, was still responsible for (i) instilling and amplifying a climate of insecurity and fear among ordinary Rwandans: it made numerous references to RPF attacks against civilians; (ii) reinforcing the association between the war of the 1990s and the Hutu Revolution of 1959–1962: it linked the RPF with the Tutsi exiles, and claimed that it wanted to reinstate the pre-revolutionary order; and (iii) strengthening the idea that action was self-defence: RTLM repeatedly emphasized that Rwandans were innocent victims of RPF aggression.

---

[36] I have RTLM broadcasts from 7, 9, 11, 13, 14, 15, and 17 April 1994.
[37] Straus (2007) reaches a similar conclusion.

RTLM played a part then in subtly priming many Rwandans and making them more susceptible to direct, face-to-face mobilizational appeals.

* * *

In this chapter, I have chosen to highlight the impact of Rwanda's civil war on the attitudes and beliefs of ordinary Rwandans rather than of the ruling political class. We have lacked evidence of the war's micro-level effects. In so doing, I have argued that Rwanda's civil war contributed to its genocide in at least four ways: (i) it increased the ethnic distance between Hutu and Tutsi; (ii) it redefined the enemy target; (iii) it enforced Hutu solidarity; and (iv) it legitimized the killing. Collectively, I have argued that these four effects indicate the extent of civilian radicalization in Rwanda. However, I have also argued that while Rwanda's civil war was a necessary condition, the security threat it represented was by itself insufficient to cause the genocide. In the next two chapters, I argue that a political opportunity was also necessary.

The findings here edge the frontier of our understanding of the genocide forward in several ways. First, the evidence suggests that most Rwandans were in fact not widely radicalized *before* the genocide. The massive and rapid mobilization that followed was not due to prior radicalization. Second, at some point after the president's assassination, however, some part of the population did radicalize. I have argued that this is because radicalization was likely both cause and consequence of violence. Some Rwandans likely radicalized as a *result* of participating in the violence. Finally, I have argued that it is possible that RTLM's role in mobilizing the population has been overstated. Most of the killing was over *before* the radio began to broadcast language to directly incite Rwandans to violence. This is not to deny the radio any role. RTLM did amplify several of the radicalizing effects of the threat created by Rwanda's civil war. However, as we shall see, micro-mobilization was more the product of immediate, local forces within communities than of inciteful radio messages from above.

4 | *Threat and Opportunity: The Dangers of Freedom*

4.1 Introduction

Political liberalization was the second macro-political factor – in conjunction with the civil war – that pushed Rwanda closer to genocide. Between 1990 and 1994, as in many parts of Africa, Rwanda took preliminary steps away from autocracy and towards democracy. This move did not ineluctably or by itself lead to mass ethnic violence. Thirty-nine other African nations underwent democratic transitions at the same time as Rwanda, yet none of these ended in genocide.[1] In Rwanda, however, the push for political freedom unusually coincided with a civil war. Rwanda's ruling elite faced twin challenges to its power: an external threat from a rebel army, and a domestic challenge from new opposition parties. The interaction of the war with liberalization escalated elite contestation and brought ethnicity to the foreground of Rwanda's politics. It enabled the rise of ethnic extremism.

Liberalization, then, simultaneously posed a threat to Rwanda's incumbent elite and created a new political opportunity for challenger elites. Together, this threat and opportunity pushed the country further down the path towards ethnic confrontation. This proposition is not new, however. Much has been written on the risks that the opening of political space posed – and continues to pose – for Rwanda. Less well-understood, however, are the precise mechanisms through which political liberalization, in conjunction with the civil war, escalated ethnic tensions in Rwanda. How and why exactly did the opening of political space intensify ethnic politics at the national and local levels? Why did politics not take a more moderate direction instead? In this chapter, I explain the operation of three common mechanisms behind liberalization. Political pluralization, competition, and participation were each powerful forces unleashed in the space of opportunity created

---

[1] See Bratton and Van de Walle (1997, pp. 30–31) for a list of the thirty-nine countries that embarked on liberalization trajectories between 1989–1992.

by liberalization. While often perceived as desirable characteristics in a political system, I show how each of these forces also manifested a darker side in the context of an ongoing security threat. Liberalization and the war would become deeply intertwined. New-found freedom carried with it risks.

I will show, first, how political pluralization led to the expression of a broad spectrum of political interests and ideologies. It gave rise to parties with Christian, Islamic, socialist, liberal, and environmental ideologies, among others. Fatefully, amid this diversity an ethnicist ideology would re-emerge in Rwanda. As we shall see, it was, however, merely a fringe ideology initially. Multiple more moderate ideologies circulated in Rwanda's public sphere. This exclusionary ideology propagated the belief that power could not be shared between Hutu and Tutsi, equated democracy with Hutu majority rule, and warned that the Hutu revolution risked reversal. Although not widespread at the outset of multipartyism, this ideology would grow in significance as the war escalated, resonating more and more against a collective Hutu memory or narrative of past oppression by Tutsi.

Second, political competition, in the context of war and weak constraints on extremism, enabled the eclipse of moderation and the rise of ethnic politics. Initially, the contestation was political in character. It took place primarily between northerners loyal to Habyarimana and southerners who wanted democratic reform and an end to regionalism. However, as the war escalated, the contestation became increasingly ethnic in nature. As the RPF made gains either on the battlefield or at the negotiating table, the divisions within the ruling party and main opposition parties evolved into ethnic extremist and moderate factions. The internal political competition interacted with the external military contestation.

These within-group and between-group dynamics escalated toward ethnic confrontation because the domestic and international constraints on extremism were weak. At home, the state institutions charged with upholding the rule of law – in particular, the judiciary and police – lacked independence. Moreover, Rwanda's most influential civil society actors – the Catholic Church and the broadcast and print media – largely failed to denounce extremism. At the international level, the absence of diplomatic denunciation, economic sanctions, prosecution threats, and robust peacekeeping all shaped the calculus of Rwanda's extremists. In short, the escalatory actions taken by parties on both sides of the civil war and the domestic political divide experienced few constraints. Together, they pushed Rwanda closer to genocide.

Lastly, political participation created a new class of challenger elites, who wanted to share in the spoils of the state, and engaged an important swathe of otherwise passive ordinary Rwandans in politics. Attacks from these political entrepreneurs weakened the authority of the ruling party, opening up an opportunity for them to mobilize ordinary Rwandans dissatisfied with their government. As we shall see, a radical sub-set of these entrepreneurs and their supporters would go on to play a key role in mobilizing the wider population again during the genocide.

This chapter is structured as follows. Section 4.2 looks at the context for liberalization in Rwanda. Section 4.3 then examines the impact of liberalization at the national and local levels in Rwanda itself. Finally, Section 4.4 explains the three mechanisms that emerge from these descriptions, and that I argue lie behind liberalization: political pluralization, competition, and participation.

4.2 The Context for Liberalization

Rwanda was not unusual in its move to liberalize politically at the time. Its transition belonged to a Third Wave of democratic energy that had swept across sub-Saharan Africa in the early 1990s following the end of the Cold War. Moreover, by conventional measures, Rwanda was also an unexceptional autocracy on the eve of its transition in 1989. Nothing at first glance would suggest that its move to more political freedom could lead to the exceptional outcome of genocide. It shared many of the features of other authoritarian regimes in sub-Saharan Africa. It had been a single-party state *de jure* since 1975, and *de facto* since 1965. In its thirty-two years since independence, it had effectively known only two heads of state. Neither of them had been a democrat: the first, Kayibanda, came to power through revolution (subsequently legitimized by election), and the second, Habyarimana, through military coup. Its legislature and judiciary represented no effective check or balance against executive power, which was highly concentrated in the presidency. The state was synonymous with the ruling party, and its political culture was neo-patrimonial. For most of its post-independence period, Rwanda had scored six out of a possible seven in the established Freedom House measure of political rights and civil liberties (seven being least free). Overall, Rwanda had little tradition of political competition, participation, or pluralism. Moreover, it was a middle-ranking authoritarian regime in sub-Saharan Africa. It ranked nineteenth (out of forty-seven) for the number of direct, competitive elections held since independence; twelfth for the percentage of the population who voted in legislative elections; and seventeenth for the number of new parties created in the continent's democratic Third Wave (Bratton & Van de Walle, 1997). Its unexceptional autocracy cannot by itself account for its quite exceptional genocide.

Rwanda's Unusual Baseline Characteristics

Yet a closer look reveals several characteristics that do set Rwanda apart. First, Rwanda's opening-up coincided with an ongoing civil war. Rwanda's ruling elite were now confronted with a dual threat. On one front was the rising expectation of greater political space. On the second front, and beginning almost simultaneously, was Rwanda's civil war. For the next four years, these two processes – the liberalization of the political arena and the resolution of the civil war – would mutually drive each other. As we shall see, their unusual interaction had an important outcome in Rwanda: the rise of ethnic extremism.

Second, as observed earlier, Rwanda had an unusual socio-demography and geography. It was one of the smallest, most densely populated, and least urbanized countries in sub-Saharan Africa. The implications of these baseline characteristics for political change may not be immediately apparent. Yet they magnified the impact of political liberalization in several ways. Rwanda's small size allowed the state apparatus, which was synonymous with the party apparatus, to extend down to the grassroots of Rwandan society. As a result, political competition between incumbents and challengers was not limited to the national level, but also arose at the most local level of Rwandan society. Contestation was not confined to the capital. In addition, the short distances between the centre and the periphery lent itself to outreach and popular mobilization. It took only three hours to travel by road from the capital to the most distant small towns in Rwanda. National-level politicians then had frequent face-to-face contact with rural communities. In a clientelist political culture, this meant patron-client relationships were strong and reciprocity – material benefits in exchange for personal loyalty – was high. Moreover, party politics were not restricted to urban centres. The overwhelming majority, 93 per cent, of Rwandans lived in rural areas. As a result, there was fierce competition to recruit party supporters on hilltops across Rwanda. As people also lived very close together, it was difficult to opt out of party politics. Individuals could not easily hide their membership – or non-membership – of a particular party. Political participation was high. Lastly, Rwanda was effectively a bi-ethnic society and one ethnic group was overwhelmingly numerically dominant. Hutu represented at least 85 per cent of the population. Elections risked the permanent exclusion of the Tutsi if liberalization did not also produce an institutional safeguard for the minority. The risk of elections legitimizing an ethnocracy was high in the Rwandan context. In short, Rwanda's unusual socio-demography was a critical baseline condition that made rapid liberalization a strategy with considerable risk.

4.3 The Impact of Liberalization on Rwanda

What then was the impact of the general drive for liberalization in Africa on the specific characteristics of the Rwandan polity? I start by summarizing the outcome at the national level, and then consider the impact of liberalization at the local level.

Liberalization at the National Level

As elsewhere in Africa, liberalization in Rwanda began with civil society's assertion of its independence from the state. The war created one of the first opportunities. State authorities had arrested some 13,000 Tutsi civilians following the initial rebel attack on 1 October 1990. A second RPF attack, on Ruhengeri on 23 January 1991, resulted in retaliatory massacres of hundreds of Bagogwe Tutsi sanctioned by northern local authorities. These heavy-handed reprisals galvanised a nascent human rights movement in defence of civil liberties as insecurity mounted.[2] At the same time, new press freedom had

---

[2] For a description of the five main human rights organizations established and their activities, see Reyntjens (1994, pp. 161–164).

led to an explosion of print media.[3] Many articulated the growing popular sentiment critical of the Habyarimana regime. Even within the Mouvement Révolutionnaire National pour le Développement (MRND), the prevailing democratic winds on the continent had emboldened calls for reform. The progressive wing of the party, composed primarily of members from the south and centre, and championed by Matthieu Ngirumpatse, sought to limit the dominance of northerners from Ruhengeri and Gisenyi. Liberalization was a force felt even within the ruling party.

Under pressure at home and from international donors, Habyarimana was compelled to accept a major institutional change that would accelerate the liberalization process. On 10 June 1991, a constitutional amendment ended the single-party state. Within a few months, fifteen new parties were created, in many cases founded and supported by disaffected MRND members. The most serious challenges came from the Mouvement Démocratique Republicain (MDR), the Parti Social Démocrate (PSD), and the Parti Libéral (PL). Each had distinct core constituencies. While the ruling MRND's powerbase comprised the north-west prefectures of Gisenyi and Ruhengeri, the opposition held sway elsewhere. Thus, the MDR drew most of its support from the centre-south, concentrated in Gitarama prefecture. The PSD was also strong in the south, but particularly in Butare prefecture. The PL was mainly an urban party, attracting business people and professionals, including many Tutsi. These parties initially displayed remarkable cohesion in their demands for change. They variously accused the ruling party of regionalism, ethnic discrimination, corruption, nepotism, clannism, and anti-democratic practices more generally. Many of these criticisms echoed the concerns of the reformist wing within the MRND, and the party in fact appended the epithet 'democratic' to its name in July 1991 and it became the MRNDD. At the same time, as the war with the RPF continued and a campaign of attacks against civilians escalated from July 1991, the Coalition de la Défense de la Réplublique (CDR) entered the political arena in February 1992. Its members, initially few in number, saw the war as an ethnic power struggle in which Hutu were defending the gains of Rwanda's revolution against the return of Tutsi feudalism and monarchy. Anti-Tutsi

---

[3] For one of the best analyses of Rwanda's media in this time period, see Chrétien (1995).

4.3 The Impact of Liberalization on Rwanda

sentiment flared again, a month later in March 1992, when several hundred Tutsi in the Bugesera region were massacred following false radio reports of a Tutsi plot to kill Hutu leaders.

Notwithstanding the emergence of the CDR, in the early stages of liberalization, political contestation was still primarily regional rather than ethnic. In April 1992, following street demonstrations orchestrated by the opposition, Habyarimana accepted the four main opposition parties into a coalition government led by Dismas Nsengiyaremye of the MDR as prime minister.[4] This action would prove highly consequential for the failure of the peace process and the escalation of the war. Nine ministries went to the ruling MRNDD while the opposition shared the remaining ten. It was a fragile coalition. Once the new government was installed, political contestation intensified. The Alliance pour le Renforcement de la Démocratie (ARD), comprising principally the MRND and the CDR, worked to bring the new multiparty government down. In contrast, les Forces Démocratiques du Changement (FDC), comprising the opposition MDR, PSD, and PL, pushed for more extensive democratic reform. The main parties also established youth wings to mobilize supporters. Both the MDR's *Inkuba* and the PSD's *Abakombozi* practised *ukubohoza* (liberation), physically coercing MRNDD members to join their parties, leading to violent clashes with the ruling party's own *Interahamwe* and the CDR's *Impuzamugambi*. Liberalization, with its implied redistribution of political power, was destabilizing. However, the fault-lines were still principally partisan rather than ethnic while the war was still in its infancy.

Instead of fomenting ethnic divisions, liberalization in fact enabled a *cross-ethnic* political alliance at the outset. The Rwandan Patriotic Front (RPF) and the opposition FDC (which also counted Tutsi among party members) stood together against the MRNDD. Both groups shared the goal of ending the ruling party's political dominance. Interests trumped identities. The two groups met in Brussels on 29 May 1992 to discuss an end to the war, without the ruling party, and issued a statement affirming their continued collaboration to expose the 'MRND dictatorial system'.[5] A few days later, on 5 June 1992, the

---

[4] The fourth party was the Parti Démocrate Chrétien (PDC).
[5] Joint press statement between FDC and RPF dated 3 June 1992. Exhibit in Prosecutor vs. Karemera et al., ICTR-98-44-T.

RPF then launched another surprise attack from the north, into Byumba. This escalation increased international pressure on the MRNDD to come to the negotiating table.

On 12 July 1992, the Organisation of African Unity (OAU), in conjunction with several regional states, formally began mediation talks in Arusha. International sponsorship of the process strengthened the prospects of a power-sharing outcome. The mediation, however, was structurally flawed in conception. It was designed as a two-way negotiation between the rebels and the government. In reality, there was a distinct third party: the domestic opposition. Yet their interests were conflated with those of the ruling party as they had formally become partners in a coalition government and Boniface Ngulinzira, from the MDR, led the government delegation as its new minister of foreign affairs throughout most of the negotiations.[6] The arrangement resulted in frequent disagreement between the delegates from the MRNDD and the delegates of the other parties.[7] The design flaw was the product of the unusual and unfortunate coincidence of the democratization effort with the civil war. As a direct consequence, as the peace process made progress, the divide within the multiparty government deepened between hardliners opposed to power-sharing and moderates supportive of it. In September 1992, a commissioned Forces Armées Rwandaises (FAR) report was released defining the primary enemy as 'extremist Tutsi within the country and abroad who are nostalgic for power'[8]; at the same time, plans to set up Radio Télévision Libre des Mille Collines (RTLM) were set in motion; in October, the CDR organized multiple demonstrations against Arusha; and in November Léon Mugesera, a renowned MRNDD ideologue, gave an ethnically inflammatory speech warning people to 'wake up' and 'not

---

[6] Following the finalization of the power-sharing protocol in January 1993, Habyarimana replaced Boniface Ngulinzira with James Gasana, the Minister of Defence and a MRNDD moderate. Ostensibly, it was because the next protocol to be agreed related to the integration of the armed forces.

[7] MRNDD delegates counted Ambassador Kanyarushoki and Théoneste Bagosora; Boniface Ngulinzira, the Minister of Foreign Affairs and delegation head, who was from the MDR; and Landoald Ndasingwa, a Tutsi and Minister for Labor, who was from the PL.

[8] FAR Military Commission report, 'Definition of the Enemy', December 1991. Exhibit in Prosecutor vs. Bagosora et al., ICTR-98-41-T.

4.3 The Impact of Liberalization on Rwanda

let themselves be invaded'.[9] Habyarimana found himself caught between opposing international and domestic pressures and his public statements vacillated between support and denunciation of Arusha.

The flawed design in the international mediation led to a flawed power-sharing arrangement. On 5 January 1993, the second Arusha protocol, on power-sharing, was amended and finalized. Twenty-two ministerial posts would be divided among the MRNDD, the RPF, and opposition parties in a formula that provided the RPF and FDC, if they remained allies, with the two-thirds majority needed to propose changes the MRNDD could not veto. Hardliners viewed it as a betrayal and believed that Ngulinzira, representing the Rwandan government, had deliberately conceded too much to the RPF. The reaction, scarcely a fortnight later, was a series of attacks against Tutsi in the north-west. These attacks would in turn provide the pretext for the RPF to launch a major attack on 2 February 1993. The offensive would displace nearly a million Rwandans and bring the RPF within 30 km of Kigali, stopped only by the reinforcement of the FAR with French paratroopers.

The RPF's strategic escalation of the war exacted a price, however. It weakened the alliance that had been forged between itself and the main opposition parties and fractured them into pro- and anti-RPF factions. Thus Donat Murego (national secretary) and Froduald Karamira (second vice-president) of the MDR, and Stanislas Mbonampeka (second vice-president) of the PL found new common cause with hardliners opposed to power-sharing within the ruling party. They no longer believed that the RPF was sincere in its commitment to a negotiated transition and that it really wanted an outright military victory because it could not win democratic elections. The distrust was not ill-founded. In local elections for eight communal councils held in the Demilitarized Zone (DMZ) in September 1993, the RPF did not win a single seat despite intensive campaigning. In fact, elections held earlier in March 1993, in 38 of Rwanda's 145 communes, suggested that the MRNDD would likely win a *national* election. Opposition parties won twenty-two constituencies but only in their strongholds in the centre and south of the country.

This weakening in the external partnership coincided with internal competition within the main political parties for positions within the

---

[9] Speech at MNRD rally, 22 November 1992. Exhibit in Prosecutor vs Akayesu ICTR-96-4.

Transitional Government envisaged by Arusha. Inside the MRNDD, northern conservatives, who placed their confidence in Joseph Nzirorera, competed with southern liberals championed by Matthieu Ngirumpatse. Liberals won a major victory at the MRNDD congress on 3 July 1993. Ngriumpatse was elected president of the party and thus became Habyarimana's potential successor as president of the Republic. Inside the MDR, the contestation was between Dismas Nsengiyaremye and Faustin Twagirumungu, who both held ambitions to become prime minister in the Transitional Government. The party split when Nsengiyaremye held an extraordinary congress on 23 July 1993 to depose Twagirumungu. Ngirumpatse, however, sought an MRNDD-MDR alliance to help contain the northern influence within his own party and, as Nsengiyaremye opposed such a partnership, the result was a collaboration between Twagirumungu's minority MDR faction and Ngirumpatse's liberal MRNDD faction. It produced a new government with Agathe Uwilingiyimana, from the MDR, as interim prime minister.

On 3 August 1993, the Arusha process produced a second, even more unbalanced outcome. Under an armed forces protocol, an integrated national army was envisaged with the Rwandan Patriotic Army (RPA) receiving 50 per cent of the officer corps and 40 per cent of the rank-and-file. The government had originally proposed only 15 per cent, but the RPF's offensive in February 1993 had made its military superiority clear and had left the government delegation, now headed by James Gasana, the minister of defence, with little leverage to bargain. The agreement gave the RPF an effective veto in politico-military terms and implied massive demobilization of FAR officers and soldiers, including the Presidential Guard. The following day, on 4 August, Arusha was signed into effect and the UN Security Council authorized the deployment of a peacekeeping mission, United Nations Assistance Mission in Rwanda (UNAMIR). The peace agreement lacked support among those sceptical of power-sharing with the RPF. However, it was the shock assassination of Burundi's first elected Hutu president, Melchior Ndadaye on 21 October 1993, by low-ranking Tutsi soldiers, that would ethnically radicalize and decisively split the main opposition parties into pro-Hutu and more moderate factions. The assassination confirmed for many in these parties that the Tutsi could not be trusted. Two days later, Froduald Karamira responded with his infamous

4.3 The Impact of Liberalization on Rwanda

'Hutu Power' speech, in which he warned MDR supporters of being 'dragged into a Hima government'.[10]

Ndadaye's assassination forged a new political alliance bringing together hardliners in the MRNDD and the new 'Power' factions of the MDR, PSD, and PL. Members of these factions joined an MRNDD rally on 16 January 1994. It was here that the moderate leader of the PL, Justin Mugenzi, famously signalled his radical shift with a speech affirming the need to 'protect the sovereignty of the people acquired during the 1959 Revolution'.[11] Contestation was now primarily between moderate and 'Power' factions within the main opposition parties to secure the two-thirds majority needed to control the transitional institutions. The principal points of contention, which would persist until the day of Habyarimana's assassination, were three-fold: (i) Prime Minister Agathe Uwilingiyimana's insistence on candidates for the Transnational National Assembly (TNA) to be taken from the PL's moderate faction, headed by Landoald Ndasingwa, over those of Justin Mugenzi's new 'Power' faction; (ii) Habyarimana's refusal to accept a member of the PL as the Minister of Justice given the risk of a future criminal indictment against himself; and (iii) the RPF's moral objection to a member of the radical CDR party as a deputy in the TNA (Guichaoua 2015). The deadlock resulted in the failure to install the new government by the appointed deadline. The UN Security Council threatened to withdraw UNAMIR if agreement was not reached. The contestation also became increasingly violent and in February 1994 the charismatic PSD leader, Félicien Gatabazi, was assassinated. Believed to be orchestrated by close associates of Habyarimana at the time, PSD activists responded the next day by killing the CDR leader, Martin Bucyana.[12] Agreement on the Transitional Government was never reached before Habyarimana fatefully boarded his plane leaving Rwanda for Dar Es Salaam on 6 April.

---

[10] Speech given 23 October 1993, Exhibit in Prosecutor vs. Karemera et al., ICTR-98-44-T.

[11] Speech given 16 January 1994, Exhibit in Prosecutor vs. Bizimungu et al., ICTR-98-50-T.

[12] An alternative theory attributes Gatabazi's assassination to the RPF. Its motive was to make way for PSD politicians more sympathetic to the RPF and/or to deepen divisions between the MRNDD and the other parties (Guichaoua, 2015, pp. 108–110).

Liberalization at the Local Level

These national-level events are well-known.[13] But what impact did liberalization have at the local level? We know less about what life was like in Rwanda's rural areas *before* the genocide. How did newfound political competition, participation, and pluralism each concretely affect the lives of ordinary Rwandans? I present an analysis of four communities in which I trace the process of liberalization and, importantly, its interaction with the war. As we shall see, the story is different between the north and the south of the country. The north was the ruling party's powerbase and was heavily affected by the war. As a result, the war overshadowed party politics, and the outcome was *inter-ethnic tensions* and ethnic extremism in the foreground. The south, in contrast, was an opposition stronghold and was largely untouched by the war. The outcome was *inter-party tensions,* and ethnic extremism in the background.

Southern Rwanda: War Distant, Party Politics Intense

Mwendo Cell, Maraba Commune, Butare Prefecture

Political competition from opposition parties in 1991 would weaken the ruling party's influence in Mwendo, but ethnic tensions would remain relatively muted in the cell. Mwendo was a long way from the frontline in the north. The closest border by far was with Burundi to the south. The largest of three cells in Tare sector, Mwendo was home to 1,497 Rwandans before the genocide. Eighty-four of these (5.6 per cent) were Tutsi. Altogether, there were seventeen distinct Tutsi-headed households in the community. Inter-ethnic marriage was also high in Mwendo. Eleven Tutsi women had married Hutu men, and seven Tutsi men had married Hutu women. Mwendo was a rural cell and agriculture was the main livelihood. There was electricity, but no telephone in the sector. But Mwendo's location, just a few minutes from a highway, meant that people and news travelled quickly to and from the cell.

---

[13] For more detailed accounts, see Guichaoua (2015, pp. 23–142); Reyntjens (1994, pp. 132–259); Prunier (1998, pp. 121–212); and Des Forges (1999, pp. 47–179).

The MDR was the most influential political party in Mwendo. Emmanuel Rekeraho, a former government soldier and MDR representative for the commune, emerged as the politically dominant authority in the community. Rekeraho kept a residence in the cell and his presence eclipsed the authority of the two official MRNDD representatives, the cell *responsable*, Ernest Mulinda, and the sector councillor, Stanislas Binenwa. His network both within Mwendo and beyond was more extensive and powerful than theirs. His two brothers, Joseph Habyarimana and Antoine Bizimana, were both influential politicians in the PSD and MDR parties respectively in other communities. In fact, the *responsable* and councillor opted out of party politics altogether, and accepted Rekeraho's superior influence locally. Here is how the *responsable* described the politics in his cell:

Did you join a political party? I did not join any political party and I stopped going to the MNRD meetings. *Why?* There would be abuse hurled between the parties. The PSD was full of young men who were all *ibirara* [juvenile delinquents]. The main problem was between Rekeraho who was in MDR and his elder brother as they were not in the same party. *Was there violence?* There was tension and bad words were exchanged, but there was no violence. *What about threats?* No one threatened me as I chose not to be associated with any parties. (*Ernest Mulinda, Hutu, aged 44, cell responsable, Mwendo cell, Maraba commune, Butare prefecture, May 2003*)

Mulinda's survival strategy then was not to defend the MRNDD, or to engage in a contest for power in Mwendo. He retained his post from the advent of opposition politics and through the genocide because he offered no resistance and because he did not seek power. Both before and during the genocide, he followed the prevailing wind. This was not unusual. Cell politics were often less contentious than commune politics. It was at the higher commune-level that more intense political competition occurred.

The burgomaster of Maraba commune (in which Mwendo cell was located) was Jean-Marie Habineza, who had taken office in September 1990, on the eve of the civil war. Despite the popularity of opposition parties in the south, he had remained staunchly MRND. Habineza personified much of what had made the ruling party unpopular. According to prefectural archives, between 1991 and 1992 alone Maraba residents had escalated fourteen complaints of personal misconduct and failure to fulfil duties against their burgomaster to the level of the prefect. These included eight allegations that he had appropriated land illegally for himself. As a result, the burgomaster often crossed swords with Butare's prefect, Jean-Baptiste Habyalimana, who moreover belonged to the opposition PL party. As a MRNDD representative, then, Habineza faced challenges from below, from Rekeraho of the MDR, and from above from Habyalimana of the PL.

While party politics took root early, ethnic politics arrived late and, in any event, existed on the fringes in Mwendo. Eloise, a Tutsi survivor, remembers that ethnic tensions were initially muted, but grew as the war advanced.

Did the political parties cause Hutu and Tutsi to separate? I remember when the parties began. They were not bad at the start. Some politicians started to say bad things about Tutsi in the middle. I don't remember when exactly. *What about Rekeraho?* He was a politician. He was encouraging people to join his MDR party. He was well-liked. But when the war started [meaning the genocide] he changed. It was as if he had been given back his rank as a soldier. He organized much of the killing. (*Eloise, Tutsi survivor, aged 30, Mwendo cell, Maraba commune, Butare prefecture, May 2003*)

So, ethnic tensions did emerge in Mwendo, but they were not particularly pronounced. It was Rekeraho himself who gradually radicalized over time and came to represent a fringe anti-Tutsi sentiment within the community. Oriel, a convicted perpetrator, describes the relationship between party politics and inter-ethnic tensions in his community thus:

Did the political parties cause Hutu and Tutsi to separate? In 1991 there were meetings of parties. Everyone tried to belong to a political party. There were parties who taught solidarity like PSD, while MDR taught otherwise. And it was in the meetings that they started to say that the PL was really the RPF disguised. *Who was saying this?* It was the MDR leader Emmanuel Rekeraho who said this. But still this hatred was not very strong. Even when Habyarimana died on the 6th [April 1994], on the 10th there was a baptism of a Tutsi businessman's son, Denis Kabandana, and both Hutu and Tutsi attended. The tensions were not very visible. But maybe they were in people's heads. (*Oriel, Hutu accused of genocide-related crimes, aged 45, primary school teacher, author-led interview in French, Butare central prison, southern Rwanda, April 2003*)

In short, tensions in Maraba then were mainly inter-party, not inter-ethnic. The opposition demanded a share of the state's power, rather than action against the Tutsi minority. Rekeraho represented one of several challenges from an emerging political class created by the opening up of Rwanda's political space. As we shall see, he would also be one of the main instigators of violence during the genocide.

Tamba Cell, Shyanda Commune, Butare Prefecture

In Tamba, as Mwendo, one individual would again emerge to challenge the ruling party's authority in the opportunity created by liberalization. Tamba too was located far away from the war and its trials. The cell was home to 803 Rwandans in 1994. Seventy-two (9 per cent) were Tutsi. Inter-ethnic marriage, while good, was less common than in Mwendo. Seven Tutsi had married Hutu – six were unions with Hutu men.

The challenger in Tamba cell, Emmanuel Karimunda, was not an opposition politician. Karimunda was in fact just a butcher, but one well-known for his bigoted views on Tutsi and his violent temper. His emergence can be traced to competition at the commune-level. In Shyanda commune (where Tamba was located), the opposition PSD had ousted the ruling MRNDD in the limited local elections of March 1993. Théophile Shiyarambere had replaced Habineza Côme as burgomaster. The election of a PSD partisan weakened the positions of the local councillors and *responsables* below, who were at least nominally MRNDD. This was the case for the local *responsable* of Tamba cell, Joseph Nkusi. Though personally well-liked within the community, Nkusi faced growing challenges to his authority from Karimunda. He sought opportunities to provoke confrontations with Nkusi. In a direct challenge, he would sell his own home-made beer right in front of the local bar that Nkusi owned and ran in Tamba. Residents interpreted this action as it was intended: a statement on where authority and power lay within the community.

Wilma, a genocide survivor, remembers Karimunda, though in her view Karimunda represented a fringe, ethnically extremist sentiment within the community. For her, ethnic tensions were not widespread or intense in Tamba as a result of the party politicking.

What happened in your community when multipartyism began? People started to become competitive with each other as they wanted everyone to join the same party. But the conflict was not very bad. People would just trade insults in bars... *Did people say bad things about the Tutsi in your community?* There was one person who was strong here and each time he saw me he would pull my nose and say he wished he could shave it now [reference to Tutsi stereotype of a long nose]. *Was this Emmanuel Karimunda?* Yes. *When did this happen?* This was before 1994 but after the *Inkotanyi* had invaded. *Did anyone else say things like him?* There was no one else in Tamba like this man Emmanuel. I don't know if there were others who disliked Tutsi. Perhaps in their huts they said things but he was the only one to reveal it to me. (*Wilma, aged 35, Tamba cell, Shyanda commune, Butare prefecture, May 2003*)

Karimunda dominated life in Tamba. He recruited his brother and his nephew to help establish his authority within the community. The three would often move together and intimidate local residents. As we shall see, this core group would go on to do the same again during the genocide as well. In fact, Karimunda became even more influential in the power vacuum created by Habyarimana's assassination, fully usurping the authority of the local *responsable* and councillor. He and several of his relatives would constitute the backbone of the attack groups during the violence. In short, it was not only political entrepreneurs like Rekeraho in Mwendo who emerged during the period of political liberalization. Ethnic entrepreneurs – racists such as Karimunda – profited as well. The most important effect of party politics then was to weaken the authority of the local MRNDD representative, and thereby to open up an opportunity for an extremist to establish himself.

Northern Rwanda: War Close, Party Politics Weak

Mutovu Cell, Nkuli Commune, Ruhengeri Prefecture

Liberalization had a limited impact on Mutovu. The target was not the ruling MRNDD party, but instead the cell's Tutsi minority. Mutovu was located close to the war's front lines, and in fact a government military base was situated within the same sector as Mutovu. As with much of the north-west, Mutovu had benefited from Habyarimana's favour over the years. The cell, unusually, had both electricity and telephone lines, and good roads leading into it. Also, unusually, among its 785 residents was a sizeable Tutsi minority. Mutovu was home to sixty Tutsi, 7.6 percent of its population, a considerable proportion for a Ruhengeri community. The prefecture as a whole was overwhelmingly Hutu. Integration was limited in Mutovu, however. There were

4.3 The Impact of Liberalization on Rwanda

only two inter-ethnic marriages in the cell – both between Hutu men and Tutsi women.

Mutovu was, like most of the north, loyal to the ruling MRNDD party. The opposition had almost no support. As the political arena opened up, the war's proximity, as well as historic loyalties, produced a different effect to the south: pressure for solidarity rather than competition. The only two parties with a visible presence in Mutovu were the ruling MRNDD and radical pro-Hutu CDR. Officials from both parties were united in their hunt for enemy collaborators at the commune-level. Unlike the south, then, suspicion of Tutsi and general anti-Tutsi sentiment were widespread in the north. The distrust also extended to Hutu who belonged to moderate opposition parties.

The man who would emerge to lead the anti-Tutsi campaign in Mutovu was Gervais Harelimana, a locally well-known businessman, politician, and bigot. He was the CDR party representative for the entire commune of Nkuli and he resided in Mutovu. His presence, given his relative importance, overshadowed both the local *responsable*, Matthieu Tibiramira, and sector councillor, Anastase Kabatura. Harelimana organized an intimidation campaign against the sixty Tutsi who lived in Mutovu. He enlisted the support of family members and his neighbours to do so. Thus Edison Munyaratama, a primary school headmaster and neighbour, and Félicien, Harelimana's younger brother, belonged to the CDR network and were active in this campaign. They would also form part of the core attack group during the genocide, along with the *Impuzamugambi*, the CDR youth militia. With the assistance of commune officials and officers from the nearby military base, Harelimana had several Tutsi arrested and detained. In neighbouring cells, Tutsi were killed in 1992 and 1993. As this Tutsi survivor explains, it was the war that provided the rationale for this anti-Tutsi campaign.

Which political parties were there in Mutovu? MRND and CDR were present in the cell. *Which party did the Tutsi belong to?* The Tutsi belonged to the MRND party, as it was stronger. *Did the parties say bad things about Tutsi?* Only the CDR said bad things about the Tutsi in Mutovu. It was when they had just started. But as it was believed that some people knew the RPF were going to attack, so more bad things were said in the newspapers like *Kangura*. *Did the political parties fight among themselves?* The political parties did not fight among themselves in Mutovu. Before Habyarimana died the political parties were instead saying that they should look for the *ibyitso* [accomplices] of the *Inkotanyi* [rebel RPF] so that they can be arrested. They suspected almost all of the Tutsi of being *ibytiso* but it was not true. They particularly suspected the educated Tutsi. But it was not true that the Tutsi were *ibyitso*. We did not know about the RPF invasion beforehand and we were not supporting them. (*Justin Ndahayo, Tutsi farmer, aged 33, Mutovu cell, Nkuli commune, Ruhengeri prefecture, July 2003*)

The war then pushed local politics against the Tutsi in the community. The suspicion extended to the MDR party, whose moderate supporters were also vulnerable to accusations of enemy collaboration. The few MDR partisans there were had to operate covertly to avoid attracting the attention of the MRNDD and CDR supporters. In fact, the opposition was so marginalized that neither the PSD nor the PL had a single representative for the entire commune.

Mutovu then was a case where the political entrepreneur and ethnic entrepreneur to emerge in Rwanda's new political space was one and the same person. Moreover, ethnic extremism was not on the margins as in the south. It had the support of state authorities. In Mutovu the sector councillor and MRND representative, Anastase Kabutura, collaborated with the extremist Harelimana. This collaboration continued during the genocide. As elsewhere, those who emerged as influential before the genocide, would rise again during it.

Ruginga Cell, Bisate Sector, Kinigi Commune, Ruhengeri Prefecture
In Ruginga as in Mutovu, the war rather than party politics once again dominated life in the cell, and ethnic tensions were high. Ruginga was located right on a front-line of the war. Situated on the perimeter of the Volcanoes National Park on the border with Zaire, it frequently suffered RPF hit-and-run attacks. Before the genocide, Ruginga was home to just thirty-five Tutsi, representing seven households descended from two family lines. None had married with their Hutu neighbours.

Ruginga's story is similar to Mutovu's. The opposition did not get a strong foothold, and the MRNDD again ruled largely unchallenged. Ruginga's location on a front line instead kept its residents in a state of high insecurity. As a result, and as elsewhere in the north, suspicion of Tutsi and moderate Hutu as enemy collaborators was widespread. In this climate, with the war so close-at-hand, there was no question of joining an opposition party in Ruginga or anywhere else in the commune of Kinigi. Dissent meant disloyalty. The CDR was the only other party to have a strong presence in Kinigi. Its representatives collaborated with MRNDD hardliners in the commune in their campaign against the Tutsi population.

The commune, under the leadership of burgomaster Thaddée Gasana, began targeting the *Bagogwe*, a sub-group of Tutsi pastoralists who had settled in north-west Rwanda, as early as 1991. Following a lightning raid by the RPF on Ruhengeri's main prison on 23 January 1991, the commune authorities had swiftly retaliated against the local Tutsi population. They arrested and detained large numbers of Tutsi civilians. They also encouraged and acquiesced in attacks perpetrated by small bands of ordinary Hutu civilians against the Tutsi.

Ruginga's seven Tutsi families were not spared in this region-wide campaign. However, the initiative to target them did not originate from within the cell. It was not the sector councillor, Faustin Rucyahana, the cell *responsable*, Dionyise Sharamanzi, or any other cell resident who organized these attacks. Instead, Ruginga suffered repeated raids from a small group of attackers originating from neighbouring Kanyamiheto sector. This small band of about a dozen raiders acted with impunity. They had the support of the commune authorities and government soldiers in the area and would terrorize the Tutsi population within the region. Opposition parties, then, had little opportunity to take root in a community whose residents were gripped by war-time insecurity, and divided by ethnic violence. Indeed, all of these events in Ruginga took place six months before political parties were first legalized in Rwanda. By June 1991, there were no longer any Tutsi living in Ruginga. In short, the war's impact eclipsed the effect of political liberalization in this community.

4.4 The Mechanisms of Liberalization

The four communities studied illustrate the impact of the interaction of the widening of Rwanda's political space with the escalation of the civil war at the grassroots level. The key analytical point to take away is that while the Hutu-Tutsi cleavage had been an important fault-line in Rwanda's history, political liberalization did not immediately or ineluctably revive it. In the two southern communities far from the war, the principal division had initially been along partisan, not ethnic lines. In contrast, in the two northern communities close to the war's front lines, politics were ethnicized from the outset. Ethnic polarization was the result of the *conjunction* of the war's escalation with the drive to democratize Rwanda. My broader survey evidence confirms this. Table 4.1 shows nearly four-fifths (79.5 per cent) of my Hutu respondents reported that multipartyism impacted their communities. Nearly four-fifths (79.8 per cent) of these individuals claimed that it created divisions. However, only 3.8 per cent indicated that these divisions had been *ethnic* in nature. In fact, only a minority of Hutu respondents (20.1 per cent) recall politicians speaking ill of Tutsi before the genocide. The majority of Tutsi respondents also confirmed that politics were not primarily ethnic. The divisions instead were primarily party political in nature.

In fact, contrary to dividing the country along ethnic lines, liberalization initially encouraged cross-ethnic appeals. The main political parties sought to attract supporters from across the ethnic divide. The MDR, for instance, made its opposition to racial discrimination a pillar of its party manifesto and dropped the 'Parmehutu' label when re-launched in 1991 to distance itself from its historical antecedent, Parti du Mouvement de l'Emancipation Hutu (PARMEHUTU), associated with Hutu nationalism at the time of the revolution. Table 4.2 shows that 28.0 per cent of Tutsi admitted to having initially supported the MRNDD, 4.9 per cent the MDR, and 9.7 per cent the PSD. This compares with 44.7 per cent, 10.9 per cent, and 16.5 per cent for Hutu respectively. So all the main political parties had some cross-ethnic support when first established.

The four communities studied support a second analytical point. Liberalization involved three observable processes at the local level. First, it stimulated political competition. In the two southern communities, this competition weakened the local authority of the ruling party and created the space of opportunity for challengers to emerge. Second, it encouraged political participation. In three of the four communities, a political entrepreneur emerged capable of mobilizing the population. As we shall see in the Chapter 5, these same three individuals would mobilize the population again during the genocide. Third, it fostered political pluralism. In the two southern communities, the MDR and PSD took root and opposed the MRNDD; in the two northern communities, the radical CDR party established itself and collaborated with the ruling party. In the next sections, I examine and theorize the operation of these three mechanisms: pluralization, competition, and participation.

Table 4.1 Impact of multipartyism at local level

	Ethnicity		Perpetrator Status		Region	
	Hutu	Tutsi	Non-perp.	Perp.	South	North

Question: Did life in your community change in any way after multipartyism began in 1991?

	(N=272)	(N=21)	(N=168)	(N=104)	(N=132)	(N=140)
Yes, life did change	79.5%	95.3%	79.4%	80.3%	92.4%	69.8%
Unable/unwilling to say	4.0%	0.0%	4.1%	1.6%	2.2%	5.0%

Question: If so, in what ways did life change in your community after multipartyism started? (open-ended, multiple answers permitted)

	(N=207)	(N=20)	(N=136)	(N=71)	(N=108)	(N=99)
Caused community divisions	79.8%	74.8%	80.0%	73.9%	76.7%	83.9%
Caused ethnic divisions	3.8%	24.8%	3.7%	7.3%	3.0%	4.8%
Caused violence/insecurity	15.9%	15.1%	16.0%	15.2%	6.8%	28.1%
Caused people to neglect their work	17.4%	10.0%	17.8%	9.4%	21.9%	11.5%

Question: Before the genocide did the politicians ever say bad things about the Tutsi in your community?

	(N=217)	(N=19)	(N=136)	(N=81)	(N=106)	(N=111)
Yes, they said bad things	20.1%	42.4%	20.1%	20.4%	28.9%	9.5%

Table 4.2 Political participation at the local level

	Ethnicity		Perpetrator Status		Region	
	Hutu	Tutsi	Non-perp.	Perp.	South	North
	(N=272)	(N=21)	(N=168)	(N=104)	(N=131)	(N=141)

Question: Many people supported political parties before the genocide. Did you support a political party and if so, which party?

No, I did not support a party	25.4%	43.5%	25.3%	27.9%	40.2%	11.1%
Yes, the MRND	44.7%	28.0%	45.7%	25.7%	9.5%	78.8%
Yes, the MDR	10.9%	4.9%	10.2%	23.9%	14.0%	7.9%
Yes, the PSD	16.5%	9.7%	16.4%	19.1%	32.4%	1.1%
Yes, the PL	1.2%	0.5%	0.5%	0%	0%	0.1%
Yes, the CDR	0%	0%	0%	0%	0%	0%
Yes, MDR-Power	0%	0%	0%	0%	0%	0%

Question: If so, why did you support this party? (open-ended, multiple answers permitted, most common answers listed)

	(N=199)	(N=10)	(N=119)	(N=80)	(N=76)	(N=123)
It was the dominant party	26.7%	9.9%	26.8%	25.4%	22.0%	29.7%
I believed in its ideology and/or policies	26.3%	30.5%	26.3%	25.3%	42.7%	16.1%
I had to join to protect myself	11.9%	29.6%	12.5%	0.5%	6.4%	15.3%
I have always known the MRND	9.9%	0.0%	9.9%	9.3%	0.9%	15.5%
I knew someone in the party	6.3%	20.2%	5.9%	13.6%	8.2%	5.1%
It was the party for people of my ethnicity	0.2%	0.0%	0.0%	4.5%	0.6%	0.0%

Question: Did you participate in political party meetings in your community?

	(N=266)	(N=21)	(N=165)	(N=101)	(N=129)	(N=137)
Yes, I participated in party meetings	52.9%	33.6%	52.1%	67.5%	51.6%	54.2%

Political Pluralization

Political liberalization unsurprisingly pluralized the landscape of Rwanda's civil and political society. The country experienced an explosion in print media, political parties, and human rights organizations. Rwanda's new parties and publications reflected a wide spectrum of political interests and ideologies. Fifteen political parties registered in Rwanda in response to the new law of 18 June 1991. As their names suggest, they covered a wide set of interests: from the environment and workers, to religion and women.[14] The proliferation was the result of a very low institutional bar set for forming a party. The most important legal constraint was simply that 'in its principles, programs and actions, no political party may institute discrimination based on ethnic, regional, or religious affiliation.'[15] There was no threshold number of signatures demanded, and no approval from the Minister of the Interior required. As a consequence, with the exception of the MDR, PSD, PL, and PDC, most parties only enjoyed marginal popular support.

Pluralism touched the media too. In addition to the profusion of political parties, Rwanda also experienced a multiplication in its print publications. From 1 January 1990 at least seventy-two more newspapers, magazines, and journals appeared for sale in Rwanda, on top of the eight already in circulation. As with the parties, these publications also reflected a wide range of ideological orientations and political viewpoints. Some were supportive of the ruling party; others affiliated with an opposition party. Ideologically, certain publications were associated with a particular religion; a few defended the interests of a particular ethnic group; and others espoused political ideologies from Marxist to libertarian. Fifteen could be classified as independent.

---

[14] The fifteen parties were the MDR (Mouvement Démocratique Republicain), PSD (Parti Social Démocrate), PL (Parti Libéral), PDC (Parti Démocratique Chrétien), PSR (Parti Socialiste Rwandais), RTD (Rassemblement Travailliste pour la Démocratie), PDI (Parti pour la Démocratie Islamique), PECO (Parti des Ecologistes), PPJR (Parti Progressiste de la Jeunesse Rwandaise), PADER (Parti Démocratique Rwandais), PARERWA (Parti Révolutionnaire du Rwanda), MFBP (Mouvement des Femmes et du Bas-Peuple), PADE (Parti Démocrate), and CDR (Coalition pour la Défense de la République). Finally, there was the RPF (Rwandan Patriotic Front), the rebel movement in Rwanda's civil war.

[15] Loi 28/91 'Partis Politiques', Official Journal of Rwanda, 18 June 1991.

Fourteen were openly Hutuist or extremist in orientation and four more would radicalize in this direction over time.[16]

Amid this dazzling diversity, extremist interests and an extremist ideology would also emerge. 'Hutu Power', as ethnic extremism would become known in the Rwandan context, was one of the many offspring of Rwanda's newly fertile political space. Yet, as we shall see, it was initially a fringe ideology with limited support. Rwanda had other competing ideologies that were more moderate and inclusive in orientation.

Against Ideological Singularity

A consensus is forming in comparative work on genocide and mass violence on the theoretical importance of ideology – and ideas more broadly – in explaining why leaders and regimes choose elimination over other options to deal with groups they perceive as problematic (Kiernan, 2009; Sémelin, 2005; Straus, 2015; Weitz, 2005). Ideology, by which I mean simply a set of coherent beliefs about the world at-large (Gerring, 1997), can both provide *ex ante* motivation and legitimation and *ex post* rationalization for the extermination of groups (Costalli & Ruggeri, 2015; Leader Maynard, 2014). This shift towards the role of ideas in shaping elite decisions is a welcome counterbalance to the rationalist, institutionalist, and materialist approaches that have dominated in explanations of genocides and mass killings (Besancon, 2005; de Figueiredo & Weingast, 1999; Krain, 1997; Rummel, 1995; Valentino, 2004; Wayman & Tago, 2010). Yet to say that ideology matters overlooks an important fact and begs a crucial question. First, as a matter of fact, there are often multiple, differing, and even conflicting ideologies in circulation within the public sphere at any one time. Rarely is there a single, exclusionary ideology that is unambiguously dominant. Second, if the public sphere is ideologically plural, how and why does extremism come to prevail over myriad other ideological currents, including more inclusive and more moderate creeds? I begin by documenting the existence of multiple ideological frames in Rwanda's public sphere on the eve of the genocide. I then present a theory of how competition between extremists and moderates resolves and show how strategic interactions both between *and*

---

[16] This description of Rwanda's new media landscape is derived from the classification undertaken by Chrétien (1995, pp. 383–386).

within parties, in the absence of domestic and international constraints, facilitated the triumph of extremists in Rwanda. An extremist ideology was a necessary condition for the genocide, but it was neither inevitable that it would prevail nor sufficient by itself to cause the violence.

Ideological Pluralism in Rwanda
Ethnic extremism was not the sole or even the dominant ideology in Rwanda between 1990 and 1994. At the outset of the liberalization period, only one of sixteen political parties (the CDR), and only twenty of eighty print publications in circulation could be described as pro-Hutu or anti-Tutsi in character.[17] Rwanda was not in the grip of widespread Hutu nationalism. Nor was it burning with extensive ethnic hatred against Tutsi. As we shall see, extremism would rise in prominence as the war escalated. It was through complex contestation both within groups and between groups, and through the weakness of domestic and international constraints, that extremism would prevail over moderation.

Before the war and liberalization began, at least three ideologies had had a longstanding impact on Rwanda's public sphere: (i) the revolutionary and emancipatory ideology of Kayibanda's First Republic (1959–1973); (ii) the unifying and nationally inclusive rhetoric of Habyarimana's Second Republic (1973–1994); and (iii) the pacifist and ethnically equivocal messaging of the Catholic Church. None of these ideologies was hegemonic before the genocide.

Kayibanda's Revolutionary and Emancipatory Ideology
Grégoire Kayibanda's ideological perspective on ethnicity and power in Rwanda was classically essentialist. He viewed Hutu, Tutsi, and Twa as distinct races and did not see distinctions within these groups between the elite who wielded political power and ordinary individuals who did not. For Kayibanda, the quest for political power in Rwanda was a struggle between ethnic groups. In this regard, Kayibanda's ideological mindset most closely resembled that of the extremists behind the genocide. The *Bahutu* manifesto, published in 1957 and of which Kayibanda was one of the nine signatories, baldly stated that 'the problem above all is the political monopoly held by one race: the

---

[17] A list of these publications can be found in Chrétien (1995, pp. 383–386).

Tutsi'. The language is noticeably similar to that used by Théoneste Bagosora thirty-eight years later, when he would describe the civil war as a 'secular conflict between Hutus and the Tutsi minority, who are still seeking to monopolize power at all costs'.[18] The manifesto, drawing on Enlightenment ideals of equality, liberty, and justice, would provide the ideological motivation for Rwanda's social revolution that followed it two years later.

For Kayibanda, the revolution, by abolishing a feudal monarchy and establishing a republic, ended Tutsi privilege and liberated the Hutu majority. The name of Kayibanda's party, the PARMEHUTU, literally signified the party for the emancipation of the Hutu. Although the party would drop the ethnic identifier, Parmehutu, when political parties were legalized once more in 1991, it still maintained in its founding statutes that 'the fundamental principle of the MDR is the defence and safeguard of the gains of the socio-political revolution of 1959, to wit: democracy and the republic'.[19]

The themes of feudalism and monarchy would appear and would be contrasted frequently against those of democracy, republicanism, and emancipation in Kayibanda's presidential addresses.[20] They were the core tenets of his political ideology. For Kayibanda, democracy signified Hutu majority rule. The first republic was in effect a Hutu ethnocracy.

Democracy means recognizing the masses and giving them the chance to exercise their rights and to strengthen their position in all areas of national, political, cultural, social, economic, familial, and even religious life. Democracy signifies freedom and if we do not achieve freedom in these many aspects, democracy is only futile noise. (Kayibanda, Labour Day, 1 May 1963)

The Rwandan people have been emancipated from servitude; feudalism has collapsed; and colonialism has departed [...] but the objective of

---

[18] See Bagosora's essay entitled 'The final Tutsi operation to gain power in Rwanda by force', dated 30 October 1995, Exhibit in Prosecutor vs Bagosora, ICTR-96-41-A.

[19] See article 3 of MDR statutes, Exhibit in Prosecutor vs. Bizimungu et al, ICTR-99-50-T.

[20] A database of speeches by presidents Kayibanda and Habyarimana is maintained by Scott Straus at the University of Wisconsin. faculty.polisci.wisc.edu/sstraus/african-presidential-speeches-database/rwanda-speeches/. Accessed 8 January 2018.

4.4 The Mechanisms of Liberalization

emancipating the masses is a project that will take time. (Kayibanda, Independence Day, 1 July 1967)

Despite his essentialist perspective on identity, Kayibanda rarely used the terms 'Hutu' and 'Tutsi' in his presidential speeches. In fact, in fifteen national presidential addresses given between 1962 and 1973 on Independence Day, Labour day, and the New Year, he used the term 'Tutsi' on only one occasion, following massacres of Hutu in Burundi in 1972.[21] Kayibanda purposely avoided ethnic or racial language when speaking in French and for external audiences. It was instead implicitly understood by Rwandans that references to feudalism and monarchy meant the Tutsi; and that references to democracy and republicanism meant the Hutu. However, when he spoke directly to Rwandans and in Kinyarwanda, this ethnic equation would become explicit. His language particularly ethnicized in response to the security threats created by the *Inyenzi* attacks of the 1960s. Thus, Kayibanda famously made an address in 1964, entitled 'Power and Democracy', explicitly to the Tutsi inside Rwanda in which he simultaneously warned and entreated them. He told his Tutsi citizens:

Tell me sincerely, if the Hutus had been that wicked to exterminate the Tutsis, would he have waited for the *Inyenzi* to attack? Is it untrue that some of you assert: 'If the Tutsis had won, no Hutu would be alive, except the one who would withstand the ten feudal chores.' We have made our will known to you in our speech of July 1st 1963. Embrace democracy and become the disciples of the new Rwandan system. We want that all citizens should be brothers. We will be lenient to you, as long as you cooperate. (*Kayibanda*, Power is Democracy, 29 March 1964)

At the same time, he also appealed to them.

The objective of the feudalist *Inyenzi* is to set you at odds with the country that has opted for democracy. They want you to be rooted to your Tutsi ethnic group (you know the meaning in good Kinyarwanda) [...] Our constant concern is to instil a veritable spirit of brotherhood amongst all Rwandans as well as establish democracy for all Rwandan citizens. (*Kayibanda*, Power is Democracy, 29 March 1964)

Kayibanda's revolutionary ideology would have been internalized particularly by the generation who had achieved political consciousness at

---

[21] He also used the term 'Hutu' twice, but only in stating the meaning of his party, the PARMEHUTU.

the time of the revolution. It would, then, have been particularly strong among those aged 45 and over at the time the war began in 1990.

Habyarimana's Unifying and Nationally Inclusive Rhetoric

In contrast with Kayibanda, Habyarimana sought to reconcile veneration of the 1959 revolution with unifying appeals to a shared Rwandan national identity in his presidential addresses. His ideology was more inclusive and integrationist than that of Kayibanda, whose views on ethnicity Habyarimana considered divisive and overly essentialist. Habyarimana instead attributed the injustice and inequality in the pre-independence era in impersonal terms to the abstraction of the feudal monarchy.

> Their cries were not heard. The little people continued to suffer degrading and humiliating treatment. Arrogance, contempt, and affront were at the root of the popular social revolution of 1959, which allowed the Rwandan people, oppressed for so long, to be rid of this corrupt feudal power. The social revolution allowed a democratic society to be built that cared for the interests of the popular masses. (Habyarimana, 20th anniversary of Rwanda's independence, 1 July 1982)

Habyarimana purposely avoided group homogenization and made a careful distinction between the erstwhile Tutsi ruling elite and ordinary Tutsi. As he stated in an Independence Day anniversary speech in 1987, 'Our young people today know that our struggle was directed against an outdated hegemonic feudal system and not against one ethnic group as such.'

It was this intra-ethnic distinction that allowed Habyarimana simultaneously to extol the virtues of the revolution and to include ordinary Tutsi in his nation-building rhetoric. He promoted a common Rwandan identity that transcended, though was not intended to eliminate, ethnic differences.

> We are of course born of different families and we come from different parts of the country. But we also all share a common homeland: our dear Rwanda. How could we not be united, all of us who share a common cultural heritage, who support the principles of the MRND which banished all discrimination based on sex, religion, ethnicity, origin, profession, and social status? (Habyarimana, 20 December 1985)

Habyarimana linked this national unity to the country's development and portrayed his coup in 1973 as a 'moral' revolution that ended the regional discrimination that characterized the Kayibanda era, in

4.4 The Mechanisms of Liberalization

contrast with the 1959 'social' revolution that ended the ethnic discrimination that defined the pre-independence era.

You all have a duty to work to re-establish peace and national unity. It is in your own interest; for the good of your own families; it is for the prosperity of the entire nation. Love your compatriots regardless of their ethnic or regional origin. Reject all propaganda that preaches regionalism. (Habyarimana, 6 July 1974)

It was to re-instate peace and national harmony that the moral revolution of July 5th 1973 happened. Since that date our country has known a period of peace and national stability which has contributed a great deal to our economic and social progress. Peace and national unity are necessary first steps before we can devote the bulk of our efforts towards our development. (Habyarimana, 25th anniversary of Rwanda's independence, 1 July 1987)

Despite his promotion of a Rwandan national identity and although he rarely used the terms 'Hutu' and 'Tutsi' in his national addresses, Habyarimana nonetheless maintained that Hutu, Tutsi, and Twa were distinct ethnic groups. In an interview with the magazine, *Jeune Afrique*, he was asked, if his view of ethnicity did differ from that of Kayibanda's, why he had not abolished ethnicity on identity cards.

It would not bother me to do so, but what is more important: to do away with a written notation or eliminate the complex in the minds of individuals? Just because I am identified as a Hutu on my ID card does not mean I think I am superior to others. But whether they mention it or not, I am a Hutu and a Tutsi will always be Tutsi! (Habyarimana, interview with *Jeune Afrique*, October 1990)

Once the war began in October 1990, Habyarimana continued to avoid ethnically homogenizing and essentializing language in his national addresses, even though more radical members of his own party increasingly defined the threat in ethnic terms and Tutsi civilians were increasingly targeted for arrest, detention, and violent attack. In a speech given in December 1990, he carefully distinguished between the Tutsi inside Rwanda, the refugees who supported the monarchy and left Rwanda in 1959, and the rebel RPF, the subset of refugees who sought armed return. As the war progressed, although Habyarimana wavered in his commitment to the Arusha peace process, his pleas for national unity remained constant. In fact, he would maintain the refrain of unity up until the very eve of the genocide.

Let all the events we have gone through, the disasters we have talked about, be a lesson for us to remain united despite the various parties to which we belong, despite the various regions we were born in and despite our ethnic affiliations. We all are and we all remain Rwandans, all equal, with equal rights... (Habyarimana, 24 February 1994)

Habyarimana's ethnically inclusive and nationally unifying messages would have influenced most strongly the generation that first attained political consciousness at the start of the Second Republic. These individuals would have been between 30 and 45 years old at the start of the war in 1990.

The Catholic Church's Pacifist and Ethnically Equivocal Ideology
Non-violence, and its related precepts of compassion, love, and fellowship, along with non-discrimination, and its concomitant ideas of equality, tolerance, and justice, both feature strongly in Christian teachings. Yet in the Rwandan context of politicized ethnicity, the Catholic Church's position on these issues had historically been ambivalent. It was caught between the moderating tendencies of its religious principles and the constraints imposed by its ties to the state and political power.

As is well-known, the first Catholic missionaries in Rwanda, the White Fathers, believed that Hutu and Tutsi represented distinct races with a clear racial hierarchy. They saw the Tutsi at the apex as Hamites; then the Hutu as Negroids; and finally, the Twa as Pygmoids. Instead of non-discrimination, the Church practised ethnic favouritism at first in Rwanda. The early generations of missionaries, keen to expand the Church's influence, cultivated their relationship with the Tutsi, whom they perceived as the politically dominant and naturally superior ruling class. Tutsi overwhelmingly received educational opportunities and were selected for training into the priesthood over Hutu. However, following World War II, a new generation of missionaries, animated by ideas of racial equality and justice, questioned the Church's historical alliance with the Tutsi. Adopting a more classically Christian attitude, they shifted sympathies and support towards the poorer, more disadvantaged Hutu. This led to the emergence of a new, educated generation of Hutu who challenged the socio-political order in which Tutsi were ascendant. Following the revolution that toppled this order, Kayibanda, as one of the Church's Hutu protégés, would

4.4 The Mechanisms of Liberalization

maintain a close relationship between his regime and the Church. The Church's ties to political power led to its adoption of another position inconsistent with Christian ideals of pacifism and compassion: its overwhelming silence in the face of anti-Tutsi violence during the revolution and reprisal killings following the *Inyenzi* attacks in the 1960s.

Under Habyarimana, the Church's messaging on ethnic discrimination and violence improved compared with its muteness under Kayibanda. Divergent viewpoints, however, still existed within the institution, reflecting in part the gap between its senior leadership, predominantly Hutu and largely sympathetic to the regime, and its lower and middle orders, predominantly Tutsi and more critical. Seven of nine Archbishops were Hutu and the Archbishop of Kigali, Monseigneur Nsengiyumva, in fact sat for many years on the MRNDD's Central Committee. In contrast, the majority, one estimate suggests 70 per cent (Des Forges, 1999, p. 39), of its priests were Tutsi. One of the Church's means of communicating its positions down the clerical ranks lay in the issuance of pastoral letters.[22] In February 1990, eight months before the war began, it published 'Christ, our Unity'. The letter reaffirmed the Church's commitment to Christian unity and non-discrimination:

The Church, for its part, does not cease to preach unity [...] There are some Rwandans who reject these teachings and continue to support ethnic rivalries through all sorts of speeches and manoeuvres. One sometimes hears people complain that, for reasons of ethnic origin, they have been refused a job or a place in school, they have been deprived of benefits, or that justice has not been impartial in their regard [...] The Twa, the Tutsi, the Hutu, the foreign guests, all of us are children of God and we possess one and the same father: God. (Pastoral Letter, *Christ Our Unity*, February 1990)

Notwithstanding its apparent message of solidarity, priests from the diocese of Nyundo published a reply to this letter in April 1990 criticizing it for explicitly recognizing Rwanda's ethnic distinctions. They viewed the prominence accorded to ethnicity in the letter as

---

[22] The pastoral letters were originally published in the *Recueil des Lettres et Messages de la Conference des Evêques Catholiques du Rwanda Publies Pendant la Period de Guerre (1990–1994)*. I am indebted to T. P. Longman (2010) who reproduced and translated all the letters cited in this chapter.

reproducing Habyarimana's political ideology and reinforcing rather than transcending ethnic identities.

Once the war began, the ideological divisions within the Church became more apparent. Its senior leadership published another pastoral letter, again, seemingly, with a message of moderation.

> At the ethnic level, our Christian solidarity ought to be manifested by good understanding, tolerance, and complementarily. All Rwandans, whatever ethnicity they are part of, have the right to live and grow in all tranquillity in the heart of the national community. (Pastoral Letter, *Happy are the artisans of peace*, November 1990)

Despite its outwardly pacifist character, however, the letter's message was again ambiguous. It did not mention or condemn the massacres of Tutsi in Kibilira that had just taken place in October 1990 in reprisal for the RPF's invasion. Another pastoral letter, entitled 'Peace and Reconciliation for Rwandans', published later in the war in 1993, referred to the 'injustice, ethnic and regional discrimination that have characterized the sharing of power' and the 'limited respect accorded to the human person at the point of spilling blood and, too often, that of innocents'. Again, its message was equivocal. It did not specify the authors or the victims of the discrimination and failed to reference the several massacres of Tutsi that had already taken place, let alone condemn those responsible for them.

In contrast with the equivocation by the Church's senior leadership, other Church actors spoke out clearly against the regime on matters of conscience. Statements in the influential Catholic newspaper, *Kinyamateka*, edited by André Sibomana, specifically denounced civilian attacks committed by *both* the RPF and FAR/Interahamwe (Sibomana et al., 1999, pp. 44–45). Kinyamateka, Rwanda's oldest newspaper, belonged to the Episcopal Conference and was financially independent of the Catholic Church. The bishop and clergy of Nyundo diocese also exhibited independence from the regime. They issued a statement in December 1993 challenging the government to explain why arms had been distributed in certain communes and to arrest those who carried them.[23] In fact, the Church actively sought to promote peace between the warring parties. In early 1992, in conjunction with Protestant and other religious organizations, it facilitated

---

[23] Exhibit in Bagosora et al., ICTR-98-41-T.

contact between the RPF and the government. These early talks would lend important momentum to the establishment of the formal Arusha negotiations.

The Catholic Church, then, was not a unitary actor but rather an organization composed of individuals with differences in their religious ideological commitments. It was also a highly significant and influential social institution in Rwanda with direct and longstanding relationships with local communities across the country through its nationwide network of dioceses. Eighty-six per cent of Rwandans identified as Christian in 1991, of whom roughly 60 per cent were Catholic, 18 per cent were Protestant, and 8 per cent were Adventist.[24] While we do not know what exactly priests preached from the pulpit each Sunday, the Church was not simply an echo-chamber for Habyarimana's government. It also contained voices that preached Christian unity, peace, and non-discrimination.

The Primacy of Moderation

Even before liberalization began then, Rwandans had not been exposed to a single, dominant ideology. To the contrary, Rwandans had received multiple, conflicting, and ambiguous ideological messages that ranged from ethnically essentialist to ethnically inclusive. Liberalization pluralized further the multitude of political ideologies that circulated within Rwanda before the genocide. Moreover, the clear majority of these creeds that first manifested in 1990 were ethnically moderate in orientation.

Rwanda's largest opposition political parties, the MDR, PSD, and PL, all initially emphasized national unity over ethnic differences in their public statements. All three sought cross-ethnic support and counted Hutu and Tutsi among their members. The MDR, whose historical precursor, the PARMEHUTU party, was known for its Hutuist orientation, made its opposition to racial discrimination a pillar of its party manifesto. Its statutes listed as the party's first objective 'the peaceful coexistence of Rwanda's ethnic groups in the spirit of equality and mutual respect in order to preserve a republican nation, peaceful, united, and indivisible'.[25] The party's leadership also

---

[24] See Government of Rwanda (1994).
[25] See article 4 of MDR statutes, Exhibit in Prosecutor vs. Bizimungu et al, ICTR-99-50-T.

issued communiqués, in February 1992 and then February 1993, each following major Tutsi massacres, unequivocally condemning the killing and holding the ruling party responsible.[26] The president of the PL, Justin Mugenzi, also made a high-profile speech in July 1993 explicitly denouncing ethnic ideologies.[27]

> We don't have a Tutsi ideology. Our ambition is to assemble a majority around an ideology made of all the Rwandan sociological components. We want a majority built on an ideology. Our ideology does not make any mistake, we are a Liberal party and liberalism is defined in the specific case of Rwanda by a broadening to all these ethnic groups. (Justin Mugenzi, PL President, July 1993)

Moderate messages also featured prominently in radio broadcasts, the main means of mass communication in Rwanda. Jean-Marie Higiro, appointed by moderate MDR Prime Minister Agathe Uwilingiyimana, took up the position of Director of Radio Rwanda in July 1993, the same month that RTLM began broadcasts. He implemented a strict editorial policy for what content could be aired, prohibiting, for instance, the use of the ethnically pejorative term *Inyenzi*. The RPF also broadcast its eight-point programme, a précis of its political manifesto, on its own Radio Muhubura. Its first point was the 'restoration of unity among Rwandans'. Even RTLM aired content that advocated inter-ethnic unity. Charles Nkurunziza, a former Minister of Justice under Habyarimana, for instance, made public appeals for ethnic co-existence on RTLM as late as December 1993.

> Now that we are approaching the year 2000, we should understand no ethnic group should monopolize power. Things must change. There must be a different culture. No ethnic group was born to rule at the expense of the other. In fact, democracy is a culture. It is the people who are sovereign and they must choose their leader without considering his/her ethnic origin. (*Charles Nkurunziza, former Minister of Justice, RTLM broadcast, 12 December 1993*)

In sum, there was no shortage of ideologically moderate messages propagated during the liberalization period. Ethnic extremism was but one of many ideological currents and it initially existed only on the fringes of Rwanda's political arena and as a minority viewpoint. So the

---

[26] See exhibits in Prosecutor vs Karemera, ICTR-98-44-T.
[27] See exhibit in Prosecutor vs. Bizimungu et al., ICTR-99-50-T.

4.4 The Mechanisms of Liberalization 157

question this evidently raises is how and why would extremism come to prevail over such pervasive moderation in Rwanda? The answer, as we shall see next, lies in the competition that liberalization sparked both within and between parties in the context of war and weak domestic and international constraints to contain the competition. However, before theorizing how this competition led to the victory of extremists, I first examine the ideas and beliefs that ordinary Rwandans had in fact internalized from Rwanda's ideologically plural public sphere.

Ideological Beliefs 'From Below'
In Chapter 3 I presented survey evidence that Rwanda's Hutu population possessed a very strong collective memory of past Hutu oppression and Tutsi privilege. A total of 70.3 per cent believed that the Tutsi monarch, the *Mwami*, had favoured the Tutsi at the expense of the Hutu. In addition, 75.4 per cent felt that institutions associated with the monarchy, notably *ubuhake*, a form of feudal clientship, had unfairly exploited Hutu. In fact, Hutu victimhood was only one of three widely held ideological beliefs concerning ethnic relations that I encountered.

The first belief emphasized that Hutu and Tutsi were fundamentally different. Ethnic consciousness was instilled from early on in Rwandans. As Table 4.3 shows, the average age at which Hutu children become aware of their ethnic identity was usually between eleven and twelve years old. Tutsi became ethnically conscious a little earlier, at the age of nine or ten. When asked *how* they came to know their ethnic identity, the majority of Hutu respondents stated that it was either through school (43.1 per cent) or from their parents (33.2 per cent). In practice, these were often one and the same way. In almost all these cases, respondents remembered a moment when a schoolteacher had asked students to stand up in class and to identify themselves by ethnicity. As most did not know their ethnicity at that early age, they were required to go home and ask their parents. So the state had an important role in instilling ethnic consciousness, and in shaping inter-ethnic relations, through the national educational system.

The second belief stressed that Tutsi were foreigners. According to this, the Tutsi had settled in Rwanda as pastoralists after earlier settlement by Hutu farmers. By implication, Tutsi had a weaker tie to Rwanda. This idea in part lies in the Hamitic Hypothesis that

Table 4.3 Beliefs concerning ethnic consciousness and Tutsi indigeneity and privilege

	Ethnicity		Perpetrator Status			Region	
	Hutu	Tutsi	Non-perp.	Perp.		South	North

Question: How old were you when you first learned what ethnicity you were?

	(N=270)	(N=21)	(N=167)	(N=103)		(N=132)	(N=138)
Age (mean years)	11.8	9.5	11.8	11.0		11.0	12.6

Question: How did you find out what ethnicity you were?

	(N=267)	(N=21)	(N=166)	(N=101)		(N=130)	(N=137)
At school	43.1%	24.3%	24.8%	14.5%		30.6%	18%
From my family	33.2%	44.0%	42.9%	65.5%		48.8%	39.3%
Some other way	23.7%	31.7%	32.3%	20%		20.6%	42.7%

Question: At the time of the genocide, where did most people think Tutsi came from originally? (open-ended)

	(N=267)	(N=21)	(N=165)	(N=102)		(N=131)	(N=136)
Outside of Rwanda	58.6%	71.5%	58.9%	53.1%		63.3%	56.4%
Indigenous to Rwanda	3.7%	4.6%	3.6%	6.4%		1.7%	6.2%
Unwilling/unable to say	37.7%	23.9%	37.5%	40.5%		35.0%	37.4%

Question: At the time of the genocide, where did most people think Hutu came from originally? (open-ended)							
	(N=262)	(N=20)	(N=163)	(N=99)	(N=126)	(N=136)
Outside of Rwanda	32.7%	15.1%	33.0%	27.5%	23.4%	38.1%
Indigenous to Rwanda	16.1%	29.9%	16.6%	6.0%	21.9%	13.3%
Unwilling/unable to say	51.2%	55.0%	50.4%	66.5%	54.7%	48.6%

Question: In your community before the genocide, did most Tutsi families have either more land or more cows or both than most Hutu families?

	(N=270)	(N=21)	(N=167)	(N=103)	(N=132)	(N=138)
Not materially better off	32.6%	28.7%	33.0%	26.1%	36.8%	27.7%
More land, more cows, or both	55.5%	66.6%	54.5%	72.5%	58.1%	55.1%
Unable/unwilling to say	11.9%	4.7%	12.5%	1.4%	5.1%	17.2%

Question: If Tutsi were better-off, why were they so?

	(N=269)	(N=21)	(N=166)	(N=103)	(N=131)	(N=138)
Hard work	30.8%	63.1%	30.2%	42.4%	35.4%	26.7%
Special treatment	48.6%	36.9%	49.0%	41.8%	46.4%	22.6%
Unable/unwilling to say	20.6%	0.0%	20.8%	15.8%	18.2%	50.7%

underpinned Belgian racial science during the colonial era. The hypothesis claimed that Tutsi, as the biblical descendants of Ham, were naturally superior and fit-to-rule Rwanda because they had a racial origin distinct to that of the Bantu Hutu. When asked where they believed Tutsi originally came from, the majority of Hutu (58.6 per cent) believed that Tutsi had come from outside of Rwanda. When asked to specify the area, the most common answer (45.3 per cent) was that Tutsi had originated in Ethiopia or Abyssinia.

The third belief concerned Hutu oppression and Tutsi privilege. In addition to the questions regarding Hutu subjugation above, I also asked Hutu respondents whether most Tutsi in their own communities had either more land or more cows – two of the most important material assets in Rwanda – than most Hutu families. The majority (55.5 per cent) said yes. I then asked them what they believed was the cause of the Tutsi's materially superior status. The question was designed to elicit an opinion on the legitimacy of outgroup success. More (48.6 per cent) were willing to state openly that this success was illegitimate, the result of privileges Tutsi had enjoyed historically, than because of their hard work (30.8 per cent).

Many scholars have interpreted such beliefs as the basis of anti-Tutsi sentiment that has been variously described as a racist ideology, ethnic prejudice, racism, inter-ethnic antipathy, and longstanding hatred.[28] It is worth noting that I found Tutsi shared many of these beliefs too: 52.8 per cent believed that the Mwami had favoured Tutsi; 61.9 per cent believed that Hutu had been unfairly exploited; and 71.5 per cent believed that Tutsi originated outside of Rwanda. Moreover, these answers were given in the socio-political context of an authoritarian government intent on minimizing ethnic differentiation. These beliefs are, on the face of it, difficult to reconcile with Habyarimana's 'we're all Rwandans' rhetoric and the Catholic Church's message (albeit ambivalent) of 'Christian solidarity'. How did Rwandans receive and resolve these multiple and conflicting ideological messages?

The answer lies in recognizing that it is possible for conflicting beliefs to co-exist within a given individual. An individual's ideological

[28] Uvin uses the terms 'racist ideology', 'racial prejudice', 'ethnic prejudice', and 'racism' inter-changeably. Braeckman writes of 'longstanding hatred'. Straus refers to inter-ethnic antipathy, while minimizing its importance in explaining individual participation in the genocide. I prefer to use the broader term 'anti-Tutsi sentiment' to encompass all of these terms.

4.4 The Mechanisms of Liberalization

outlook need not comprise a consistent and stable system of beliefs. Psychological theory has long recognized that individuals frequently encounter conflicting cognitions in their lives. Cognitive dissonance theory argues that individuals will always seek out ways to resolve such inconsistencies (Festinger, 1957). One response to dissonance is to ignore a conflicting belief or else reduce its salience relative to the other belief with which it conflicts. Understood in this way it becomes possible for someone to believe that Tutsi were ethnically different, not indigenous, and historically privileged, and at the same time believe in a Rwandan national identity, inter-ethnic unity, and non-discrimination. Either the inclusive or exclusionary beliefs become more salient in the individual's belief system. Individuals radicalize and de-radicalize. Ancient tribal hatred, a phrase used in early media accounts of Rwanda's genocide, misleadingly characterizes Hutu–Tutsi relations because it wrongly implies a constancy in the salience of anti-Tutsi beliefs across Rwanda's history. Similarly, ethnic hate narratives or myths (Kaufman, 2001), while necessary to mobilize groups, do not deterministically lead to violence. They exist passively in the background, alongside other narratives and beliefs, until activated.

Elite strategic communications can alter the salience of individual beliefs and activate particular narratives. Before the genocide, Habyarimana's rhetoric of national unity and Hutu–Tutsi solidarity contrasted sharply with extremist messages that framed military confrontation as necessary to prevent the reversal of the revolution and the reinstatement of the monarch. Such extremist views were minoritarian at the start. Most political parties and media outlets espoused more moderate views and, as we saw in the Chapter 3, Rwanda's civilian population was not widely radicalized before the genocide began. Yet as the war escalated, these messages gained in salience. They resonated more and more against the latent beliefs that the Tutsi had been privileged, were alien, and had subjugated the Hutu. This begs the question of why the salience of more moderate messages declined. Why did elite moderate communications not resonate against beliefs in a Rwandan national identity, in Christian solidarity, or in non-discrimination and non-violence, for example? The answer lies in the failure of domestic and international constraints to contain the competition that took place both between and within parties. Having documented the existence of competing ideological positions in Rwanda, in the next section I present a theory of how this competition played out before the genocide.

Political Competition

The second effect of liberalization was to enable political competition in the new space of opportunity created. Liberalization induced two political cleavages in Rwanda. First, competition divided Rwandan politics into *conservatives* who sought to preserve the status quo in which the ruling party and a small clique of northerners dominated; and *reformers* who challenged this political order. Opposition political parties were formally established in 1991 and informal liberal-conservative factions, mirroring primarily a north-south divide, appeared within the ruling party. However, as the war progressed, competition produced a second schism: between hardliners who believed only military victory would end the conflict, and moderates who advocated negotiated settlement. Breakaway 'Power' factions emerged within the main opposition parties, the MDR, PSD, and PL; and moderates were sidelined within the ruling party.

The contestation then was complex. Competition took place both *between* parties: between the opposition and the ruling parties. It also took place *within* parties: between reformist and loyalist blocs initially, and then between hardliner and moderate factions eventually. Contestation implies contingency and uncertainty. It was not inevitable that hardliners would prevail. Moderates, who were in fact ascendant at the outset, could well have won out too. Liberalization then did not deterministically ethnicize Rwandan politics and lead to genocide. It was liberalization's interaction with the war that would enable the rise of extremism. These two processes reinforced and drove each other. The internal political competition that liberalization enabled became entwined with the external contestation created by the war.

Theorizing Contestation

Can we predict then how such contestation will play out? I theorize that inter-group and intra-group conflict rarely occur independently of each other. The contestation *within* parties, usually between moderates and extremists, often drives the contestation *between* parties. In turn, the outcome of between-group contestation often impacts the moderate-extremist contestation *within* parties. Contestation then

4.4 The Mechanisms of Liberalization

involves dynamic and strategic interactions between and within actors. For instance, a surprise military attack by rebels in violation of a ceasefire (between-group contestation) may strengthen the position of the hardliner faction within the government (within-group contestation). Hardliner distrust of the rebels is vindicated. If regime hardliners publicly denounce the peace process in response, rebel hardliners will likely believe that continued military confrontation is the only way forward. As a consequence, the conflict escalates.

Contestation between moderates/reformers and hardliners/extremists is a common theme in studies of war and genocide. However, what is meant by moderate and extremist is often left unspecified. I offer then a formal definition. In the Rwandan context, moderation and extremism refer to a spectrum of ideological beliefs measurable along three dimensions. First, actors differ in their commitment toward military confrontation and negotiated settlement. Extremists believe that only military force will resolve the conflict; moderates believe that accommodation and power-sharing are possible. Second, actors differ in how they frame the conflict. Extremists tend to perceive the conflict in essentialist and ethnic terms. It is a war between Hutu and Tutsi. Moderates tend to see it in political, non-ethnic terms. It is a war between the rebels and the government. Third, actors differ in their beliefs regarding violence against civilians. Extremists argue that civilians may become legitimate targets; moderates believe it is never permissible to kill non-combatants. The more intensely held each of these three beliefs, the more radical the actors.

In applying this definition, two important theoretical points must be made. First, these ideological beliefs are not immutable. Attitudes on each of the three dimensions may intensify and moderate over time. Actors evidently radicalize and de-radicalize. The idea of attitude mutability is integral to the idea of the escalation and de-escalation of conflict. As the security threat intensifies, attitudes will radicalize. Increasingly, actors advocate military confrontation over negotiated settlement, frame the threat in ethnic rather than non-ethnic terms, and accept the targeting of civilians as well as combatants. The second important point is that not all political actors can be classified as moderate or extremist. Their ideological outlook may have led them to espouse other issues. These actors may simply not yet have formed beliefs on each of the three dimensions. Such individuals belong more accurately to a third category of 'uncommitted' actors. Their position is not yet established. As the threat escalates, however, the pressure to take a position increases. Individuals must choose whether to advocate for a negotiated peace, to frame the conflict in non-ethnic terms, and to denounce violence against civilians. Political choice is reduced to these dichotomies.

The idea that genocide is the outcome of a process of escalation has gained traction in the theorization of genocide (Straus, 2012). Genocide is believed to be the product of a sequence of escalatory actions that evolve over time. Yet less well-understood is why competition should escalate events in a particular direction and specifically towards extremism and violence? Why do the forces of moderation not succeed and de-escalate tensions in the direction of inclusion and cooperation? The answer, I theorize, has to do with the external constraints – both domestic and international – that the actors face. These constraints shape the calculus of what extremists believe they can get away with.

Domestically, state institutions and civil society actors may each serve to check extremist, escalatory behaviour. State institutions charged with enforcing the rule of law have an especially important role. The police have the power to investigate and arrest in relation to incidents of insecurity and disorder. Party political violence, targeted assassinations, and civilian killings are common occurrences in democratic transitions and civil wars. Similarly, the judiciary has the power to adjudicate and resolve disputes. It may intervene to proscribe speech as hateful, ban demonstrations likely to turn violent, or outlaw political parties that violate codes of conduct. The independence and strength of these institutions then shape extremist calculus. If weak, extremists feel emboldened; if strong, they may be deterred.

Civil society may also constrain extremism. In sub-Saharan Africa, the Church is a particularly influential actor. Its voice is a moral compass for its followers. Its silence in the face of hateful rhetoric or extremist violence is powerful. The media also possesses prodigious power to shape public opinion. How the broadcast and print media frame violence will likely affect public support for one side or the other. Other civil society actors – professional associations, human rights organizations, trade unions, and business associations – each have the capacity to organize and mobilize people. Through collective action – demonstrations, strikes, and civil disobedience – they too can signal their opposition to state policies.

4.4 The Mechanisms of Liberalization

Internationally, statements and actions by actors at this level also affect extremists' calculus. As countries liberalize politically, diplomatic rhetoric and external material support in favour of moderates or against extremists may influence the ascendance of one over the other. Silence and inaction often advantage the latter. In civil wars, international mediation, economic sanctions, peacekeeping, and the threat of criminal prosecution may each affect the strategic calculations made by hardliners intent on escalation. International disinterest or inaction often works to the advantage of those committed to violence.

In the face of weak external constraints, I theorize the outcome of inter-group and intra-group contestation will turn on the relative material capabilities of each party. Each actor's relative capacity for coercion, communication, and coordination will ultimately decide the outcome. In the case of intra-group contestation, for instance, if extremists command the security services, the airwaves, and the civilian bureaucracy, they would be in a structurally advantageous position vis-à-vis moderates. The conflict will likely escalate into violence.

Moderate-Extremist Contestation in Rwanda

How well then does this model of contestation fit Rwanda? In Rwanda, the principal actors were the Rwandan government and the rebel RPF at the international level; and then the main opposition parties and the ruling party, who had formed a coalition government, at the national level. Within each of these actors, moderate and extremist factions emerged – in both the civilian and military spheres – as the war and liberalization processes interacted and the threat escalated. Individuals radicalized at different escalatory moments.

Within the ruling party, Théoneste Bagosora, *Directeur de Cabinet* at the Ministry of Defence, and Léon Mugesera, MRNDD ideologue and vice-chairman for Gisenyi prefecture, articulated extremist beliefs from early in the war. Bagosora headed a military commission whose report published in September 1992 would define the primary enemy as 'extremist Tutsi within the country and abroad who are nostalgic for power...'. Mugesera famously told MRNDD party members in November 1992 that Rwandans would send the Tutsi back to Ethiopia via the Nyabarongo river. In contrast, James Gasana, the Minister of Defence, was an unequivocal MRNDD moderate. He sought to disarm the militia groups and steadfastly advocated for a negotiated settlement with the RPF until death threats forced his flight from the country in

July 1993. However, many senior MRNDD party figures – including the principal power-brokers Joseph Nzirorera, the MRNDD national secretary, Matthieu Ngirumpatse, the MRNDD president, and Édouard Karemera, the head of the National Synthesis Commission – fall into the 'uncommitted' category for much of the pre-genocide period. Their moment of radicalization came only with the assassination of Habyarimana in April 1994. It was only then that they made their commitment to the extremist cause clear.

Among the opposition parties, the MDR, PSD, and PL espoused strong moderate positions when first established. They committed to power-sharing with the RPF and informally allied with the rebel group from early 1992. However, a major schism – into pro- and anti-RPF factions – progressively developed in 1993 following, first, the major RPF military offensive in February that came within striking distance of Kigali and, second, the conclusion of the Arusha Accords in August. Senior political figures such as Donat Murego, the MDR national secretary, Froduald Karamira, the MDR second vice-president, and Jean Kambanda, MDR vice-president for Butare, as well as Stanislas Mbonampeka, the second vice-president for the PL, become increasingly hostile toward the RPF whom they suspected of being intent on outright military victory. In contrast, Agathe Uwilingiyimana, the prime minister in the coalition government just before the genocide, and Faustin Twagiramungu, the prime minister designate, both from the MDR, and Landoald Ndasginwa, the first vice-president from the PL, remained committed to cooperation with the rebel group. The schism decisively ethnicized with the assassination of Melchior Ndadaye, Burundi's first elected Hutu President, by Tutsi soldiers in October 1993. The PSD, PL, and PDC then followed the MDR and split into Hutu Power and moderate factions. Justin Mugenzi, the president of the PL, famously signalled his radicalization with a speech in January 1994, openly extolling the Hutu Revolution.

Within the RPF, radicalization occurred early. Moderation died with the RPF's military commander, Fred Rwigyema, killed on the war's second day.[29] Rwigyema had been open to negotiating the repatriation of refugees and the integration of RPF officers into the FAR. However,

---

[29] The circumstances of Rwigyema's death remain disputed. The RPF's official line is that he was killed by a stray bullet. Historian Gérard Prunier initially corroborated this version of events but later retracted this claim and instead alleged that Rwigyema was killed by two of his own sub-commanders, Peter

his replacement, Paul Kagame, possessed a much more hard-line disposition. The RPF continued to negotiate hard in Arusha and secured major victories at the table. It also maintained its official position on ending ethnic politics and promoting national unity in Rwanda. However, Kagame brooked no dissent and, and according to one RPF insider, members of the RPA High Command and of its Political Bureau all came to believe in the possibility of absolute victory on the battlefield and of capturing Rwanda entirely.[30] We may never know the truth of the RPF's commitment to a negotiated settlement. The extent of its radicalization before the genocide may always remain unclear. Yet it is improbable the RPF – which was after all a Tutsi-dominated organization – would knowingly sacrifice the entire Tutsi population inside Rwanda to secure an outright military victory. That would have been a truly radical choice. A more plausible explanation is that it underestimated the scale and the speed of the civilian killings that would follow its decision to re-engage the war. While it likely foresaw some reprisal violence, it did not anticipate genocide.

Escalation and De-escalation in Rwanda

How then did the interactions both within and between actors – moderates and extremists – affect the trajectory of the conflict? Figure 4.1 presents a graphical chronology sequencing events from the start of the war in October 1990 until the genocide in April 1994. The timeline distinguishes between *inter-group* (left-hand side) and *intra-group* actions (right-hand side). It also distinguishes escalatory (shaded boxes) and de-escalatory actions (white boxes). *Between* groups, escalatory actions typically comprised military offensives, civilian massacres, and targeted assassinations; de-escalatory actions involved negotiations, ceasefires, and peace agreements. *Within* groups,

---

Banyingana and Chris Bunyenyezi, possibly at the behest of Paul Kagame (Prunier, 2005, pp. 13–14).

[30] Theogene Rudasingwa, former RPF secretary-general, explains that, once the war began, the RPF did not experience internal contestation between hardliners and moderates as Rwanda's political parties did. He attributes this cohesion to three factors: (i) the RPF was overwhelmingly a Tutsi organization; (ii) the refugee experience had been unifying; and (iii) Kagame's absolutist leadership style tolerated no dissent. He points out that although Alexis Kanyarengwe was the nominal head of the RPF and the RPA was formally subordinate to the Political Bureau, the RPF negotiators at Arusha called Kagame to obtain authority to agree terms. Kagame fused military and political power.

168 *Threat and Opportunity: The Dangers of Freedom*

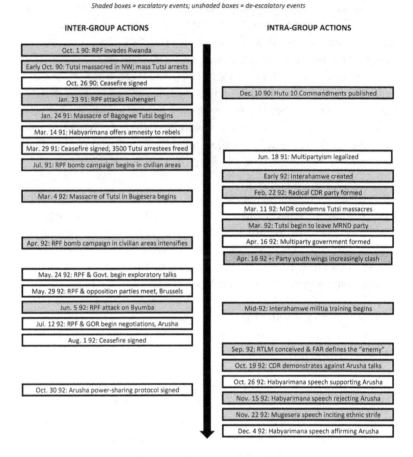

Figure 4.1 Pre-genocide timeline of escalatory and de-escalatory events

escalatory actions comprised the emergence of ethnically defined party factions, the making of ethnically divisive speeches, and protests and riots against ethnic power-sharing; de-escalatory actions involved moderates assuming leadership positions, conciliatory, inclusive speeches, and the arrest and denunciation of ethnic extremists. As the timeline suggests, the contestation was complex. However, it can be deconstructed into identifiable pivot points that exemplify the contingent nature of the escalation and de-escalation process. I focus here on

4.4 The Mechanisms of Liberalization

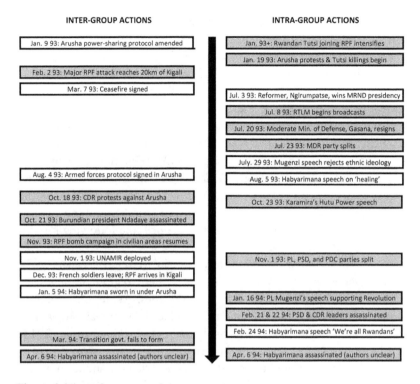

Figure 4.1 (cont.)

the more important escalatory and de-escalatory moments in the war and peace processes.

Inter-group contestation
Inter-group contestation took place principally between the Hutu-dominant government and Tutsi-dominant rebel group. In response to the RPF's opening attack in October 1990, the Rwandan government arrested and detained some 13,000 Tutsi civilians across Rwanda while local authorities also organized a massacre of 367 Tutsi in the north-west of the country.

At the same time, French, Belgian, and Zairean governments sent military support to Habyarimana. With Uganda widely believed to be supporting the RPF, the conflict was at risk of widening and escalating. However, action at the international level helped constrain it. The presidents of Uganda, Rwanda, and Tanzania meet in Dar Es Salaam and a ceasefire agreement was later signed on 26 October.

The RPF, having regrouped under the leadership of Paul Kagame, then made a second and more audacious attack on 23 January 1991, this time on Ruhengeri town where it liberated inmates from the central prison. In reprisal, the following day, local authorities again organized massacres targeting 500–1,000 Bagogwe, a Tutsi subgroup in north-west Rwanda. The war escalated. International intervention provided restraint again, however, as the OAU, regional heads of state, and the United Nations High Commission for Refugees (UNHCR) convened a summit in Dar Es Salaam in February 1991 to discuss the refugee problem. It led to the RPF agreeing a ceasefire and the government of Rwanda releasing 3,500 Tutsi detainees the following month. The conflict de-escalated.

The conflict heated up again, however, in March 1992 when 277 Tutsi civilians were massacred in the southern region of Bugesera, again with the involvement of local authorities. At the same time, a campaign involving bombs and mines placed in civilian areas was initiated. The RPF was most likely behind it (Guichaoua, 2015, p. 67). In June 1992, the RPF launched another offensive, this time in Byumba. International intervention de-escalated the situation again, however. Under western diplomatic pressure, the government entered formal peace talks with the RPF in Arusha in July 1992 and another ceasefire was agreed. The negotiations led to agreement on a first protocol relating to the rule of law in August 1992 and then on a second protocol setting out a power-sharing arrangement between the government, the RPF, and the opposition political parties in October 1992.

These steps forward in the peace process were short-lived, however. Following an amendment to the power-sharing protocol in January 1993, several hundred Tutsi civilians were again massacred in the north of the country. The RPF responded by launching a major offensive in February that came within 30 km of Kigali and that displaced nearly one million Rwandans. The move dramatically shifted the balance-of-power in favour of the rebels. Notwithstanding the ceasefire violation, the peace process continued and culminated in the signature of the Arusha Accords in August 1993. UNAMIR began deployment in November 1993 and this ceasefire held until Habyarimana's assassination in April 1994.

In short, each of the four major RPF military offensives during the war – October 1990, January 1991, June 1992, and February 1993 – were either immediately followed or preceded by the targeting of Tutsi civilians. Hard-line actions from both sides – RPF ceasefire violations and Tutsi reprisal killings – escalated the conflict. External interventions, in contrast, de-escalated it.

Inter- to Intra-group contestation
Three pivotal events exemplify how this between-group contestation in turn shaped within-group dynamics. First, the formal opening of the Arusha peace talks in July 1992 between the RPF and the government divided the ruling party into hardliner and moderate factions. Hardliners advocated continued military confrontation. Moderates believed that power-sharing with the RPF was conceivable. Second, the major RPF military offensive in February 1993 fractured the main opposition parties into pro-RPF and anti-RPF factions that respectively favoured and rejected continued peace negotiations. The offensive was a decisive moment in the civil war as it confirmed for many that the RPF was intent on military victory and its commitments at the negotiating table could not be trusted. Third, the conclusion of the Arusha Accords in August 1993 legally bound the ruling party and the army to the terms of the power-sharing and armed forces protocols. It widened the division within the MRNDD and the FAR between those who believed the peace agreement should be disregarded and those who wanted it implemented. In all three instances, within-group divisions expanded even though the inter-group interaction in the first and third cases had been conciliatory in character and confrontational in the second. Within-group radicalization resulted from both escalatory *and* de-escalatory actions between groups.

Intra to Inter-group contestation
Within-group contestation in turn drove the between-group contestation. The hardliner-moderate fractures that emerged in first the ruling party and then the main opposition parties confirmed the RPF's distrust in the peace process. They also weakened the government. The schism within the ruling party put Habyarimana in a difficult position. He had to hold his party together at the national level and at the same time maintain his diplomatic commitment to a peaceful resolution of the conflict at the international level. As a result, his public speeches

vacillated between support and disavowal of the Arusha process. On 26 October 1992, four days before the signing of the protocol on power-sharing, Habyarimana affirmed his commitment to Arusha. Sixteen days following the protocol's promulgation, in a speech in Ruhengeri, he then described it as a 'scrap of paper'. Nineteen days following this speech, Habyarimana then re-affirmed his support for Arusha. This oscillation naturally gave the RPF reason to doubt Habyarimana's willingness and ability to honour any peace deal and made a military resolution more likely. It also encouraged the RPF to foment and exploit divisions within its politically weakened opponent. Similarly, the formal split and creation of 'Power' factions within the MDR, PSD, PL, and PDC in October 1993, just a week after Ndadaye's assassination, disrupted the implementation of Arusha. Factions fought over who would fill positions in the Transitional Government. The resulting deadlock, which persisted right up until April 1994, increased the prospects of a military resolution to the conflict.

Explaining Escalation: Weak Constraints and High Impunity
Why then did these inter- and intra-group interactions lead to escalation rather than de-escalation of the conflict? As the event timeline in Figure 4.1 shows, moderate actions also occurred – sometimes nearly simultaneously with more radical actions – but the conflict nonetheless escalated. In my theory of contestation, conflict escalates in the absence of external domestic and international constraints to contain it. At the domestic level, each of the major episodes of violence against Tutsi civilians – in October 1990, January to February 1991, March 1992, and January 1993 – represented significant moments of escalation in the conflict. However, Rwanda's state institutions – notably its gendarmerie and judiciary – failed to hold to account those responsible for inciting or tolerating the killings. The Catholic Church, the institution with the greatest moral weight in Rwanda, in its pastoral letters issued during the war failed to mention the massacres, let alone condemn those responsible for it. And Radio Rwanda, the official government broadcaster, instead of calming ethnic tensions, incited the violence in Bugesera by falsely propagating rumours that Tutsi were plotting to kill Hutu leaders. In short, Rwanda's state institutions and civil society offered little constraint. Extremists acted with near impunity.

At the international level, mediation both constrained and enabled the escalation of the conflict. Each of the major ceasefires agreed – in

October 1990, March 1991, August 1992, and March 1993 – represented important moments of de-escalation. Yet no intervention force capable of enforcing these ceasefires existed. UNAMIR did not deploy until November 1993 and was in any event unequal to the task of militarily restraining either side. The ceasefires were consequently violated – principally by the RPF – with impunity. Furthermore, the Arusha Accords, while ostensibly a major achievement in the peace process, in fact escalated the intra-group contestation within the government. Regime hardliners saw it as a victory gifted to the RPF.

The *intra*-group contestation between moderates and hardliners also escalated in the absence of external constraint. Separate factions within the opposition MDR and PL emerged and triggered leadership contests. Each faction claimed to be the rightful representative of the party. This in turn stymied the peace process. Agreement could not be reached on the appointment of deputies to the Transitional National Assembly (TNA) because each faction believed it held the power to nominate representatives. The disagreement could not be resolved by Rwanda's Constitutional Court, the appropriate state institution, because its president, Joseph Kavaruganda, was not perceived by hardliners as independent. He had openly switched his party allegiance from the MRNDD to the opposition MDR.

In sum, in the face of weak constraints and high impunity, hardliners both within the regime and among the rebels succeeded in escalating the war. In Chapter 5, I examine how the relative material capabilities of hardliners and moderates within the regime at the time of the president's assassination ensured the victory of the former. Extremist success at the national level meant that the outcome of the war would also turn on material coercive capabilities of each actor at the international level. The RPF proved to be stronger on the battlefield than the government.

Political Participation

The third and final effect of Rwanda's liberalization was to encourage Rwandans to participate more actively in political life. In particular, it facilitated the rise of a new class of challenger elites. These political and ethnic entrepreneurs would rival incumbents in their ability to mobilize the population. A radical sub-set of them and their supporters – 'critical masses' – would play an instrumental role in committing violence, and in mobilizing their communities during the genocide. Participation levels in Rwanda's new party politics were high. As mentioned, the country's small size and dense settlement contributed to this. A total of 74.6 per cent of my survey respondents stated that they supported a party. Many also attended party meetings. Table 4.2 shows that 52.9 per cent admitted to having attended such meetings in their communities. However, having known only single-party rule, few from Rwanda's post-independence generations had had experience in freely making individual political choices. The new legal freedoms had not had time to mature into a democratic political culture. The survey evidence indicates that many Rwandans still made choices that reflected their lack of knowledge of and experience with the democratic process. As Table 4.2 shows, only 26.3 per cent of respondents stated that they chose to support a party for its particular ideology or policies. The majority cited other reasons: the party's dominance, a sense of obligation to the party they have always known, a personal tie to someone in a party, or the necessity of joining a party to prevent being targeted. The desire to evaluate independently the merits of a party and its program reflected a minority viewpoint among respondents. In short, Rwanda's political culture reflected its old neo-patrimonial politics more than new democratic practices. In such a culture, patronage networks still prevailed over individual freedom of choice.

What changed, however, was the emergence of a new class of political and ethnic entrepreneurs also capable of mobilizing ordinary Rwandans. Political entrepreneurs, such as Rekeraho in Mwendo, were interested in exploiting the new opportunity to accrue personal power. Ethnic entrepreneurs, such as Karimunda in Tamba, were driven more by racist sentiment – ethnocentric interests. Sometimes these interests, power and race, converged, as with Harelimana in Mutovu. These entrepreneurs also did not act alone. They depended upon small bands of hardcore supporters within their communities. As we shall see in the next chapter, they drew these supporters from their social networks, calling upon family and friends to assist them. In Tamba, Karimunda would receive aid from his brother and his nephew. In Mutovu, Harelimana would co-opt a brother and several neighbours. It was a sub-set of these entrepreneurs and supporters, a radical minority, who would succeed in the power struggle to control the state in the vacuum created by Habyarimana's death. These

4.4 The Mechanisms of Liberalization

'critical masses' would form the backbone of attack groups during the genocide and would mobilize the rest of the population to participate as well.

* * * * *

Political liberalization, representing simultaneously a threat and opportunity, was the second factor, after the civil war, that contributed to the genocide. Liberalization involved political pluralization, competition, and participation whose effects were amplified against the unusual geographic and socio-demographic baseline Rwanda represented. Yet liberalization did not by itself ethnicize Rwandan politics. Contrary to existing accounts of the genocide that emphasize the widespread assimilation of racist or exclusionary ideology, at the outset ethnic extremism had minority support in Rwanda. Moderate, more inclusive political ideologies were in fact ascendant. Rwanda's public sphere was ideologically plural. Explanations that point to racist ideology overlook the diverse and even conflicting messages that competed for attention in Rwanda during the liberalization period. It was liberalization's unusual conjunction with the civil war, however, that gradually increased the popular salience of beliefs in historical Tutsi privilege, subjugation, and alien origin, relative to beliefs in an inclusive Rwandan identity, national unity, and non-discrimination. The contestation at the international level, between the government and rebels, interacted with the contestation at the national level, between the ruling and opposition parties. The outcome was the emergence of a moderate-hardliner schism *within* each of the domestic parties that in turn impacted the contestation *between* the government and rebels. In the absence of domestic and international constraints capable of containing the contestation, it escalated in favour of hardliners and military confrontation. While an extremist or racist ideology was a necessary condition for the genocide, it was not by itself sufficient to cause the violence. Its adherents were not destined to prevail. The intensifying security threat posed by the civil war and the absence of external constraints enabled their eventual triumph.

These findings have a number of implications. First, several commentators have argued that Rwanda represents a cautionary tale in promoting democratization as a strategy for ending civil wars (Clapham, 1998; Paris, 1997). The violence that followed appears to call into question the prevailing liberal international model for peacebuilding of a grand coalition followed by a transition period to national elections. But there is a crucial distinction in the case of Rwanda. Whereas power-sharing and transitional elections are envisaged to *follow* the conclusion of the peace agreement, liberalization in Rwanda began *before* the war ended. Opposition parties and, most consequentially, a coalition government were created *before* the Arusha accords were signed. The timing was in large part due to the wave of democratic movements washing across Africa following the end of the Cold War. The divisions within the coalition government between the opposition and ruling parties were all too evident at the negotiating table with the RPF and undermined faith on all sides in the ability of the peace process to deliver an agreement that would be honoured. Had the ruling party negotiated for itself and a coalition formed *subsequent* to the end of the war, the peace deal may have had more legitimacy.

Second, Rwanda's post-genocide regime points to the experience with democratization in the 1990s as the reason for its tight control over political space today. It cites the risk of the re-emergence of ethnic divisions and genocidal ideology. Yet I found liberalization initially encouraged the main parties to make cross-ethnic appeals to attract supporters from both sides of the ethnic divide. It was the war, in conjunction with the move to multipartyism, that escalated ethnic sentiments. The security threat was a critical contextual factor. More precisely, the absence of external constraint capable of containing the internal extremist-moderate contestation fomented by the war enabled the rise of ethnic extremism. Liberalization was destabilizing. However, the divisions were initially partisan, not ethnic.

Lastly, having argued that political *contestation* was central to the rise of ethnic extremism and the escalation toward military confrontation, it raises the question of when the genocide – a plan to eliminate the Tutsi in entirety – was first conceived. Conspiracy proponents point to earlier Tutsi massacres; the preparation of lists bearing Tutsi names; and the training of militia groups. Yet each of these facts is susceptible to an alternative plausible interpretation. Early Tutsi massacres may not have been part of a 'rehearsal' for the genocide (Des Forges, 1999, p. 70). The killings usually occurred in *response* to rebel military advances. Reprisal violence has deep roots in Rwanda's history, beginning with the *Inyenzi* attacks of the 1960s. Similarly, lists

4.4 The Mechanisms of Liberalization

may have been prepared not to eliminate individuals, but to monitor RPF supporters and regime opponents. In fact, the lists for whose existence there is evidence indicate that only certain Tutsi men or Tutsi 'intellectuals' were named. Tutsi women and children did not appear on them.[31] Lastly, militia may have been created not only to implement a genocide, but also as part of a civilian defence program to resist a rebel movement believed to be intent on outright military victory. Furthermore, as we shall see in the next chapter, the position of extremists in the ruling party, the military, and the civilian administration was far from dominant, even on the eve of 6 April 1994. They faced considerable resistance at the national and local levels. An extremist faction then could not be certain it would prevail and be able to implement a genocide. In all, I believe, as the International Criminal Tribunal for Rwanda (ICTR) also concluded, that the evidence does not clearly point to a conspiracy to commit genocide before 7 April 1994.

Contestation has a second implication: contingency. Both sides had opportunities to de-escalate the conflict. The RPF knew its military offensives, in violation of ceasefires, would deepen the divide between moderates and hardliners within the ruling and opposition parties. Hardliners similarly knew that attacks on Tutsi civilians would motivate the RPF to respond militarily. Yet both chose these escalatory actions. While primary responsibility for the genocide must lie with those who organized and executed it, hardliners on *both* sides were nonetheless culpable of undermining the peace process and pushing the country ever closer to the fateful military finale.

---

[31] See Prosecutor vs. Kajileli, ICTR 98-44-A, paragraphs 439–441.

5 Opportunity II: Death of the Nation's Father

5.1 Introduction

Juvénal Habyarimana's assassination on 6 April 1994 was the third and final macro-political factor, after the civil war and political liberalization, that pushed Rwanda to genocide. Habyarimana was one of twenty-eight presidents assassinated in office in sub-Saharan Africa since the end of colonial rule.[1] This number is not insignificant. It represents nearly 8 per cent of the region's 361 post-independence rulers.[2] However, two things distinguished Habyarimana's assassination. First, it was the assassination of – by far – the longest-serving post-independence ruler to be killed in office in sub-Saharan Africa. Habyarimana had held office for 7,580 days, four times longer than the average term of the others assassinated.[3] Second, the timing was special. The loss of the president's authority occurred in the midst of a period of unprecedented uncertainty in Rwanda. The regime faced simultaneously an external, military challenge from a rebel group, and an internal, political challenge from newly legal opposition parties. Not one other country in sub-Saharan Africa – bar Burundi – had experienced the conjunction of a civil war and political liberalization,

---

[1] See Table 5.1 for the list of the twenty-eight individuals killed in office. In constructing the dataset on assassinations, I am indebted to the compilers of the Rulers database (www.rulers.org) from where I drew the names and dates-in-office of the region's post-independence rulers.

[2] I included as rulers only those who held the highest national office and in whom state power was most concentrated. In practice, this meant that in twenty of the twenty-eight cases, the rulers were presidents of Republics. In four cases, they were prime ministers: Burundi in 1965, Nigeria in 1966, South Africa in 1966, and the Republic of Congo (Leopoldville) in 1960. South Africa and Burundi were not yet Republics, and in the Congo, upon independence in 1960, power was balanced between the prime minister and the president. In four cases, the countries were Republics (Ghana in 1978 and 1979, Nigeria in 1966 and Burkina Faso in 1987) but their military rulers did not take the title president.

[3] The average term of those assassinated in office was 1,866 days.

5.1 Introduction

with the assassination of the head of state. Their concurrence created an equally unprecedented political opportunity in Rwanda. Whereas political liberalization had created several, small, and incremental opportunities, Habyarimana's assassination created a single, sudden, and massive one.

Habyarimana was not simply deposed; he was physically eliminated. While his assassins' identities remain the subject of debate today, in Rwanda it was widely believed at the time that the RPF was responsible.[4] Both facts mattered. Had it instead been a coup from within, and Habyarimana removed but left alive, the genocide would likely not have happened.[5] The reason is this. The putschists would not have been able to command the elite military units and militia deployed to eliminate their moderate rivals and the Tutsi population in the capital if it was believed that they had betrayed Habyarimana. The commanders of the Presidential Guard, the Para-Commando and Reconnaissance battalions, as well as the leadership of the Interahamwe National Committee – collectively the core coercive power in Kigali – were all loyal to the president.[6] Were Habyarimana still alive, they would have taken orders from him. Habyarimana's assassination – and the belief that the RPF were responsible – were causally necessary for the extremists to capture the state and thereby carry out the genocide.

The president's assassination produced a power vacuum. Habyarimana had ruled Rwanda autocratically and uninterruptedly for nearly twenty-one years. In that time his persona had become synonymous with authority, and his ruling party synonymous with the state. In such a deeply entrenched autocratic and neo-patrimonial culture – as against a more institutionalized and democratic one – it was not

---

[4] RTLM, for instance, stated on 8 April 1994 'Not only do the facts point to the RPF being implicated in the assassination of Habyarimana, but they rushed, the RPF rushed, to restart the war and liquidate Hutu leaders like Kanyarwenge...'.
[5] While the genocide was unlikely to occur if Habyarimana had not been assassinated, the possibility cannot be ruled out entirely. If Habyarimana himself was intent on genocide, it then could have been accomplished without his death. Yet, at the same time, if Habyarimana were committed to genocide, the extremists logically would not then have needed to eliminate him.
[6] Majors Protais Mpiranya and Aloys Ntabakuze, commanders of the Presidential Guard and Para-Commando battalion respectively, were among the first individuals to visit the presidential residence to pay respects to the president's family the night of the plane crash (Guichaoua, 2015, p. 155).

obvious that succession would be determined through formal rules and processes. His death created political uncertainty and consequently an opportunity. An extremist faction exploited both to install a president of its choosing. To satisfy the appearance of following formal procedure, extremists also manufactured legal ambiguity. They argued that Rwanda's 1991 constitution, not the 1993 Arusha peace accord, governed Habyarimana's succession. They could do so because the timing of his assassination was special. Rwanda was in the midst of a political transition. The civil war and political liberalization had resulted in a power-sharing deal brokered just eight months earlier between the ruling party, the rebel group, and main opposition parties. However, it was unclear whether the transition phase envisaged under Arusha had formally begun and it was consequently debatable whether the Arusha Accords were the applicable legal regime to govern Habyarimana's succession. In fact, as Table 5.1 shows, the unusual timing of Habyarimana's death created a political opportunity that had no parallel in the continent's history. Rarely has a head of state been killed during both a civil war and a move to democratize. And not one has been assassinated in the window between the formal settlement of the war and the start of the post-war transition arrangement.

This unusual political opportunity played out in the following way. The political uncertainty created by the Chief Executive's assassination triggered a power struggle. In the absence of external constraints, the struggle escalated. Almost immediately, extremists organized strategically targeted assassinations, began killing Tutsi civilians, and installed an unlawful civilian government. Yet, inside Rwanda, the state's security institutions neither protected civilians nor apprehended the killers. Elements of the Presidential Guard and other battalions were in fact complicit in the killing. Outside Rwanda, the international community failed to acknowledge the ethnic character of the killings or to attribute responsibility for them initially. It also failed to denounce the new, unconstitutional extremist government. Extremists then acted with impunity.

In the absence of external constraints domestically or internationally, the power struggle resolved according to the relative capabilities of each party. At home, neither moderates nor extremists were in an advantageous position in terms of their political power at the outset. Both controlled important positions in the civilian and military state apparatus. However, extremists held the advantage in terms of

Table 5.1 Assassinations of African (sub-Saharan) heads of state in context

Country	Name	Entry in Office	Exit from office	Term (days)	Democratic transition?	Civil war ongoing?[1]
Rwanda	Juvénal Habyarimana	5 Jul 1973	6-Apr-1994	7580	Yes	Yes
Burkina Faso	Thomas Sankara	4 Aug 1983	15 Oct 1987	1533	No	No
Burundi	Melchior Ndadaye	10 Jul 1993	21 Oct 1993	103	Yes	No
Burundi	Cyprien Ntaryamira	5 Feb 1994	6 Apr 1994	60	Yes	Yes
Burundi	Pierre Ngendandumwe	7 Jan 1965	15 Jan 1965	8	No	No
Chad	François Tombalbaye	11 Aug 1960	13 Apr 1975	5358	No	Yes
Comoros	Ali Soilih[2]	3 Jan 1976	13 May 1978	861	No	No
Comoros	Ahmed Abdallah	3 Oct 1978	27 Nov 1989	4073	No	No
Congo-Brazz	Marien Ngouabi	1 Jan 1969	18 Mar 1977	2998	No	No
Eq. Guinea	Francisco Nguema[2]	12 Oct 1968	3 Aug 1979	3947	No	Yes
Ethiopia	Aman Mikael Andom	12 Sep 1974	17 Nov 1974	66	No	Secessionist
Ethiopia	Tafari Benti	28 Nov 1974	3 Feb 1977	798	No	Secessionist
Ghana	Ignatus Acheampong[2]	13 Jan 1972	5 Jul 1978	2365	No	No
Ghana	Fred Akuffo[2]	5 Jul 1978	4 Jun 1979	334	No	No
Guinea-Biss	Joao Bernardo Vieira	1 Oct 2005	2 Mar 2009	1248	No	No
Liberia	William R. Tolbert, Jr.	23 Jul 1971	12 Apr 1980	3186	No	No
Liberia	Samuel K. Doe	12 Apr 1980	9 Sep 1990	3802	No	Yes
Madagascar	Richard Ratsimandrava	5 Feb 1975	11 Feb 1975	6	No	No
Mozambique	Samora Moise Machel	25 Jun 1975	19 Oct 1986	4134	No	Yes
Niger	Ibrahim Maïnassara	7 Aug 1996	9 Apr 1999	975	No	No

Table 5.1 (*cont.*)

Country	Name	Entry in Office	Exit from office	Term (days)	Democratic transition?	Civil war ongoing?[1]
Nigeria	Abubakar Balewa	1 Oct 1960	15 Jan 1966	1932	Yes	No
Nigeria	Johnson Aguiyi-Ironsi	16 Jan 1966	29 Jul 1966	194	No	No
Nigeria	Murtala Mohammed	29 Jul 1975	13 Feb 1976	199	No	No
Somalia	Abdirashid Shermarke	10 Jun 1967	15 Oct 1969	858	No	No
South Africa	Hendrik F. Verwoerd	3 Sep 1958	6 Sep 1966	2925	No	No
Togo	Sylvanus Olympio	27 Apr 1960	13 Jan 1963	991	No	No
Zaire/DRC	Laurent Kabila	17 May 1997	16 Jan 2001	1340	No	Yes
Zaire/DRC.	Patrice Lumumba[3]	24 Jun 1960	5 Sep 1960	73	Yes	Secessionist

[1] I distinguish civil wars for control of the state from secessionist wars where rebels seek a separate state.
[2] Ali Soilih, Francisco Macias Nguema, Ignatus Kutu-Acheampong and Fred Akuffo were all first deposed and subsequently executed within the year.
[3] Lumumba was executed 134 days after his dismissal as prime minister. The legality of his dismissal, however, is contested.
Source: Author-compiled dataset. Data on terms in office come from the Rulers database: www.rulers.org

5.1 Introduction

coercive power. They controlled superior forces in the security apparatus. They used them to eliminate moderate rivals and to kill Tutsi civilians. As before, the within-group contestation drove the between-group contestation. The RPF responded by re-engaging the war. It also imposed conditions for a ceasefire that moderates on the opposing side could not possibly fulfil. The between-group contestation then also drove the within-group contestation. The RPF decision to resolve the conflict on the battlefield undermined the moderates' position in the opposing side. At the international level, the constraints were also weak. The Security Council did not act until too late and the United Nations Assistance Mission in Rwanda (UNAMIR) lacked the capability to enforce Arusha. The between-group contestation at the international level would again turn on the relative coercive capabilities between parties. Ultimately, the RPF proved militarily superior on the battlefield.

At the local level, the window of opportunity was exploited in one of two ways. First, in areas where extremists controlled the state as prefects or burgomasters, they used the state's authority and resources to mobilize the population. Violence was immediate. In some localities, the violence even pre-dated the resolution of the power struggle at the national level and extremists' capture of the centre. Second, where extremists did *not* already control the state, racists and opportunists (ethnic and political entrepreneurs) from within society – some of whom had emerged earlier in Rwanda's transition to multiparty politics – arose and either replaced or co-opted the moderate resisters in these communities. This power struggle took time to resolve and the violence in these communities was delayed. Violence, however, was not the outcome of only elite contestation. In communities where inter-ethnic integration was high, violence was also delayed as it took time to break these social bonds and to divide the population.

To mobilize the population, these violence entrepreneurs employed two tactics to great effect. First, they relied on small bands of hardcore supporters in their individual communities to catalyse the violence. These 'critical masses' often comprised supporters drawn from family members, friends, or neighbours: individuals tied to them through dense social networks. These radical minorities initiated the looting, property destruction, and violence. Second, the entrepreneurs also used these small groups to police the wider population. They enforced participation at the beginning, coercing would-be bystanders through physical, financial, and social sanctions. While coercion jump-started the violence initially, Rwandans quickly adapted to the new circumstances and opportunity. Many would develop other motives for participating. These, I argue, were the micro-mechanics of mass mobilization in Rwanda.

The chapter is structured as follows. In section 5.2, I describe what happened in the window of opportunity created by Habyarimana's death at the macro, meso, and micro-levels. In section 5.3, I then analyse the factors that emerged from these descriptions that I believe explain the rapid and massive mobilization in communities across Rwanda. The final section 5.4 explains the links between this extraordinary mobilization and the country's extraordinary socio-demography and geography.

5.2 The Window of Opportunity

I present several levels of analysis in the description of events that followed Habyarimana's assassination. As in Chapter 4, the focus is primarily on the micro-perspective, but I also embed these micro-events within events first at the macro- (international and national) level and then at the meso- (prefecture and commune) level.

Macro-level Analysis

I begin by weaving several sources together to establish a detailed sequence of events at the national level.[7] At 8.25pm on 6 April 1994, two surface-to-air missiles were fired at the presidential plane coming in to land at Kigali airport. One made its mark, killing both Habyarimana and President Ntaryamira of Burundi. Habyarimana's sudden death created a power vacuum in Rwanda. This was the unusual political opportunity that is the subject of this chapter. Over the course of the next two weeks, several critical decisions occurred in the space of that opportunity that set the country on the path to genocide.

Within-Group Contestation
The first critical decision was the initiation of a power struggle for control of the state's civilian and military apparatus. The contestation involved loyalists and hardliners on the one hand, determined to

---
[7] The national-level narrative draws on accounts by Booh-Booh (2005); Dallaire and Beardsley (2004); Des Forges (1999); Guichaoua (2015).

5.2 The Window of Opportunity

avenge Habyarimana's death and to avoid sharing power with the RPF; and moderates on the other, keen to avert renewed military confrontation. These factions existed within both the civilian and military echelons of the state. The struggle began less than an hour following Habyarimana's assassination. At 9pm, at an informal meeting of the FAR High Command, the *Directeur de Cabinet* at the Ministry of Defence, Colonel Bagosora attempted to impose military rule and to appoint his man, Augustin Bizimungu, for the now-vacant position of army chief-of-staff. He was rebuffed on both counts by the moderate faction on the High Command. Marcel Gatsinzi, a southerner from Butare, was appointed by virtue of his seniority, over Bizimungu, a northerner from Byumba. This moderate faction, supported by UNAMIR Force Commander Roméo Dallaire who arrived at around 10.30pm, was clear that military rule would amount to a coup. They also made clear that the UN Special Representative, Jacques Booh-Booh, should be consulted. At his home at 11.30pm, Booh-Booh told Bagosora unequivocally that Arusha must be followed and that the prime minister, Agathe Uwilingiyimana, remained the legitimate head of government. He also advised Bagosora to convene the Mouvement Révolutionnaire National pour le Développement (et al Démocratie) (MRNDD) senior leadership as, under article 48 of the amended power-sharing protocol, a new president must be selected from the ruling party.

The next morning, 7 April, at 8.00am, the four most senior figures in the MRNDD, its president, Matthieu Ngirumpatse, its national-secretary, Joseph Nzirorera, and its two vice-presidents, Edouard Karemera and Ferdinand Kabegema, duly met with Bagosora and Ndindiliyimana. The meeting's minutes show the politicians: (i) believed the president's succession should be decided with the other political parties, but not with the current cabinet members as it included opposition party figures sympathetic to power-sharing with the RPF; and (ii) accepted Bagosora's plan to declare a 'state of emergency' and take 'exceptional measures' to allow the Forces Armées Rwandaises (FAR) to establish security and prevent the Rwandan Patriotic Front (RPF) from executing whatever plan it had.[8] However, two hours later at 10.00am, at the first formal meeting

---

[8] MCC meeting minutes of 8 April 994 available online as annex 65 of Guichaoua (2015): http://rwandadelaguerreaugenocide.univ-paris1.fr/wp-content/uploads/2010/01/Annexe_65.pdf. Accessed 1 September 2018.

of the FAR High Command, Bagosora's plan faced a setback. While members agreed to the creation of an interim 'Military Crisis Committee' (MCC), they opposed Bagosora's chairmanship of it because he was militarily retired and, as *Directeur de Cabinet,* a political appointee. Instead Major-General Augustin Ndindiliyimana, chief-of-staff of the gendarmerie, was appointed. The High Command also authorized a communiqué in which it publicly committed to continue with the Arusha peace process. What most present did not know, however, was that a series of strategic assassinations, carried out by the Presidential Guard, had already begun at 6.00am that morning. The most important victim was the moderate Mouvement Démocratique Républicain (MDR) prime minister, Agathe Uwilingiyimana. Her plan to address the nation and to establish her authority early that morning was scuppered when she was assassinated and the Belgian contingent of her UN bodyguard captured. The ten Belgian peacekeepers would be brutally murdered later that day. These assassinations had the effect of undermining the multiparty government's will to function – its ministers were understandably fearful – and convincing the international community to reconsider UNAMIR's mandate. The newly constituted MCC then formally convened at 7.00pm that evening where it re-affirmed the commitment to Arusha and discussed how to end the fighting with the RPF that had started at 4.00pm when the contingent stationed in Kigali broke out of their cantonment at the Conseil National Démocratique (CND) building.

The next day, 8 April, towards the end of the morning, the MCC met again. Its discussion now centred on how to end the civilian killings that had begun in Kigali the day before. Just before 1.00pm, the MCC also met with UNAMIR to discuss how to end the fighting with the RPF. The MCC, at least ostensibly, wanted to restore peace and security in the country. Meanwhile, Bagosora, in conjunction with the MRNDD's four senior leaders, had also organized a meeting of the political parties to select candidates for an interim government. However, all opposition party candidates were drawn from the 'Power factions' and Jean Kambanda of the MDR was chosen as the new prime minister. The MCC was presented with this *fait accompli* at a meeting in the late afternoon of 8 April. The minutes show that it was Matthieu Ngirumpatse who announced that the 1991 constitution, not the Arusha power-sharing protocol, should determine the president's succession.[9] The presidency would fall then to the president of the CND, Théodore Sindikubwabo, an elderly and politically weak figure, to take up the post. The RPF unsurprisingly decried the interim government (IG) as unlawful and a mere puppet. Yet, importantly, at the outset the IG attempted to stop the killings now underway across the country. On 10 April, President Sindikubwabo made a speech, broadcast on Radio Rwanda, directly appealing to Rwandans in which he made clear his opposition to the violence:

People of Rwanda, what therefore are we asking of you as your contribution? Your contribution is to understand that no one has the right to endanger the life of another person, or to seize or damage his property [...] Everybody must be the guardian of peace. The roadblocks which are not authorized by the authorities must disappear immediately [...] Once again we denounce and publicly condemn those who have attacked other people and those who are still harbouring ill feelings.[10]

Between 10–12 April, its members went on a 'pacification tour', albeit unsuccessfully, of Kigali to try to stop the militia groups who had erected roadblocks and were targeting Tutsi. It was not until 12 April when the IG relocated to Gitarama and with violence now occurring across the country that its members appeared to reverse their position and accept the killing of Tutsi civilians. Calls to stop the violence are conspicuous by their ambivalence, ambiguity, or absence in the various speeches, written directives, and correspondence made by members of the IG from that point on. The IG then used its *de jure* authority to co-opt, coerce, or replace local authorities opposed to the genocide. By 17 April all resistant burgomasters and prefects had been eliminated. President Sindikubwabo then led another 'pacification tour' whose purpose this time was to encourage the population to mobilize against their Tutsi neighbours in the south. At this point, the moderates had lost the power struggle. The civilian apparatus state had been captured at the national and local levels. Extremist control of the military was achieved shortly thereafter. The army's interim chief-of-staff, Marcel Gatsinzi, was replaced on 18 April by hardliner Augustin Bizimungu.

---

[9] MCC meeting minutes of 8 April 994 available online as annex 65 of Guichaoua (2015): http://rwandadelaguerreaugenocide.univ-paris1.fr/wp-content/uploads/2010/01/Annexe_65.pdf. Accessed 1 September 2018.

[10] Exhibit D350C, Prosecutor v. Nyiramasuhuko et al., ICTR 98-42-T.

Analysis of these events reveals a similar pattern of intra-group contestation as before the assassination: a sequence of escalatory and de-escalatory actions undertaken by competing elite factions. Moderates attempt to place their people in positions of authority and make public commitments to peace, power-sharing, and protection of (Tutsi) civilians from violence. Extremists similarly manoeuvre for position and, covertly, assassinate their rivals and organize civilian killings. Figure 5.1 provides a graphical chronology of these escalatory (shaded boxes) and de-escalatory (white boxes) actions. It again distinguishes between intra- and inter-group contestation. As before, the contestation escalated in the absence of external constraint. Rwanda's security institutions failed to stop the violence or to apprehend the killers. To the contrary, the Presidential Guard and the Para-Commando and Reconnaissance battalions were deeply implicated in the killing. Rwanda's judicial institutions also failed to mediate the contestation for positional advantage. Extremists deliberately created legal ambiguity over whether the 1991 constitution or the 1993 Arusha accord should govern the president's succession. No one foresaw the situation of the president having been sworn in but the Transitional National Assembly (TNA) and the Broad-Based Transitional Government (BBTG) not in place. It was not clear then whether the country had formally entered Arusha's transition phase. However, there was no ambiguity in the illegality of installing an entirely new government. The assassinations of the president, prime minister, and three ministers did not prevent the continuity of the state constitutionally. Sixteen of nineteen ministers and the prime minister designate under Arusha, Faustin Twigaramungu, were still alive. Installation of the IG then amounted to a coup.[11] Yet Rwanda's Constitutional Court was not given the opportunity to adjudicate on the legality of the president's succession or the establishment of a new government. The court's president, Joseph Kavaruganda, had openly declared his allegiance to the opposition MDR and was among the first to be assassinated on 7 April. At the international level, no government denounced the new president or new government. The extremists' delegation was in fact permitted to continue to represent Rwanda at the United Nations. In the absence of external constraints on the extremists' actions, the contestation would

---

[11] Only ten of the nineteen ministerial portfolios were given to new individuals. Nine continued in office from before.

5.2 The Window of Opportunity 189

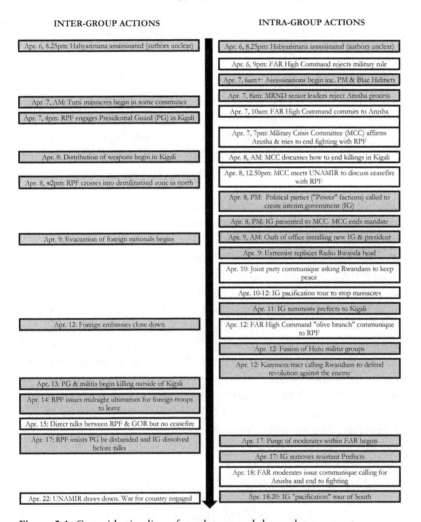

Figure 5.1 Genocide timeline of escalatory and de-escalatory events

resolve in accordance with their capabilities relative to those of the moderates.

Yet neither extremists nor moderates had an obvious positional advantage in either the civilian or military apparatuses of state immediately after Habyarimana's death. Moderates held ten of nineteen ministries; were ascendant in the FAR High Command; controlled the post of chief-of-staff of the armed forces; commanded about 4,000 troops in Kigali, and had the support of UNAMIR. In contrast, hardliners held nine ministries, including the Ministry of Defence under Augustin Bizimana (though he was out of the country at the time); and enjoyed the loyalty of the Presidential Guard under Protais Mpiranya, the Para-Commando battalion under Aloys Ntabakuze, the Reconnaissance battalion under François-Xavier Nzuwonemeye, and the militia groups. Their political power was relatively equal. Extremists, however, had a clear advantage in terms of their coercive, material power. The Presidential Guard and Para-Commando and Reconnaissance battalions loyal to the extremists together comprised about 2,000 elite, frontline-capable, combat soldiers who also possessed heavy weaponry. The security forces under the command of the moderates, in contrast, comprised a lightly armed gendarmerie battalion, two military police battalions, two logistics battalions, and an artillery battalion. They were no match for the extremists' forces.

This intra-group contestation also reinforces, once more, the contingent and uncertain nature of the event sequence leading up to the genocide. It again raises the question of when the decision to execute a nationwide genocide was made. Initial actions suggest that the immediate priority was to avenge Habyarimana and to prevent a coalition government involving the RPF. Those assassinated were all individuals who had either previously crossed Habyarimana or who supported power-sharing.[12] Moreover, the IG in fact attempted to stop the killing of Tutsi up until 11–12 April. While these actions do not rule out the possibility of a long-premeditated genocidal plan to eliminate the Tutsi population in entirety, it was far from clear before 12 April whether such a plan could have been executed given moderates' formal control of the military high command and the initial uncertainty over the IG's willingness to allow the killing of civilians (Guichaoua, 2015, pp. 219, 236). However, at some point within the first few days, a small group of extremists, coordinated by Bagosora,

---

[12] Those assassinated included Agathe Uwilingiyimana, (Prime Minister, MDR, Hutu); Joseph Kavaruganda (President of the Constitutional Court, MDR, Hutu); Boniface Ngulinzira (GOR negotiator at Arusha, MDR, Hutu); Frederic Nzamurambaho (Minister of Agriculture, PSD, Hutu); Faustin Rucogoza (Minister of Information, MDR, Hutu); Landoald Ndasingwa (Minister of Labour, PL, Tutsi); Félicien Ngango (President-designate TNA, PSD, Hutu); and Vénantie Kabageni (Alternative President-designate TNA, PL, Tutsi).

the senior MRNDD party leaders, and several loyal military officers, committed to genocide and manoeuvred to take control of first the civilian state apparatus by installing on 9 April a new interim government, and ultimately the military apparatus with the replacement of moderate Marcel Gatsinzi as army chief-of-staff on 18 April.

Between-Group Contestation
The second critical decision was to restart the civil war. It is unclear which party first broke the ceasefire, in place since February 1993. Kagame called Dallaire at 2.00pm on 7 April from RPF headquarters in the north, warning him that he will move if the killing of civilians in Kigali did not stop by sunset or if the RPF contingent at the CND in Kigali were attacked. Neither condition was met. FAR, for its part, stated implausibly that it was facing a mutiny. It claimed that 'rogue elements' of the Presidential Guard and Para-Commando and Reconnaissance battalions, acting out of grief and anger for Habyarimana's assassination, no longer responded to the chain-of-command. It is very doubtful, however, whether the assassinations of prominent political figures would have occurred without high-level authorization. At about 4.00pm, Dallaire brokered a phone call between Seth Sendashonga of the RPF, and Bagosora and Ndindiliyimana in a final, unsuccessful attempt to prevent the war from restarting. However, at 4.30pm, following sustained direct fire, the RPF contingent in Kigali broke out of the CND and engaged the Presidential Guard. The following day, 8 April, at around 2.00pm, Kagame's northern forces crossed into the demilitarized zone (DMZ).[13] The ceasefire was over.

Various efforts to broker a new ceasefire failed in the face of intransigence by both the RPF and regime hardliners. Earlier on 8 April, Dallaire met with the RPF at the CND where the RPF restated its preconditions for negotiations. These included the disarming and arrest of the Presidential Guard – a condition that was infeasible given the lack of FAR units in Kigali capable of doing so – and an end to the civilian slaughter. On 12 April, FAR's moderate faction, led by Leonard Rusatira and Marcel Gatsinzi, then signed a communiqué

---

[13] Dallaire, as UNAMIR force commander, received situation reports from his Military Liaison Observers stationed in the DMZ in the north. They informed him of the time Kagame's forces crossed into the DMZ (Dallaire & Beardsley, 2004, p. 269).

asking to meet with the RPF and offering a unilateral ceasefire the following day, a promise it clearly could not keep.[14] A meeting nonetheless took place on 15 April where the RPF refused to budge on its preconditions and while the regime's extremists refused to rein in their forces committing atrocities. Gatsinzi tried once more to establish peace by writing a letter to Booh-Booh on 17 April and signing another communique on 18 April calling for an end to combat and the installation of the BBTG.[15] These actions, viewed as a betrayal by extremists, resulted in his removal as army chief-of-staff on 18 April, marking the end of any moderate resistance within the military. Subsequent meetings between both sides on 18 April in Kigali and then on 23 April in Arusha, as part of the peace process (where the GOR delegation fails to show up), achieved nothing. It was clear that hardliners on both sides were intent on a military outcome. The war continued as the RPF's pincer attack, simultaneously advancing from the north and east, pushed FAR forces slowly towards Kigali for a major confrontation. Following a prolonged battle beginning on 4 May, the capital finally fell to the RPF on 4 July.

Analysis of these events again reveals how the intra-group contestation – the power struggle between moderates and extremists in the civilian and military spheres – once again helped drive the between-group contestation. Extremist success in installing a civilian interim government, composed of individuals opposed to power-sharing, unsurprisingly resulted in its rejection by the RPF who made its dissolution a condition for ending combat. Similarly, within the military, the inability of moderates to control the Presidential Guard and Para-Commando and Reconnaissance battalions who were carrying out systematic assassinations and civilian massacres, led to the RPF making their disarmament and arrest another precondition for ceasefire negotiations. The RPF went so far as to offer to send two battalions to assist FAR moderates in containing the allegedly rogue extremist units. This level of cooperation would have required an improbable

---

[14] Communiqués of the FAR and Army chief-of-staff of 12, 17 and 18 April 1994, available online as annex 71 of Guichaoua (2015): rwandadelaguerreaugenocide.univ-paris1.fr/the-communiques-of-the-rwandan-armed-forces-and-the-army-chief-of-staff-of-12-17-and-18-april-1994/. Accessed 2 September 2018.

[15] See note 14.

degree of trust given the risk that the enemy's battalions could subsequently be used to seize the capital.

As with the moderate-extremist contestation within the regime, the absence of external constraints permitted the escalation of the between-group contestation involving the RPF and the government. UNAMIR did not have the forces to disarm either side and Dallaire had been ordered by the Department of Peacekeeping Operations (DPKO) in New York not to take the side of any one faction within the government. Rwanda's security institutions also failed to stop the civilian slaughter. Moreover, as we shall see in the next section, the lengthy inaction and silence at the international level in the face of atrocities did nothing to deter the extremists. In the absence of external constraint, the situation would again turn on the relative capabilities of the parties. The RPF proved to be the stronger party.

Dynamics at the International Level
The third critical decision was that of the international community in response to the violence. Its prolonged inaction and belated recognition of genocide worked to the extremists' advantage. Its first response was decisive, however: evacuate expatriates. On 9 April, with remarkable speed, the first of a force of what would become 1,400 elite Belgian and French troops landed in Kigali and began the removal of foreign civilians. The evacuation was complete by 12 April. With fewer diplomats, journalists, aid workers, and other foreign nationals on the ground, there would be fewer eyes and ears to report and record the extremists' actions and to mobilize public opinion internationally. Next, the UN Security Council, following protracted deliberation, chose to weaken instead of reinforce UNAMIR. Between 7 April and 21 April, the Security Council took no action. Members disagreed over what to do. Their disagreement centred primarily over whether to withdraw UNAMIR and, if so, how many peacekeepers to leave behind. The question of *strengthening* the mission to protect Rwandan civilians was raised only by Nigeria (Des Forges, 1999, p. 479). In the interim, the UN's Department of Peacekeeping Operations limited UNAMIR's rules of engagement. On 7 April Kofi Annan, its head, verbally instructed Dallaire that UNAMIR should only fire if fired upon (Dallaire & Beardsley, 2004). Yet its formal rules of engagement permitted 'necessary action to prevent crimes against humanity' and to use 'all available means' to halt 'ethnically and politically motivated

criminal acts'.[16] On 13 April, Belgium then officially announced the withdrawal of its contingent of 440 peacekeepers. If the murder of the ten Belgian peacekeepers was a calculated tactic, it paid off. The Belgian peacekeepers represented the backbone of the force and their departure jeopardized the entire mission. Willy Klaes, Belgium's foreign minister, in fact lobbied other Security Council members for a full withdrawal. On 15 April, the US announced that it concurred. Eventually, on 21 April, the UN Security Council adopted resolution 921, which would leave a token force of 270 on the ground to help mediate a ceasefire. As it turned out, Dallaire would retain 454 of the original 2,500 odd blue helmets of UNAMIR. It was a number hopelessly unequal to the task of protecting civilians in Kigali, let alone elsewhere in the country. Yet the presence of even these few peacekeepers would save the lives of the thousands who sought refuge with them.

Anti-Tutsi Violence
The fourth critical decision was to begin targeting the Tutsi civilian population. The killing began as soon as the morning of 7 April. The violence, however, did not begin in Kigali and then radiate outwards as has been sometimes suggested. Simultaneously, in multiple locations across the country – not only the capital – Tutsi and moderate Hutu became the targets of violence. As we will see, at the local level both extremist control of the state apparatus and the strength of inter-ethnic relations determined when violence broke out across Rwanda's 145 communes. The violence, however, did not become a *nation-wide* extermination campaign until 12 April when the new IG ended its 'pacification tour' of Kigali and relocated to Gitarama. Over the next hundred or so days, this campaign would involve not only soldiers, gendarmes, and militia, but in many instances ordinary Rwandans. The RPF stopped the killing as it advanced, but for most Tutsi they arrived too late. The bulk of the killing occurred within the first two weeks.

As the war intensified and the government army was forced to retreat, on 23 June a French intervention force entered Rwanda

[16] See *International Decision-Making in the Age of Genocide: Rwanda Briefing Book, Vol. 2–73*, compiled by the National Security Archive at George Washington University for the Critical Oral History Conference, The Hague, 2014. Available online nsarchive2.gwu.edu/ageofgenocide/. Accessed 15 August 2018.

5.2 The Window of Opportunity

through its western border with Zaire. The stated goal of Operation Turquoise was to protect the civilian population. In fact, the operation had a military as well as a humanitarian objective. President Mitterand wanted to prevent a total RPF victory. Ultimately, when the reality of the atrocities committed became apparent to forces on the ground, France chose not to engage the RPF. It withdrew its forces from the north-west where the extremist government was located and instead established a safe zone in the south-west of the country. On 4 July, the RPF captured Kigali. Two weeks later, on 17 July, they took Gisenyi in the north-west and the extremist government, the army, and militia, accompanied by several hundred thousand Hutu civilians crossed the border into Zaire.[17] The civil war was effectively over, the genocide had been stopped, and the rebels were now in charge.

Analysis of the violence suggests complexity in its immediate origins and subsequent trajectory. It was neither *entirely* state-initiated nor *entirely* state-directed. The violence did not spread from the centre to the periphery. Rather, it was instigated by extremists in various locations across the country. As we shall see, some of these persons did hold state office. However, others held no official position. Sometimes party loyalists, sometimes political opportunists, these individuals emerged from within *society* and then moved to capture the *state* and appropriate its authority locally. In Kibungo prefecture, for instance, the violence began on 7 April. Yet Kibungo's prefect, Godefroid Rusindana, who belonged to the PSD and opposed the violence, was not removed until 17 April and subsequently killed. By this time, however, all twelve of Kibungo's communes were already engulfed in violence. So, anti-Tutsi violence began early despite the opposition of its highest-ranking state official. In Kibungo, the pressure for violence did not originate from the top.

The origination of violence in multiple locations *before* extremists had captured the centre suggests pressure from below in addition to direction from above. The extremist elite itself recognized the existence of popular pressure for violence. In a speech broadcast on Radio Rwanda on 19 April, Froduald Karamira, a senior figure in the MDR 'Power' faction, attempted to distinguish between legitimate and illegitimate targets:

---

[17] For maps tracing the advance of the RPF over time, see Des Forges (1999, pp. 692–693).

Our position is that no one who is not guilty of a crime should be victimized because of his ethnicity. In fact, the population has respected our instructions but unfortunately in some cases people overreacted. People may overreact when faced with unexpected situations.[18]

This early violence was limited in its geographic ambit. The killing only became nationwide *after* the centre fell to extremists. Genocide then became state policy and the state's symbolic authority and material capabilities then weaponized to deadly effect.

What Was Known Outside Rwanda?
The international community has been widely criticized for failing to recognize the violence for what it was and to denounce its perpetrators in time. The UN Security Council conspicuously avoided characterizing the violence as organized and ethnic in nature, let alone as genocide, for the first *three* weeks. Concern for the legal and moral obligations of invoking the term 'genocide' was high. It instead portrayed the violence as part of a civil war (Des Forges, 1999, p. 635). Yet Dallaire and Booh-Booh had both informed DPKO of the deliberate targeting of Tutsi civilians almost immediately. Dallaire's cable of 8 April read, in capitals:

The appearance of a very well planned, organized, deliberate, and conducted campaign of terror initiated principally by the Presidential Guard since the morning after the death of the head of state has completely reoriented the situation in Kigali. Aggressive actions have been taken not only against the opposition leadership but against the RPF (by firing at the CND), against particular ethnic groups (massacre of Tutsi in Remera) [...][19]

Booh-Booh's cable to Annan the following day read 'As many as thousands may have lost their lives. This cannot be verified in our present situation. But the killings are continuing in government-controlled areas. The victims are mostly Tutsis and Hutus from the south from non-MRND/CDR political parties.'[20] Dallaire sent an even

---

[18] Exhibit P243B, Prosecutor vs. Karemera et al., ICTR 98-44-T.
[19] *Supra International Decision-Making in the Age of Genocide: Rwanda Briefing Book*, Vol. 2–127.
[20] Exchange of cables between Booh-Booh/Dallaire and DPKO, available online as annex 77 of Guichaoua (2015): rwandadelaguerreaugenocide.univ-paris1.fr/wp-content/uploads/2010/01/Annexe_77.pdf Accessed 16 August 2018.

5.2 The Window of Opportunity

more explicit cable to the UN Secretariat on 17 April that read, again in capitals:

Ethnic cleansing continues and may in fact be accelerating. Behind RGF [Rwandan Government Forces] lines massacres of Tutsi and moderate Hutus and sympathizers with opposition parties is taking place. Bodies litter the streets and pose a significant health hazard.[21]

UNAMIR did not know in the first few days, however, that Tutsi massacres had already started outside of Kigali. Moreover, no one, other than the RPF, had suggested that genocide was being committed until 19 April when Human Rights Watch presented evidence to the Secretary-General. Nonetheless, in the first few days, the UN Secretariat had been presented with evidence that in Kigali at least (i) Tutsi were being targeted, possibly in their thousands; (ii) the targeting was organized; and (iii) it was happening in areas under the control of the IG. The Secretariat had also previously been told, in Dallaire's now infamous 'genocide fax' of 11 January 1994, that a trusted UNAMIR informant 'has been ordered to register all Tutsi in Kigali. He suspects it is for their extermination.'[22] While it was not evident that genocide was underway in the first two weeks, there was evidence at least of gross human rights violations, if not crimes against humanity.

Despite this evidence, the Security Council not only failed to acknowledge the organized and ethnic nature of the civilian killings, it refrained from holding anyone responsible for them. The Security Council's first resolution, on 21 April, stated that it was 'Appalled at the ensuing large-scale violence in Rwanda which has resulted in the death of thousands of innocent civilians, including women and children' (United Nations Security Council, 1994a). However, it did not suggest that the IG was responsible for these deaths or mention the ethnicity of those being killed. The Security Council, having accepted the 'civil war' frame provided by the UN Secretariat, instead believed that the priority was to broker a ceasefire. It did not want to take sides by condemning one party. It was not until 29 April that the organized and ethnic nature of the civilian violence was formally recognized as distinct from the civil war. The president of the Security Council issued

---

[21] *Supra International Decision-Making in the Age of Genocide: Rwanda Briefing Book*, Vol. 3–28.

[22] *Supra International Decision-Making in the Age of Genocide: Rwanda Briefing Book*, Vol. 2–75.

a statement indicating that 'the killing of members of an ethnic group with the intention of destroying such a group, in whole or in part, constitutes a crime punishable under international law'.[23] He also specified that the deaths were occurring in areas controlled by the IG. The language of the 1948 Genocide Convention then was invoked, though the word 'genocide' itself was avoided. On 17 May, the Security Council passed Resolution 918 to expand UNAMIR's mandate 'for humanitarian purposes' and authorized the deployment of 5,500 peacekeepers (United Nations Security Council, 1994b). It again warned that the killings might be crimes punishable under international law. However, it was not until 8 June that the Security Council finally adopted Resolution 925 that mentioned 'acts of genocide' and strengthened the mandate of UNAMIR II to include 'the protection of displaced persons, refugees, and civilians at risk' (United Nations Security Council, 1994c). It was too little, too late, however. Most of the killing had occurred in the first two weeks. It would take another month for the peacekeepers and resources needed to operationalize UNAMIR II even to reach Rwanda.

Could the International Community Have Done Anything?
Analyses of the role of external actors – the UN Security Council, the US, France, and Belgium in particular – have also generally asserted that they could have done more to stop or minimize the killing. The list of possibilities includes: (i) keep UNAMIR in place and expand its mandate to protect civilians; (ii) reinforce UNAMIR with 5,000 more peacekeepers; (iii) use the foreign evacuation force to contain the military units committing atrocities; (v) jam the radio signal of RTLM; and (vi) impose economic sanctions on the regime. Most of these claims have been assessed and challenged (Kuperman, 2001). The main counter-arguments have been: (i) the violence escalated too quickly and it was militarily infeasible to mobilize troops and material in time to reach Rwanda; (ii) UNAMIR lacked the manpower and munitions to protection civilians; (iii) the violence was also occurring outside of Kigali. While these counter-arguments have merit, my analysis points to two other plausible interventions.

---

[23] *Supra International Decision-Making in the Age of Genocide: Rwanda Briefing Book*, Vol. 5–147.

5.2 The Window of Opportunity

First, there existed a window of opportunity to strengthen the moderates' position and to isolate extremists – both civilian and military – in the first two weeks. The key to this would have been the resurrection of the lawful civilian government and international denunciation of the illegally formed interim government. Although established by extremists, the latter was not an irreversible *fait accompli*. Sixteen of the government's nineteen ministers were still alive as well as Faustin Twagarimungu, the prime minister designate, who was in fact already under UNAMIR's protection. The other moderate members of the government were in hiding. Had either UNAMIR or the Belgian component of the foreign evacuation force been instructed to find and protect these moderates, they could have established a seat of government either in Kigali or outside of Rwanda and asserted their executive authority in the first few days. Instead, Dallaire was instructed by UN DPKO not to promise security to a faction within one side as it risked compromising the UN's neutrality (Dallaire & Beardsley, 2004, p. 260). Had the lawful government been resurrected, the international community could have recognized its authority and also denounced the extremists' IG. Extremists' capture of the local civilian apparatus would then have been impeded as they would have lacked the legal authority to issue orders to prefects and burgomasters and to remove those who resisted. The lawful government would instead have issued orders. However, with orders emanating only from a single source – the IG – it left moderates in the military and at the local level little room for manoeuvre.

In fact, the UN Security Council *never* publicly stated that it did not recognize the IG, even after the Secretariat unequivocally learned from Dallaire's 17 April cable that 'ethnic cleansing' was occurring in areas controlled by it. To the contrary, it allowed the IG's representative to continue to occupy Rwanda's seat at the Security Council. Moreover, it is not naïve to think that extremists did not care whether external actors recognized the IG's legitimacy. The meeting minutes of the MCC and the IG show that the opinion of the international community was very important to them.[24] In fact, the IG would send multiple

---

[24] See schematic overview of IG activities in annex 97 of Guichaoua (2015), available online rwandadelaguerreaugenocide.univ-paris1.fr/schematic-overview-of-the-activities-of-the-interim-government-april-november-1994/. Accessed 15 September 2018.

delegations to foreign capitals to plead their position for the duration of the genocide.

With an alternative, lawful, internationally recognized civilian government in place early on, moderates within the FAR high command would then have been in a stronger position to challenge their extremist rivals for control of the military. Gatsinzi, as army chief-of-staff, would have received support to order the removal of the Para-Commando and Reconnaissance unit commanders who had allegedly gone rogue, denounce the actions of the renegade units in Kigali, and order the other army units in the capital that still followed the chain-of-command to protect civilians. These included two military-police battalions, two logistics battalions, one artillery battalion, and a gendarmerie battalion, representing about 4,000 men altogether in Kigali (Kuperman, 2001, p. 150). While it is unlikely that these forces could have contained the elite and better-equipped Presidential Guard and the Para-Commando and Reconnaissance battalions, who numbered about 2,000 altogether, there were combat battalions elsewhere in Rwanda – including two battalions that Gatsinzi had personally commanded in southern Rwanda, only three hours by road to the capital, and the Rebero battalion in Kigali-rural, less than two hours away. These units in fact were redeployed to Kigali later on, but only in response to the RPF's advance. Instead of the subordination of the unlawful IG to extremists in the military, it would have properly been the subordination of moderates in the military to a lawful civilian government.

Second, safe havens and safe passage could feasibly have been established. UNAMIR, with a symbolic force of only 454 blue helmets, protected tens of thousands of Rwandans in strategic locations across Kigali. The Amahoro stadium sheltered 20,000 civilians alone. In each of Rwanda's eleven prefectures, similar sports stadia and other potential refuge points existed in prefectural capitals. While such safe havens could not have saved all of Rwanda's estimated 800,000 Tutsi, eleven stadia alone could have accommodated about 200,000. Moreover, the French, in Operation Turquoise, were able in short order to deploy forces to establish safe passage for several hundred thousand Rwandans to cross Rwanda's western border into what was then Zaire. As we shall see, in southern Rwanda, the prefectures of Gitarama and Butare resisted violence for two weeks. In this time, a corridor for civilians to cross Rwanda's southern border into Burundi could also have been established. The decision to bring UNAMIR's military observers back to Kigali left the UN without eyes or ears at the periphery. The potential upside to such a corridor was not insignificant. The two prefectures were home to nearly one third of Rwanda's Tutsi population and had drawn many more from other prefectures who saw Butare and Gitarama as places of final refuge during the bloodshed.

Who Killed Habyarimana?

The question of who assassinated Habyarimana remains the subject of enduring speculation largely because of the ill-founded belief that his assassins bear primary responsibility for the genocide that followed. Yet the assassination does not morally absolve or negate the agency of those individuals who organized the genocide and who chose to kill. Moreover, the assassination alone did not 'cause' the genocide. Its conjunction with other factors – the context of the civil war and political liberalization – was necessary. Nonetheless, the question has prompted three major investigations: (i) French investigative judge, Jean-Louis Bruguière's 2006 ruling; (ii) the GOR-appointed Mutsinzi 2010 commission; and (iii) French investigative judges Marc Trévidic and Nathalie Poux's 2012 report. The first investigation asserted RPF responsibility; and the latter two suggested that it was members of Habyarimana's own regime. I present here the most persuasive arguments from these investigations – discounting those which depend on the considerable and conflicting witness evidence – for readers to evaluate for themselves the possible motive, means, and opportunity of each party to eliminate Habyarimana. My personal assessment is that it is improbable that the assassination was the result of a coup from within.

Both sides had motive. The RPF was in a strong position politically on 6 April 1994. Under the Arusha Accords, it would receive five cabinet positions – the same number as the ruling party – half of the officer positions in an integrated army, and 40 per cent of its rank-and-file. This far exceeded what its social base, rooted in the Tutsi refugee and resident population, merited. Military parity gave it a veto as well as safeguard. Yet Arusha envisaged a short transition period of only twenty-two months before national elections. The RPF had resoundingly lost local elections in the eight communes it contested in September 1993. A general election risked undoing the achievements of years of struggle in exile and war. According to advocates of rebel culpability, the RPF believed that the military balance-of-power was in its favour. It didn't need to share power and couldn't win it democratically. While this calculation implied acceptance of some reprisals against Tutsi civilians, it is not evident that the RPF would have foreseen violence on the massive scale and speed that ensued.

Motivation for an intra-regime – or more strictly an intra-party – coup was also plausible. The innermost circle of power, the *Akazu*, based mainly on close kinship ties, was cohesive.[25] It was against its interest to eliminate Habyarimana as its position and influence directly depended on him. However, there existed two fractures within the MRNDD outside of this group. The first schism was between loyalists, who wanted the Habyarimana-dependent status quo, and reformers who sought to reduce northern influence and to liberalize the party. The latter were led by Matthieu Ngirumpatse who had displaced Habyarimana as president of the party in 1993; and the former by Joseph Nzirorera, who became the party's national secretary. The second cleavage was between hardliners who distrusted the RPF's commitment to power-sharing and believed that a military resolution to the conflict was unavoidable; and moderates who, while also distrustful, preferred a negotiated settlement to continued war. While various party elites tended to the hardliner position, Théoneste Bagosora, *directeur de cabinet* at the Ministry of Defence, was conspicuous among them. He is on record for his hostility to the Arusha Accords, his perception of the war in ethnic terms, and his militant anti-Tutsi views.[26] In short, both civilian and military factions existed

---

[25] Beyond President Habyarimana and his wife, Agathe Kanziga, the most influential members of the *Akazu* comprised Protais Zigiranyirazo, Colonel Élie Sagatwa, and Séraphin Rwabukumba (the president's three brothers-in-law and respectively ex-prefect of Ruhengeri, private secretary to the president, and the head of *La Centrale*, an important private enterprise); Colonel Laurent Serubuga (former deputy chief of staff of the FAR); Dr Séraphin Bararengana (dean of the Faculty of Medicine at the National University of Rwanda and the president's brother); Dr Charles Nzabagerageza (the president's cousin and ex-prefect of Ruhengeri); Alphonse Ntilivamunda (director-general of the Ministry of Public Works and the president's son-in-law); and Joseph Nzirorera (godfather to president's daughter and general-secretary of the MRND). See Guichaoua (2015, pp. 49–50).

[26] Bagosora's views may be inferred from two documents: (i) a 1992 military commission report entitled 'The Definition and Identification of the Enemy' of which Bagosora was the most senior co-author; and (ii) a 1995 essay he

5.2 The Window of Opportunity

within the regime with motives either to eliminate Habyarimana and/ or to scupper Arusha.

Also, both sides probably had the *means* to bring down the plane. The question of means has centred on whether each side possessed surface-to-air missiles and the training needed to fire them. The Mutsinzi commission adduced documentary evidence that FAR had placed orders between 1991–1992 to five countries for SA-16 missiles and launchers, though not proof that the orders were fulfilled.[27] The commission further names FAR specialists who had received anti-aircraft training abroad. Bruguière found that FAR did not possess SA-16s but did have SA-7s and French *Mistral* missiles capable of downing the plane. However, Bruguière also found, albeit based on the testimony of five RPF defectors, including Abdul Ruzibiza who claimed to be part of the assassination team, the RPF obtained two SA-16s from the USSR via sale to Uganda and that at least four members had received training in their use in Uganda.[28] Belgian scholar, Filip Reyntjens, also claims the five-digit serial numbers for the two missiles fired begin with the same three digits as missiles in the Ugandan military's arsenal. In short, both the RPF and the FAR had the capability to shoot down the plane. Analysing 'means' is also inconclusive.

The question of opportunity has focused on the location from which the two missiles were fired. Both the Mutsinzi and Trévidic/Poux investigations commissioned experts to visit the crash site and ascertain the likely launch location. Both suggest that the most likely area was the environs of the Kanombe military camp in Kigali, rather than nearby Masaka hill where two missile launch tubes were allegedly found.[29] If correct, this would rule out the RPF. It is improbable that rebels infiltrated the area surrounding a key FAR military base

---

single-authored entitled 'The Final Tutsi Operation to Regain Power in Rwanda by Force'. Both documents are exhibits in Bagosora's ICTR trial, case number ICTR-98-41-T.

[27] See Mutsinzi pp. 145–155.

[28] See paragraph 281 of Bruguière's ruling. Ruzibiza later recanted his testimony but re-affirmed it just before his death in 2010. Trevidic and Poux received subsequent evidence from General Kayumba Nyamwasa, the most senior military defector from the RPF, who states that Kagame ordered the attack and details how the RPF obtained the missiles.

[29] Trevidic and Poux considered six possible firing locations including nearby Masaka hill but rule the latter out for several technical reasons. See pp. 336–337.

neighbouring the presidential palace. Yet closer examination suggests caution. Mutsinzi's two experts, including an explosives specialist, relied heavily on assessing witness credibility to determine possible firing locations. Trévidic/Poux's five ballistic experts and one acoustic expert simulated the firing of missiles but did not use SA-16s, and did not do so at the crash site in Rwanda, but in France whose different topography may have affected the acoustic results. The expert findings are suggestive, not conclusive.

Assessing motive, means, and opportunity then provides no definitive answer. The evidence we have is largely circumstantial. If it were an intra-party coup with Bagosora as mastermind, the speed of the response would be consistent with this. The Presidential Guard deployed and the strategically targeted assassinations of moderates began as early as 6.00am on 7 April, less than ten hours following Habyarimana's death. This suggests prior high-level authorization. In addition, Bagosora's conduct immediately after the crash is suggestive. Within an hour, he attempted to impose military rule and to assert himself as the central decision-maker in excess of his *de jure* authority. Moreover, he also had the connections and influence to organize a missile attack having previously personally commanded the anti-aircraft battalion and the Kanombe military camp.

Yet there are a number of reasons to doubt it was a coup from within. First, if Bagosora or some other senior insider had orchestrated the assassination, he would almost certainly have lost the support of the Presidential Guard. This force, by far the best-equipped and best-trained unit in Rwanda, was personally loyal to Habyarimana. A coup would have been an unforgiveable betrayal. The coup's architects needed the Presidential Guard if their objective was to restart the civil war and/or to implement a genocide. It was the Presidential Guard that engaged the RPF contingent in Kigali, thereby breaking the ceasefire on 7 April; and it was the Presidential Guard, on the same day, that carried out the strategically targeted assassinations of Habyarimana's rivals and of political moderates and the systematic elimination of Tutsi civilians in the capital. Second, if it were a pre-meditated coup, events certainly did not go to plan. Bagosora faced two serious setbacks in the first twenty-four hours. He failed to establish military rule and he failed to appoint his preferred candidate as army chief-of-staff. The decision to maintain civilian rule and appoint a new interim cabinet and a new president in accordance with the 1991 Constitution

5.2 The Window of Opportunity

were improvised responses to these setbacks. They were not planned in advance. Third, some of the senior figures that we now know led and organized the genocide at the centre involved individuals who had been bitter political rivals before Habyarimana's assassination. It is improbable, for instance, that Joseph Nzirorera and Matthieu Ngirumpatse, who represented opposing factions within the MRNDD and who had been competing to succeed Habyarimana as president, conspired to overthrow him. It was Habyarimana's assassination that united them and led to their unlikely collaboration. Fourth, Habyarimana himself had shown high trust in Bagosora, a fellow native of Bushiru. He had even tried to promote him, unsuccessfully, to army chief-of-staff. The president's family also continued to exhibit confidence in Bagosora after Habyarimana's death. He visited the family at their home and was in telephone communication with them throughout the night of 6 April. Betrayal without suspicion would have been difficult. Moreover, there is the stark contrast between the now many RPF defectors who have accused Kagame and the absence of comparable accusations from within Habyarimana's fractured regime. The well-documented attempts to silence witnesses with evidence against the RPF also invite the question as to why such efforts were necessary.[30] The circumstantial evidence then, in my view, means it is unlikely that Habyarimana's assassination was part of a coup from within.

Meso-level Analysis

I move down one level of analysis now to consider what happened at the prefectural and communal levels. The research design involved a sub-national comparison and I contrast how the genocide unfolded in the north and south of the country.[31]

Early Violence Onset: Mukingo Commune, Ruhengeri Prefecture, Northern Rwanda

In Mukingo, violence began on the morning of 7 April, the day immediately after the president's assassination. Mukingo was one of sixteen communes making up Ruhengeri prefecture in northern

---

[30] See Rever (2018), chapter 13.
[31] More detailed accounts of how the genocide unfolded in the north and south of the country may be found in McDoom (2014).

Rwanda. Ruhengeri was the place where anti-Tutsi violence seemed most likely to break out. Historically, it had been part of a region comprising Hutu principalities that had resisted central control by the Tutsi monarchy (Nahimana, 1979). It had the smallest Tutsi concentration (0.5 per cent) in the country and a low level of inter-ethnic marriage. It was on the frontlines of the civil war and its population had suffered. Politically, Ruhengeri was overwhelmingly loyal to Habyarimana, who himself hailed from the north, and to the ruling MRNDD party. All sixteen of Ruhengeri's burgomasters and its prefect, Sylvester Bariyanga, were Hutu and longstanding members of the ruling MRNDD.

From the war's outset, Mukingo's Tutsi community, numbering just under 600 or 1.3 per cent of the population, immediately faced distrust and discrimination. Juvénal Kajilijeli, Mukingo's burgomaster from 1988–1993 and during the latter half of the genocide, had drawn up lists of Tutsi men in the commune. In January 1991, in reprisal for an RPF attack on Ruhengeri's capital, hundreds of Bagogwe Tutsi were killed across Ruhengeri including in Mukingo. Kajilijeli was removed in 1993 during peace talks at the request of the RPF for his alleged involvement in Tutsi massacres. Unsurprisingly then, many Tutsi had fled the region long before the genocide. Mukingo was also located close to the war's frontline. An important military camp, Mukamira, had been established in its neighbouring commune, Nkuli. The camp trained *Interahamwe* during the war and supplied weapons to them during the genocide.

The introduction of multipartyism in 1991 changed little in Mukingo. The MRNDD ruled unchallenged and no party, other than the radical Coalition pour la Défense de la République (CDR), operated openly within the commune or prefecture. Kajilijeli had also personally trained a group of eighty *Interahamwe*, whose coercive power far exceeded that of the nine communal policemen, and whose presence intimidated the few supporters of the rival Mouvement Démocratique Republicain (MDR) who met in secret. The MRNDD's influence within Mukingo was also assured by a prominent native son, Joseph Nzirorera, the party's National Secretary, who was Kajilijeli's longstanding friend and patron. As the civil war escalated, Nzirorera travelled regularly on weekends to Mukingo and chaired meetings with the commune's local elite. The commander of Mukamira military camp, Augustin Bizimungu, also attended these meetings, along with

Lieutenant-Colonel Ephrem Setako, a native of Nkuli and Head of Legal Affairs in the Defence Ministry. Bizimungu would go on to become overall army chief-of-staff during the genocide.

When news of the president's assassination reached Mukingo on 6 April, Kajilijeli quickly convened a meeting in a local canteen next to Nkuli's commune office that same evening between 10.00 and 11.00pm. Several witnesses recall Kajilijeli addressing those present saying 'you very well know that it was the Tutsi that killed – that brought down the Presidential plane. What are you waiting for to eliminate the enemy?'[32] Following this address, several of the local elite, including Nkuli commune's burgomaster, agreed a plan to eliminate the local Tutsi population. The next morning, 7 April, Kajilijeli brought weapons from the Mukamira camp and distributed them to the *Interahamwe* from Nkuli and Mukingo communes. Over the next two days, under the direction of Kajilijeli, these *Interahamwe* eliminated the majority of the Tutsi in the two communes. Mukingo's burgomaster, Emmanuel Harerimana, died under mysterious circumstances on 8 April, possibly at the hand of Kajilijeli, who then acted as *de facto* burgomaster until officially reinstated on 26 June. Events in Mukingo were replicated elsewhere in Ruhengeri. MRNDD hardliners either in control of communes as incumbent burgomasters, or else in a position to take control, immediately used the local state apparatus to mobilize *Interahamwe* and elements of the civilian population, to hunt down and eliminate Tutsi families, often in collaboration with soldiers. The result was a rapid and comprehensive extermination of Ruhengeri's small Tutsi population.

Late Violence Onset: Taba Commune, Gitarama Prefecture, South-Central Rwanda

In Taba genocidal violence began on 19 April 1994, nearly two weeks after the president's assassination. Taba was one of seventeen communes making up Gitarama prefecture. Located in the centre of the country, Gitarama was home to roughly 83,000 Tutsi in April 1994, the third largest number of all Rwanda's eleven prefectures. Historically, inter-ethnic relations had been strong. The Hutu of the central and southern prefectures of Gitarama and Butare, collectively known as the

---

[32] See Prosecutor v. Juvénal Kajelijeli, International Criminal Tribunal for Rwanda, Case No. ICTR-98-44A-T, Judgement and Sentence.

Abanyanduga, had collaborated with the Tutsi monarch's conquests of the *Abakiga* in the predominantly Hutu north. Politically, Gitarama was also the stronghold of the opposition MDR, the successor of the MDR-Parmehutu, the party that had first ruled Rwanda following independence in 1962. Fourteen of its seventeen commune burgomasters and its prefect, Fidèle Uwizeye, were party members.

The start of the civil war in 1990 had little impact on inter-ethnic relations in Taba, partly due to its distance from the warfront, and partly due to its historically strong ethnic cohesion. The commune was home to an estimated 4,680 Tutsi in April 1994, just over 8 per cent of the population. Unlike Mukingo, no incidents of ethnic violence occurred in Taba before April 1994. In contrast, the advent of multipartyism in Rwanda in June 1991 directly impacted social relations. The divisions, however, followed partisan rather than ethnic lines. In March 1993, in commune elections, 41-year-old Taba native, Jean-Paul Akayesu of the MDR defeated incumbent Silas Kubwimana to become burgomaster, ending two decades of MRND rule. Although Akayesu enjoyed widespread support within the commune, Kubwimana continued to oppose him actively throughout his tenure.

When news of Habyarimana's death reached Taba, Akayesu initially called for ethnic solidarity and opposed violence. He turned his commune offices into a safe haven for incoming Tutsi refugees and assigned three of the commune's ten policemen to protect them. Consistent with the commune's historic ethnic solidarity, Taba's residents heeded their burgomaster. Hutu and Tutsi stood together and organized civilian day and night patrols and jointly manned checkpoints to prevent pro-violence elements from entering Taba. They resisted attempts from outside to subvert the commune's peaceful order.

As time passed, however, pressure from outside mounted. At first, Taba's geography protected it from external incursion. Its northern border with Kigali-rural prefecture, where violence had begun early, followed the Nyaborongo river and this limited contagion effects from the north. The three other communes that bordered Taba were situated within Gitarama and also opposed the violence. As the number of Tutsi refugees increased, however, so too did the number of outside armed incursions. In two notable incidents, solders and *interahamwe* militia attacked the Tutsi sheltering at the commune office but were repelled by the communal policemen. In other incidents, collaborators from inside Taba helped outside attackers enter the commune and target Tutsi homes. Solidarity and resistance were weakening.

Pressure from the centre also mounted. Prefect Uwizeye struggled to maintain his authority as his fellow party members and his administrative and security staff divided into extremist and moderate factions. When the IG moved to Gitarama on 12 April 1994, political control of the prefecture effectively passed from moderates to extremists. A thousand or so *interahamwe* accompanied the relocation and, with their arrival, military control also passed to extremists. On 18 April 1994, Rwanda's new prime minister, Jean Kambanda, summoned burgomasters to a meeting in its new Gitarama offices where he, his new ministers, and extremist party leaders directly addressed the prefecture's resistant leaders. Kambanda read a prepared statement calling for national unity and was followed by senior MRND party leaders who threatened the burgomasters more directly.

The meeting had the desired effect. Akayesu switched positions. Immediately the next day, the burgomaster addressed a gathering of Taba residents and urged them to unite against the 'accomplices' of the enemy. Over the next two days, Taba's Tutsi population was hunted down and killed. Akayesu also welcomed his former political rival, Silas Kubwimana, who had become an honorary vice-president of the *Interahamwe*. The militia and the military occupied Akayesu's commune offices and led attacks with the collaboration of Taba residents. The situation continued until 27 June 1994 when Akayesu fled the commune ahead of the rebels' arrival.

Explaining Variation in Violence Onset
So, important variation existed in when violence started across localities in Rwanda. I extended an existing dataset establishing the start date of genocidal violence in each of Rwanda's 145 communes and categorized onset into seven distinguishable time periods, each three days in length, from 16 April to 26 April.[33] Table 5.2 summarizes these data and distinguishes between communes controlled by the ruling party/government and those controlled by the political opposition/rebels. Two characteristics of the violence immediately stand out: its

---

[33] I am indebted to Straus (2006), who built the original dataset using six sources to establish a best estimate of the onset date for 124 of 145 communes. For more information on his methodology, see Straus (2006, p. 249). I added data for the missing twenty-one communes through further fieldwork conducted in 2009.

Table 5.2 *Number of communes that experienced genocidal onset in each time period*

| | | Elite control (political) || Elite control (military) ||
Time period	Onset	Ruling party	Opposition party	Govt. control	Rebel control/DMZ
6–8 Apr.	60	54	6	52	8
9–11 Apr.	25	19	6	22	3
12–14 Apr.	8	7	1	6	2
15–17 Apr.	4	2	2	4	0
18–20 Apr.	13	3	10	13	0
21–23 Apr.	17	5	12	17	0
24–26 Apr.	7	4	3	7	0
No onset	11	11	0	1	10
Total	145	105	40	122	23

nationwide ambit and its extraordinary speed. Only 11 of Rwanda's 145 communes did not succumb to violence. All but one were either controlled by the RPF or were part of the DMZ at the time of the president's assassination. Furthermore, nearly 60 per cent of those communes that did experience violence did so within the first six days (two time periods) following the president's assassination. The violence ignited rapidly.

But why did some communes break into violence early and others later? Did the violence follow some predictable pattern or did it emerge and spread randomly? Multivariate analysis points to the violence having systematic determinants.[34] The time it took for violence to emerge was a measure of a commune's susceptibility to violence. Two factors were particularly consequential: (i) elite control of the commune from above and (ii) the extent of inter-ethnic integration from below.

First, if the commune was controlled by a burgomaster who belonged to an opposition party, violence was likely delayed. The within-case analyses of Mukingo and Taba suggest that the reason

---

[34] Results are based on proportional hazards models using the speed of onset as the dependent variable. More detail on the empirical strategy followed and the results found may be found in McDoom (2014).

5.2 *The Window of Opportunity* 211

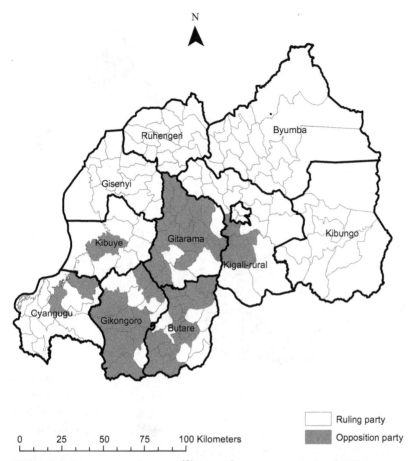

Figure 5.2 Burgomasters' party affiliations by commune in April 1994

was the local replication of the national-level power struggle between extremists and moderates that arose in the space of opportunity created by Habyarimana's death. This contestation took time to resolve. In fact, across Rwanda the struggle for control locally played out in several ways. Moderate burgomasters either (i) failed to act and were succeeded *de facto* by other figures in the commune as the new authority; (ii) were replaced *de jure* by the IG; (iii) switched position and actively pursued the extremist program; or (iv) were killed.[35]

---

[35] In Butare prefecture, for instance, Symphorien Karekezi of Kigembe commune was replaced *de facto* by Bonaventure Nkundabakura (local MDR-Power head)

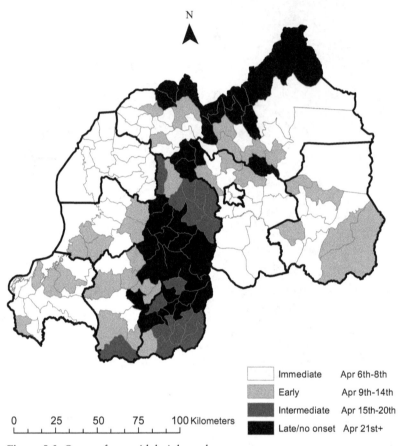

Figure 5.3 Onset of genocidal violence by commune

Once extremists established control of the commune, they mobilized communities and the violence began. Figure 5.2 shows the political affiliation of the commune burgomasters and Figure 5.3 shows how quickly violence started across Rwanda.[36] The darker areas on each

---

and Bernard Mutabaruka (local CDR head). Burgomasters replaced *de jure* included Celestin Rwankubito of Ndora commune; Chrysologue Bimenyimana of Muganza; and Vincent Rukeribuga of Rusatira. Burgomasters killed – because they were Tutsi or suspected Tutsi – include Narcisse Nyagasaza of Ntyazo (Tutsi) and Jean-Marie Vianney Gisagara of Nyabisindu (Hutu). See Guichaoua (2005, pp. 258–292).

[36] The burgomasters' political affiliations are derived primarily from two sources: (i) Guichaoua (2005, pp. 238–241); (ii) the International Criminal Tribunal for

5.2 The Window of Opportunity

map indicate areas controlled by the opposition, and areas where the violence began late. This is most visible in Gitarama prefecture, largely under MDR control, and Butare prefecture, largely under both Parti Social Démocrate (PSD) and MDR control. In these areas, most of the violence begins after 18 April. In the rest of the country, mostly under MRNDD control, the violence began almost immediately, between 6–11 April 1994. The exception appears to be Gikongoro prefecture, immediately adjoining Butare to the west. Here, as Figure 5.2 shows, the MDR and PSD had some influence. However, the violence began early. It may well be that the MDR and PSD burgomasters in Gikongoro were themselves extremist rather than moderate in orientation. The better explanation is that pressure at the prefectural level overcame the resistance at the communal level. Gikongoro's prefect and sub-prefect were MRNDD loyalists who quickly aligned themselves with the extremists at the centre (Des Forges, 1999, pp. 240–241).

The importance of elite control supports the consensus on the top-down, state-directed nature of Rwanda's violence. This explanation, however, is incomplete. The strength of social forces below was a second important determinant of onset timing. Social cohesion also mattered. I estimated the extent of local cross-ethnic ties using measures of spatial segregation.[37] Figure 5.4 maps the spatial integration across Rwanda's 145 communes. In the multivariate analysis, I found that communities where Hutu and Tutsi were well-integrated experienced violence later. Again, the centre and south of the country stand out. Hutu and Tutsi lived in particularly close proximity in Butare, Gitarama, and Kigali-rural. Inter-ethnic exposure was also high in the west of the country – in Gigonkoro, Cyangugu, and Kibuye prefectures – though the violence broke out early there. In the case of Cyangugu and Kibuye, political control by the ruling party from above likely dominated social cohesion from below. This social cohesion meant that it took time to break social bonds and divide communities

---

Rwanda (ICTR)'s in-house research conducted by a team of Rwandans resident in 1994. A copy of their research is on file with the author. Where there were a few discrepancies, I turned to other sources to help resolve them.

[37] I construct a segregation index using data on ethnicity at the commune and sector levels from Rwanda's 1991 census hitherto unavailable. Conceptually, the index estimates inter-ethnic exposure, and consequently interaction, by measuring the likelihood that a randomly selected member of one group would live in the same geographic neighbourhood as a randomly selected individual of the other group. See Lieberson (1981) for more information on the index.

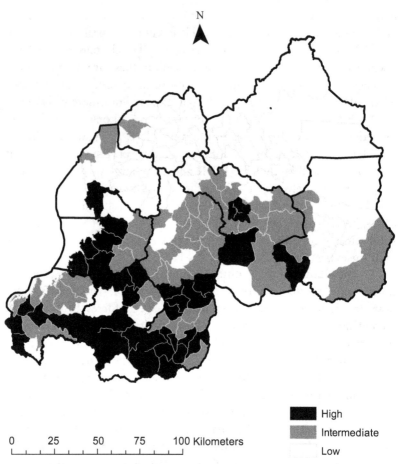

Figure 5.4 Spatial integration of Hutu and Tutsi by commune

along ethnic lines. In Taba, for instance, we saw that Hutu and Tutsi initially stood together in a display of ethnic solidarity. They conducted night patrols and manned roadblocks jointly. It was only when the burgomaster switched sides that local resistance was broken. In short, both elite agency *and* social structure were important. In contrast, none of my proxies for deprivation – literacy, wealth, and population density – was significant. Violence was triggered more by political than economic or demographic factors.

The analysis also revealed important spatial dynamics to the violence. Neighbouring communes affected each other. Violence was contagious. As the number of adjoining communes beset by violence in an earlier time period increased, the likelihood of a particular commune succumbing to violence in a later time period also increased. Contagion operated through several mechanisms: (i) demonstration: communities were inspired to follow the example of other communities; (ii) linkages: individuals had ties that crossed communities and influenced individuals in other communes; and (iii) mobility: proximity facilitated the movement of people and materials across community boundaries. In Taba and Mukingo, mobility mattered most. In Taba, the contagion effect was weak because the Nyabarongo river limited incursions and because neighbouring communes were also anti-violence. In Mukingo, pro-violence military and militia were present in neighbouring Nkuli commune and faced no constraint to enter and commit violence next door.

Micro-level Analysis

Having reviewed the situation at the macro- and meso-levels, I zoom in now to focus on events in four local communities – Rwandan administrative cells – that I had also examined in Chapter 4. I had chosen each site according to the level of violence each experienced: two with high violence and two with comparatively low violence. Table 5.3 presents a profile of all four communities.

Mwendo Cell, Maraba Commune, Southern Rwanda: Low Violence

Mwendo could be reached after a thirty-minute drive, almost all of it along a tarmac road leading from Butare, Rwanda's second town, toward Gikongoro prefecture. Mwendo was home to nearly 1,500 Rwandans in April 1994, of whom eighty-four (5.6 per cent) were Tutsi. It enjoyed a high proportion of inter-ethnic marriages. Prior to April 1994, the community had experienced no inter-ethnic confrontations or ethnic violence following the start of the war in 1990.

The genocide in Mwendo began late compared with the rest of Rwanda: thirteen days after Habyarimana's plane was brought down. But it was early compared with the rest of the prefecture, a few days prior to violence in many other Butare cells. The cell was also the site of relatively little violence. Of the eighty-four Tutsi who were resident, only seven (8.3 per cent) would meet their death within its borders. However, the intensity, as against the onset of violence, proved to be a poor indicator of dynamics in the cell. The majority of Tutsi had in fact fled the cell early on. They took sanctuary in the nearby Rugango

Parish church, where they would be massacred *en masse* several days later. In total, fifty-one (60.7 per cent) of Mwendo's Tutsi would be killed outside the cell. Only twenty-six (30.9 per cent) altogether would survive the genocide.

When the news of Habyarimama's death reached Mwendo over the radio the next day, the general reaction was anxiety and fear. It was a Thursday, ordinarily a day for *umuganda,* Rwanda's compulsory labour service. But on that day, Mwendo's residents stayed home, as the radio advised. Over the next few days they continued to live in uncertainty, attempting to interpret competing signals. On the one hand, word of violence breaking out in Kigali had reached Mwendo. In addition, Mwendo's residents could see homes burning on neighbouring hillsides across the frontier with Gikongoro prefecture. Violence had erupted early there. But it was not entirely clear in either case that the Tutsi were the targets at the start. On top of this, the local extremist, Emmanuel Rekeraho, immediately began to incite people to take action. Rekeraho, it may be recalled, was prominent in the community before as the MDR representative. As this resident described it:

What did people in Mwendo say after Habyarimana died? When Habyarimana died, the politicians said they had killed our leader. Then people's hearts changed more. *Who was saying this?* It was the extremist Emmanuel. He said 'Your father [*umubyeyi* refers to Habyarimana] has been killed. We should wake up and fight for our survival.' (*Interview with Leopold, secretary of the gacaca committee, aged 32, April 2003*)

At the same time, running counter to these signals were the voices calling for unity and calm. Butare's prefect, Jean-Baptiste Habyalimana, had resisted pressure from Kigali, now controlled by an extremist minority, to target his Tutsi civilian population. Maraba's burgomaster, Jean-Marie Habineza, held a meeting on Saturday 9 April in nearby Gako to reassure people and to appeal to them to resist the burning and destruction they could see in Gikongoro. The sector councillor, Stanislas Binenwa, carried this message and repeated it to his own community. As late as 14 April, he summoned residents to the local school and told them 'not to involve themselves in such matters'. In fact, in contrast with what happened elsewhere in much of Rwanda, under the direction of their *responsable,* Ernest Mulinda, Mwendo residents – both Hutu and Tutsi – collaborated in these early days. They erected and manned roadblocks together at strategic points in Mwendo to prevent the violence from entering their own community.

Here is what Oriel, a primary school teacher from Mwendo, said about the initial few days in his own written narrative:

> In the beginning, the population was not for the attacks, not for the looting, and not for the destruction. In fact, on the hills, the population held meetings whose purpose was to take measures to counter attacks that might come from Gikongoro. But that did not stop the sectors Kabuye, Shanga, and Maraba which bordered Gikongoro from going up in smoke. But remember, up until that point, there had not been a single instance of killing in the commune. Though that would not last long. (*Oriel, Hutu accused of genocide-related crimes, aged 45, primary school teacher, self-written narrative.*)

Thus, the tide began to turn in Mwendo as the violence from Gikongoro approached. Maraba's proximity to the border made it vulnerable to contagion. But it was still not entirely clear what was happening.

> In a few days we started to see smoke from Gigonkoro from burning houses. After a few days everyone was afraid – both Hutu and Tutsi. Who was burning the houses? They said those who were doing the burning had covered themselves in banana leaves so you could not see who it was. When they found out what was happening, the fear of Hutu decreased while the fear of Tutsi increased as they now knew who was the enemy. (*Interview with Leopold again, April 2003*)

It was the arrival of Tutsi fleeing Gikongoro that removed any remaining ambiguity surrounding the target of the violence. The Tutsi refugees began to assemble in thousands at the Simba Parish Church in Maraba commune. On Saturday, 16 April, Mwendo's Tutsi community made the decision to flee too. A group left that morning for the Rugango Parish Church. Like Simba, Rugango had also been a sanctuary during the violence of 1959. That same evening, the pillage began in Mwendo. Rekeraho and a group of his supporters looted the homes the Tutsi had just vacated. However, the trigger for violence was the visit of Rwanda's newly appointed president, Theodore Sindikubwabo, the following day.

On Sunday morning, the 17th of April 1994, the president of the Republic Theodore Sindikubwabo passed through the Maraba commune on the way to Gikongoro, with the mission, it was said, of 'pacification'. Upon his return, he stopped at the Simbi parish where many Tutsi had taken refuge, and he then visited the commune offices where he met the burgomaster, Jean-Marie Vianney Habineza, and his close collaborators. Upon his departure, later that evening the population mobilized to attack Simbi. But the Tutsi

Table 5.3 Genocide profile of four selected cells

Prefecture	Butare (southern Rwanda)		Ruhengeri (northern Rwanda)	
Cellule	Mwendo	Tamba	Ruginga	Mutovu
Demographics				
Population (Hutu, Tutsi, Twa)	1497	803	969	785
Resident Tutsi	84 (5.6%)	72 (9.0%)	35 (3.6%)	60 (7.6%)
Ethnic cohesion (inter-ethnic unions before genocide)				
Tutsi male partner	7	1	0	0
Tutsi female partner	11	6	0	2
Victims				
Resident Tutsi killed (total)	58 (69.0%)	61[a] (84.7%)	8 (23%)	53 (88.3%)
Resident Tutsi killed *within* cell	7 (8.3%)	41 (56.9%)	1 (2.8%)	46 (77%)
Resident Tutsi killed *oustide* of cell	51 (60.7%)	20[b] (27.8%)	7 (20%)	7 (11.7%)
Tutsi from *outside* cell killed *within* cell	10	9[c]	4	0
Tutsi survivors	26 (31.0%)	11 (15.3%)	27 (77.1%)	7 (11.7%)
Hutu killed (not by RPF)	2	0	0	0
Perpetrators (individuals in categories I and II under Rwandan Gacaca Law of 2004)[d]				
Prison *gacaca* number	63 (16.8%)[e]	48 (24%)	2 (0.8%)	9 (4.6.%)
Community *gacaca* number	Unknown	Unknown	1 (0.4%)	11 (5.6%)
Perpetrators from *outside* cell	Unknown	Unknown	19	24

218

	Genocide Timeline				
Genocide start (days after Habyarimana's assassination)	13	18	Before 1994	1	
Genocide end (date of RPF arrival)	4 Jul 94	2 Jul 94	7 Apr 94	15 Jul 94	

State Authorities

Ethnicity of *responsible*	Hutu	Hutu	Hutu	Hutu
Responsable implicated in genocide?	Yes	No	No	No
Present situation of responsible	Imprisoned	Dead (naturally)	At liberty	Dead (naturally)
Councillor implicated in genocide?	Mixed evidence	Mixed evidence	No	Yes
Ethnicity of councillor	Hutu	Hutu	Hutu	Hutu
Present situation of councillor	At liberty	Dead (suicide)	At liberty	Imprisoned
Burgomaster implicated in genocide?	Yes	Yes	Yes	Yes
Ethnicity of burgomaster	Hutu	Hutu	Hutu	Hutu

[a] Rwanda initially had both an official *gacaca* process involving the community, and a parallel, unofficial *gacaca* process involving prison inmates. This is the prison *gacaca* figure. The community *gacaca* figure is 59 victims.
[b] This is the prison *gacaca* figure. The community *gacaca* figure is 18 victims.
[c] This is the community *gacaca* figure. The prison *gacaca* figure is 7.
[d] Categories I and II broadly cover the organization of the genocide, sexual torture and rape, homicide, and serious bodily harm. See Chapter 7 for more specific information.
[e] This is the proportion of adult Hutu males. I assumed that they represented one quarter of the community's overall population.

seemed better armed than the Hutu and the attack was postponed until the next morning, reinforced by the commune police and gendarmes from Gikongoro under the direction of sub-Lieutenant Nyabyenda Narcisse. It was this same officer who attacked the Rugango Parish on the 21st, and several days later, Ruhashya. (*Oriel, written narrative again*)

This was the turning-point that tipped the entire commune into violence. President Sindikubwabo, a native of Butare himself, made a speech at the Simbi Parish to the population. This was the signal from above, from the highest authority, that the Hutu must fight a war against the Tutsi. A transcript of this speech does not exist, but the following is an excerpt from the address he made in Butare town just two days after visiting Maraba. It exemplifies the language of mobilization in Rwanda:

Dear Butare fellows, I have to beg your pardon because I do not normally talk with such vigour in my voice but these days I have no choice. I do not want you to take our messages, speeches, and lessons as mere words in the air. They are important messages since we are in a time of war [...] There is no shortage of good workers willing to serve their country. You know the traitors who have trained to use guns to exterminate us. I do know them. The person who knows them should tell us so that we can be rid of them. As the Prime Minister indicated, we have to fight and win this war since as he pointed out it is the final one. As it is the final one you have to make your choice soon and spare us the trouble of wasting our energy. Either we lose it or we make the right choice and win it. We will win it if you rid us of those 'irresponsible people'. They should look for these irresponsible people who trained to kill us. Rid us of them. We the conscientious Rwandans shall move on and win this war.[38]

The president frames his call-to-action in the language of war and self-defence. His speech does not use the terms 'Hutu' and 'Tutsi'. Instead, characteristically, he chooses ambiguous alternatives such as 'conscientious Rwandans' and 'irresponsible people'. If similar language was employed in Maraba, its meaning was not ambiguous for his audience. Hutu immediately moved against the Tutsi gathered in the Parish following Sindikubwabo's visit. At the same time Sindikubwabo co-opted the burgomaster, Habineza. Following his visit, Habineza

---

[38] This English translation of his speech originally in Kinyarwanda can be found in *Prosecutor v. Nyiramasuhuko et al.*, ICTR, Case no. ICTR-98-42, Exhibit no. D.2790.

5.2 The Window of Opportunity

switched from an anti-violence to a pro-violence position. He would be present during the attacks at Simbi. Later that Sunday evening, Butare's Tutsi prefect, Jean-Baptiste Habyalimana, who had been opposed to violence, was removed from office over the radio. It was now clear to Mwendo residents that the state authorities – at the macro- and meso-levels – were in favour of violence.

The burgomaster's switch would have an important consequence in Mwendo. His defection effectively undermined the lower authorities at the micro-level. The sector councillor and Mwendo's *responsable*, who had both urged calm until then, found themselves wrong-footed. Their authority had been weakened. Rekeraho, the local extremist, and his close collaborators, would instead arise to become the *de facto* authority in the community. A former government soldier who had fought the *Inyenzi* attacks in the 1960s, he donned his military uniform again. He eclipsed the *de jure* figures of authority and drew upon his social network for his hardcore supporters. Thus Jean-Baptiste Hakelimana and a certain Kaguja, both former soldiers-turned-farmers who were living in Mwendo, would move with Rekeraho. This group now represented the new law of the land.

Tell me more about Rekeraho. During the genocide he killed for killing's sake. One evening there was too much noise at a local bar and there was a rule that after 18.30 you could not be there. But there was a group making noise and when Rekeraho came and asked who was responsible for this, this young man presented himself and said 'It was me.' Rekeraho shot him there and then. *Who was this young man? When was this?* This was in June and he was a Hutu. You could not stop him [Rekeraho] during the genocide. He was a member of the self-defence committee at the prefecture. He was wearing his military uniform again. (*Oriel again, author-led interview in French, Butare central prison, Southern Rwanda, April 2003*)

The capture of the state was now complete at all levels. On Rekeraho's orders, the anti-Tutsi campaign began. It commenced with the organization of the men in Mwendo into an attack group. Interviewees referred to these groups as *ibitero* in Kinyarwanda, a term connoted with royal hunting parties in the era of Rwanda's monarchy. Ernest Mulinda, officially the cell *responsable* but no longer in charge, followed the example of the burgomaster and also switched his position. He joined the attack group. Having looted Tutsi homes on Sunday, 17 April, this newly formed group burned them on Monday,

18 April. On Thursday, 21 April, the attack group converged with groups from elsewhere upon the Rugango Parish where most of their Tutsi neighbours had sought sanctuary. With the aid of gendarmes, the attackers killed almost all of them. These few days in the first couple of weeks represented the period of the most intense violence in the community.

Over the next two months, the manhunt continued. At the start, the attack group assembled early every morning, routinely, and then decided where to go. As time passed and as the number of Tutsi left alive dwindled, they met only when summoned. Rekeraho, though a resident of Mwendo, did not lead all of these attacks.[39] He in fact had received an appointment to the new prefectural self-defence committee (Guichaoua, 2005, p. 314). His influence would now extend over the entire prefecture. Instead, other individuals from within Mwendo would rise to take the opportunity to lead the attack groups in the community.

A few Tutsi families chose not to flee and remained in Mwendo. Household by household they were targeted. One family survived until early May. There was some doubt as to the ethnicity of the household head. Though Tutsi, Jacques Biremba had moved relatively recently to Mwendo, and his wife was Hutu. He told his family they should stay. If they were to die, better to die together.

What happened to your family during the genocide? My husband [Biremba] was killed here by this house. They took him out of the house and told him that they were having a meeting and when they reached the path, they killed him. *And you?* I was at home. We fled immediately after they took him out of the house. *When was this?* It was the 8th of May that he was killed. *But why didn't you flee before?* We did not flee before then because before they were looking for Tutsi who were born here in Mwendo but we were born in Huye [another commune]. Afterwards they came to look for those they had doubts about. My husband was Tutsi but I was not. I fled to my father's house. They came to look for me at my father's house. But we survived by the grace of God. You see when Habyarimana died, he was not buried. People would come to you and say they will make you escort him. *What do you mean?* They mean kill you too. Just like the king used to be escorted in death by people who were killed so as to accompany him. *Who was in the group that killed your husband?* There were more than fifty people who came to look

---

[39] Rekeraho's registered domicile was Huye commune but he kept his actual residence in Mwendo, Maraba commune.

for my husband. There were three attack groups that came together. It was being led by Kazungu [a nickname] who was also a farmer and another called Gaspari. The one who actually killed him was Nsabimana. (*Aurelie, aged 30, genocide survivor. Author-led interview in Kinyarwanda in her home, April 2003. Her brother-in-law is also present.*)

As this sad story shows, the violence was not a spontaneous flash of emotion, but highly organized and sustained in Mwendo. This state of affairs would persist until the RPF finally reached Mwendo on 4 July, eighty-nine days later, and too late.

Tamba Cell, Shyanda Commune, Southern Rwanda: High Violence

Tamba, located deep in the heart of Shyanda commune, was the remotest of the four cells I researched. It was a good hour's drive from the main road, slowly along dirt tracks that were almost impassable after rain, even in a four-wheel drive. It was also the last to experience violence. The killing did not begin until Sunday, 24 April 1994, some two and a half weeks after Habyarimana's death. It was far from the commune offices and a sixty-minute walk to the nearest church, secondary school, and health clinic. The absence of electricity and a telephone reinforced the cell's isolation. Tamba was home to 803 Rwandans in 1994. Seventy-two (9 per cent) were Tutsi. Forty-one (56.9 per cent) of them would be killed on its territory. Only eleven (15.3 per cent) would ultimately survive.

Tamba residents reacted to the news of Habyarimana's death in much the same way as residents of Mwendo. Most felt shock, fear, and uncertainty. The reaction of the civilian authority figures was also similar. The burgomaster, Théophile Shiyarambere, the sector councillor, Antoine Ngirabanyigina, and the cell *responsable*, Joseph Nkusi – all Hutu – each made efforts to keep order and to prevent looting, burning, and violence from engulfing their community. In part through the signals they sent, and in part because there had been no serious ethnic incidents previously, Hutu and Tutsi cooperated in Tamba to assure the security of the cell at the outset. They participated in security patrols and manned barriers on the cell's frontiers together. Instead of ethnic division, Habyarimana's death initially prompted inter-ethnic cooperation in the face of what was first seen as a threat external to Tamba.

At the beginning when Antoine [the sector councillor] first saw the houses burning in the communes nearby, he gathered people and put them at the borders that evening to stop this bad air from coming in to our place. Then he said: 'Let us wait and see how the authorities are reacting.' The following morning, on the 24th April, as I live close to the border I saw a roadblock had been erected between Ndora and Shyanda communes. We thus protected our cell from disturbances coming from these places. (*Simon, Hutu, self-confessed perpetrator. Author-led focused group interview in Kinyarwanda in Butare central prison. Two other self-confessed perpetrators present.*)

Despite the strong appeals for calm and unity, as in Mwendo, Tamba's residents faced conflicting signals. Within Tamba, the local bigot, Emmanuel Karimunda, had immediately begun to call for action against the Tutsi. Karimunda, a butcher by trade, was well known for his racist views and was also widely feared within the community for his violent nature. He had been asserting his personal authority over the cell *responsable*, Joseph Nkusi, long before 6 April. But it was not only signals coming from within Tamba to which its residents were exposed. Reports of events outside the cell also filtered in. Rumours of looting and killing in neighbouring communities were in circulation. Several Tutsi refugees observed fleeing through the cell had the effect of reinforcing the rumours. In short, as in Mwendo, there were competing signals at play in Tamba: those encouraging violence and those resisting it. The tension and uncertainty are captured in this account by a Tamba resident.

What happened in your community after Habyarimana died? After Habyarimana died, there was a state of fear. Some of the big politicians were being killed in Butare town. We saw people fleeing from different places and we were praying that it would not reach us here in Tamba. When we asked people why they were fleeing they could not explain it. They were saying they were burning Tutsi houses. We told them not to cause panic here as you have no evidence. People in Huye [another commune] started to say the same things. But we said that the reason it was in Huye was because it was close to the authorities in Butare town. It will not come here. Do not be afraid. One person who was working in Save [name of commune that succeeded Shyanda after genocide] said Rwaniya Joseph, a politician, was attacked and his house burned. That evening we saw houses burning in the nearby area. When it came close to us, because we knew where people used to live, we could tell whose houses were being burned. We saw it was only Tutsi houses being burned. When we saw this type of burning we remembered in 1959 that Tutsi houses were being burned but that they would come back and people would do *umuganda* [compulsory labour service] to rebuild their

5.2 The Window of Opportunity

homes afterwards. (*Marcel, Hutu, aged 44. Author-led interview in Kinyarwanda in his home.*)

Marcel, then one of the five members of the cell committee, indicates initial disbelief at the prospect of the burning and violence reaching Tamba. He thought the cell would be spared because of its remote location, far from the political centre of gravity in Butare town. Yet, through rumours and other signs, any uncertainty that all Tutsi were the target would diminish in Tamba. It was on the Saturday, 23 April, that events took a definitive turn in Tamba. The background was the pressure building on Shyanda's burgomaster to join the genocidal program. Théophile Shyirambere was a member of the opposition PSD party and a moderate who did not share the extreme anti-Tutsi views of Rwanda's new central government in Kigali. Five days earlier he had attended the inauguration ceremony of Sylvain Nsabimana, who had replaced Jean-Baptiste Habyalimana as Butare's prefect. It was on this trip to Butare town that Shiyarambere met with Rwanda's new president, Sindikubwabo, the prime minister, and several other ministers. It was then that he also attended a prefectural security meeting with most of Butare's burgomasters the next day. Following these meetings, there would be no doubt in his mind as to what was expected of the burgomasters. To add to the pressure, Shiyarambere would also receive visits from Rwanda's new interim minister of the interior, Callixte Kalimanzira.

Once back in Shyanda, following these events in Butare town, Shyanda's burgomaster held meetings with all of the sector councillors. In consequence of this, action began in Shyanda on Friday, 22 April. Théophile's assistant burgomaster, Déo Banguwiha, led a raid that evening at about 6.00pm with the support of a group of villagers drawn from the vicinity of his private residence. They targeted a Tutsi family's home in Rwanzana cell, neighbouring Tamba, where they slaughtered and ate a cow. In fact, this attack was part of a wider series of attacks on several other communes that had also been resisting violence: Ngoma, Mbazi, Ruhashya, Mugusa, and Ndora. The following day, Déo led an even larger raid, this time aided by another assistant burgomaster, Innocent Uwimana, a teacher known as Jean-Paul, the Rwanzana cell *responsable*, Jean-Baptiste Mazimpaka, and even more villagers from the area. They were even more destructive on this occasion. The group attacked two Tutsi families, burned four Tutsi homes, and looted and stole even more.

These outside raids, led by high-level authority figures, would set the example inside Tamba. The next day, Sunday, 24 April, Déo visited the cell in a commune vehicle and reportedly asked Tamba residents publicly 'Why are you not working?' Emmanuel Karimunda, the local racist, immediately organized a group to hunt down the Tutsi in Tamba. Encouraged by the 'green light' from above, he sidelined Tamba's *responsable*, Joseph Nkusi, who had opposed the violence. Nkusi would lose his authority within his community.

What did the local authorities do in Tamba? They did not stop the genocide because it was supported by the high authorities. They were saying: 'The high authorities have more powers than us and then they would kill us too.' One time, the *responsable* Nkusi asked the people why they were going to kill and loot at a certain home. They responded that: 'The leniency you show is trying to sabotage our program.' So, he was also afraid and was even told by the group leader [Karimunda] that he was no longer the *responsable*. (*Interview with Marcel again, April 2003*)

On that Sunday, however, most Tutsi were not in their homes. They had suspected that danger was looming and had gone into hiding the night before.

Tell me how the killing began in Tamba: The following Saturday the councillor told us [Tutsi] not to flee – and we even went out to attend our fields. That same day at about 2.00pm we saw houses burning across the hill and we saw it was only the Tutsi houses. We did not sleep at home that night. We slept out on the hills. When I was hiding in the sorghum fields, I heard gunshots but later I learned that they were just making noise to scare people into running so that they would be killed. In the morning we went back to our house and then Emmanuel [Karimunda] came. He wanted to take the cows of my husband. My husband refused and then he took the cows by force. That was in the morning. Then at around 3.00pm, that is when all my family members were killed – except my husband who was killed two days later on Tuesday. *Where did this happen?* My family members were killed near to where they were hiding in the sorghum plantation. My husband was killed where you left your car – by the cabaret [local bar]. (*Véronique, genocide survivor. Author-led interview in Kinyarwanda in her home, May 2003.*)

Few Tutsi would be killed that Sunday. Instead, their homes were looted and their cows slaughtered for meat. However, the next day, a Monday, on Karimunda's order the attack group gathered again at

7.00am by the local *cabaret* (bar). Karimunda's right-hand men were his nephew, Jacques N., and his brother, Pierre S. They divided into several groups to hunt down the remaining Tutsi hiding in the sorghum fields. Almost all the forty-one Tutsi killed from the cell met their end that day. The Tamba villagers buried their bodies the following day. Having killed most of the local Tutsi, there would be no more attacks conducted in Tamba, but several members would participate in attacks on other areas. This would continue until the RPF arrived on 2 July.

Mutovu Cell, Nkuli Commune, Northern Rwanda: High Violence
Mutovu bordered a tarmac road and was an easy twenty-minute drive from Ruhengeri town. As with much of the north-west, it had benefited from Habyarimana's favour over the years. Its 785 residents included sixty Tutsi, 7.6 per cent of its population, a considerable minority for a Ruhengeri community. The sector, Mukamira, comprising five cells altogether, was also home to a military camp. Its presence in part explains the devastating speed and completeness of the killing in Mutovu. Soldiers and Mutovu residents together targeted Tutsi immediately on 7 April. By 8 April, forty-six (77 per cent) had been killed within the cell and another seven (11.7 per cent) met their end in the military camp itself.

Unlike the two southern communities, inter-ethnic tensions had surfaced in Mutovu long before 6 April 1994. The community's proximity to the frontlines of the civil war had led to early accusations against Tutsi civilians of collaboration with the rebel army. Anti-Tutsi activity began as soon as the war started in October 1990 and it ebbed and flowed with the tide of the combat. Thus, in January 1991, following an RPF raid on the Ruhengeri prison, the burgomaster arrested and detained two Tutsi men from the cell. This caused several other Tutsi men to flee the cell, leaving their families behind. It was initially believed that only educated men were being targeted for enemy collaboration. But then in February 1993, in reprisal for a rebel violation of a ceasefire, soldiers aided by civilians burned a family of seven Tutsi alive in their home, all women and children, in the neighbouring cell, Rugeshi. By this time, the movements of the remaining Tutsi in the cell had been restricted by the vigilance of their suspicious Hutu neighbours. This young Hutu man described it thus:

What happened to the Tutsi in your community after the war started? There were no Tutsi killed in Mutovu but there were some arrested and imprisoned before Habyarimana died. *Why were they arrested?* There were two men. They were seen as *ibyitso* [collaborators] as they looked like intellectuals [someone with secondary level education] in that area. *Who arrested them?* The authorities and the police arrested them. *And who reported them?* We do not know who reported them. We saw only that the police came. My father talked to the burgomaster as he was someone known to the authorities so these two were then released. *When did this happen?* It was in 1992 that they were arrested. *What about Tutsi outside of Mutovu between 1990–94?* In Mukamira between 1990 and 1994, there were some Tutsi who were killed but I do not know who. It was in cell Rugesha. *Who did this?* I don't know the names of who did this. But there were villagers involved. In Mutovu the Tutsi were being hassled and threatened because they were Tutsi. Villagers from Mutovu were saying they would kill them. *Who was saying this?* Gervais Halerimana was behind the intimidation. He was a businessman who is now dead. But there were many who supported him. He was also the President of CDR in Nkuli commune but he lived in Mutovu cell. (*Vincent, aged 42, Hutu. Author-led interview in Kinyarwanda conducted in sector office. Office vacant at time, May 2003*)

Asked the same question, this young Tutsi survivor corroborated his story. He survived because he had fled the cell in January 1994.

What happened to Tutsi in your community after the war started? The relationship changed between Hutu and Tutsi in Mutovu. Those who liked each other started hating each other [Hutu and Tutsi]. *Did everyone hate the Tutsi?* No, it was not everyone who hated the Tutsi. *Did anyone attack the Tutsi then?* There were no Tutsi harmed in Mutovu during this time. But there were some Hutu who were saying to the Tutsi that: 'It is you who have invaded Rwanda' as they made the association with the *Inkotanyi*. Nothing else much happened in Mutovu. We were afraid in 1990 as we were afraid the Hutu might kill us. *What was life like before the war?* Before 1990 things were OK between Hutu and Tutsi. There was a normal hatred between the groups but there was no desire to kill. There was even intermarrying. We could see this normal hatred. For example, there would be quarrelling or sometimes fighting but then they would make peace. They would sometime quarrel because they were drunk or sometimes they would fight over their land. (*Jerome, Tutsi survivor, aged 33, farmer. Author-led interview in Kinyarwanda, in sector office. No persons present at time, May 2003.*)

Anti-Tutsi sentiment then was palpable in Mutovu long before Habyarimana's assassination. It was in part attributable to the war

5.2 The Window of Opportunity

which had led to charges of Tutsi complicity with the enemy. Though, as Jerome reminds us, anti-Tutsi sentiment in the north-west predated the civil war. Vincent and Jerome further tell us that it was not only the commune authorities but also elements of the civilian population that were against the Tutsi. Thus, the CDR party was active within the cell. Its popularity was in part due to the presence of a prominent individual, Gervais Harelimana, who kept a private residence in the cell. As it may be remembered, Harelimana was the CDR party representative for the entire prefecture and a renowned racist. He was assisted by: Edison Munyaratama, a primary school head teacher, a CDR supporter, and his neighbour; Felicien, Gervais's younger and poorer brother; and Habimana, a CDR party representative for Nkuli commune. They, in turn, would be aided by Mutovo's young men. Interviewees confirmed the presence of the *Impuzamugambi*, the CDR's youth wing, and the *Interahamwe*, the MRND's youth-wing-turned-militia.

It is more difficult to build a solid picture of what precisely happened in the cell immediately *after* Habyarimana's death. In part, this is because the violence was so rapid. It lasted only two days. It also involved mostly outsiders, soldiers from the nearby military camp. Twenty-six of the thirty-seven perpetrators of violence came from outside of the cell. But it is also because there are simply no survivors to tell the tale who were in the cell at the time. All who had remained were killed. Of the forty-six victims, thirty-five were children, five were women, and only three were men. Most of Mutovu's Tutsi men had in fact already fled, having been harassed by the commune authorities following the start of the civil war. However, we know a few things for certain. On 7 April, a lieutenant from the nearby Mukamira military camp, accompanied by soldiers, rounded up Tutsi in the vicinity of the camp, brought them back to the base, and executed them. At the same time, the sector councillor, Anastase Kabutura, led attack groups assisted by *Interahamwe* and *Impuzumugambi* militia, and systematically killed all the remaining Tutsi in Mutovu. These same groups would also participate in the massacre at the church in Hesha, an adjoining cell. The following is a typical account of events post-Habyarimana's death in Mutovu.

What happened in your community after Habyarimana died? On the 7th they said on the radio that no one should leave their homes. After two days we started to see new faces that we were not used to seeing in the area and we saw smoke coming from the areas where the Tutsi were living. Because we were close to the road where the market was, we would see that houses were burned and the iron sheets removed. Tutsi we used to know we never saw them again as the RPF advanced. In July we fled to Zaire and we heard that there was no Tutsi that was spared. When the RPF took the government, we crossed over to Zaire. We fled before the RPF arrived as other people reached us in Mukamira telling us about the advance of the RPF. *Who was doing the killing in your community?* Those killing the Tutsi in Mutovu were the young men from Mutovu and people from outside. *Who were they? The people from outside?* We heard gunshots so it could be a mixture of soldiers and villagers. But some villagers were also given guns. *Who led the villagers?* It was being organized and directed by the councillor at the time and he was the only authority in the area. The *responsable* from Mutovu refused to take a gun and to distribute guns. *Where did the guns come from?* It was the officer in charge of the military camp who was distributing the guns. The civilian authorities including the burgomaster did not have any say. It was the soldiers and the *Interahamwe* who had power. For the real *Interahamwe*, we did not have them. But we had neighbours who had the hearts of killing like the real *Interahamwe*. (*Interview with Vincent again, May 2003*)

Vincent used careful and oblique language to describe the killing at first. He did not state explicitly that Tutsi were killed and that soldiers were the perpetrators at the start. He described instead 'people we had not seen before' or 'smoke coming from where Tutsi lived'. This probably reflected the context. *Gacaca*, the local justice process for genocide crimes, was ongoing at the time, and my questions were sensitive. In all, an astounding 88 per cent of all Tutsi resident in Mutovu would be killed and all within the first two days. The intensity and rapidity of the violence had much to do with the cell's geography. Proximity to the civil war had fuelled anti-Tutsi sentiment and the proximity to the Mukamira military camp placed the civilians within easy range of soldiers.

Ruginga Cell, Kinigi Commune, Northern Rwanda: Low Violence
In contrast with Mutovu, Ruginga's Tutsi population escaped relatively unharmed from the genocide. Of the thirty-five Tutsi who were resident, twenty-seven (76 per cent) would survive. In addition, only one of the eight victims would be killed in the cell itself. The high survival rate was due to the cell's geography. Situated on the perimeter of the Parc National des Volcans, the mountain gorillas' sanctuary, it

5.2 The Window of Opportunity

was a relatively short and unobstructed journey through the park and across the unmarked border with what was then Zaire. Refugees did not have to run the gauntlet through other communities to escape. By 6 April 1994, all of the seven Tutsi homes in the cell had been abandoned, their occupants having fled in 1991. There were simply no Tutsi left to kill.

Unfortunately for Ruginga's residents, the cell was also located on a frontline of the civil war, a full hour's drive away from Ruhengeri town. The national park provided excellent cover for the rebels to conduct guerrilla strikes. Whenever the RPF attacked, it targeted the small military outpost situated in Ruginga itself. The rebels would advance and occupy the cell on two occasions in the course of the war, forcing many of Ruginga's population to flee until government forces re-took the area. On the second occasion, the RPF held ground for as long as three months. The overall effect on the local community was dramatic. Residents lived in a state of heightened insecurity and fear – even for a northern community. They lived precarious lives.

Life changed. Villagers did not have enough security and the talk of that period was of the war and when you met people you would talk about where we would flee to this time. (*Robert, Hutu, self-confessed perpetrator. Author-led interview in Kinyarwanda, Ruhengeri central prison, May 2003.*)

The impact of the war on the population translated directly into anti-Tutsi sentiment. The Hutu population, as elsewhere in the north, suspected the Tutsi in their community of supporting and helping the RPF. They also blamed them for the hardship of having to spend nights patrolling the bushes for infiltrators and also for being displaced by the RPF advances. The following two accounts typify the suspicion and resentment towards Ruginga's Tutsi residents.

What happened in your community after the war started? Here in Ruginga people started to say that they [the rebels] were going to bring back the monarchy and people even started to suspect the Tutsi here in Ruginga. They called all the Tutsi here *ibyitso* [collaborators] (*Sebastian, Hutu, aged 30, tailor. Author-led interview in Kinyarwanda in his home. May 2003.*)

When the *Inkotanyi* [rebels] invaded Umutara [a Rwandan prefecture] people said that those who invaded are too weak and that they cannot take over the government. They even said that they had tails like the devil but after a while we saw that they were just like us. Then the Hutu started to say the Tutsi are going to bring the back *Mwami* [Tutsi monarch]. *Did people threaten or attack the Tutsi in Ruginga?* I did not see cases of Hutu from

Ruginga threatening the Tutsi but they did have a suspicious eye for them. (*Dionyise Sharamanzi, Hutu, cell responsable, aged 60. Author-led interview in Kinyarwanda in his home. May 2003.*)

The anti-Tutsi sentiment followed the pattern of RPF attack, then anti-Tutsi reprisal. Ruginga's Tutsi community was small – merely 3.6 per cent of the whole population. They had moved to Ruginga after the revolution, when the area was declassified as protected national forest. They had come from Gisenyi prefecture and, like everyone else in the area, had received a generous two hectares of land through the government's new *paysannat* scheme. The seven Tutsi households in Ruginga in 1994 were in fact really just two families, headed by Kayihura and Ndizi. Their children had built homes nearby when they married and they all lived within a few minutes' walk from each other. Anti-Tutsi reprisals began in Ruginga as soon as the initial RPF invasion in October 1990. It was the Tutsi family of Kayihura who were first targeted. He, his wife, and his son Jean Gacumbitsi were taken forcibly by a group of villagers from the neighbouring sector, Kanyamiheto, to the commune offices. This was in fact part of the wave of approximately 8,000 arrests that had swept the country following the invasion. Thaddée Gasana, Kinigi's burgomaster, had been particularly vindictive. Once in the hands of the commune authorities, the three were beaten and imprisoned for a week before being released. Kayihura's daughter remembers it vividly:

What happened in Ruginga after the war started? When the war broke out, they started to harass us [Tutsi] in Ruginga. My father and my mother and Gatwa my brother were imprisoned and were beaten in prison. They were said to be *ibyitso* [collaborators]. But it was not true that they were *ibyitso*. *How did it happen?* Some villagers came and took them as they were ordered by the burgomaster. *Who took them?* It was a group of many people all from Kanyamiheto sector. Then the second time they came in 1991 it was to kill. *Who did this?* It was again those people from Kanyamiheto. (*Willene, Tutsi survivor, aged 35. Author-led interview in Kinyarwanda in her home, Ruhengeri town, June 2003.*)

Willene alludes to the second major event in the war that brought reprisals against Ruginga's Tutsi population. The RPF's lightning one-day strike on Ruhengeri town on 23 January 1991 brought tragedy to Ruginga. In response to the attack, the same group of villagers from the neighbouring Kanyamiheto sector targeted the same family in Ruginga. But this time they had violence in mind. According to

5.2 The Window of Opportunity

Willene, in their first attempt they were not enough to overpower Kayihura's family as his relatives had come to their assistance. However, the group returned later that day, reinforced. On this second attempt, the family locked themselves in their hut and the attack group then stoned it. Eventually the door opened and Gatwa, the son, ran out only to be pursued by the group who caught and killed him with several machete blows to the head. At this point, the group took fright at having killed a man and dispersed by themselves. This second event resembled the first. As before, the order for the attack had originated with the burgomaster of Kinigi, Thaddée Gasana. Also, as before, it was part of a series of coordinated actions against the commune's *Bagogwe* Tutsi in response to the RPF raid on Ruhengeri.

From this moment onwards, life considerably deteriorated for Ruginga's small Tutsi community. Following the first attack in January, those remaining of Kayihura's and Ndizi's family, lived under the careful watch of their Hutu neighbours. It was almost a form of house arrest. Not long after Gatwa's death, in February 1991 the Kanyamiheto radicals returned to Ruginga. This time they targeted Ndizi. They told him that the commune had summoned him for questioning but instead they took him to Kanyamiheto where they promptly killed him. In the same month, Kayihura was also killed. Soldiers forcibly took and executed him outside Ruginga. His two other sons were murdered in Gisenyi where they worked. Another Tutsi, a man from outside the community, was caught fleeing through Ruginga. Three villagers from neighbouring Ndubi cell captured and killed him.

Up until this time, the target of violence had always been men. The women and children who remained found their movement highly restricted. They survived through the kindness of a few sympathetic neighbours.

Not all the villagers suspected us after the war started. We still had some friends who would share with us. There were some who would bring water for us and others food as once the war started we could not move. *What happened to them?* They were also being harassed for doing this by the other villagers from Ruginga. They would ask them what did they want from *ibyitso* houses? (*Interview with Willene again, June 2003.*)

However, the mounting violence soon convinced the remaining women and children that they must find an opportunity to flee. By July 1991, there were no Tutsi left in the cell. When Habyarimana was assassinated, on 7 April 1994, the day afterwards the RPF moved to occupy the sector causing part of the population to flee again. The rebels would be driven back by a FAR counter-attack several days later. However, while there were no Tutsi in Ruginga left to kill, a Tutsi woman with her three children from another community came in search of the RPF encampment only to find that she had arrived too late. She and her children fell into the FAR hands instead. The soldiers killed all four. The final death toll in Ruginga would stand at eight: one – Gatwa – killed within the cell and another seven killed outside. This would include Gatwa's wife and two children who fled to Gisenyi in 1991 only to be killed in 1994. Much of the violence had been committed by outsiders – in particular, villagers from the neighbouring Kanyamiheto sector. Only one resident of Ruginga would stand accused of violent crime. But another thirty-five stood accused of looting following the flight of the Tutsi from their homes.

5.3 The Micro-mechanics of Mobilization

The first part of this chapter provided some insight into what transpired in the window of opportunity created by Habyarimana's death. His assassination triggered power struggles for control of the state at the macro-, meso-, and micro-levels in which extremists and opportunists ultimately prevailed. In the second part of the chapter, I explain in more depth how, once state capture at the centre and periphery had been achieved, the extraordinary mobilization of Rwanda's civilian population followed. The micro-mechanics of Rwanda's rapid and massive mobilization of the population beg explanation. Mobilization is particularly puzzling in the south where we have seen earlier that state and society were not widely radicalized against Tutsi beforehand. The extremist ideology of Hutu Power had only shallowly penetrated Butare prefecture. Yet in a very short space of time, minority behaviour became majority behaviour in many communities.

Analysis of the events in the four cells points to mobilization as a process. It began first with the emergence of ethnic and political entrepreneurs. In each community, there was a central figure who rose up and sought to mobilize the community into violence. These entrepreneurs relied either on existing mobilization structures, such as the party youth wings in the north, or else drew on their social networks as in the south, to establish a small number of like-minded supporters in favour of action. Family members, friends, and neighbours were drawn into the genocide through their links to the dominant entrepreneur in their community. Together, these entrepreneurs and their supporters constituted a critical mass of individuals in favour of violence locally. This radical minority then jump-started the mobilization of a broader swathe of the local population using peer pressure and other forms of coercion. They were aided in this process by Rwanda's unusually high population density, which amplified the social forces of coercion and co-optation. In the following sub-sections, I expand upon each of these steps in the mobilization process and, where available, draw upon additional data to help show that these findings were not unique to the four communities researched.

The Emergence of Ethnic and Political Entrepreneurs

The mobilizing agents at the local level comprised both longstanding bigots and political opportunists. These ethnic and political entrepreneurs were the first-movers in their communities. Some already held positions of state authority before the plane went down. They were commune burgomasters, sector councillors, and cell *responsables*. Others, however, were not state officials. They had emerged early on as local political figures as a result of Rwanda's liberalization process and then engaged in power struggles locally to establish themselves as the state authority figures. In the north, we saw that mobilization was immediate. In Mutovu cell, Gervais Harelimana, who held strong anti-Tutsi views, had first emerged as a prominent politician following the start of multipartyism when he became the president of the radically anti-Tutsi CDR party for Nkuli commune. After Habyarimana's assassination, the *Impuzamugambi,* the CDR youth wing whom Harelimana commanded, and the *Interahamwe*, controlled by the sector councillor, immediately began eliminating the cell's Tutsi population. In Kinigi, its hard-line burgomaster, Thaddée Gasana, had targeted Tutsi for violence even *before* 6 April. Extremists already controlled the state in Kinigi before Habyarimana was assassinated. In the two southern communities in contrast, mobilization was delayed. We saw Karimunda, a well-known racist, and Rekeraho, a political opportunist, rise up and eclipse the hesitant *responsables* and councillors in Tamba and Mwendo respectively. Rekeraho had first emerged as a prominent MDR politician in Maraba commune following the legalization of opposition parties. In both communities, these local entrepreneurs supplanted the local state officials only after Butare's moderate prefect, Jean-Baptiste Habyalimana, had been removed and the burgomasters had defected to the new IG at the centre. Habineza, the burgomaster of Maraba commune, switched to support violence on 18 April. Théophile Shiyarambere of Shyanda commune did so on 23 April following a meeting with Butare's new hard-line prefect. In both north and south, then, popular mobilization followed state capture at the local level.

We see also that there was resistance to the violence within the state apparatus. There were burgomasters at the meso-level and sector councillors and cell *responsables* at the micro-level who either opposed action or else hesitated to act. This was particularly true in the south where Butare exemplified this resistance. It was the 'rebel prefecture' (Guichaoua, 2005). More interestingly though, we also see that there was support for violence from actors unconnected to the state. Thus, there was Karimunda, the extremist butcher in Shyanda commune; Rekeraho, the opportunist opposition politician in Maraba; and Harelimana, the extremist and opportunist opposition politician in Nkuli. None of these figures was in the employ of the state. These political and ethnic entrepreneurs instead came from within Rwandan *society*. In the opportunity created by Habyarimana's assassination, they moved first to become the new *de facto* or *de jure* authorities in their communities. They replaced the incumbent authority figures who either hesitated or resisted.

Survey data corroborate that this did not only happen in these four communities. When asked whether the incumbent local authority figures continued to exercise authority during the genocide, Table 5.4. shows that only 60.7 per cent of Hutu said this was so of their burgomasters; 69.9 per cent said this was so for their sector councillors; and 65 percent said this was so of their cell *responsables*. By implication, for between 35–40 per cent of ordinary Rwandan Hutu, local state authority figures had lost their authority in their constituencies.

These other individuals – the entrepreneurs of violence – came from diverse walks of life. I collected data on 160 named, local entrepreneurs in twenty different sectors across Rwanda. These were individuals who had organized or led the genocide in their communities. I confirmed their identities with confessed perpetrators in prison as well as non-perpetrators at liberty, who had lived in the same communities during the genocide. Table 5.5 summarizes the profile of these

Table 5.4 Power of local state authority figures during the genocide

Question: During the genocide, in your opinion, which of the following individuals continued to have authority in your community?

	Ethnicity		Perpetrator Status		Region	
	Hutu	Tutsi	Non-perp.	Perp.	South	North
	(N=223)	(N=21)	(N=156)	(N=67)	(N=95)	(N=128)
Commune Burgomaster	60.7%	71.1%	60.8%	56.8%	54.9%	66.8%
Sector Councillor	69.9%	85.6%	70.0%	67.1%	71.9%	67.8%
Cell Responsible	65.0%	80.8%	64.8%	69.9%	60.4%	69.9%

Table 5.5 *Profiles of 160 grassroots leaders of Rwanda's genocide*

	Total (%)	Butare (%)	Ruhengeri (%)
Gender			
Male	160 (100%)	102 (100%)	58 (100%)
Female	0	0	0
Age Range			
<20	0	0	0
20–29	33 (22.5%)	11 (11.7%)	22 (41.5%)
30–39	58 (39.5%)	43 (45.7%)	15 (28.3%)
40–49	41 (27.9%)	26 (27.7%)	15 (28.3%)
50+	15 (10.2%)	14 (14.9%)	1 (1.9%)
Unknown	13	8	5
Occupation before Genocide			
Farmer	72 (47.1%)	43 (42.6%)	29 (55.8%)
Civilian admin. authority (*responsable*, councillor, burgomaster)	32 (20.9%)	23 (22.8%)	9 (17.3%)
School teacher	8 (5.2%)	6 (5.9%)	2 (3.9%)
Other local government employee	11 (7.2%)	9 (8.9%)	13 (2.0%)
Police or other civilian security personnel	9 (5.9%)	8 (7.9%)	8 (1.0%)
Soldier	3 (2.0%)	1 (1.0%)	7 (2.0%)
Former/reserve soldier	5 (3.3%)	3 (3.0%)	12 (2.0%)
Private sector employee (e.g. driver, mechanic, cook, guard)	4 (2.6%)	2 (2.0%)	10 (2.0%)
Businessman/self-employed (e.g. owns bar, restaurant, shop)	3 (2.0%)	2 (2.0%)	1 (1.9%)
Professional (e.g. doctor, lawyer, university professor)	2 (1.3%)	2 (2.0%)	0
Student	1 (0.7%)	0	1 (1.9%)
Semi-skilled artisan (e.g. mason, potter, carpenter, tailor)	3 (2.0%)	2 (2.0%)	11 (1.0%)
Unknown	7	1	6

5.3 The Micro-mechanics of Mobilization

Table 5.5 (*cont.*)

	Total (%)	Butare (%)	Ruhengeri (%)
Political Party Affiliation			
MRND	81 (57.5%)	46 (50.6%)	35 (70.0%)
MDR	35 (24.8%)	30 (33.0%)	5 (10.0%)
PSD	11 (7.8%)	11 (12.1%)	0
PL	1 (0.7%)	1 (1.1%)	0
CDR	10 (7.1%)	0	10 (20.0%)
No party/party unknown	22	14	11
Residence of Origin during Genocide			
Inside the community (sector)	119 (79.9%)	73 (76.0%)	46 (86.8%)
Outside the community (sector)	30 (20.1%)	23 (24.0%)	7 (13.2%)
Unknown	11	6	5

local genocide leaders. What is most telling is that less than half (44.5 per cent) of all those identified were employees of the state – either civilian or military. By this I mean burgomasters, councillors, *responsables*, other commune employees, schoolteachers, gendarmes, policemen, soldiers, and military reservists. In contrast, 55.5 per cent of all those who led the genocide came from Rwandan society. They had nothing to do with the state. Moreover, it was not simply the rural elite.[40] Certainly there were local businessmen, professionals, salaried private sector employees, and secondary and university-level students among this number. However, the majority were non-elites. In fact, 47.1 per cent were ordinary farmers. In short, it was not only extremists from within the state apparatus who pushed for violence. It was also extremists and opportunists from below, from within Rwandan society as well.

---

[40] Straus (2006, p. 91) makes one of the most explicit cases that it was the rural elite who took advantage of the opportunity created by Habyarimana's assassination.

We need to refine the claim of the role of the state. The model of the genocide in which the pressure spread from the top to the bottom, or from the centre to the periphery is incomplete. It did not simply start with an order at the top that was then loyally implemented at various levels below. There was resistance to violence *within* the state apparatus, as well as support for it from *outside* of it. The impetus for violence moved in both directions. Radical challengers from within Rwandan society, in collaboration with extremist incumbents within the state, mobilized the population.

Critical Masses: The Importance of Small Groups

These local ethnic and political entrepreneurs did not act alone. They were assisted by small bands of hardcore supporters in their communities. In the north, the MRNDD and CDR youth wings, the *Interahamwe* and *Impuzumugambi*, represented existing mobilization structures that entrepreneurs could draw on. However, particularly in the south, they also relied on mobilizing persons in their social networks. Thus, in Mwendo, Rekeraho – who was a former soldier – was aided by two friends who were also former soldiers, Habimana-Kirenga and Kayihura. In Tamba, Karimunda's right-hand men were his brother, Pierre S., and his nephew, Jacques N. Family members, friends, and neighbours were to be found among an entrepreneur's most loyal supporters. Collectively, they represented 'critical masses' of individuals in favour of violence in their communities. These violence entrepreneurs then used these active minorities to mobilize the otherwise inactive or 'uncommitted' majority, the large numbers of residents who did nothing either to oppose or to support violence.[41] To reverse an adage: all it took for good to fail was for a few bad men to do something.

Survey data corroborate the existence of such critical masses elsewhere in Rwanda. Table 5.6 shows that 56.3 per cent of Rwandan Hutu confirmed that there were individuals in the attack groups who were exceptionally enthusiastic for violence in their community. According to these respondents, such individuals on average numbered between one and ten in their communities. These critical masses of committed supporters willing to use violence were essential to the mobilization of the population.

---

[41] Marwell et al. (1988) first applied the notion of the 'critical mass' to collective action.

Table 5.6 *Identifying committed killers or 'critical masses'*

	Ethnicity		Perpetrator Status		Region	
	Hutu	Tutsi	Non-perp.	Perp.	South	North

Question: *If there was a group organized in your community, how many – if any – in that group would you say were enthusiastic to kill?*

	(N=229)	(N=15)	(N=143)	(N=86)	(N=98)	(N=131)
None	32.7%	0	33.7%	12.6%	1.5%	57.8%
1–10	56.3%	93.5%	55.7%	68.4%	81.2%	36.2%
11–20	6.2%	6.5%	5.6%	17.0%	9.4%	3.6%
21+	4.8%	0	5.0%	2.1%	7.9%	2.4%

Harnessing Group Forces: Ingroup Policing and Peer Pressure

These critical masses – the small minority of individuals most willing to commit violence – were 'critical' because they triggered a chain reaction that ultimately culminated in mass mobilization. They relied on coercion to jump-start this process. This coercion involved not only the threat or actual application of physical force. It also comprised subtler forms of duress, notably: (i) financial sanctions: individuals were fined money or goods for not participating; and (ii) social stigma: non-participants were just labelled enemy collaborators. These were the metaphorical weapons with which radical minorities policed the wider population.

Mwendo provided one example of how coercion worked in practice. Rekeraho, the central figure within the community's critical mass group, enforced participation by drawing up a list of the able-bodied men. At the start, early every morning these men were required to assemble at a crossroad in the community where they would decide where they would go to hunt the enemy. It was a roll call. The names of those who did not show up were noted. The group would then call upon this person's home and demand a fine. It could be money, it could be beer, or it could be food. In one instance, they took a whole cow.

Mwendo was not unique. Coercion – at least to jump-start mobilization – was widespread. I asked survey respondents two open-ended questions regarding sanctions: (i) what happened if somebody refused to participate in an attack group? and (ii) what happened if someone was caught helping a Tutsi? Table 5.7 shows that about half responded

Table 5.7 Importance of ingroup policing and peer pressure during the genocide

	Ethnicity		Perpetrator Status		Region	
	Hutu	Tutsi	Non-perp.	Perp.	South	North

Question: During the genocide, were there people from your community, other than the elderly and sick, who refused to participate in the attacks or to hunt for the enemy?

	(N=263)	(N=21)	(N=164)	(N=99)	(N=126)	(N=137)
Yes, there were people who did nothing	75.4%	90.5%	75.3%	77.3%	91.2%	60.1%

Question: If so, what, if anything, happened to these people who did not join the attacks or hunt for the enemy? (open-ended, multiple answers permitted, post-coded)

	(N=194)	(N=18)	(N=128)	(N=66)	(N=114)	(N=80)
Nothing happened	53.3%	49.7%	53.7%	46.3%	45.1%	65.4%
Seen in bad way or called 'collaborator'	16.9%	22.4%	17.3%	9.1%	19.7%	12.6%
Fined money	11.5%	5.7%	10.3%	33.9%	16.5%	4.1%
Property looted/destroyed	7.9%	5.4%	7.1%	24.2%	9.6%	5.4%
Chased out of the cell	4.5%	5.7%	4.7%	0.5%	6.3%	1.9%
Forced to participate in some anti-Tutsi activity	0.9%	0.0%	0.8%	4.3%	0.4%	1.8%
Physically threatened	11.4%	22.0%	11.7%	6.5%	9.4%	14.3%
Physically harmed	9.8%	11.3%	10.2%	2.3%	11.4%	7.5%
They were killed	9.2%	16.8%	9.5%	4.3%	13.0%	3.6%
Something else happened	6.2%	0.0%	6.3%	4.3%	9.2%	1.8%

Question: What happened to people caught helping Tutsi? (open-ended, multiple answers permitted, post-coded)

	(N=169)	(N=17)	(N=102)	(N=67)	(N=115)	(N=54)
Nothing happened	42.1%	29.4%	42.3%	38.8%	46.9%	30.8%
Seen in bad way or called 'collaborator'	6.9%	0.0%	6.9%	6.4%	8.5%	3.1%
Fined money	19.7%	29.2%	18.7%	34.2%	21.6%	15.4%
Property looted/destroyed	13.3%	23.4%	13.7%	8.3%	12.7%	14.9%
Chased out of the cell	2.9%	0.0%	2.9%	2.0%	2.8%	3.0%
Forced to participate in some anti-Tutsi activity	6.2%	6.0%	5.0%	22.6%	8.7%	0.2%
Physically threatened	12.8%	6.0%	12.5%	17.8%	4.4%	32.7%
Physically harmed	11.9%	6.0%	12.7%	0.9%	9.3%	18.0%
They were killed	13.9%	23.4%	14.7%	1.7%	14.6%	12.3%
Something else happened	0.9%	0.0%	1.0%	0.0%	1.3%	0.0%

that nothing happened. However, the other half gave a wide range of sanctions. In order of frequency, in response to the first question Rwandan Hutu said that these individuals: (i) faced accusations of being collaborators (social stigma); (ii) were physically harmed or killed; (iii) were physically threatened; (iv) were fined money; or (v) had their property looted or destroyed. The list was the same but the order almost reversed for the second question.

These sanctions represented a form of ingroup policing, or more coercive peer pressure. They were all the more effective in densely populated Rwanda. It was difficult for an individual to opt out as action and inaction could be easily observed. As we shall see in Chapter 6, however, coercion does not explain the full scale of mobilization. It did not account for everyone's participation. It only *jump-started* the violence. Mobilization was a continuum that began with these critical masses who used coercion to trigger a chain reaction. As more and more people joined in the violence, the risks of participation diminished and the costs of non-participation increased. And as more people joined in, the reasons for participation diversified and transformed. There was a multiplicity of motives people gave for their own actions and those of others. I shall examine these other motives, and how they evolved, in Chapter 6. Ultimately, while coercion was important to catalyse the violence, many different micro-motives would come to sustain it.

Mobilization Amplifiers

As noted already, the civilian mobilization, and ensuing violence, were extraordinary in their scale, speed, and scope in Rwanda. I estimate that one in five Hutu men committed an act of violence; much of the killing occurred in the first two weeks following Habyarimana's assassination; and it took place in almost every community where Tutsi lived. Rwanda's unusual mobilization and violence can be traced to a number of unusual demographic and geographic characteristics. These operated in several, unobvious ways.

First, Rwanda's small territory, high population density, and remarkable road network collectively implied small, easy-to-traverse distances between communities. These amplified contagion effects in Rwanda. Violence spread rapidly. Mwendo was among the first communities to succumb to violence in Butare prefecture because Maraba

5.3 The Micro-mechanics of Mobilization

commune borders Gikongoro prefecture, where the genocide was already underway. Conversely, Tamba was among the last in Butare because it was so remote. It took longer for news, looting, burning, and other external triggers to reach its residents. Such spill-over effects were not limited to Mwendo and Tamba. As Table 5.8 shows, 72.3 per cent of surveyed Hutu said individuals came from *outside* their community to commit violence within it. Similarly, 68.7 per cent said individuals from their own communities travelled to other places to commit violence. So, cross-contamination was important. Small distances also amplified the centre's opportunity to mobilize the periphery. The hardliners who succeeded in capturing the central state apparatus travelled frequently and easily to Rwanda's rural communities during the genocide, often to their prefectures and communes of origin where their local influence was greatest. The facility in movement within Rwanda also enabled violence as soldiers, gendarmes, and militiamen could readily reach communities to overcome local resistance and jump-start the killing.

Second, Rwanda's unusual settlement pattern – Hutu and Tutsi lived side-by-side throughout the country – directly magnified the scale, speed, and ambit of the violence. It facilitated the surveillance of the Tutsi population. It also made it easier to identify and target them. Tutsi could not easily escape. Identification was reinforced by high rural immobility. Rwanda was one of the least urbanized countries in sub-Saharan Africa. Families often lived in the same rural communities, often on the same hill, for generations. This meant that neighbours had intimate knowledge of each other. Anonymity would have been impossible and ethnicity difficult to conceal. Contact theory (Hewstone & Swart, 2011) predicts that spatial proximity would encourage positive inter-ethnic attitudes, but only if groups enjoy equal status and share common goals. Hutu and Tutsi, in contrast, were ranked groups whose members likely suspected each other of supporting opposing parties in the war. Under these conditions, contact engendered conflict not co-existence.

Lastly, Rwanda's exceptional population density amplified the effects of peer pressure and social networks. The forces of coercion and co-optation are strong in communities where people live closely together. It was difficult to avoid scrutiny – either as a Tutsi seeking to escape or as a Hutu wishing to avoid having to kill. This has been aptly named the difficulty of 'exit' in Rwanda (Straus, 2006, p. 8).

Table 5.8 Contagion effects of the violence

	Ethnicity		Perpetrator Status		Region	
	Hutu	Tutsi	Non-perp.	Perp.	South	North

Question: During the genocide, did people from outside your cell come to hunt for the enemy inside your cell?

	(N=249)	(N=21)	(N=155)	(N=94)	(N=122)	(N=127)
Yes, people from outside came into our cell	72.3%	90.3%	72.6%	65.8%	89.3%	54.1%

Question: Did people from inside your cell go to hunt for the enemy in other cells?

	(N=226)	(N=19)	(N=136)	(N=90)	(N=115)	(N=111)
Yes, people went to other cells	68.7%	100.0%	68.8%	66.1%	87.4%	45.9%

Question: Were the leaders of the attack groups in your cell from your cell or from elsewhere?

	(N=182)	(N=21)	(N=127)	(N=55)	(N=105)	(N=77)
From the cell	23.9%	42.9%	23.0%	47.7%	30.1%	13.9%
From elsewhere	21.5%	14.2%	21.1%	33.5%	14.1%	33.5%
From both places	54.5%	42.9%	55.9%	18.8%	55.8%	52.5%

5.3 The Micro-mechanics of Mobilization

In Chapter 6, I will examine more closely how the dense social networks created by Rwanda's extreme population density mattered for the violence.

* * * * *

This chapter has examined the third and final macro-factor that I argue was behind Rwanda's genocide: a political opportunity. My goal was to understand how communities moved to violence so quickly and so massively in the space of opportunity created by Habyarimana's assassination. In explaining mass mobilization, I refined two common claims about the genocide. The first concerns the state-centric, top-down interpretation of the violence. The power of the Rwandan state was indeed important for implementing the genocide. However, this overlooks: (i) the resistance within the Rwandan state apparatus itself; and (ii) the contribution of Rwandan society. The resistance is better-known, and confirmed in the power struggle for control of the state at the macro- meso-, and micro-levels after the president's death (Guichaoua, 2005; Straus, 2006). But the role of Rwandan society is less well-articulated. Yet there was clearly pressure from below. In my sample of 160 men who came to lead and organize the genocide in their communities, more than half were unconnected to the state. These were extremists and opportunists from within Rwandan society. Moreover, they were not just local elites. As we have seen, almost half of them were ordinary farmers.

The second claim concerns Rwanda's unusual geography and demography. I find that these mattered not so much because they created a neo-Malthusian resource crunch – as would happen when demographic pressure collides with ecological scarcity. They mattered because they amplified the effects of (i) contagion; (ii) coercion; and (iii) co-optation. Living in such close proximity to each other where distances were small meant that (i) violence spread quickly; (ii) it was difficult to avoid scrutiny; and (iii) people had multiple inter-personal connections to each other that could draw them into action. So, Rwanda's unusual geography and demography were in part the reason for the unusual scale and speed of its popular mobilization.

6 | *Authority: Rwanda's Privatized and Powerful State*

6.1 Introduction

The conjunction of war with liberalization and assassination provided the motive and opportunity for genocide. The state in contrast represented the *means* for the crime. The focus on the state in genocide is not unwarranted. The modern state, or more precisely the elite who control it, is specially and powerfully positioned to kill large numbers of its own citizens. In the twentieth century alone, thirty-one of thirty-seven cases of mass killings, that is the intentional killing of at least 50,000 civilians over five or fewer years, involved the state acting against its own citizens.[1] In contrast, non-state actors were complicit in only eight instances of such mass killings, of which seven were committed by rebel or insurgent groups during civil wars.[2]

---

[1] These thirty-one cases are drawn from Valentino's (2004) dataset on mass killings. I included only those cases where the state targeted its own citizens. The locations and dates for each event are as follows: the Soviet Union (1917–1923), Soviet Union (1928–1933), China (1949–1972), Cambodia (1975–1979), Turkey (1915–1918), Soviet Union (1941–1953), Germany (1939–1945), Yugoslavia (1941–1945), Eastern Europe (1945–1947), Bangladesh (1971), Burundi (1972), Indonesia in East Timor (1975–1999), Bosnia-Herzegovina (1990–1995), Rwanda (1994), Namibia (1904–1907), China (1927–1949), Spain (1939–1943), Algeria (1954–1963), Sudan (1956–1971), Tibet (1959–1960), Iraq (1963–1991), Guatemala (1966–1985), Ethiopia (1974–1991), Angola (1975–2002), El Salvador (1979–1992), Sudan (1983–2002), Somalia (1988–1991), Burundi (1983–1998), Russia in Chechnya (1994–2000), Spain (1936–1939), and Nigeria (1967–1970).

[2] The seven cases of mass killing committed by organized non-state actors in the context of internal wars occurred in: China (1927–1949), Algeria (1954–1963), Vietnam (1954–1975), Angola (1975–2002), Mozambique (1975–2002), Algeria (1992–2002), and Spain (1936–1939). Note two cases, Algeria (1954–1963) and Angola (1975–2002), involved both state and non-state actors. The eighth case occurred in the unusual context of India's Partition in 1947 in which Hindu and Muslim civilians attacked each other during their relocation to and from newly created Pakistan.

6.1 Introduction

Existing explanations of why the state is so frequently implicated in genocide have overwhelmingly highlighted its enormous material power (Horowitz, 2002; Rummel, 1995; Straus, 2006). Proponents point first to the state's *coercive* capabilities. These include the state's formal security apparatus: the army and the police, in both regular and specialised variants, constitute its backbone. However, 'violence specialists' with more ambiguous ties to the state – paramilitaries, death squads, militia groups, and youth wings of political parties – are often also implicated in civilian killings.[3] The state's *coordination* capabilities also matter. The civilian administrative machinery of state is capable of killing by creating policies or deliberately failing to relieve conditions that starve, exhaust, or expose to disease its civilian population. The state has created prison camps, forcibly relocated populations, and induced famines, as a result of which massive numbers of civilians have died.[4] The concentration of power in the modern state and the concomitant rise in its bureaucratic and administrative capabilities has led some to see genocide as a product of modernity (Bauman, 2000).

Yet explanations of genocide that emphasize the state's material capacity miss other aspects of its power that matter for mobilization and violence. It is, moreover, unsurprising that the state has unrivalled power of life and death over its civilian population. Even states with military capabilities that are weak vis-à-vis other states are strong vis-à-vis their own societies. The state represents a technology that can be instrumentalized and its considerable resources readily deployed against large numbers of defenceless civilians. It is a weapon of potential mass destruction *par excellence*. Existing explanations, however, overlook two other fundamental dimensions of the state's power that matter for genocide: the state's autonomy and its legitimacy. First, the

---

[3] Tilly (2003) first coined the term 'violence specialist'.
[4] Communization was responsible for many of the most brutal civilian policies. In the Soviet Union, Stalin established Gulag prison camps to accommodate those deemed criminals and traitors of the state (1929–1953). The brutal conditions claimed millions of lives. In the Ukraine, collectivization resulted in a massive famine (1932–1933) in which millions starved. Stalin used the famine to crush Ukrainian nationalism. In Cambodia, the Khmer Rouge forcibly relocated millions of the residents of its major cities to the countryside to work. Many were executed or else perished from starvation or exhaustion. Pol Pot also saw the forced displacement as an opportunity to eliminate potential elite opponents to the regime.

state's autonomy, by which I mean the independence of its institutions from capture by private social and political forces such as extremism, is central to resisting commands and policies that wrongly target individuals and groups for elimination. Its considerable material resources cannot be deployed if individuals who hold state office feel constrained by formal rules on how they may be lawfully used. Second, the state's legitimacy is key to public acceptance of and participation in policies that target civilians. Were the state and its institutions perceived as illegitimate, its commands would lack authority. Its officials and citizens would feel only a weak urge to comply voluntarily with them.

In studies of the genocide, the remarkable capacity of the Rwandan state has become well-known and the use of its power to deadly effect well-documented. It has been described as a Leviathan in a continent comprised overwhelmingly of weak states (Straus, 2006). Its unusual strength has been used to explain civilian participation in the violence as primarily the product of coercion. The state's remarkable capacity to surveil the population and to enforce its authority at the periphery made 'exit' from the violence costly. This 'Leviathan' argument challenges earlier claims that Rwandans were culturally inclined to obey authority (Prunier, 1998, p. 248; Reyntjens, 1996, p. 245). It credits Rwandans with agency but argues that individuals calculated they had no choice other than to comply given the state's power to monitor and punish those who did not. However, this Hobbesian-inspired explanation is incomplete. It is not simply that the Rwandan state had unusually strong capabilities. Coercion does not fully explain the massive mobilization. As we shall see, the Rwandan state additionally had high legitimacy and low autonomy. It was this tripartite combination of strong capacity, high legitimacy, and low autonomy that was highly unusual for a modern African state. Collectively they contributed to the unusual mobilization during the genocide. Each dimension mattered in different ways at the micro-level. As we shall see in Chapter 7, there was heterogeneity in the reasons for participation. High capacity affected 'compliers' who felt coerced into participation; high legitimacy mattered for 'conformists' who respected the state's authority and heeded its orders; and low autonomy enabled 'extremists' and 'opportunists' who felt authorized by the state to act.

In this chapter, I trace the origins of these three facets of the Rwandan state's power and explain the ways in which each contributed to the extraordinary scale, speed, and ambit of the mobilization. First,

6.1 Introduction

I show that the state's low autonomy, while not unusual for a modern African polity, was nonetheless necessary to allow extremists and opportunists to capture and instrumentalize its institutions and resources. Its origins lay, in part, in the continuity of the precolonial informal institution of political clientelism, which co-existed with formal political institutions in the postcolonial era. Rwanda had a neo-patrimonial political culture in which power was personalized within ostensibly impersonal institutions. It lay in part also in the weakness of Rwanda's civil society and its inability to serve as a counterweight to the state and hold its officials accountable for their decisions. Most of all, however, the state's autonomy was circumscribed by the remarkable machinery of the ruling party, whose organization mirrored and penetrated the state down to its lowest administrative level. While liberalization weakened the party's *legitimacy*, its organizational *capacity* remained strong. The party operated on the strength of clientelist ties and privileged personal, kinship, and regional loyalties. It expected its members who held state office to subordinate their official obligations to the interests of the party. The party represented the instrument through which society, or rather elite factions of society, privatized and politicized the state.

Second, the modern Rwandan state's high symbolic authority or perceived legitimacy was unusual for a postcolonial African state. I will argue that it can be traced first and primarily to the revolution on the eve of its independence. The revolution ended oppressive monarchic and chieftain rule associated with the Tutsi minority and legitimized a new republican state associated with the Hutu majority. Rwanda's unusual ethnic composition – a bi-ethnic division in which one group, the Hutu, were overwhelmingly numerically dominant – reinforced the legitimacy of the majority group's exclusive control of the state. Second, the broad institutional continuity in authority structures across the precolonial, colonial, and postcolonial eras strengthened the state's symbolic authority. Its modern-day prefects and burgomasters resembled the traditional chiefs and sub-chiefs. Lastly, the modern state was not an artificial colonial construction replete with alien institutions. It was the successor of an already highly developed precolonial kingdom whose territorial borders had remained relatively constant since the nineteenth century. The rulers of the Rwandan polity had been governing largely the same people – the Banyarwanda – throughout its history.

Finally, the state's high capacity, as others have observed, was also unusual on the continent. It has rightly been linked to Rwanda's high population density, open landscape, and hilly topography. These geographic and demographic particularities facilitated the projection of power from centre to periphery as Rwandans could be easily found and could not easily evade state obligations (Straus, 2006). However, I point to four other often-overlooked sources of the state's material strength: the location of its capital in the country's geographic centre, its small territorial size, its extensive road network, and its homogenous ecology. I shall show how these characteristics contributed to the mobilization and violence by reinforcing the state's capacity for both compliance and coordination.

Table 6.1 summarizes Rwandan state power on these three dimensions across the precolonial, colonial, and postcolonial eras. As can be seen, the state's autonomy has been consistently low and its capacity consistently high. However, it is worth noting that its legitimacy has varied. Legitimacy begins to fluctuate once the equation between exclusive political power and ethnicity is made. Belgium first established ethnocratic rule and began to undermine the state's legitimacy through the favour it showed Tutsi in appointments to state office. The revolution of 1959 was primarily a response to this ethnic monopoly and it imbued the successor republican state with revolutionary legitimacy in the eyes of the Hutu majority. As we shall see, the extremist Hutu elite invoked the defence of the revolution's gains and ordinary Hutu cited the respect of the post-revolutionary state's authority as an important rationale for their participation during the genocide.

Table 6.1 *Dimensions of Rwandan state power across time*

	Precolonial (1860–1897)	Colonial (1897–1962)	Postcolonial (1962–1994)
Autonomy	Low	Low	Low
Legitimacy	High	Initially high for all, later low for Hutu	High for Hutu; low for Tutsi
Capacity	High	High	High

6.2 Dimension I: Weak State Autonomy

Low state autonomy, by which I mean the independence of state institutions from capture by private political and social forces, made it possible for extremists and political opportunists to instrumentalize the state's material resources and to appropriate its symbolic authority. The distinction between the state and the regime was weak in Rwanda. In fact, few countries in sub-Saharan Africa approached the Weberian ideal of a state composed of formal, impersonal institutions and run by impartial officials and administrators acting autonomously of their political masters and social groups. While the extent to which state power is personalized and accountability to formal rules varies across countries, it is generally low in Africa. Rwanda was not exceptional in this regard. Nonetheless low state autonomy was a necessary condition for state capture. When state autonomy is low, private social and political forces more easily instrumentalize the state's authority and resources. In contrast, when the state's autonomy is high, its officials protect its institutions, comply with its formal rules, and resist efforts by ethnic groups and political parties to commandeer its authority and resources for their private ends. Contrary to the Marxist conceptualization, the state is not necessarily the instrument of the dominant class or an arena wherein class struggles are fought (Skocpol, 1979, pp. 27–32). Moreover, bureaucratic autonomy is a dimension of governance distinct from bureaucratic capacity (Fukuyama, 2013). The Rwandan state was 'soft' (lacking in autonomy), but it was not 'weak' (lacking in capacity) (Myrdal, 1967).

Continuity in Clientelist Governance

Low state autonomy did not manifest suddenly with the creation of the postcolonial state in Rwanda. It was in part the product of an institutional legacy. In the precolonial era, political power had been personalized. There was no distinction between the office and the individual who held it. Power vested in the person of the *Mwami*, whose word was law. Patrimonial rule, as Weber characterized authority that fused the public and private spheres, continued into the colonial era. Both the German and Belgian colonial administrations preserved the Tutsi monarchy and with it survived the traditional institution of political clientelism. At its core, political clientelism comprises an asymmetric relationship between the patron who offers privileges or benefits to his or her client who in return provides his or her political loyalty. The *Mwami* granted positions, chieftaincies and sub-chieftaincies, to his clients in exchange for their political allegiance (Lemarchand, 1972). Kinship ties based on (i) lineages (*umulyango*); (ii) clans (*ubwoko*); and (iii) sub-clans (*ishanga*) were often, though not invariably, privileged in the choice of clients. Ensuring loyalty was paramount. While the birth of the modern Rwandan state coincided with the abolition of the monarchy, it did not signify the end of clientelism, however. Formal state institutions co-existed with the informal traditional institution of political clientelism. The tension within society created between the value placed on traditional clientelist rule and the value placed on modern institutional rule is, I argue, at the heart of Rwanda's neo-patrimonial political culture. The stronger the attachment to clientelism, the weaker the autonomy of the state.

The Party-State

The institutional dualism implicit in neo-patrimonial rule was manifest in the relationship between party and state in Rwanda. In both the First and Second Republics, the two ruling parties, first the Parti du Mouvement de l'Emancipation Hutu (PARMEHUTU) and then the Mouvement Révolutionnaire National pour le Développement (MRND), became synonymous with the state. Within the party, position was secured primarily through clientelist means. Within the state, position could be achieved through the formal rules governing selection and election, but it could also be obtained through party ties. The ties that particularly mattered for intra-party advancement, beyond evidently ethnicity, were (i) regional and (ii) clan-based. The principal regional allegiance was either to the *Abayanduga* or to the *Abakiga*, terms that broadly referred to people from the south and north of Rwanda respectively. Within these broad groupings, more localized ties – such as commune of birth – were often consequential. The second important basis of allegiance continued to be the clan, which often overlapped with the geographic ties. In the Second Republic, clans from Buhoma and Bukonya in Ruhengeri prefecture and from Bugoyi and Bushiru in Gisenyi prefecture were highly represented in the inner circles of power. The importance of party ties for public position was the means

6.2 Dimension I: Weak State Autonomy

through which private social and political forces penetrated and captured the state.

The party then privatized the state. The state's hierarchical and extensive organization, comprising four sub-national levels – prefectures, communes, sectors, and cells – has been credited with its remarkable capacity to control society (Straus, 2006). Yet the *party's* machinery also deserves recognition. Its organization and functioning have been underestimated in accounts of the state's role in the genocide. While its *authority* had been challenged by liberalization, its organizational *capacity* remained strong. The party mirrored the state apparatus down to the smallest administrative unit. At the prefectural, communal, sector, and cell levels, the party's apparatus comprised three bodies: (i) a deliberative body, known as an assembly or congress; (ii) a smaller planning body termed a committee; and (iii) a yet smaller executive body known as a bureau.[5] In fact, the party surpassed the state in its organization. The cell was first a unit of organization created by the MRNDD before it became an official administrative unit of the state.[6] Figure 6.1 shows how the party's organization paralleled the state's structures of authority. State officials at the various levels of government were, until the introduction of multipartyism in 1991, almost all MRNDD representatives in parallel party structures at the same organizational level. The party was omnipresent within the state. The fusion of party and state lies at the root of the state's weak autonomy. The party became the instrument through which private interests controlled the public sphere and through which power remained personalized as it had been in the precolonial and colonial eras. The party was the principal means through which clientelist governance persisted in post-independence Rwanda

The Weakness of Civil Society

In modern states, a key role often played by civil society, the community of actors outside of the state, the market, and the family, is to hold individuals in public office accountable for their exercise of the state's authority and for their use of the state's resources. In states with low

---

[5] See statutes of the MRNDD, Rwanda Official Journal, 15 August 1991. Copy on file with the author.
[6] See Rwanda Law no. 31/91 of 5 August 1991.

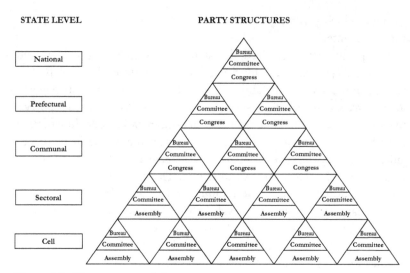

Figure 6.1. The structure of the party-state
(Author-compiled based on MRNDD statutes)

autonomy, government officials and civil servants who fail to distinguish between the private and public realms in the exercise of their duties may be called out by civil society. Yet in Rwanda, the plethora of cooperatives, farmers' organizations, tontines, and other NGOs that flourished, especially in the Second Republic, were never truly independent of the state.[7] Many were the creatures of the government or foreign donor organizations, and did not evolve organically from within society itself. Moreover, most of these civil society organizations did not operate in the political sphere. Many limited themselves to activities in the vast rural development sector. Between 1965 and 1990 there were few human rights organizations, trade unions, and social movements in Rwanda to speak out against abuses of state power.

Rwanda's limited media sector, instead of challenging the individuals who controlled the state, for the most part bolstered their position. The Fourth Estate lacked pluralism and lacked independence. Before 1990, it comprised three official government organs: Radio Rwanda (which enjoyed a monopoly), and *Imvaho* and *la Relève*, weekly and

[7] For a superior analysis of Rwanda's civil society after independence, see Uvin (1998, pp. 163–179).

6.2 Dimension I: Weak State Autonomy

bi-monthly publications respectively dating from the 1960s. All three faithfully supported the government. The two main and oldest non-government voices both came from the Catholic Church: *Kinyamateka*, a Church newspaper in print from 1933, which had shown brief periods of independence, and *Dialogue*, a quarterly journal dating from 1967, which had been less critical. The government would show little tolerance for freedom of expression. In 1985, it shut down the short-lived secular publication, *Umunyamuryango*, and would harass and intimidate outspoken editors of *Kinyamateka*.[8]

The Catholic Church, given the number of its adherents, its natural authority, its deep roots in the countryside, and the length of its presence in Rwanda, could have posed the strongest counterweight to those who commanded the state's power.[9] In pre-independence Rwanda, the Church had indeed been politically engaged. Having initially matched Rwanda's colonial administrators' preference for the Tutsi minority, it would transfer its allegiance to a new Hutu counter-elite and would support the Hutu revolution. Following independence, however, the Church would become closer and more subordinate to those who controlled the state. Kayibanda was the first to clip its wings. He brought the entire educational system – previously the preserve of the Church – under the control of the state in 1967. Under Habyarimana, the activities of the Church's newspaper, *Kinyamateka*, would face strictures. Sylvio Sindambiwe, an editor from 1980 who had been critical of his regime, was forced to resign in 1985. A second editor, André Sibomana (1988–1997), would face trial for breaking a story on government corruption. By the time of the genocide, while most of the lower-level clergy remained Tutsi (about 70 per cent in 1990), seven of its nine bishops were Hutu. The Archbishop of Kigali was particularly close to Habyarimana, having served on the MRND Central Committee until forced to resign in 1985.[10] The Catholic Church for the most part remained either politically mute, or else sided

---

[8] For a good overview of Rwanda's media before 1990, see Chrétien (1995, pp. 19–24).

[9] According to Rwanda's 1991 Population Census, 62.6 per cent of Rwandans were Catholic, 18.8 per cent were Protestant, and 8.4 per cent Adventist. Catholic missionaries first arrived in Rwanda at the end of the nineteenth century. Church edifices can be found in almost all local communities across Rwanda.

[10] See Longman (2010, p. 89 and more generally) for an excellent analysis of the Catholic Church's role during the genocide.

with incumbent regimes in post-independence Rwanda. The two civil society actors then best-placed to hold state officials to account, the media and Catholic Church, did not play this role and their default contributed to the low autonomy of the Rwandan state.

6.3 Dimension II: High State Legitimacy and Symbolic Authority

The modern Rwandan state had unusually high symbolic authority for a sub-Saharan African country. In keeping with a Lockean, consent-based conception of the state, its natural authority helped to legitimize the decisions and actions of its officials and to encourage the assent of its citizens to its policies. During the genocide, its legitimate authority made the identification of the Tutsi as an enemy threat more credible and the participation of Hutu in countering the threat justifiable. As we shall see in Chapter 7, while motivation was heterogeneous, the state's authority was an oft-cited factor in Rwandans' explanations of their participation in the violence.

Postcolonial states in sub-Saharan Africa, widely perceived as artificial colonial constructions, typically suffer from a legitimacy deficit. Upon independence, many of their key political institutions, inherited or imported from European states, were alien. Furthermore, their geographic borders, reflective of the balance-of-power in late nineteenth-century Europe, were unconducive to governing the culturally diverse peoples they encompassed. The juridical existence of these states had been protected by an international state system built on a European conceptualization of the nation-state that venerated state sovereignty and territorial integrity (Englebert, 2009; Jackson & Rosberg, 1982). So Rwanda's legitimacy can in part be traced to the continuity in its institutional structures and territorial boundaries as well as to its cultural homogeneity. However, the primary source of its legitimacy in fact lay elsewhere and is often overlooked. Its legitimacy originated principally in the revolution the country experienced that accompanied the birth of the modern independent state.

A Post-Revolutionary State

Rwanda's revolution was an exceptional event in the history of African decolonization. The political energy for independence was not directed externally against the colonial ruler – as occurred with decolonization movements in most of sub-Saharan Africa – but rather internally against an indigenous authority. Rwanda's revolution overturned the Tutsi monarchy. To put this into perspective, not one other country in sub-Saharan Africa had experienced such a revolution prior to its independence. The closest equivalent was Zanzibar. There, a few weeks after independence from Britain, on 12 January 1964, the Arab minority that controlled the island-state was violently disempowered and the majoritarian Afro-Shirazi party was installed as Zanzibar's new government.[11] Rwanda's revolution had two important consequences for the postcolonial Rwandan state. First, it bestowed the state with revolutionary legitimacy and, second, it eliminated any competition between itself and traditional authority.

Rwanda's revolution imbued the newly independent republican state with legitimacy because it ended a monarchy whose own legitimacy had been eroded by a colonial administration that had ruled indirectly through it. The revolution, as we have seen, became part of the ideological discourse during the genocide: Hutu were fighting in 1994 to protect the achievements of the revolution, and to prevent a return to the pre-revolutionary order in which a Tutsi elite had dominated and exploited them. Through Belgian indirect rule, colonial extraction had taken place in the name of the Tutsi monarchy. The increasingly exploitative nature of quasi-feudal institutions such as *ubuhake* and *ubeletwa*, along with the Tutsi quasi-monopoly of power, and ideology of racial superiority, had each damaged the legitimacy of Royal power in the eyes of the ethnic Hutu majority. They had also stimulated popular anti-Tutsi feeling.

Rwanda's revolution of 1959–1962 was the unusual culmination of this inequitable system. It destroyed *de facto* an oppressive grip on power by a Tutsi elite and empowered for the first time in Rwanda's history a Hutu-controlled government. The successor modern institutions of state were the beneficiaries of the damage inflicted on the monarchy's natural authority by colonial indirect rule. But they also owed their legitimacy in part to the fact that the process that created

[11] Guinea-Bissau's independence from Portugal in 1974 has also been characterized as the product of a revolutionary struggle by the PGAIC led by Amilcar Cabral. However, in this case, the Fula minority who collaborated with the Portuguese had not subjugated the country's other groups and were not definitively displaced from power following independence.

them, a social revolution, was widely perceived as popular and indigenous – even though the Belgians had arguably some part in facilitating it. These institutions were not simply imposed from without upon independence, but in fact came from within and pre-dated independence. Moreover, the elites who assumed control of the state following the revolution and who inherited it upon independence had genuine popular support from below. In a state with low autonomy, the distinction between the elite who constituted the regime and the institutions that constituted the state was weak. Both the popularity of the revolutionaries and the indigeneity of the revolution were important characteristics that reinforced the symbolic authority of the modern Rwandan state that the revolution had ushered in.

More than forty years after the monarchy's abolition, ordinary Hutu continued to think of the *Mwami*'s rule as inequitable, even though very few were old enough to have had direct knowledge of it. As previously documented in Chapter 3, 70.3 per cent of my Hutu survey respondents believed that the *Mwami* had favoured the Tutsi over other ethnic groups. The actual figure is likely higher, as another 12.2 per cent said they could not or would not answer this sensitive question. I had also asked Rwandans what they thought of the revolution. Due to the importance of the revolution in the genocidal discourse, many Hutu were unwilling to speak candidly about it. Only 23.3 per cent of surveyed Hutu were willing to state that the revolution was a 'good thing'. However, nearly all of those who did, said it was because the revolution had emancipated the Hutu or else had brought democracy. Following the revolution, democracy became synonymous with Hutu majority rule, even though the two Republics that succeeded the monarchy were single-party states.

It is also likely that this narrative of Tutsi subjugation and Hutu emancipation grew stronger *after* the end of the monarchy, reinforced in school systems and through the official discourse of the state. Elias, who was sixty-eight when I interviewed him, had a more nuanced memory of the *Mwami* and the chiefs. His testimony is important because he was old enough to remember the actual events leading up to the revolution.

Tell me what people thought of the Mwami and the chiefs before the revolution: Before 1959, the sub-chief here was called Nzamuye and he was responsible for Mutovu. He was Tutsi and was appointed by the chief,

6.3 Dimension II: High State Legitimacy and Symbolic Authority

Rwabulidi, who was responsible for Buhoma-Rwankeri. The chief treated the people well and he dealt with Hutu and Tutsi in the same way. The chief was better-liked than the sub-chief. The sub-chief used to punish those who committed crimes by whipping them. In 1959 the house of the sub-chief was burned down but the house of the chief was not. He was saved by both Hutu and Tutsi. *And the Mwami?* The Hutu here at that time liked the *Mwami*. *What about the Belgians?* During that time there were no intellectuals. The people did not care about the Belgians. They were only concerned with the *Mwami*. *What happened in your community in 1959?* Before the burning [of houses] began, there were papers distributed by the political parties. *Which parties?* I remember PARMEHUTU and RADER. In these papers they were saying what their political parties stood for. The parties were saying that they wanted the Hutu to be in government. *Did they say anything about the Mwami?* They did not say much bad about the *Mwami* as he had given back everything and had already abolished *ubuhake*.[12] The parties were fighting only to be in the government. But they were saying bad things about the Tutsi. They said the Tutsi had colonized the Hutu and had made them into *mugaragu* [slaves] and did not allow them to enter the house of government. And it was true that the government then favoured the Tutsi. There were poor Tutsi who did hard work like the Hutu but there was a class of Tutsi that was richer. They were the ones who were more like the sub-chief. (*Interview with Elias, aged 68, Hutu, former councillor for Mutovu, Ruhengeri, northern Rwanda, August 2003*)

Elias corroborates the survey data: the pre-revolutionary order with its inherent pro-Tutsi bias was resented. It was this resentment that was to legitimize the revolution, and the two Republics that followed it. However, Elias does not share the undifferentiated perspective that characterizes the beliefs of those who learned of this history afterwards. He distinguishes between individuals within the system: the persons of the *Mwami*, at that time Mutara Rudahigwa, and the local chief he suggests were well-liked, whereas the sub-chief was not. The narrative rigidity of those who were not old enough to remember suggests the important influence of post-revolutionary discourse on their beliefs propagated by the government that ruled them at the time.

The second consequence of the revolution that contributed to the modern state's authority was the elimination of any challenge to it from the traditional bases of social power. The institutions of the *Mwami*, the *abiru* (court ritualists), and the chiefs and sub-chiefs were abolished *de facto* and *de jure*. This was unusual. Postcolonial states in

---

[12] The *Mwami* finally abolished *ubuhake* on 11 November 1953.

sub-Saharan Africa, whose authority is usually concentrated at the centre in the capital and other urban areas, often compete for influence at the local level with individuals, usually in outlying rural areas, who enjoy traditional or customary authority that pre-dates independence . Mamdani (1996) has argued that indirect rule exacerbated this competition in Africa. It constructed a racially distinct identity between colonials and natives, but reinforced ethnic or tribal identities *among* natives. When 'racially distinct' colonials disappeared upon independence, Africa's new ruling elite faced ethnically divided rural societies led by 'decentralized despots'. Boone (2003) has refined this argument, emphasizing local variation in the balance of power between state and society. Where traditional rural elites enjoy popular influence locally and are economically autonomous, society then represents the strongest challenge to state power. Where, however, rural elites are neither autonomous nor influential, the state's authority is greatest, and society becomes an ally instead of a challenger to the state. After its revolution, however, there was no source of traditional authority left in Rwanda to challenge the post-independence state, and it could extend its authority uninterrupted to the rural periphery.

Geography, or more specifically territorial reorganization, further reinforced the emasculation of traditional social power. Kigali, in the centre of the country, became the capital upon independence in 1962, moving the centre of power away from the Royal Court in Nyanza in south-west Rwanda. In addition, Rwanda's 45 chiefs and 558 sub-chiefs in charge of chieftaincies and sub-chieftaincies became 229 burgomasters and 2,896 councillors in charge of communes and sectors in 1960 (Reyntjens, 1985, p. 269 and 281). Changing the boundaries, the number, and the loci of power of the country's territorial units ruptured existing political and social relations and ensured that no legacy of traditional authority survived into the post-independence era.

Institutional Continuity

In most of sub-Saharan Africa, the political institutions established in the colonial and postcolonial periods were imported from Europe and had shallow roots in the histories and cultures of the African peoples governed under them. Englebert (2000, p. 77), who has theorized and measured the degree and effect of the legitimacy challenge in Africa extensively, describes it in this way,

6.3 Dimension II: High State Legitimacy and Symbolic Authority

The foundations of political authority in the new African states in the 1960s bore little resemblance to those in precolonial societies. Rarely, either, had the colonial state borne any relation to the economic systems, political organizations, and networks of social identification of the indigenous peoples [...] As a result of their genesis these states lacked legitimacy vis-à-vis the societies, norms, and institutions they contained, however diminished were those that survived the colonial episode.

By this reasoning, the Rwandan state's legitimacy should have been negligible. Its main indigenous institutions – the Tutsi monarchy and chieftaincies – did not survive independence. However, their abolition was the exceptional result of a largely indigenous process: revolution. As noted previously, this social revolution on the eve of Rwanda's independence legitimized the new state and the institutions born of it because the antecedent institutions (the monarchy and chieftaincies) had been progressively delegitimized through their instrumentalization by Belgian colonial rulers. Strictly, it was the revolutionary elite who led the liberation effort against the monarchy, rather than the republican state and its political institutions, upon whom legitimacy was bestowed. Kayibanda and his supporters did not come from a minority group and represented a narrow social base. They were representatives of the Hutu majority. However, given the longstanding low autonomy of the state, the weak distinction between the ruling elite and the state meant that both enjoyed the legitimacy born of their revolutionary origins. Moreover, the institutional structure of authority and the nature of power in postcolonial Rwanda were very familiar to ordinary Rwandans. Lemarchand (1970, pp. 264–286) astutely described the First Republic as 'the kingdom reborn', its president as the modern incarnation of a *Mwami*, and the prefects and the burgomasters as the modern replacements of the chiefs and sub-chiefs. The individuals who occupied these positions continued to exercise power personally but through the façade of impersonal, rational institutions. The modern state had not discarded all of its traditionalist markings.

Boundary Continuity

Boundaries are arguably a special case of institutional continuity discussed above. Africa's postcolonial borders were largely the product of nineteenth-century European geopolitics and rarely considered the political, economic, and social realities on the ground that had naturally defined the boundaries of precolonial African polities. Following decolonization, these borders became fixed by an international state system that consecrated the norms of territorial integrity and state sovereignty and preserved the 'juridical' form of postcolonial polities even though many did not 'empirically' function well as modern states (Jackson & Rosberg, 1982). Englebert (2009) has argued that the international recognition of these states provided their ruling elites with the power of legal command and obviated the need for them to build domestic support and legitimacy. This legal recognition also ensured material support from the international community in the postcolonial era, especially in the form of foreign aid, which helped otherwise illegitimate regimes to endure. So, fixed and unsuitable borders lay at the heart of the crisis of legitimacy that afflicted many postcolonial states in sub-Saharan Africa.

The postcolonial Rwandan state, however, was an exception. It ranks second out of forty-two sub-Saharan states in an index designed specifically to measure boundary continuity (island-states excluded).[13] Only Swaziland ranked higher, with its tiny population of 846,000 and surface area of 6,640 square miles in 1993. As a result of this high continuity, Rwanda's postcolonial rulers for the most part governed the same people, the Banyarwanda, as its precolonial rulers did on the eve of European occupation.[14] The new polity did not forcibly bring together many disparate groups that had different institutions of authority and whose respective elites would then vie for power, as occurred in many newly independent African states. In addition, the new polity did not fracture individual groups across borders and thus divide the loyalties of constituents between different sources of authority. The Banyarwanda, on the whole, were able exceptionally to maintain their group composition as it stood just before the advent of colonialism. Put differently, boundary continuity meant that Rwanda was the same state and the same society for much of its history.

---

[13] The index of boundary continuity may be found in Englebert (2000).
[14] The exception was the north and north-west region of Rwanda, composed of autonomous Hutu principalities, which were forcibly annexed with German and Belgian assistance.

Demographic Particularities

As noted in Chapter 2, Rwanda possessed several unusual demographic characteristics. Two, in particular, reinforced the state's high symbolic authority. First, Rwanda is, by one measure, the least ethnically diverse of forty-two sub-Saharan states. It was home to only three groups: Hutu, Tutsi, and Twa. Moreover, despite the existence of multiple groups, Rwanda was culturally homogenous. The three ethnic groups shared a common religion, language, and a set of cultural beliefs. This was unusual. Ethnic groups in sub-Saharan Africa each typically possess their own tribal authority structures and distinct cultural beliefs and practices. As noted before, this multiplicity of traditional authorities ordinarily represented a challenge to the modern authority of the postcolonial state. However, Hutu, Tutsi, and Twa had historically recognized a common authority: the *Mwami*, his chiefs, and sub-chiefs. They had been governed as one people, a fact reflected in their cultural homogeneity, and it is for this reason that it has been suggested that the three groups were, at least historically, more distinct castes than distinct tribes or ethnic groups (Maquet, 1961). A historic respect for a single authority then was advantageous for the authority of the successor modern state.

Second, Rwanda ranks first among sub-Saharan states in a measure of ethnic dominance. The Hutu represented, by one estimate, at least 85 per cent of the population in 1994. In the years leading up to independence in colonial Africa, the new zeitgeist was not only self-determination and African nationalism. Ideas of democracy and equality had entered the consciousness of Rwanda's modernizing Hutu elites, largely through the Church's influence, to challenge the 'premise of inequality' that had characterized racial science in the colonial era.[15] In this new context, the Hutu's overwhelming numerical superiority reinforced the legitimacy of the two Republics that were Hutu-controlled. Hutu majority-rule became synonymous with democracy and Tutsi minority-rule equated with dictatorship. *Ethnos* and *demos* coincided. This majority-minority discourse was reproduced during the genocide, as this speech by Rwanda's new president, Jean Kambanda, broadcast over Radio Télévision Libre des Mille Collines (RTLM) illustrates (my italics):

---

[15] The term 'premise of inequality' comes from Maquet (1961).

Kambanda I think you know what is at the root of this war that has lasted almost four years since it began on October 1st 1990. The reason for this war is that the *majority* took power away from the *minority* in 1959. The *minority* did not want to give it up. Since 1961 these people [Tutsi] still believed in dictatorship and, full of arrogance, they launched attacks on Bugesera, Bweyeye, and Nshili and elsewhere, with the aim of taking power from the *majority* for themselves. At that time, the Government, led by his Excellency Grégoire Kayibanda, resorted to arms to repel the *Inyenzi*. He trampled on, disarmed, and defeated them once and for all. The *majority* then felt safe being in the Rwanda of their ancestors. But after their defeat the *Inyenzi* did not disarm. The war we have known since 1990 is being fought by the children of the *Inyenzi*, who try to hide who they are by calling themselves *Inkotanyi* [...]They have not yet understood that power has come back to its rightful owners and that they are not going to give it up. To you, our soldiers, to you all Rwandans who have mobilized to defend the integrity of our country! Courage! *(Jean Kambanda, President of Rwanda, RTLM broadcast, 5 June 1994)*

Low ethnic diversity and high ethnic dominance each operated to support the authority of the modern, Hutu-controlled republican state.

6.4 Dimension III: High Material Capacities

While it is now widely accepted that Rwanda in 1994 was a highly capable and effective state in a continent of 'lame Leviathans', less well-understood are the reasons for its remarkable strength. Similarly, little attention has been paid to which specific capacities of the state mattered – and in what ways – for the remarkable mobilization and violence during the genocide. While states are credited with many capabilities – from extraction, coercion, and regulation to monitoring, organization, and planning among others – these various capacities may be distilled into two core competences: the capacity for compliance and the capacity for coordination. Compliance refers to the ability of the state to ensure that both its agents and its citizens observe the obligations it imposes. Coordination refers to the ability of its agents to work together to attain the objectives it sets. I argue that Rwanda's strength in these two areas was remarkable and the result of several unusual geographic and demographic characteristics whose linkages with state power have yet to be explicitly articulated, as well as of several institutional characteristics. These characteristics explain much of the genocide's other distinctive characteristics, notably the speed of the violence and of the mobilization as well as the extensive geographic ambit of the killing.

Evidence of the State's Compliance and Coordination Capabilities

One useful indicator of compliance and coordination capacity, to be found in the relationship between state and society, lies in the extent of social control the state enjoys. While compliance may also be achieved through incentives and norms, Rwanda's high level of social control was due largely to its remarkable coercive power vis-à-vis its citizens. In terms of its formal security apparatus, counting gendarmes and soldiers, Rwanda had an estimated 39,000 individuals at the time of the genocide.[16] This made it the fourteenth largest security force in sub-Saharan Africa in 1993 in absolute terms. In relative terms, Rwanda had 1 state security agent for every 193 civilian individuals, ranking it twelfth of forty-two states. Rwanda was a heavily securitized state.

A state's superior ability to control its civilian population physically, however, is hardly surprising. A more useful indicator of the state's compliance capacity lies in its ability to extract taxes from the population. Yet if we take direct monetary taxes, that is, the taxes levied on the income of individuals and corporate entities, Rwanda was not exceptional. By my own calculation, the state extracted on average just under seventeen dollars per person from its population in 1993, which would make Rwanda only the twenty-fifth most 'extractive' state of thirty-two sub-Saharan states for which

---

[16] This comprised twenty-three infantry battalions (13,000), two Commando Battalions (1,000), one Para-Commando Battalion (1,000), one Armored Reconnaissance Battalion (690), one Presidential Guard Battalion (600), Support Units at Headquarters (4,770), Training Battalion (600), ten Gendarmerie Territorial Groups (5,300), one Gendarmerie Territorial Company (400), two Gendarmerie Intervention Battalions (920), one Route Security Company (200), one Gendarmerie Air Assault Company (200), Gendarmerie Headquarters Staff (200). The data are taken from the National Intelligence Daily report from the United States Central Intelligence Agency for 26 April 1994. A declassified copy was submitted to the International Criminal Tribunal for Rwanda (ICTR) in its case against Bizimungu et al. (ICTR 99-50-II). Copy on file with the author.

such data exist.[17] However, Rwanda had an unusual form of tax that escapes conventional measures: labour. In Rwanda, the state had been extracting labour from its population as a form of taxation since the precolonial era.

In the precolonial period, a labour tax known as *ubeletwa* was imposed for the first time on farmers in the late nineteenth century. In addition to a share of their produce, farmers were required to contribute half of their time in services to the chief (Vansina, 2004, p. 134). Under Belgian rule, *la corvée*, as the tax became known, continued but became yet more onerous as it was transformed from a collective into a more individual obligation. Its post-independence successor, *umuganda*, continued as an individual obligation but was performed only once a week. Labour as a form of taxation on society has deep historical roots in Rwanda.

As it became more inequitable, ordinary Rwandans increasingly resented the extraction of their labour as a form of taxation. Yet many still complied. As Table 6.2 indicates, 74.4 per cent of Rwandans surveyed stated that they always performed *umuganda*. In case these answers were self-serving, 52.2 per cent said the same even for other people. The state could mobilize on a weekly basis a significant proportion of its adult population. Compliance with this state-imposed obligation provides us with an important insight for understanding compliance with the order to kill during the genocide.[18] Not all Rwandans complied because they respected the state's legitimate authority and had internalized a cultural norm to obey this authority. Compliance should not be confused with obedience. Rwandan society had its share of law-defying as well as law-abiding citizens. In addition to its symbolic authority, the state had the means to identify and punish those who refused to comply. Compare these two opinions – both from village authority figures – on participation in *umuganda* in their community before the genocide.

---

[17] Direct taxes are taxes paid by individuals directly to the government and include income tax, corporate tax, and transfer tax. Indirect taxes refer to taxes paid first to an individual who then pays it to the government and include goods and services tax or value added tax. This figure was calculated using several variables from the World Bank's African Development Indicators' database and is adjusted for purchasing power differences across countries.

[18] For another good analysis of the importance of *umuganda* in understanding Rwandans' compliance with authority, see Straus (2006, pp. 217–218).

Table 6.2 Measuring the Rwandan state's social control and mobilizational power

	Ethnicity		Perpetrator Status		Region	
	Hutu	Tutsi	Non-perp.	Perp.	South	North

Question: Before the genocide, were there times when you refused to do umuganda (compulsory state labour tax), other than when you were sick?

	(N=240)	(N=21)	(N=157)	(N=83)	(N=107)	(N=133)
No, I always did umuganda	74.4%	76.1%	74.5%	71.3%	73.8%	75.0%

Question: Were there times when other people refused to do umuganda, other than when they were sick?

	(N=270)	(N=20)	(N=166)	(N=104)	(N=131)	(N=139)
No, they always did umuganda	52.1%	45.1%	51.4%	64.4%	59.6%	44.6%

Question: Were people in your community punished if they did not do umuganda?

	(N=221)	(N=13)	(N=132)	(N=89)	(N=99)	(N=122)
Yes – *sometimes* punished	52.7%	61.6%	52.6%	53.8%	70.4%	38.6%
Yes – *always* punished	40.6%	30.8%	40.6%	40.2%	25.8%	52.4%

Table 6.2 (cont.)

	Ethnicity		Perpetrator Status		Region	
	Hutu	Tutsi	Non-perp.	Perp.	South	North

Question: In your view was umuganda fair or unfair?

	(N=268)	(N=21)	(N=164)	(N=104)	(N=128)	(N=140)
Umuganda was fair	76.7%	62.3%	76.1%	87.4%	73.4%	77.0%

Question: Why was it fair or unfair? (most common answers)

	(N=258)	(N=20)	(N=154)	(N=104)	(N=127)	(N=131)
Fair, as it developed or benefited our community	44.1%	35.1%	43.4%	54.5%	41.7%	46.6%
Unfair, as we were forced to do it and it was unpaid	13.3%	25.1%	13.7%	7.8%	14.4%	12.2%
Fair, as it was our duty	9.9%	9.8%	10.3%	1.9%	7.5%	12.3%
Fair, as it united the villagers as everyone participated	8.5%	0.0%	8.4%	10.0%	8.4%	8.7%
Fair, as it was not excessive	8.2%	10.2%	7.9%	13.0%	14.7%	1.5%
Unfair, as some did not have to participate	3.9%	9.8%	3.9%	3.1%	4.0%	3.7%

6.4 Dimension III: High Material Capacities

Did the villagers always do umuganda? People participated well in *umuganda*. There was no problem. Of course, there were those people who would not do *umuganda*. Like the young men who were stubborn and wild. *Were they many?* There were about seven young men like this where I lived. *Did the villagers respect your authority?* In general, the villagers would respect the *responsable* and councillor. There were stubborn people as I said. But you cannot fail to have such people in any community. People have different characters. Some accept what they are told and some do not. You could see this in the *umuganda*: some would not come to work or some would not come to the village meetings. (*Interview with Vermont, member of cell committee, aged 42, Hutu, Mutovu, northern Rwanda, June 2003*)

Did the villagers always do umuganda? Before the war, the villagers were quite committed to *umuganda*. Those who missed it though were punished. In general, the villagers listened to me and for those who were stubborn, I would report them to the councillor and he would punish them. I would see this stubbornness in *umuganda* sometimes. Some people would not come to do the work. Then the punishment given would depend on the number of times the person missed *umuganda*. If it was one day, maybe it was 50F and if it was one week, then it could be 500F. (*Interview with Dionyise Sharamanzi, cell responsable, aged 60, Hutu, Ruginga cell, Kinigi, northern Rwanda, July 2003*)

These accounts illustrate that while many Rwandans appeared to respect the state's authority, there were also individuals who refused to do *umuganda* and whom the state punished as renegades. The survey data in Table 6.2 corroborate the existence of dissenters: over 23 per cent of respondents would state they felt that *umuganda* was not fair. When dissenters were asked why they resented *umuganda*, the most common answer was that people were given no choice and that they were unpaid for their labour. The survey also confirmed that dissenters were usually punished for their non-compliance: 40.6 per cent of all respondents said individuals were always punished and an additional 52 per cent said it happened at least sometimes. In short, the evidence suggests that in addition to its symbolic power to instil respect for its authority, the Rwandan state had sufficient coercive power to extract this labour, even from unwilling and resentful segments of the population.

A third indicator of Rwanda's exceptional control over its people may be seen in its power to immobilize its population. Upon independence most sub-Saharan states experienced urbanization, mainly in the flow of people from the country to the city in search of opportunities. Yet Rwanda did not. In 1993, it was the least urbanized country in sub-Saharan Africa. To put this into perspective, just 7 per cent of its population lived in urban areas in 1993 compared with a mean urban population of 31 per cent for the rest of sub-Saharan Africa. Much, though not all, of this was the result of a state policy of keeping Rwandans on their farms. Rwanda's ruling elite had two motives for preserving a large rural population. First, many depended on receipts from the country's two largest export-earners, coffee and tea, for their wealth. Both crops required intense rural labour to produce them, and the government had at times forced Rwandans to plant them over subsistence crops. Second, they wished to avoid the risk of a large urban population that could be readily mobilized politically to challenge the regime. The ruling elite preferred to minimize popular participation in the political process by keeping a distance between cities – often the centres of political activity – and the population.

A final indicator of the pre-genocide state's remarkable coordination and compliance capabilities may be seen in its success in implementing public immunization programmes. These nationwide campaigns, organized by the Ministry of Health and involving hundreds of health workers, aimed to reach every child in every community across the country. In 1993, Rwanda had managed to vaccinate 83 per cent of its infants against diphtheria, polio, and tetanus. This achievement placed Rwanda ninth out of forty sub-Saharan states (excluding island states) for which data exist in 1993 (World Bank, 2003). In contrast, Rwanda's GDP in 1993 was 261USD per capita, ranking it the twenty-fifth poorest nation in sub-Saharan Africa of forty-two. The achievement then was not due to advanced economic development. The state, in short, had considerable power to reach its citizens and enjoyed a remarkable degree of social control in Rwanda. In the next sections, I set out the geographic, demographic, and institutional characteristics that I believe amplified the Rwandan state's compliance and coordination capacities.

Amplifier I: Favourable Geography and Demography

The link between the Rwandan state's remarkable strength and the country's unusual geography has already been recognized. The explanation has centred on Rwanda's status as Africa's most densely

6.4 Dimension III: High Material Capacities

populated country. Not only did this facilitate the state's capacity to broadcast or project its power to the periphery (Herbst, 2000), it also amplified its ability to monitor its citizens' behaviour and to hold them to account for non-compliance with its obligations (Straus, 2006). I believe that the logics of projection and surveillance are correct, though I argue in Chapter 7 that Rwanda's high population density mattered also for *horizontal* – not only vertical – accountability. Where people lived and worked side-by-side dense social networks emerged, tying people to each other in multiple ways. Through these social networks, individuals became accountable to their neighbours for their action and, during the genocide, their inaction. As we shall see, this spatial proximity amplified peer pressures and facilitated co-optation and coercion into violence during the genocide.

However, the focus on population density misses several other related and distinctive geographic and demographic features that also amplified the state's compliance and coordination capacities. As noted in Chapter 2, with a surface area of 24,670 sq.km, Rwanda is the fourth smallest country in continental sub-Saharan Africa and the distances between any two locales was consequently small. Relatedly, Rwanda ranked first in sub-Saharan Africa in 1993 for its road network density with 0.57 km of road per square kilometre making it a highly accessible country within which to move. Rwanda is also the fourth least ecologically diverse country in sub-Saharan Africa with no deserts or coastlines and little savannah or forest with which state-planners had to contend.[19] Finally, Rwanda's geographic centre also became its administrative centre following the decision to relocate the capital from Astrida to Kigali upon independence. Collectively, this set of four unusual geographic characteristics contributed to the state's power in two ways. First, they enhanced its capacity for compliance by strengthening the state's *omnipresence*. The small distances and the absence of inhospitable and varied terrain lowered the costs of building the physical infrastructure of the state at the periphery. Local government offices could be found in all 145 communes and in most of its 1,545 sectors. These outposts of the state helped ensure that directives issued from the top could be executed locally and compliance with them observed and recorded. Rwandans, in their own perceptions,

---

[19] See Table 2.1, and Chapter 2 more generally, for the basis and calculation of each of these claims.

Table 6.3 *Perceptions of the state's provision of public goods in Rwanda*

Question: Who provided each of the following services in your community? (multiple answers permitted)

	State (%)	Church (%)	NGO (%)	Villagers (%)	No one (%)
Education	88.1	9.5	5.4	23.8	4.8
Health	73.5	3.3	10.9	7.8	6.1
Roads	77.9	1.0	5.5	58.6	3.8
Water	77.5	2.8	16.2	29.2	9.2
Agricultural extension	84.4	1.4	13.2	30.9	4.2
Justice	96.9	0.7	0.3	26.6	2.0
Security	93.8	1.7	1.0	40.4	4.1

confirmed the omnipresence of the state. As Table 6.3 shows, when asked who provided the most important public goods and services in their community – education, health, roads, water, agricultural extension, justice, and security – rural Rwandans overwhelmingly responded the state. It would be difficult to imagine such responses in some of Africa's larger states such as the DRC, the Sudan, Chad, Ethiopia, or Angola. Even in the furthest of communities, the state had a local presence – stronger than Churches and NGOs. The reach of the state was formidable.

Second, these four geographic characteristics also enhanced the state's capacity for coordination. Decision-making was not only administratively but also geographically centralized in Kigali. This geographical centralization, along with small distances and high road accessibility, facilitated communication and the flow of information more generally between the centre and the periphery, making the latter more accountable to the former. During the genocide, the extremist central government often summoned local prefects and burgomasters to the capital for private meetings and ministers often travelled to the provinces to co-opt or replace hesitant local officials and to mobilize the population. Return trips from every single one of Rwanda's 145 communes to the capital could be completed within one day. They also facilitated the rapid movement of the state's resources. Again, during the genocide, soldiers, militia, and gendarmes, along with weapons, were transported rapidly around the country to reinforce the civilian population. The small distances and high accessibility implied also meant that the genocide had 'contagion effects'. As we saw in Chapter 5, what happened in one community quickly became known and occurred in other communities. Local extremists, usually with a small hardcore of supporters, rapidly moved to other places to commit and incite violence there. In short, this aspect of Rwanda's physical geography explains much of why the genocide happened so quickly and why it happened almost everywhere in the country.

Rwanda's demographic particularities, its low ethnic diversity and cultural homogeneity, also reinforced the state's coordination capacity. In ethnically heterogeneous societies, coordination is challenging because ethnic groups often have competing preferences or tastes that may hinder state decision- and policy-making (Habyarimana et al., 2007). Cultural pluralism may also make governing inefficient as communicating and collaborating across ethnic boundaries is often more costly (Deutsch, 1966). Furthermore, as potentially distinct interest groups whose internal cohesion is assured by shared identities and loyalties, ethnic groups often also compete for disproportionate shares of state-controlled resources and this often leads to perverse or suboptimal policy outcomes (Bates, 1974; Easterly & Levine, 1997). By these several logics the individuals in control of the Rwandan state were in a strong position to govern. Rwanda was home to only three ethnic groups, whose language was identical and whose culture was similar. Rwandans shared a set of longstanding and widely shared beliefs, values, and customs. It is these similarities that helped their leaders to govern and ultimately to mobilize them.

Amplifier II: Institutional Configuration

The institutional configuration of Rwanda's First and Second Republics also bolstered the state's compliance and coordination capacities by strengthening (i) the omnipresence of the state and (ii) the centralization of power. First, the Rwandan state was visible and felt almost everywhere – down to the lowest level of society. As already mentioned, the country's small size aided this. However, this in turn enabled an impressive territorial hierarchy to be built. It comprised four administrative layers: 11 prefectures, 145 communes, 1,545 sectors, and 9,000+ cells, headed by identical numbers of prefects, burgomasters, councillors, and *responsables* respectively. Their presence ensured that the state was able to exercise its authority at all levels of society.[20] The smallest territorial unit, the cell, was home to about 200 households on average. The cell *responsable* lived among the population, and usually knew each individual family in their community by name. He was also the head of a committee of five elected local residents. In some regions, the hierarchy in fact extended down to a fifth level: the *nyumbakumi* – associations of ten households with a single head.

These representatives of the state and its ruling party had frequent and intensive interactions with ordinary Rwandans. Here is how Ernest, who was the *responsable* for Mwendo cell in the south, describes this contact.

Tell me what the relations between the authorities and the villagers were like: The councillor lived in Gashikili. He would come to Mwendo to collect reports from me and to give me the programme for *umuganda* [state compulsory labour]. *How often did he come?* He came twice a week. Once on Monday to tell me about *umuganda* on Tuesday and then on Wednesday for the *umuganda* on Thursday. The young men and girls, and older men in general would do work on Tuesday and on Thursday it was all women. *What was in the reports?* The reports would contain information about *umuganda*, the villagers' problems, the meetings of the cell committee – which was once a week – and also the meetings of the whole village, which was once a month. *What happened in these meetings?* The cell committee would meet first to decide the agenda and then the whole village met once a month. When the whole village met, it was in order to tell them to pay the personal contribution tax and the tax for livestock. We also told them how they should look after their coffee and how to fight soil erosion. *Did everyone pay taxes?* No, we had *ibirara* [young, delinquent men]. These persons would refuse to pay taxes and they would say 'We don't have a home, or a wife, why should we pay?' They had no jobs. *Were there many?* There were five who were really stubborn. They were young men who do not want to work. They spent most of their time before the genocide at the market in Gako where they would just roam around.' (*Interview with Ernest Mulinda, cell responsable for Mwendo, Hutu, aged 44, southern Rwanda, May 2003*)

Ernest's description reveals both the hierarchical, as well as intrusive nature of the state in the lives of ordinary Rwandans: the sector

---

[20] These figures are taken from Rwanda's 1991 Population Census.

councillor held Ernest, the cell *responsable*, accountable for reporting on the activities of the villagers. Ernest, in turn, assembled the villagers on a weekly basis to work for the state and then on a monthly basis to pay taxes and to receive instructions from the state on how to farm. Through this administrative organization, the state's ability to ensure compliance reached down to the very grassroots of Rwandan society. As we saw in the survey evidence earlier, those who missed the weekly *umuganda* were fined for their absences. As we shall see in Chapter 7, during the genocide those who refused to participate in the group attacks also faced fines. Such interventions by the state in the lives of Rwandans would simply be impossible to achieve in many developing African nations, and would be unthinkable encroachments on individual freedoms in liberal democracies.

In addition to its omnipresence, a second institutional characteristic of the state was the concentration of power at the centre. There were no effective checks on Executive power in either Republic. At the national level, the autocratic nature of both Republics manifested in several ways. There was no process of competitive selection for the position of president. Kayibanda assumed power through popular revolution in 1961 and ruled for eleven years; Habyarimana came to power through a military coup in 1973 and ruled for twenty-one years. Furthermore, neither Republic had any independent legislative oversight of the Executive. Habyarimana did permit a Conseil National pour le Développement in 1981 but its constitutional powers were highly circumscribed. Lastly, each Republic was a single-party state. Kayibanda had eliminated *de facto* opposition parties by 1965, and Habyarimana outlawed them under the constitution from 1975 to 1991. His own party, the MRND, had cells throughout the country, counted every Rwandan automatically as a party member, and provided the candidates for all local prefects and burgomasters positions. Habyarimana would run unopposed in a series of presidential elections in which he won consistently close to 100 per cent of the vote. The often-made parallel with the traditional rule of Rwanda's *Mwami* is a strong one (Lemarchand, 1970, pp. 269–272; Prunier, 1998, p. 58).

At the local level, central control of Rwanda's rural periphery was assured in two main ways. First, the president held the power to nominate and to dismiss each of the burgomasters who headed

Rwanda's 145 communes.[21] The burgomasters were the most important representatives of state power in rural areas. Second, local government lacked economic autonomy vis-à-vis the central authorities. The communes had very limited powers to raise taxes, and were dependent on central government for most of the financial resources needed to fulfil their responsibilities.[22] A 1992 report written by Rwanda's own National University found that communes were woefully underfunded and the majority were in debt.[23]

6.5 State Power and Perpetrator Heterogeneity

How then do macro-constructs such as state autonomy, legitimacy, and capacity translate into individual behaviour at the micro-level? Unsurprisingly, the focus on the Rwandan state's unusually high capacity in existing scholarship has led to explanations that emphasize coercion in accounts of individual participation in the genocide's violence. Individuals had no choice because the state was remarkably capable of monitoring citizens' compliance with its directives and of punishing non-compliance. Yet not everyone participated out of coercion. As we shall see in the Chapter 7, I find there was heterogeneity among perpetrators. Some individuals willingly and even enthusiastically participated in the violence. I term these individuals 'extremists' and 'opportunists'. For them, the Rwandan state's low autonomy was important. Low autonomy enabled them to appropriate the state's authority to justify the violence and to mobilize others. They became the new figures of state authority at the local level and felt 'authorized' not 'coerced' to kill. I also found individuals who explained their participation by referring to the state's authority. I heard the phrase

---

[21] In the First Republic, burgomasters were initially elected directly by the population. However, by a Law of 19 May 1969 they came to be nominated by the president from among the communal councillors upon their recommendation. In the Second Republic, the president continued to nominate, but it was now upon the recommendation of the minister of interior. See Rwandan Law of 12 September 1973.

[22] The commune could levy only the Minimum Personal Contribution tax, a cattle tax, local contributions for certain commune-financed development projects, and several other insignificant taxes that generated little revenue. See *Etude Sur La Commune du Rwanda*, Université Nationale du Rwanda, Report of 31 March 1992, pp.189–193 on file with the author.

[23] *Etude Sur La Commune du Rwanda*, Université Nationale du Rwanda, Report of 31 March 1992 p.188.

6.5 State Power and Perpetrator Heterogeneity

'it was the Law' (*amateka* in Kinayarwanda) repeatedly in my interviews. For some of these individuals, the Rwandan state's legitimacy was genuinely important. 'Conformists', as I call them, respected the state's authority. They tended to follow its rules and to heed its commands. While the claim that Rwandans were culturally programmed to obey is an overstatement, I believe for some Rwandans the state's legitimacy was an important factor in the justification of their participation. Were the state's authority illegitimate, they would have felt entitled to disregard its authority and orders. Rwandans scored very highly in the World Values survey when asked whether obeying their rulers was an essential characteristic of democracy. Out of sixty-one countries surveyed in 2012, Rwanda ranked tenth in how highly its citizens valued obedience to legitimate authority.

So, each of the three dimensions of the Rwandan state's power mattered during the genocide. This multi-dimensional conceptualization of state power speaks to an ongoing debate on civilian participation in the genocide. To what extent was the violence the product of elite manipulation from above and to what extent mass agency from below? The notion of elite instrumentalism, which is the dominant view, neatly dovetails with the proposition that Rwandans are socially conformist and tend to respect authority. In contrast, the notion of popular pressure from below resonates more with the idea that ordinary Rwandans felt 'authorized' to act. I argue that the two propositions are not incompatible with each other. As I show in the next chapter, some Rwandans 'conformed' to authority; others participated because the state granted them impunity for their actions. The idea that there would be variation within a population in individual orientations to authority would not be surprising to a student of psychology. The temptation to treat Rwandan perpetrators as an undifferentiated mass should be resisted.

* * * * *

In this chapter, I have argued that what distinguished the Rwandan state in sub-Saharan Africa was not merely its widely recognized capacity to compel its citizens. It was the conjunction of its remarkable capacity with its high symbolic authority and low autonomy that set it apart. Each of these three dimensions of the state's power would matter for the genocide. Furthermore, it was not simply the Rwandan state's capacity to *coerce*, but also its capacity to *coordinate* that was remarkable. I explained the sources of these three facets of the Rwandan state's power and argued that they originated in a set of unusual historical, geographic, demographic, and institutional characteristics. These distinctive features amplified the state's power vis-à-vis society and in turn contributed to the remarkable scale and speed of civilian mobilization, as well as extraordinary scale and speed of the violence observed during the genocide. While the importance of several of these characteristics has already been acknowledged, others, however, have been hitherto unrecognized. The unusual legitimacy of the postcolonial state, for instance, can be traced not merely to historic continuity in territorial borders, but also in large measure to the popular Hutu revolution that ushered in the country's independence. Similarly, the state's low autonomy was not simply the product of a pervasive neopatrimonial culture, but also of the state's penetration and privatization by a remarkable party apparatus. This multi-dimensional conceptualization of the state's power also helps to understand the challenge to the claim that the state primarily coerced Rwandans into participation. As we shall see in the next chapter, people participated for a wide variety of reasons. It was not simply because the state could readily monitor and punish non-compliance. The state's power also mattered because it could authorize the violence for those who desired it and legitimize the violence for those uncertain of it.

7 | *Why Some Killed and Others Did Not*

7.1 Introduction

Why did Rwandans kill? And how different – if at all – were those Rwandans who did kill from those who did not? The urge to distance ourselves from the perpetrators of atrocities is strong, perhaps equal to our desire to hold individuals to account for such extraordinary violence. But did the killers have unusual characteristics that distinguished them and disposed them to violence? Or were they, as the current scholarly consensus contends, ordinary individuals faced with simply extraordinary circumstances? As we shall see, I estimate one in four Hutu men committed an act of violence during the genocide. This is a shocking statistic. But it still means that three-quarters did not. Why did this minority participate but so many others not?

Genocide scholars have conventionally approached this question as a theoretical choice between dispositional and situational forces. Proponents of disposition point to distinctive traits or innate characteristics and infer motivations from them to explain why some kill and others not. They have suggested that ideological commitments, ethnocentric attitudes, deep-seated grievances, conformist inclinations or else more deviant dispositions such as narcissistic characters, authoritarian personalities, and sadistic tendencies among others were factors.[1] Situationists, in contrast, point to extrinsic, impersonal forces in explaining why perpetrators kill. They argue that perpetrators are quite ordinary and it is extraordinary opportunities and circumstances that select them into violence. They have pointed to macro-situational pressures: war-time threats, acute economic hardship, political upheaval, and demographic and environmental stresses among

---

[1] Mann has referred to individuals who match almost all these characteristics, and indeed others. See Mann (2005, pp. 27–28). On narcissism and sadism, see Baumeister & Campbell (1999). On authoritarianism, see Suedfeld and Schaller in Newman & Erber (2002, pp. 68–91).

others;[2] and also to micro-situational forces: peer pressure, conformity, group dynamics, and exposure to authority, for example.[3] Hannah Arendt's (1963) perspective on evil's banality, Philip Zimbardo's (1973) famous prison simulation, and Stanley Milgram's (1963) experiments in authority and obedience are all closely associated with the situationist position. A clear scholarly consensus has since formed in favour of situationist and 'ordinary men' explanations (Browder, 2003; Browning, 1992; Waller, 2002). This has also been the conclusion regarding Rwanda's *génocidaires*.[4]

Yet neither approach adequately explains what I found in Rwanda. I did not find a single, distinct profile that separated perpetrators from non-perpetrators. The notion of an unusual or deviant disposition seems, in any event, implausible in the face of mass participation. I also found that not everyone responded to the same opportunities and circumstances in the same way. Situationism over-predicts participation as, logically, it implies that all individuals, when faced with similar situational pressures, would succumb and commit violence.

Instead, what I found supported four conclusions about Rwanda's killers. First, there was dispositional heterogeneity among perpetrators. They were not *all* 'ordinary men'. Individuals varied in their commitment to the violence and had a multiplicity of motives. I found that individuals could be grouped broadly – according to their commitment to the violence – into extremists, opportunists, conformists/compliers, and pacifists. Second, individual motivations changed over time and, more specifically, through the act of violence. Those who joined reluctantly initially, did so more willingly subsequently, for instance.

---

[2] On the impact of wars, and other political opportunities, see Krain (1997). On political upheaval, see Melson (1992). On acute economic hardship, see Staub (1989, p. 44). On environmental pressures, see Newbury (1994) and Uvin (1996).

[3] On peer pressure, see for example Browning (1992, pp. 175–176) On conformity, see Asch & Guetzkow (1951). On group dynamics, see Staub (1989, p. 77) and Tambiah (1996, pp. 266–308) On the effects of authority, see Milgram (1974).

[4] Straus interviewed 210 sentenced, self-confessed perpetrators and concluded that 'Rwanda's killers were ordinary in all but the crimes they committed.' (Straus, 2006, p. 119). Mironko, a Rwandan himself, interviewed about one hundred self-confessed perpetrators and describes them among the 'countless ordinary civilians – men, women, and children – who were more informally persuaded to take part in the killing, but who may in fact have killed more innocent people than all the other forces combined'. (Mironko, 2004, p. 177). Fujii interviewed eighty-two Rwandans, of whom at least eight she describes as 'joiners' who 'were, in every sense of the word, ordinary men (and women).' (Fujii, 2009, p. 17).

7.1 Introduction

It accounts, in part, for the sadistic cruelty and sexual violence observed during the genocide. Not all perpetrators killed because they were sadistic or fanatical; some perpetrators became sadistic or fanatical because they killed. Third, situation still mattered, in addition to disposition. I found that settlement patterns – ethnic geography – contributed to selection into the violence. Living in close proximity to other killers increased the likelihood of being drawn into the violence. Fourth, social ties also determined participation. Killers were not only better-connected than non-killers but they had also had more ties to other killers. Conceptually then, participation appeared to be a complex interaction of dispositional, situational, and *relational* forces. Who you were, where you lived, and who you knew all contributed to selection into the violence.

I reached these conclusions through an evaluation of multiple pieces of evidence. First, I surveyed and compared perpetrators systematically against non-perpetrators to test a number of hypotheses on why individuals commit violence. I found few significant differences other than age and gender. There is no bright line separating killers from non-killers. However, this statement requires an important qualification. Those surveyed proved to be neither the individuals who organized the violence nor the hardcore serial killers. They were more conformists than extremists. Second, I looked at why Rwandans *say* they killed: their own rationales, justifications, and stated motives. Triangulating the responses highlights the role of authority, security, and opportunity – the book's three central themes – as the most common explanations given. However, a powerful state, a civil war, and a president's assassination still do not explain differential selection into the violence. These macro-situational factors are better conceptualized as permissive or facilitative contextual conditions for participation. Lastly, given the unanswered question of differential selection, I pursued a different tack and mapped the geographic location of every household in one community and compared the social networks of a sub-set of perpetrators and non-perpetrators within this community. I found clear patterns in spatial settlement and clear differences in social ties between those who killed and those who did not.

Before presenting this evidence, I address two contentious questions about the genocide that continue to be debated today. How many Rwandans participated and how many were killed in the violence?

7.2 Counting the Killers and Victims

Estimates of perpetrator and victim numbers are invariably politically sensitive and emotionally charged in cases of mass violence. The stakes are high. Perpetrator and victim groups have powerful incentives to maximize and minimize these numbers in opposing directions. For perpetrators, an individualized tally is important to avoid the attribution of collective responsibility for the violence to the entire ethnic or national group. The actions of a few can easily reflect negatively upon the many, even though the perpetrators may not always enjoy the wider support of their group or society.[5] In post-genocide Rwanda, the perception of a large criminal Hutu majority also magnifies the threat to internal security and legitimizes, albeit thinly, authoritarian measures taken by the administration. Moreover, a belief in widespread complicity impedes forgiveness and reconciliation. If distrust and resentment extended to all members of the group they could, given the opportunity, contribute to a cycle of revenge violence. For victims, the civilian death toll shapes public perceptions of who is the victim and who is the aggressor. A high victim count on one side can make the other side appear belligerent, making more implausible the framing of violence as a 'just war' or as self-defence. Moreover, victim status evokes sympathy, and also guilt among those who failed to prevent the violence. This sympathy and guilt make the victim group difficult to reproach and those who are critical risk being accused of supporting the persecutor. Making reliable, defensible counts then is important to minimize the opportunity for both sides to promote numbers that serve their particular agenda.

The Perpetrators

Estimates of the number of Rwanda's perpetrators vary by as much as an order of magnitude. At one end stands the government's official figure of nearly one million individuals (Government of Rwanda, 2005).[6] At the other end, it has been claimed that as few as 25,000

---

[5] Valentino (2004, pp. 31–39) makes this point well.
[6] See Marijke Verpoorten (2012a) for an assessment of the reliability of the central government's official *gacaca* data on perpetrators.

7.2 Counting the Killers and Victims 285

could have accomplished the killing.[7] Between these two extremes lie several estimates that run into the hundreds of thousands.[8] One of the better scholarly estimates, based on field evidence and an explicit methodology, places participation at between 175,000 and 210,000 Rwandans (Straus, 2004). The absence of a scholarly consensus is problematic. The estimates at the two extremes, for instance, suggest radically different pictures of the genocide. Was it the work of a small, highly active minority? Or were communities indeed involved extensively and intimately?

Methods and Evidence

I drew on two sources to estimate perpetrator numbers. First, micro-data from the pilot of Rwanda's truth, justice, and reconciliation program known as *gacaca*; and second, micro-data from Rwanda's last census before the genocide, in 1991, hitherto missing.[9] *Gacaca* was a traditional conflict resolution institution that Rwanda's government had adapted to deal with the massive scale of perpetration. Its defining feature was the empowerment of local communities to try and to sentence those of their members who had participated in the genocide.

In order to eliminate the possibility of *post hoc* manipulation of the data by the centre, I relied on data from *gacaca* pilots and only on numbers established at the *local* level.[10] Since 2004, three categories of

---

[7] Jones (2001, pp. 39–41) claims that such a low figure is theoretically possible but realistically believes that the extremists were probably aided by 50,000 'henchmen'.

[8] See Des Forges (1999, p. 2); Mamdani (2001, p. 7); Scherrer (2002, p. 106).

[9] While the 1991 Census *report* is widely available, it provides aggregated data mainly for Rwanda's 11 prefectures, and occasionally for its 145 communes. It does not have data disaggregated to the level of the administrative sector. The raw data, according to the head of Rwanda's Service National de Récensement in 2003, had been lost during the genocide. The same individual, Daniel Mugabo, however, later admitted to having the 1991 data, but claimed he could not vouch for its authenticity, and thus would not share the data. However, after two years of searching elsewhere, I finally obtained the raw sector-level census data from a source who asked to remain unnamed. These data are sensitive for many reasons, not least because they provide the most comprehensive micro-level data on Rwanda's ethnic composition just before the genocide.

[10] I obtained these data directly from local *gacaca* coordinators and, taking a sample, I manually verified the numbers they provided against individual names to ensure that they tallied. *Gacaca* had been piloted in 118 of 1,545 sectors (representing 751 cellules) and across all 11 of Rwanda's prefectures representing a healthy sampling fraction of 1 in 13 sectors. The criteria by which

crimes existed under Rwanda's *gacaca* law and each pilot community had compiled a list of individuals by category.[11] Category I crimes were the most serious, and broadly applied to those who organized or led the genocide; those who distinguished themselves by their zeal for violence; and those who committed sexual torture. Category II covered violent crimes against the person – typically homicide and assault. Category III addressed crimes against property – usually looting and property destruction.

I drew on these community lists to establish the number of perpetrators in each sector, factoring in a most likely acquittal rate based on data from completed *gacaca* trials.[12] I then used the census data on the number of Hutu resident in each pilot sector in April 1994 to calculate what percentage of the community had mobilized. I then extrapolated these figures to the prefectural and national levels to establish an overall estimate of the number who killed. Reliance on *gacaca* data carries risks, however. Observers have reported instances of false confessions, false accusations, witness intimidation, as well as the corruption of judges.[13] We have no evidence of how widespread or systematic these problems are. Some measure of irregularity should be anticipated amid the nearly two million cases tried by *gacaca* courts. Nonetheless, I believe the *gacaca* data – at least tabulated at the local level – remain the best source we have or are likely ever to have to estimate perpetration.

Findings

I estimate 367,000 individuals committed at least one act of violence against the person resulting in either serious injury or death during Rwanda's genocide. This is the estimate for Category II criminals. It represents 19.5 per cent, or nearly one in five, of all Hutu males aged between 15 and 54 years old. Furthermore, I estimate an additional 56,000, or 3.6 per cent of Hutu males aged 15–54, were guilty of the

---

pilot sectors were chosen were not fully enumerated by the Rwandan government. However, selection was not random. The possibility that extrapolations from the pilot data may suffer from bias then cannot be definitively ruled out.

[11] See Organic Law No. 16/2004 in Rwanda's Official Journal of 1 July 2004.

[12] The acquittal rate of 22.4 per cent is based on the independent observation of 277 trials of accused *génocidaires* across 10 prefectures. Sixty-two were acquitted. See Avocats Sans Frontières (2007, p. 52).

[13] See, for example, Penal Reform International (2005).

7.2 Counting the Killers and Victims

Table 7.1 *Perpetrator estimates by category of crime and prefecture*

Region (Prefecture)	Category I perpetrators Gacaca pilot data estimate	% of Hutu men aged 15–54	Category II perpetrators Gacaca pilot data estimate	% of Hutu men aged 15–54	Category III perpetrators Gacaca pilot data estimate	% of Hutu men aged 15–54
Butare	5,959	3.54	56,935	33.82	17,500	10.40
Byumba	5,627	2.88	38,227	19.54	27,127	13.86
Cyangugu	7,637	5.92	37,617	29.14	9,993	7.74
Gikongoro	7,155	7.37	34,994	36.07	27,902	28.76
Gisenyi	2,769	1.48	15,107	8.07	11,269	6.02
Gitarama	9,668	4.57	95,775	45.31	19,699	9.32
Kibungo	9,729	5.87	48,355	29.17	28,848	17.40
Kibuye	7,025	6.31	43,981	39.49	13,647	12.26
Ville de Kigali	5,194	9.72	8,502	15.91	2,953	5.53
Kigali-Ngali	9,946	4.46	85,709	38.46	35871	16.09
Ruhengeri	1,856	1.00	8,117	4.39	6,652	3.60
Total/Average	**72,564**	**4.69**	**473,230**	**25.07**	**201,461**	**10.84**
After Acquittal	**56,310**	**3.64**	**367,296**	**19.45**	**156,333**	**8.41**

more serious Category I crimes. Together then, 423,000 or nearly one in four Hutu men aged 15–54 participated in Rwanda's violence. I also estimated how many committed property crimes alone and find that 156,000 fall into Category III. This represents 8.4 per cent of Hutu males aged 15–54. This number, however, is likely a significant underestimate as individuals who had reached amicable settlements with their victims were not prosecuted for property crimes. Table 7.1 details these findings for each of the three categories of perpetrator, and for each of Rwanda's eleven prefectures.

The estimates for categories I and II, based on local *gacaca* pilot data, are in line with the central government's official, published figures of 50,937 and 320,803 respectively.[14] The correspondence

---

[14] Government figures were published online at www.gacaca.rw, accessed 4 June 2018. I exclude individuals who appealed their convictions and were acquitted.

between the local and central data suggests fears of *post hoc* political manipulation of the data – at least for the more serious crimes against the person – may be unfounded. However, for Category III – crimes against property – a major disparity exists. The central government puts the figure at 1,264,069 individuals, eight times higher than my estimate. A large proportion of these cases relate to looting, the opportunistic theft of property belonging to individuals who had fled or been killed. It is likely that my estimate, using pilot data collected nine years before *gacaca* officially ended in June 2012, was too early and that it took more time for these less serious crimes involving significant numbers of community members to be exposed and enumerated. It is also possible that individuals, knowing some measure of restitution would be required, eventually learned that it was profitable to make false accusations. We do not have evidence to allow us to assume that those who looted also supported the killing. We can only safely say that participation in the violence was limited to roughly one quarter of the Hutu adult male population.

What the Data Tell Us
First, these numbers clearly confirm that the scale of civilian participation was indeed a distinguishing characteristic of Rwanda's genocide. The vast majority of killers were not 'violence specialists'. While soldiers, gendarmes, police, and militia were implicated, most of these perpetrators were civilians.[15] Rwanda then is a remarkable case study of mass mobilization and collective violence. Second, the data reinforce the idea of organization behind the genocide. An observable pattern in the violence is that the number of perpetrators in a community appears to be quite closely correlated with the number of Tutsi who were resident there. Where there were many Tutsi, there were many perpetrators. Where few Tutsi lived, few individuals mobilized. Figure 7.1 illustrates this relationship more clearly. The two exceptions appear to be the northern prefectures of Ruhengeri and Byumba where relative mobilization was higher. Anti-Tutsi sentiment may have been higher there due to the region's location on the war's frontlines and to its historically strong Hutu identity and political loyalty to Habyarimana.

---

[15] By virtue of the authority that their official positions in the security apparatus of the state gave them, many of these 'violence specialists' would be classified as Category I criminals.

7.2 Counting the Killers and Victims

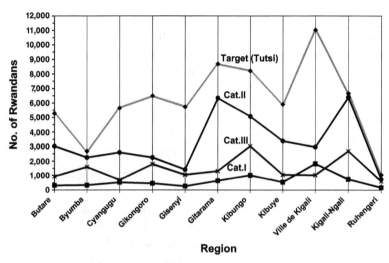

Figure 7.1 Relationship between numbers of perpetrators and targets

The close correlation nonetheless helps us to choose between two perspectives on the violence. In one view, it was a popular and spontaneous explosion of emotions from below. In the opposing view, the genocide was an organized and calculated strategy. The data here suggest some degree of organization as just enough Rwandans were mobilized to do the job. Finally, the data suggest that in the face of the particular opportunity presented by the genocide, individuals responded differently. Rwanda's civilian, rural population was not an indistinguishable mass. Although the categorization is crude, the *gacaca* data give us some sense of the relative distribution of behaviour in the perpetrator population: 10 per cent committed violence willingly and zealously (Category I perpetrators); about 25 per cent acted opportunistically with a view to personal enrichment (Category III); and the remaining 65 per cent majority fell somewhere in-between (Category II).

The Victims

Claims concerning the genocide's death toll have differed dramatically in respect of two fundamental aspects of the violence: the number and the ethnicity of the victims. At the high end, Rwanda's post-genocide government puts the number killed at just over one million

(Government of Rwanda, 2001). At the other end, two American political scientists, Christian Davenport and Allan Stam, have in the past suggested that as few as 250,000 Rwandans may have been killed.[16] In between these two figures lie various other estimates including that of (i) Human Rights Watch, an international human rights organization, which put the figure at 507,000 Tutsi, and unspecified thousands of Hutu dead (Des Forges, 1999, pp. 15–16); (ii) the French historian, Gérard Prunier, who estimates 800,000–850,000 were killed (Prunier 1998, p. 265); and (iii) Belgian economist, Marijke Verpoorten, who calculated that the toll lay between 512,000 and 662,000. The differences then are considerable.

The second controversial claim concerns the identity of the victims. What proportion of those killed were Tutsi, and what proportion Hutu? The Rwandan government claims that nearly 94 per cent of the million victims it identified were Tutsi. In contrast, Davenport and Stam have suggested that as few as 50,000 Tutsi and as many as 540,000 Hutu may have been killed.[17] If true, these latter numbers invite us to revise the common characterization of the violence as genocide. Claims of a politicide and a 'double genocide' have become politically and emotionally charged issues in post-genocide Rwanda. The country's post-genocide government has viewed them as attempts to deny, minimize, or equate the genocide with other violence. In response, it revised the country's constitution to specify that the events of 1994 constituted a genocide of Tutsi only. It insists on the moral singularity of the violence suffered by this ethnic group. In contrast, the regime's critics believe that violence targeting Hutu civilians has been underestimated. They argue that the Hutu experience has been inadequately recognized and deserves also to be remembered.

Estimating a reliable toll for all those wrongly killed – whether Tutsi or Hutu - is not simply a matter of establishing an accurate historical record. At stake are also questions of justice and reconciliation. Accountability rests on recognizing the full extent of the crimes committed and attributing full responsibility for them. Without it, inter-

---

[16] Christian Davenport cites a 2010 source jointly authored with Allan Stam in a 2014 blog entry where he gives a range for the death toll of between 250,000 and 890,000 Rwandans killed. See politicalviolenceataglance.org/2014/10/24/measuring-denying-trivializing-deaths-in-the-case-of-rwanda/, accessed 15 June 2019.
[17] Prunier 1998.

7.2 Counting the Killers and Victims

ethnic reconciliation may be an unrealistic expectation. The number and identities of the dead matter also for perceptions of aggressor and victim. More crudely, they shape beliefs about the 'good guys' and the 'bad guys'. Finally, it is worth noting that continued contestation over the identity of the victims serves also to preserve the power of ethnicity as a force in Rwandan society and politics.

Methods and Evidence

Two methods are commonly practised in estimates of victims of mass killings: counting the dead and counting the survivors. The Rwandan government's genocide census employed the former technique and declared the number of genocide victims as 1,074,017, of whom 93.7 per cent (1,006,032) it believes were Tutsi (Government of Rwanda, 2001).[18] The accuracy of this figure, however, is questionable. The government also conducted a census of survivors in which it identified 309,000 individuals of whom at least 278,000 were Tutsi (Government of Rwanda, 2008). If we combine the government's figures for Tutsi victims and Tutsi survivors, it would imply the pre-genocide proportion of Tutsi in Rwanda stood at 17.8 per cent, slightly more than the colonial-era percentage. This would mean that the Hutu revolution that marked the end of the colonial period never created a Tutsi refugee population. The estimates of both Human Rights Watch, Prunier, and Verpoorten, in contrast, rely on the latter technique but are over 300,000 apart. The disparity in estimates is due to their sensitivity to one highly contested statistic: the number of Tutsi living in Rwanda just before the genocide.

In calculating the pre-genocide Tutsi population, extrapolation from the 1978 and 1991 population censuses, which put the national proportion of Tutsi at 9.8 per cent and 8.4 per cent respectively, produces the figures of 714,000 and 647,000 Tutsi in Rwanda on the eve of the genocide. Critics believe, however, that both censuses significantly underestimated the Tutsi population because (i) Rwanda's pro-Hutu

---

[18] The census report distinguishes between 'enumerated' and 'declared' victims. A victim is enumerated only if the enumerator obtained responses for all questions on the questionnaire. The enumerated figure is lower at 934,218 victims. The report is unclear, however, whether the 93.67 per cent refers to the declared or enumerated total. The estimate of over one million Tutsi dead is based on the declared total. If the enumerated total is used, the figure becomes 875,000 Tutsi dead.

government misrepresented the percentage to justify ethnic quotas limiting Tutsi representation in education and the civil service; and/or (ii) many Tutsi identified as Hutu to avoid harassment and discrimination. They point to colonial-era censuses in which Tutsi represented 16.7 per cent, 17.5 per cent, and 16.6 per cent of the population in 1933, 1952, and 1956 respectively and suggest that these data should be employed to calculate the pre-genocide Tutsi population.[19] Significant uncertainty exists, however, over the number of Rwandans, mainly Tutsi, who fled the country between 1959 and 1964 following the Hutu revolution. A 1964 UN High Commission for Refugees (UNHCR) census put the number of Rwandan refugees at 336,000 but subsequent estimates have differed dramatically.[20] This uncertainty makes estimations based on the colonial-era data problematic.

A better check is a comparison of the 1978 and 1991 national census data against local administrative records on births, deaths, and migration established independently of the central government.[21] Communes collected these data more frequently, usually several times a year, and enumerators were often local administrative figures, cell *responsables* or the *nyumbakumi*, who knew the households personally, making it unlikely a Tutsi household could pass itself off as Hutu. I located eleven annual reports from prefectural office archives dating between 1965 and 1991 for Butare and Ruhengeri. This allowed me to observe any suspicious change in the Tutsi proportion over time. In Butare in 1965, 1975, 1983, 1985, and 1988 the proportion of Tutsi was 18.3 per cent, 18.5 per cent, 18.3 per cent, 18.3 per cent, and 17.8 per cent respectively. The 1991 national census reported a slightly lower figure of 17.3 per cent. In Ruhengeri in 1965, 1973, 1981, 1985, 1988, and 1991, the proportions were 0.8 per cent, 0.7 per cent, 0.7 per cent, 0.7 per cent, 0.6 per cent, and 0.6 per cent respectively.[22] The national census figure was again only slightly lower at 0.5 per cent.

---

[19] For the 1933 data, see Mamdani (2001, p. 98). For the 1952 data, see Des Forges (1999, p. 40). For the 1956 data, see Reyntjens (1985, p. 28).

[20] André Guichaoua (1992, p. 26) documents the variation in the official estimates of the Rwandan refugee population.

[21] Marijke Verpoorten (2005) also relies on local population data to estimate the death toll in one province, Gikongoro.

[22] The gentle decline in Tutsi proportions observed within the local data is likely due to the lower fertility rate for Tutsi women. Hutu women had on average 6.2 children in their lifetime, whereas Tutsi women had 5.1.

7.2 Counting the Killers and Victims

So, the local data for the Tutsi proportion in Ruhengeri and Butare appeared stable over twenty-five years. I then drew on the administrative records to establish the pre-genocide Tutsi population. I had obtained these data for all of Rwanda's eleven prefectures for the year 1983.[23] The national proportion of Tutsi according to these data was 10.8 per cent. Projecting the 1991 census data forward to April 1994, and assuming that it did not mis-state Rwanda's total population, I conclude that the estimated number of Tutsi alive in April 1994 would have been almost exactly 800,000.

Did the national census purposely undercount the number of Tutsi? While the national census data were slightly lower than the local administrative data, I believe that this was unlikely to be the result of central government manipulation and rather the consequence of Tutsi identifying themselves as Hutu. I base this conclusion on three facts. First, the earliest reports are from 1965 and pre-date the establishment of the ethnic quota system and thus the incentive to under-estimate the Tutsi population. Second, the under-estimation was greater in Ruhengeri where Tutsi had a stronger incentive to identify as Hutu given the stronger discrimination in the north, than in Butare in southern Rwanda. Third, a comparison of the local administrative against the national census data for Ruhengeri indicates that the latter overstated the Hutu population by 1.07 per cent but understated *both* the Tutsi and Twa populations by 14.5 per cent and 9.2 per cent respectively. As there was no incentive for the government to manipulate the Twa proportion given their historic under-representation in the civil service and educational sector, it suggests that some Tutsi and Twa chose instead to identify as Hutu to escape state-instituted discrimination and harassment.

Findings

Having established the pre-genocide Tutsi population, the number of Tutsi killed could be readily calculated by subtracting the number of Tutsi survivors. However, the survivor estimates we have also differ considerably. The first figure of 150,000 survivors is based on unofficial or unsupported estimates of Tutsi living in refugee camps, hiding in

---

[23] The 1983 data had been submitted in evidence to the International Criminal Tribunal for Rwanda (ICTR) in the case against Bizimungu et al. (ICTR 99-50-II). Copy on file with author.

Rwanda, and having escaped into Zaire or Tanzania in July 1994.[24] The number appears to be an intelligent guess and not based on actual headcounts. A second figure of 202,000 is based on the official *gacaca* data published by the Rwandan government.[25] However, when compared against data on the Tutsi killed that I obtained for 20 administrative sectors in Butare and Ruhengeri prefectures directly from the communities themselves, there are significant discrepancies. A third figure comes from a census of survivors conducted by the Rwandan government in 2006, which counted 309,000 individuals (Government of Rwanda, 2008). I believe this figure to be the most reliable of the three. The census was conducted by the National Institute of Statistics of Rwanda, and not by the government agency responsible for survivors whose budget depended on the number of survivors. As the census defined survivor to include Hutu widows of Tutsi partners, I subtracted the total number of widows. The number of Tutsi survivors then ranged from 278,000 to 309,000 persons.

I conclude then between **491,000** and **522,000** Tutsi were murdered in Rwanda between 6 April 1994 and 19 July 1994 given a pre-genocide Tutsi population of 800,000 and a likely survivor range of 278,000 to 309,000. It is important to specify the temporal and spatial boundaries surrounding this estimate and to be clear that it refers only to Tutsi victims. Rwandans – both Hutu and Tutsi – have been killed in other major periods of violence throughout the 1990s and the 2000s, and both inside and outside of Rwanda. These periods include (i) Rwanda's civil war leading up to President Habyarimana's assassination (October 1990 to April 1994); (ii) the immediate consolidation of power by the Rwandan Patriotic Front (RPF) following the genocide (August 1994–1995); (iii) the pursuit of Hutu refugees by the Rwandan government in the first Congo war (1996–1997); (iv) the insurgency and counterinsurgency in Rwanda's north-west (1997–1998); and (v) authoritarian repression inside Rwanda (2000 onwards).[26] Moreover, most of these other instances of violence did

---

[24] See Prunier (1998, p. 264) and Des Forges (1999, p. 15).
[25] The Rwandan government initially released the data via a web page that is no longer accessible. However, Belgian economist, Marijke Verpoorten, had downloaded the data and generously shared them with me.
[26] I adapt this periodization from Straus (2019).

not occur in isolation of each other. They were related.[27] Nonetheless, while the broader historical and regional context is valuable, it should not obscure the fact that a genocide occurred between 6 April and 19 July 1994 inside Rwanda.[28]

Establishing the Number of Hutu Victims

Was Rwanda simply and purely a genocide of Tutsi? Few dispute Hutu died as well, but uncertainty over the number killed has allowed speculative characterization of the violence as: (i) a double genocide; and (ii) politicide.[29] The former characterization implies widespread killing of Hutu civilians, in addition to Tutsi. The latter characterization implies that people were killed for political reasons, and not because of their ethnicity. The number matters. Neither the *gacaca* courts nor the ICTR investigated RPF killings of Hutu civilians and few RPF soldiers have been convicted at home in Rwanda for crimes committed during the genocide.[30] The perception of victor's justice is a serious impediment to national reconciliation efforts, as well as a source of popular resentment.

Claims of a double genocide have centred primarily around two time periods and two locations: (i) Rwanda in 1994; and (ii) the Democratic Republic of Congo (DRC) between 1996 and 2003. For killings inside Rwanda during and immediately after the genocide, existing scholarly estimates range from tens to hundreds of thousands – though these

---

[27] For an overview of the various episodes of violence in the Great Lakes in the postcolonial era, and the connections between them, see McDoom (2010).

[28] Rwanda's Organic law 08/96 on the Organization of Prosecutions for Offences constituting the Crime of Genocide or Crimes against Humanity defines a genocide victim and sets temporal boundaries from 1 October 1990 to 31 December 1994. It is generally acknowledged, however, that a state-sponsored policy to eliminate *all* Tutsi was not implemented until after President Habyarimana's assassination on 6 April 1994. It ended with the flight of the IG and government soldiers into what was then Zaire and the creation of a new government by the RPF on 19 July 1994.

[29] For the claim of politicide, see, for instance, the transcript of the presentation 'Understanding the Rwandan Genocide' made by Allan Stam to the Ford School of Public Policy at the University of Michigan on 18 February 2009. Copy on file with author. For the claim of double genocide, see, for example, Ruzibiza & Vidal (2005).

[30] Nearly a decade following the genocide, Rwandan military tribunals had tried only twenty RPF members for war crimes committed in 1994, acquitting three, and convicting twelve with prison terms of one to three years. See Waldorf (2006, p. 60).

claims are not supported by verifiable evidence.[31] UNHCR conducted a mission to Rwanda in August 1994, not to investigate these killings, but its lead consultant, Robert Gersony, unofficially estimated that the RPF killed 25,000–45,000 Hutu civilians between April and August 1994.[32] This is likely a low estimate. Gersony visited only 41 of 145 of Rwanda's administrative communes. Moreover, RPF reprisal killings were not the only forms of violence to occur other than genocide. To these we must add combatant deaths in a civil war; the targeted assassinations of moderate politicians; the killing of Hutu who aided or supported Tutsi; and private disputes between Rwandans settled under the cover of the genocide, among others. We have little systematic evidence to quantify all these other deaths. A household survey of 1,795 Rwandans in three of Rwanda's eleven prefectures found that while 92.7 per cent of the Tutsi households surveyed suffered losses, only 9 per cent of Hutu households did so.[33] Weighing all this evidence, I believe it would be more accurate to characterize RPF killings of Hutu civilians in this first time period as massacres or atrocities, but not genocide.

The killing of Hutu civilians in the DRC, primarily during the first Congo war (1996–1998) that toppled Joseph Mobutu and installed Laurent Kabila, appears more serious, however. Several early reports alluded to the possibility of a genocide, but it was the 2010 report of a UN mapping exercise that presented the most compelling evidence (United Nations, 2010). The mapping exercise, conducted in 2008, lasted six months and deployed a team of thirty-three staff in five field offices across the DRC to investigate human rights violations committed in the DRC between 1993 and 2003. To highlight its most persuasive findings, it documented that 104 of the 617 incidents reported were against Hutu refugees; that the majority of the victims were

---

[31] Des Forges (1999, p. 558) suggests a minimum death toll of 25,000–30,000, but acknowledges that the figure may include combatants as well as civilians. For the claim of possibly hundreds of thousands, see Reyntjens (1996, p. 248).

[32] UNHCR chose not to publish the report, which has never been officially released. For more detail, see Des Forges (1999, pp. 553–559).

[33] Verwimp acknowledges that his figures may be an under-estimate as it excludes those prefectures where most rebel-perpetrated violence allegedly occurred. Of the 1,620 Hutu surveyed, he found that forty-three died violent deaths: twenty-one at the hands of the rebels, nine by Hutu militia, one by Rwandan government troops, and five by other, unspecified individuals. For seven individuals, the killers were unknown. See Verwimp (2003b).

women, children, the elderly, and sick; that the perpetrators, the Alliance des Forces Démocratiques pour la Liberation du Congo (AFDL) rebel group and Rwandan and Burundian armed forces, made few efforts to discriminate between civilians and combatants; and that those killed included both Hutu refugees from Rwanda and Hutu native to DRC, suggesting the deliberate targeting of an ethnic group. To be clear, the final version of the report, revised after objections by the Rwandan government, did not conclude that a genocide had been committed. This, it states, requires a judicial determination. At the same time, the report is also clear the scale of the killing was not equivalent to the killings of Tutsi in Rwanda. It put Hutu victims in the 'tens of thousands'. Others, however, have claimed a death toll in the vicinity of 200,000 refugees.[34] The report was also clear that the Rwandan government had repatriated tens of thousands of Hutu refugees to Rwanda in the same time period and had pursued only those who chose not to return. None of these facts, however, negates the possibility that genocide occurred.

Irrespective of whether these killings meet the legal definitions of war crimes, crimes against humanity, or genocide, the fact remains that large numbers of Hutu civilians were killed in the DRC and that their deaths have yet to be investigated judicially. The absence of proper recognition and accountability for them remains an obstacle to inter-ethnic reconciliation and a continuing grievance for the Hutu community.

7.3 Comparing Perpetrators and Non-perpetrators Systematically

How different then, if at all, were the one in four Hutu men who participated in the genocide from the three in four who did not? A major challenge in answering this question satisfactorily is methodological. It is not easy to identify reliably and then gain access to perpetrators. Interviews are rare, and they raise practical and ethical issues. When interviews have been possible, they have always been after the event. At that point, it is impossible for us to know which characteristics existed or mattered *ex ante* and which ones emerged *ex post*. Rarely are baseline interview data on perpetrators collected

---

[34] See Straus (2019, p. 513) and Emizet (2000, p. 163).

before they commit violence. Related to this, perpetrator testimony after the fact is vulnerable to attempts to minimize personal responsibility, or else to construct socially acceptable narratives. Memory loss should also not be under-estimated. Each of these methodological challenges is difficult for researchers to overcome.

Yet other methodological issues exist that can be more readily resolved. First, and most conspicuously, has been the tendency to look only at the perpetrators. The methodological risk is that, without a non-perpetrator comparison group, it is difficult to know how different from their wider society the selected perpetrators are. It may cause researchers to find what appear to be unusual characteristics in the killers. Some research addresses this by comparing perpetrators with census data.[35] This is better, but it limits comparison to a narrow set of demographic variables. We cannot compare attitudes and opinions, for example. In social scientific terms, researchers often do not have variation on their dependent variable.

Second, there is the issue of selecting which perpetrators to examine. Sometimes we do not know the criteria, if any, by which researchers choose particular perpetrators and, if disclosed, the method is not random. Purposive selection is vulnerable to the charge of selection bias. Tied to this is the question of numbers. How many perpetrators must be in the sample to be representative of the perpetrator population? Rarely do we know the size of the overall perpetrator population to determine an appropriate sampling fraction. These issues notwithstanding, it does not mean that findings based on small, non-random groups of perpetrators are wrong. It means merely that a level of caution must be exercised in evaluating these findings that is appropriate to the methodological choices made.

My own research, of course, was not immune to these methodological obstacles. In Chapter 1, I described how I identified perpetrators and non-perpetrators for interview. To recap, I used *gacaca* data to distinguish as best as possible between the two groups. A perpetrator was any individual who committed an act of violence against another person, or joined a group that did so, during the genocide, and I required evidence that he or she appeared on the lists

---

[35] See, for example, Straus (2006, pp. 103–108) and Mann (2005, p. 222).

7.3 Comparing Perpetrators and Non-perpetrators Systematically 299

of accused of both the prison *gacaca* and hill *gacaca*.[36] I surveyed 294 Rwandans altogether: 104 perpetrators; 190 non-perpetrators, including 21 (7.1 per cent) Tutsi, in two prefectures.[37] I selected respondents using a stratified, two-stage cluster random sampling method. I did not know the perpetrator population until after the survey, but the sampling fractions turned out as follows: every perpetrator in the sample represented 738 perpetrators in the perpetrator population for the two regions; every non-perpetrator represented 8,271 non-perpetrators. I had over-sampled perpetrators and accordingly weighted the results reported to reflect the effect of this survey design.

The circumstances of the interviews themselves merit a brief description as well. For imprisoned perpetrators, I conducted the interviews myself, with the aid of my interpreter, unless the interviewee was well-educated and comfortable in French. Despite initial reluctance from some prison authorities, I obtained a private room for this purpose. In the case of non-perpetrators, who came from the same communities as the perpetrators, I used trained enumerators to cover the wide geographic area of the sample. I chose individuals who already knew the community in which they would be working. None of course was implicated in the genocide, and they usually conducted the interview in the privacy of the respondent's home.

Lastly, I should say a word about the reliability of responses. Most of the interviews in this project took place in 2003, nine years after the genocide. Some perpetrators would likely have constructed their own narrative – either intentionally or unconsciously – concerning the events of 1994. To mitigate this, I tried several techniques. First, I gave more weight to statements-against-interest. Self-incriminating or socially unfavourable responses were likely to be more credible. Second, I evaluated the many 'I don't know' responses to sensitive questions in two ways: both literally, and also as evidence that the

---

[36] In another major survey of *génocidaires* conducted in 2002, Straus interviewed sentenced, confessed perpetrators only. He reasoned that they would have least incentive to lie. See Straus (2006, pp. 99–100). I decided against this approach given the possibility of biasing the sample in favour of individuals most willing to confess. Ultimately, both approaches have advantages and disadvantages.

[37] I excluded Tutsi responses in the perpetrator-non-perpetrator comparison. The two prefectures were Butare and Ruhengeri, representing the south and north of the country respectively.

individual held a socially or politically unfavourable opinion. At the time of the survey, the RPF was the dominant partner in Rwanda's post-genocide government, the *gacaca* process had begun, and ethnicity was a taboo subject. Some self-censorship had to be anticipated. Third, I also asked questions indirectly. I sometimes asked respondents what *others* were thinking – partly to find about others and partly to allow the interviewees the opportunity to project their own thoughts and actions into their answers. Lastly, I triangulated responses. Typically, I would compare Hutu answers against those of Tutsi. None of these methods, however, is fool-proof. Ultimately, I present the data, rough edges and all, and give them my best possible interpretation.

In the next sections, I test some of the main theories for why people kill in wars and genocides using the survey data. The central question driving this analysis is simple. Were perpetrators measurably different from non-perpetrators?[38] I grouped related theories into five clusters: (i) those that point to disaffected male youth; (ii) those that emphasize deprivation, such as poverty, ecological scarcity, relative deprivation, inequality, exclusion, and structural violence; (iii) those that emphasize ethnicity, which include social identity, ethnic prejudice, racism, and ethno-nationalist ideologies; (iv) those that focus on threats, such as the security dilemma and myth-symbol complexes; and finally (v) those that point to what I term influence, including obedience, authority, social influence, peer pressure, ingroup policing, and conformity. I begin with basic demographic profiles of both perpetrators and non-perpetrators.

Demographic Profiles

What did Rwanda's killers look like? As Table 7.2 reveals, the most conspicuous characteristic is that almost all the perpetrators sampled were male. 94 per cent in fact were Hutu men. Women did commit genocide-related crimes, but in far fewer numbers than men. They represented less than five per cent of the population in the prisons that I had sampled.[39]

---

[38] I test for significant differences using: (i) Pearson's chi-square statistic; and (ii) univariate logistic regressions.
[39] Butare central prison was home to 10,665 inmates of whom 445 were women. Ruhengeri central prison housed 1,902 *génocidaire*s, of whom 84 were female. I excluded inmates who were detained for non-genocide crimes in the census.

Table 7.2 Demographic profiles of killers and non-killers

	All Hutu	Non-perpetrator		Perpetrator		Statistical Difference	
	%	N	%	N	%	Chi Square	Logit (s.e.)
Sex (male)	74.5	169	73.4	104	93.9	9.82***	5.63 (3.48)***
Age in years (mean; s.d.)	37.8	167	38.0 (0.9)	104	35.7 (0.86)	na	0.98 (0.01)*
Marital status (married)	87.7	168	88.1	104	80.5	2.09	0.56 (0.23)
Children (mean; s.d.)	4.0	168	4.0 (0.24)	104	3.3 (0.19)	na	0.92 (0.04)**
Landless	11.9	164	11.5	96	18.9	1.41	1.79 (1.17)
Education (years)	4.5	na	4.5 (0.26)	na	3.8 (0.41)	na	0.94 (0.04)
Occupation: Farmer <3.5Ha.	75.3	168	75.6	104	70.8	0.59	0.78 (0.25)
Religion:							
Catholic	69.8	167	70.1	102	64.3	na	na
Protestant	12.7	167	12.5	102	15.0	na	na
Adventist	12.2	167	12.0	102	15.0	na	na
No religion	1.4	167	1.2	102	4.7	na	na
Religiosity: Church attendance. (Scale 0-4: 4=least religious)	1.24 (0.12)	162	1.23 (0.13)	103	1.30 (0.12)	na	1.05 (0.13)

*** Significant at 1% level. ** 5% level. * 10% level.

On average, the perpetrators were just under thirty-six years old. But their ages ranged from as young as sixteen to as old as sixty-seven at the time of the genocide.[40] Most were husbands. 80.5 per cent were married at the time of the genocide. The majority (86.2 per cent) were also parents.[41] But neither characteristic distinguished them from non-perpetrators. On average they had between three and four children, this time slightly less than non-perpetrators. Educationally, most perpetrators had received three to four years of primary level education, again comparable to the non-perpetrators sampled. Occupationally, most (70.8 per cent) were farmers. I distinguished farmers from those who rented out their land to be farmed (defined as those having more than 3.5 hectares of land in total).[42]

But perpetrators came from diverse walks of life. As Table 7.3 shows, perpetrators count businessmen, state employees, salaried private sector employees, and artisans among them. This range reflects the occupational diversity within the wider population. Religiously, almost all claimed Christianity as their faith. Perpetrators did not come from any particular denomination. There was no distinction between Protestants, Adventists, or Catholics – the three most common confessions. They were also not more likely to be atheists or agnostics, or to have different degrees of religiosity, as measured by how often they went to church.

Overall, with the exception of being male and having slightly fewer children, Rwanda's perpetrators did not have a demographic profile that distinguished them from non-perpetrators.

Cluster I: Masculinity, Youth Bulges, Disaffected Young Men

Were young men the ones most likely to join Rwanda's attack groups and commit violence? Young men have popularly been perceived as threats in many cultures, especially when unemployed or not meaningfully occupied.[43] Scholarly work, mostly quantitative cross-national

---

[40] Rwanda's president, Paul Kagame, first ordered the provisional release of the elderly, the infirm, and minors from prisons in January 2003. My sample, however, was selected *before* the Presidential Decree took effect.

[41] There were more fathers than husbands because some men had informal unions, rather than marriages, with women.

[42] About two-thirds in fact farmed less than one hectare of land.

[43] See for example Kaplan (1994) and Zakaria (2001).

Table 7.3 *Occupations of killers and non-killers compared*

	All Hutu	Non-perpetrator	Perpetrator
	(N=254)	(N=157)	(N=97)
Farmer (<3.5 hectares of land)	78.1%	78.5%	71.5%
Farmer (≥3.5 hectares of land)	6.2%	6.0%	9.7%
Teacher	2.9%	3.0%	0.0%
Private sector employee (e.g. driver, mechanic, cook, guard)	2.0%	1.8%	6.0%
Businessman/self-employed (e.g. bar, restaurant, shop)	1.8%	1.8%	2.2%
Civilian administrative authority (*responsable*, councillor, burgomaster)	1.7%	1.8%	0.7%
Other local government employee	1.8%	1.8%	2.2%
Student	1.7%	1.8%	0.3%
Semi-skilled artisan (e.g. mason, potter, carpenter, welder, basket-maker, tailor)	1.5%	1.2%	6.9%
Shepherd	1.1%	1.2%	0.3%
Cattle-breeder	0.6%	0.6%	0.0%
No occupation	0.6%	0.6%	0.0%

studies, has also associated 'youth bulges' – the over-representation of young men in societies – with revolutions, rebellions, and domestic armed conflicts.[44] In Rwanda, certain scholars have asserted that it was bands of young, disaffected men (*isore sore* in Kinyarwanda) who did much of the killing.[45] They either already belonged to party youth wings or militia groups such as the *Interahamwe, Impuzumugambi, Abakombozi,* and *Inkuba,* or else quickly adapted to the opportunity for violence and organized themselves into similar groups.[46]

---

[44] For revolutions, see Goldstone (1991) For rebellions, see Moller (1968). For domestic armed conflicts, see Cincotta et al. (2003) and Urdal (2006).
[45] See Des Forges (1999, pp. 227–231); Prunier (1998, p. 243)
[46] These youth wings belonged to the MRND, CDR, PSD, and MDR parties respectively.

But what makes young men seemingly so prone to group violence? First, it is argued young men in particular experience frustration when deprived of opportunities for social and economic advancement, especially if their expectations have been raised from receiving education (Goldstone, 2002, pp. 392–393; Kahl, 1998). Second, it has been suggested that young men are less constrained by family and career responsibilities, and can thus afford the opportunity cost of participating in time-consuming and risky activities such as rebellion (Collier & Hoeffler, 2004, p. 569). Third, it has been argued that young men are especially susceptible to ideals and are strongly motivated by the urge for change. They are consequently more likely to engage in protests, violent or otherwise (Huntington, 2002). Fourth, young men, especially those with limited opportunity for upward mobility, may be drawn to groups that bestow them with honour, status, and purpose. Participation in violence becomes a means of restoring normative ideals of manhood (Richards, 1998). Fifth, violence has seductive or intoxicating properties to which young men are most susceptible, such as the sensation of power over individuals against whom it is directed.[47] So, there are many reasons to believe that young men would be particularly likely to kill.

Were young men over-represented among the perpetrator sample? We have already seen that men were more likely than women to participate in the violence. Being male increased the odds of being a perpetrator nearly six-fold.[48] Age, in contrast, only weakly distinguished perpetrators from non-perpetrators. Expressed probabilistically, being one year younger increased the odds of an individual being a perpetrator by only 2 per cent. I also divided the sample into five age groups (Table 7.4). I did not find that perpetrators were statistically over-represented in any age bracket, including the youngest bracket of 15–24-year-olds. They were, unsurprisingly, under-represented in the oldest age bracket: over 56 years old. The

---

[47] On the allure of violent crime, see Katz (1988) On the sensation of power in violence, see Keen (2005)

[48] Although the sample was random, women were under-represented in the non-perpetrator stratum. I suspect that enumerators often did not find the women selected for interview at home when they went there during the day, and so interviewed the alternate respondent instead. The under-sampling of female *non-perpetrators* reinforces the finding that men were more likely to be perpetrators.

Table 7.4 *Age groups of killers and non-killers compared*

	All Hutu	Non-perp.	Perp.	Statistical Difference	
	(N=271)	(N=167)	(N=104)	Chi Square	Logit (s.e.)
16–25 years old	12.2%	11.9%	16.4%	1.11	1.45 (0.51)
26–35 years old	29.3%	29.3%	28.5%	0.02	0.96 (0.28)
36–45 years old	31.8%	31.3%	40.6%	2.22	1.50 (0.41)
46–55 years old	16.5%	16.8%	11.9%	0.55	0.67 (0.36)
56+ years old	10.3%	10.8%	2.6%	5.46**	0.22 (0.16)**

*** Significant at 1% level. ** 5% level. * 10% level.

elderly or infirm would physically have been unable to participate in the attack groups.

In fact, as already noted, the average perpetrator was middle-aged, married, and a father. Rather than few responsibilities, he had many. As we shall see, however, this may be explained by thinking of participation as a risk continuum. As more individuals joined the violence, the risk of participation declined. For the risk-averse family man, non-participation could even be more perilous than participation if refusal entailed monetary or physical sanctions.

Cluster II: Deprivation-Related Theories – Ecological Scarcity; Structural Violence; Relative Deprivation; Inequality

Rwanda was the 149th poorest country in the world out of the 173 surveyed in the United Nations Development Programme (UNDP)'s 1993 Human Development Report.[49] Perhaps as a result, the notion of deprivation has been tied in different ways to its genocide. *Structural violence* has been one such suggestion.[50] A sophisticated psycho-social concept, it takes into account inequality, social exclusion, and dignity/humiliation in a society. *Ecological scarcity* has been another. Essentially a Malthusian argument, it is motivated by Rwanda's status as Africa's most densely populated nation – the result of a high population

[49] The Human Development Index combines normalized measures of life expectancy, literacy, educational attainment, and GDP per capita.
[50] Uvin (1998, pp. 103–108) applied the concept originated by Galtung (1969) to Rwanda's genocide.

growth rate and limited arable land.[51] More broadly still, the idea of *difficult living conditions* – meaning economic hardship – has been associated with genocidal violence more generally, including in both Germany and Cambodia (Staub, 1989, p. 44).

Deprivation-related theories pre-date Rwanda's genocide. The concept also lies at the heart of more generalized explanations of violent conflict. *Relative deprivation* has been one of the more enduring of these theories. In its original formulation, it is the state that arises from a discrepancy between an individual's aspirations or expectations and his/her achievements or capabilities.[52] Another longstanding argument is that *inequality* in a society also matters: both vertical – when one individual is more deprived relative to another; and horizontal – when an entire group is worse off than another.[53]

At the root of almost all these different ideas is a frustration-aggression mechanism. Faced with such circumstances, an individual becomes gradually more frustrated, and ultimately aggressive. This aggression may be channelled or displaced (Berkowitz, 1993). However, many of these deprivation-centric ideas are difficult to test. There is no consensus on operational measures for many of them. So I included a series of different questions in the survey which incorporated both (i) objective and subjective measures; and (ii) measures of personal and group deprivation.

On the whole, as Table 7.5 shows, while Rwandans did suffer privation, perpetrators were simply not more deprived than their non-violent co-ethnics. Using objective indicators, we have already seen that they were first of all indistinguishable in terms of occupation and education. Most were farmers with a basic primary level education. Perpetrator landholdings were also not any smaller than those of their non-violent ethnic brethren.[54] Both had multiple, small plots of land that they farmed. Even when re-classified into two groups – the landed and the landless – there was again no statistically significant

---

[51] See for example André & Platteau (1998).
[52] For the original formulation, see Gurr (1970) For more recent formulations, see Walker and Smith (2002).
[53] For the link between genocide and inequality, see for example Besançon (2005).
[54] I did not measure the size of respondents' land plots myself, and so the number must be treated with caution. However, respondents had no obvious incentive to misrepresent this to me, and in a land-scarce culture, Rwandans usually knew exactly how much land they owned.

Table 7.5 *Deprivation profiles for killers and non-killers*

	All Hutu		Non-perpetrator			Perpetrator			Statistical Diff.	
	%		N	%		N	%		Chi Square	Logit (s.e.)
Objective measures										
Occupation: Farmer (<3.5 hectares)	75.3		168	75.6		104	70.8		0.59	0.78 (0.25)
Occupation: Elite	16.7		167	16.8		103	15.9		0.04	0.94 (0.31)
How many plots of land did you have, and how many *intambwe* (pace ≈ 1 m) wide and long were they? (total in hectares) [mean(std.dev.)]	1.32 (0.13)		164	1.3 (0.13)		96	1.4 (0.45)		na	1.00 (0.00)
Landless (proportion with no land)	11.9		164	11.5		96	18.9		1.41	1.79 (1.17)
How many cows did you own in April 1994? [mean(std dev)]	1.36 (0.22)		159	1.4 (0.23)		104	0.66 (0.16)		na	0.78 (0.10)**
Did you have any activity, other than working on your own or others' land, to make money? (Yes)	40.3		169	41.0		104	28.5		2.24	0.57 (0.22)
Education (years)	4.48 (0.25)		na	4.52 (0.26)		na	3.76 (0.41)		na	0.94 (0.04)
Subjective measures										
Before the genocide, did you and your family have enough food and money to live on? (Yes)	47.9		167	48.4		104	38.9		0.94	0.68 (0.27)
Did you and your family have enough land to live on (Yes)	31.2		164	31.2		103	32.1		0.01	1.04 (0.36)

Table 7.5 (*cont.*)

	All Hutu	Non-perpetrator		Perpetrator		Statistical Diff.	
	%	N	%	N	%	Chi Square	Logit (s.e.)
Exclusion							
Did you and your family benefit more, less, or the same as others in your community from each of the following services? Schools; Health services; Agricultural extension; Rural credit. (Scale 1–5: 5=most excluded)	1.57 (0.19)	169	1.57 (0.20)	104	1.61 (0.10)	na	1.02 (0.13)
Vertical Inequality (intra-group)							
Before the genocide in your cell, were there some people who were getting richer while others got poorer, or did it not change? (It changed)	86.6	163	86.6	104	86.5	0	0.99 (0.49)
If it was changing, in your view was the way in which people were getting richer fair or unfair? (Unfair)	13.2	166	13.2	85	12.4	0.2	1.27 (0.69)

Horizontal Inequality (inter-group)

In general did the Tutsi in your community have either more cows or more land than other people? (Yes they had either more cows and/or more land)	55.4	167	54.5	103	72.5	3.28*	1.39 (0.66)
Unwilling to say	11.9		12.5		1.4	1.16	1.30 (0.32)
If the Tutsi in your community were better off than most people, was it because they had worked harder or because they had received special treatment at some point in time? (The Tutsi had been privileged)	43.0	166	43.9	103	27.6	7.07**	0.37 (0.14)**
Unwilling to say	18.8		19.2		11.1	5.12**	0.62 (0.14)**

*** Significant at 1% level. ** 5% level. * 10% level.

difference.[55] These findings would seem to weaken Malthusian arguments based on a resource crunch or ecological scarcity. Lastly, perpetrators were not any more likely to have income from secondary sources. This usually meant income earned from off-farm activities such as brick-making, tailoring, or petty commerce. The only respect in which the two groups differed in objective, material terms was in livestock ownership. Perpetrators usually owned fewer cows.

Subjectively, when asked whether they had enough (i) land or (ii) food and money to live, a majority in both groups reported that they did not. Most Rwandans clearly felt poor. But, again, perpetrators did not feel this any more than non-perpetrators. I also attempted to measure exclusion, an important component of the structural violence concept. I asked respondents whether they and their family benefited more, less, or the same as other families in their community from four important services: schools, health care, agricultural extension, and rural credit. I combined the responses into a single, scaled measure. Overall, rural Rwandans felt moderate levels of exclusion, but once again this did not distinguish the violent from the non-violent.

Lastly, I considered the impact of inequality, another component of structural violence. I did not have good enough data to measure income inequality, and instead I asked respondents for their *perceptions* of material differences. When asked whether the gap between rich and poor was changing in their communities, 86.6 per cent felt that it was indeed growing wider. There was then a high degree of perceived vertical inequality. But perpetrators were not prone to this perception

---

[55] Philip Verwimp (2005) has constructed a methodologically sophisticated economic profile of a perpetrator. He re-surveyed 340 Rwandans households that were originally surveyed before the genocide in an agricultural research project. Of these, he found fifty-two households were home to seventy perpetrators. He then classified all the households according to socio-economic status into three categories (based on land owned, land rented, and non-agricultural income). He found that perpetrator households were over-represented in the poorest category (twenty-one households, 23 per cent) and wealthiest category (eleven households, 28.2 per cent), but under-represented in the middle category (twenty households, 13.2 per cent). He argues then that perpetrators were likely to be those with something to gain (the poorest), or something to protect (the wealthiest). Some caution is merited, however. Verwimp placed the responsibility for identifying perpetrator households on his survey enumerators. For enumerators to ask individuals to incriminate other community members of genocide-related crimes raises issues of reliable identification.

any more than non-perpetrators. Interestingly, when asked whether they thought that this trend was unfair, only a minority (13.2 per cent) reported that they thought it was. Horizontal inequality – the difference between Hutu and Tutsi as whole groups – was also widely perceived. Most Hutu (55.4 per cent) felt that Tutsi usually had either more land and/or cows than them – even before taking into account self-censorship. When asked whether this socio-economic success was deserved, a large minority (43.0 per cent) reported that it was not. They felt that Tutsi had been privileged in the past. They challenged the legitimacy of the outgroup's success. Counter-intuitively, however, in a rare difference between the two groups, perpetrators were *less* likely than non-perpetrators to resent this perceived Tutsi advantage. All in all, however, deprivation – even in its many different conceptualizations – did not conclusively differentiate Rwanda's killers from its non-killers. There is little doubt that deprivation was high in Rwanda. But these factors did not explain why certain individuals came to commit violence and others not.

Cluster III: Ethnicity-Related Theories – Ethnic Prejudice; Racism; Social Identity; Ethno-nationalist Ideology

Ethnicity is evidently central to the idea of genocide. But how a macro-concept such as ethnicity operates at the micro-level is less clear. The individual-level mechanisms that explain how and why ethnicity influences individuals to commit violence and genocide are less well-understood. Social psychology provides a starting point. It distinguishes ingroup positivity from outgroup negativity in inter-group relations. *Positive* sentiments can be measured as pride, loyalty, and superiority, while *negative* feelings comprise contempt, hostility, and prejudice (Brewer, 1999). Translating these into terms commonly used in the ethnic conflict literature, the former suggests the importance of ethno-nationalist ideology, while the latter points to ethnic animosity and racism. Rwanda's violence has been described in all of these terms. Hutu nationalism, longstanding hatreds, and a racist ideology figure among the explanations.[56]

---

[56] On Hutu nationalism, see Mann (2005, pp. 469–470). On racial ideology, see Uvin (1998, pp. 31–38). On longstanding hatreds, see Braeckmann (1994, p. 161).

I asked a variety of questions to measure both pro-Hutu and anti-Tutsi sentiment in Rwanda. Overall, the results, displayed in Table 7.6, do not suggest that killers were any more likely to have harboured either Hutu nationalist feeling or ethnic prejudice against Tutsi. Ethnicity, of course, was a taboo subject in post-genocide Rwanda, and I anticipated self-censorship on the more controversial questions. In recognition of this, I also report the 'I don't know' responses, when there were more than usual of them. They were a barometer of the question's sensitivity. I also ran a second round of statistical tests for perpetrator/non-perpetrator differences, this time assuming that these 'I don't know' responses were really the socially unfavourable answer disguised.

I start with anti-Tutsi sentiment. I examined marital preferences to indicate ethnic bias or prejudice. In an attitudinal measure, I asked respondents whether they preferred their children to marry someone of the same ethnicity as themselves. Only a small minority (9.6 per cent) said yes. The vast majority, however, were indifferent. Moreover, perpetrators were not more likely to express an ethnic preference. In fact, counter-intuitively they were statistically *less* likely to do so. I then checked this attitudinal measure against a behavioural measure of marital preference. I looked at the number of Hutu respondents who were in fact married to Tutsi before the genocide. The advantage of this indicator is that, unlike the attitudinal measure, it could not change following the genocide. Yet once again, perpetrators were not any more likely to have a marital preference. Inter-ethnic unions were just as common among perpetrators (14.6 per cent) as among non-perpetrators (11.3 per cent). Based on marital preferences then, we cannot say that ethnic prejudice or discrimination distinguished those who committed violence from those who did not.

I then looked at racial ideology. I tested for three fundamental tenets of the ideology. These were: (i) whether Tutsi were indigenous to Rwanda; (ii) whether Hutu had been the victims of Tutsi oppression historically; and (iii) whether Tutsi had received unfair advantages over Hutu in Rwanda's pre-independence past. I found that most Rwandans, 58.6 per cent, believed that Tutsi were in fact alien to Rwanda. This proportion rises to a staggering 96.3 per cent if we assume that the huge number of respondents who replied 'I don't know' in reality believed Tutsi were foreigners. But perpetrators did not believe this any more than non-perpetrators, even after controlling

Table 7.6 *Ethnicity-related indicators for participation in violence*

	All Hutu		Non-perpetrator			Perpetrator		Statistical Difference	
	%		N	%		N	%	Chi Square	Logit (s.e.)

Anti-Tutsi sentiment

	%	N	%	N	%	Chi Square	Logit (s.e.)
Did you prefer your children to marry from a particular *ubwoko* (ethnic group)? (prefer someone of same ethnicity)	9.6	167	10.1	103	1.0	19.17***	0.09 (0.06)***
What ethnicity was your spouse? (Tutsi)	11.5	163	11.3	99	14.6	0.38	1.35 (0.65)
Where did the Tutsi originally come from? (outside of Rwanda)	58.6	165	58.9	102	53.1	0.97	0.52 (0.35)
Unwilling to say	37.7		37.5		40.5	0.96	0.71 (0.25)
Composite of 4 questions testing historical memory of Tutsi oppression and favouritism. (Scale 1–8: 8=most negative memory) [mean(std dev)]	4.79 (0.22)	164	4.77 (0.23)	101	5.18 (0.15)	na	1.24 (0.18)

Pro-Hutu sentiment

	%	N	%	N	%	Chi Square	Logit (s.e.)
Before the genocide, were you proud of your ethnicity? (open-ended) Yes, proud	72.7	167	72.5	102	76.4	0.16	1.23 (0.62)
No, I was not proud	4.1	167	22.1	102	11.8	1.75	0.47 (0.27)
It was not important to me	21.6	167	3.6	102	11.8	3.32*	3.57 (2.65)*

Table 7.6 (*cont.*)

	All Hutu	Non-perpetrator			Perpetrator			Statistical Difference	
	%	N	%		N	%		Chi Square	Logit (s.e.)
Unable/unwilling to say	1.7	167	1.8		102	0.0		nv	nv
Before the genocide, what did you think of the 1959 Hutu Revolution? (open-ended) Good thing	23.2	168	21.3		103	56.5		16.24***	4.83 (2.05)***
Bad thing	64.1	168	65.5		103	38.7		9.04***	0.33 (0.13)***
Good and bad	4.0	168	4.2		103	0.0		0.27	NV
Unwilling/unable to say	8.8	168	9.0		103	4.7		1.15	0.50 (0.33)
Why did you think this of the revolution? (open-ended) Bad, as it divided Hutu and Tutsi	13.9	149	14.1		100	10.0		0.55	0.68 (0.36)
Bad, as it brought death, violence, conflict	44.8	149	46.3		100	20.2		8.06***	0.29 (0.13)**
Good, because it ended Tutsi monarchic rule and/or brought Hutu freedom/democracy	22.5	149	20.7		100	52.5		11.86***	4.22 (1.89)***

*** Significant at 1% level. ** 5% level. * 10% level.

7.3 Comparing Perpetrators and Non-perpetrators Systematically 315

for possible self-censorship. The two groups questioned Tutsi autochthony equally. I then compiled four questions regarding historical Tutsi favouritism and Tutsi subjugation into a single, scaled indicator:[57] The higher the number, the stronger the internalization of an anti-Tutsi ideology. On the whole, as already seen, Hutu did have a strong collective, historical memory of victimization and discrimination. But once again, those who did not commit violence in Rwanda's genocide were just as likely to hold such ideological beliefs as those who did. In short, a collective memory of ethnic oppression existed in Rwanda. But it does not explain why some killed and others didn't.

Having looked at anti-Tutsi feeling, I turn now to pro-Hutu sentiment. Was a belief in Hutu nationalism the basis for the violence? Did the killers feel pride in and loyalty to their ethnic group more than the non-killers? I first asked respondents quite simply whether they were proud of their ethnicity, or whether it was unimportant to them. Nearly three-quarters (72.7 per cent) felt pride. But perpetrators (76.4 per cent) were not any more likely to be proud of their Hutu identity than the non-perpetrators (72.5 per cent). Second, I asked respondents for their opinion of Rwanda's revolution. The revolution was a critical juncture in Rwanda's history, and it could be interpreted in two quite different lights: either negatively – as it resulted in the mass exodus of hundreds of thousands of Tutsi, and set Rwanda on a collision course with the resulting refugees; or else positively – as it marked the end of Tutsi monarchic rule, and the emancipation of the Hutu. In short, the question was one of ethno-ideological loyalty. Those who felt loyalty towards Hutu as an ethnic group, or a sense of Hutu nationalism, would most likely express the latter view.

As noted previously, only a few Rwandans (23.2 per cent) were willing to characterize the revolution as a 'good thing'. Most said it was a 'bad thing' (64.1 per cent) or else 'both good and bad' (4.0 per cent). Quite a few, however, (8.8 per cent) claimed they 'did not know', suggesting that the question was indeed a sensitive one in Rwanda's post-genocide climate. Nonetheless, in a rare difference between

---

[57] The four questions were: (i) Do you think that the *Mwami* [Tutsi monarch] favoured any *ubwoko* [ethnic group]? (ii) Do you think that the Belgian colonials favoured any *ubwoko*? (iii) In *ubuhake* [a form of feudal clientship associated with the Tutsi monarchy], did the *shebuja* [master] and *mugaragu* [servant] usually belong to any particular *ubwoko*? (iv) When it existed, was *ubuhake* in your opinion fair or unfair?

perpetrators (56.6 per cent) and non-perpetrators (21.3 per cent), I found the former were much more likely to view the revolution positively. Admittedly, a high proportion of respondents were again unwilling to respond, but even taking this into account does not affect the overall result. When asked the reasons for their opinion, the top positive answer (22.5 per cent) was that the revolution had ended the Tutsi monarchy and/or brought freedom for Rwanda's Hutu. It is difficult to interpret this finding, given that it goes against all the other measures that indicate perpetrators and non-perpetrators had broadly similar attitudes towards Tutsi. It may simply be that perpetrators, many of whom had already been imprisoned for over nine years, had less to fear from the government than those still at liberty. They could speak more candidly and freely. But the possibility that it indicates a stronger sense of ethno-nationalist loyalty on the part of the perpetrators cannot be conclusively ruled out.

All in all, these findings suggest that Rwanda was indeed a country in which a racial ideology – or at least a historical memory unfavourable to Tutsi – was widely instilled. The Rwandans surveyed shared a set of beliefs that the Hutu had been the victims of Tutsi oppression and that they had been at a disadvantage historically. I argued in Chapter 4 that these beliefs were latent and co-existed with other ideas such as the importance of non-discrimination and national unity that appeared inconsistent with them. More than one narrative on inter-ethnic relations circulated in Rwanda's public sphere. However, extremists made appeals for action designed to resonate against the collective, historical memory of grievance and in so doing increased the salience of these beliefs relative to others. Having said this, I do not find that a highly developed sense of Hutu nationalism or anti-Tutsi prejudice distinguished the killers. Non-killers, in the main, were just as likely to hold pro-Hutu views and anti-Tutsi orientations. Finally, as a cautionary methodological note, it must be acknowledged that with retrospective opinion data, it is difficult to know whether the articulation of racially grounded beliefs was the *cause* or *effect* of the violence. Ideology may not only motivate and legitimize violence; it may also serve to rationalize participation after the fact.

Cluster IV: Threat-Related Theories – Security Dilemmas; Myths-Symbol Complexes; Ethnic Fears

A fourth cluster of theories emphasize the power of threats. As previously noted, these divide into two main approaches: (i) rationalist

7.3 Comparing Perpetrators and Non-perpetrators Systematically

explanations that examine strategic interactions *between* groups such as the 'security dilemma' or *within* groups when ethnic and political entrepreneurs compete for support within their ethnic constituencies; and (ii) culturalist explanations that emphasize myths, symbols, or narratives which, when combined with opportunity, cause groups to mobilize. But, also as previously noted, the main issue with these theories is that they are macro-focused and elite-centric. They do not tell us how threats work at the level of ordinary civilians and cause them to mobilize and take action. In response, I suggested four mechanisms in Chapter 3 through which war-time threat may facilitate civilian mobilization. I showed that the greater the threat: (i) the wider the ethnic distance; (ii) the greater the homogenization of the enemy outgroup; (iii) the stronger the demand for ingroup loyalty; and (iv) the greater the violence that can be legitimized. Were perpetrator responses on these four indicators measurably different from non-perpetrators? Table 7.7 summarizes the findings.

I asked respondents, first, to describe in their own words the ways in which the war had affected them. The two most common responses were consistent with the first and second mechanism. The war created security fears (32.1 per cent) and increased ethnic distance (53.4 per cent). Hutu were afraid for their physical security and they were suspicious of their Tutsi neighbours. However, perpetrators were not alone in feeling fearful for their security or distrustful of the Tutsi. Non-perpetrators felt these things too. In fact, counter-intuitively, perpetrators felt the existential threat and the ethnic distance a little *less* than their non-perpetrator counterparts.

What of the definition of the outgroup and ingroup, the third and fourth threat indicators? As I argued in Chapter 3, as the threat grows, group boundaries evolve: the enemy outgroup expands to include not only Tutsi combatants, but also Tutsi civilians; and the ingroup contracts to exclude disloyal Hutu. I first asked respondents, in an open-ended question, who most people believed the enemy to be. The answer, overwhelmingly, was that all Tutsi – both rebels and civilians – were considered the enemy (91.1 per cent). However, perpetrators (91.8 per cent) and non-perpetrators (91.0 per cent) alike attributed the threat to the Tutsi. Second, I asked who they believed the *ibyitso* or enemy collaborators to be. I classified the answers into those who replied it was the Tutsi only and those who thought it included both Tutsi and Hutu. The majority (88.5 per cent) felt that members of both

Table 7.7 Threat-related indicators for participation in violence

	All Hutu	Non-perpetrator		Perpetrator		Statistical difference	
	%	N	%	N	%	Chi-square	Logit (s.e.)
		Threat Perception & Impact					
Was your life affected negatively by the war? (Yes)	84.7	166	85.5	102	69.0	5.08**	0.38 (0.17)**
In what ways was your life affected? (i) Security impact	32.1	166	32.3	102	27.8	0.30	0.81 (0.32)
(ii) Ethnic relations impact	53.4	166	54.4	102	30.5	3.30*	0.37 (0.21)*
(iii) Economic impact	31.4	166	31.8	102	20.0	1.74	0.53 (0.26)
		Threat Magnitude					
What did people say would happen if the RPF won the war? (i) Hutu would be killed	67.8	166	69.1	102	46.6	5.71**	0.39(0.16)**
(ii) Hutu would be oppressed and/or monarchy restored	18.8	166	18.9	102	16.5	0.14	0.84 (0.39)
(iii) The rebels would govern well	6.6	166	6.1	102	15.3	3.99*	2.76 (1.46)*
(iv) Nobody thought the RPF would win	5.4	166	5.0	102	12.1	1.87	2.61 (1.90)

	Threat Attribution						
At the time of the genocide, who did most people think was the *enemy*? (All Tutsi)	91.1	166	91.0	102	91.8	0.69	0.53 (0.41)
Unwilling/unable to say	7.0	166	7.1	102	4.8	0.65	0.55 (0.42)
At the time of the genocide, who did most people think were the *enemy collaborators*? Both Hutu and Tutsi	88.5	159	88.6	98	86.2	0.15	0.80 (0.46)
Tutsi only	11.5	159	11.4	98	13.8	0.15	0.80 (0.46)
Threat & Legitimization of violence							
At the time of the genocide, do you think that most people believed that what was happening was right? (Yes)	54.2	169	54.1	99	55.9	0.19	1.20 (0.51)
Unwilling/unable to say	12.8	169	12.6		15.2	0.15	1.09 (0.24)
If so, why did they think it was right? (They were defending themselves against enemy)	22.7	131	22.9	82	21.3	0.00	1.01 (0.42)
They personally profited from it	16.4	138	17.2	97	2.0	10.17***	0.10 (0.09)**
The authorities had ordered it	10.9	149	10.7	87	10.4	1.63	2.09 (1.23)
Threat Resonance							
Composite of 4 questions testing historical memory of Tutsi oppression and favouritism. (Scale 1–8: 8=most negative memory)[mean(std dev)]	4.79 (0.22)	164	4.77 (0.23)	101	5.18 (0.15)	na	1.24 (0.18)

*** Significant at 1% level. ** 5% level. * 10% level.

319

ethnic groups could be called enemy accomplices. Perpetrators (86.3 per cent) were statistically no more likely to feel this than non-perpetrators (88.6 per cent). Ingroup loyalty was important in the minds of both groups.

Next, I asked Rwandans for their perceptions of the violence's legitimacy. I showed in Chapter 3 that, in the face of a threat, violence is legitimized as self-defence: the greater the threat, the greater the violence that can be justified. A majority of Rwandans (54.2 per cent) felt that the consensus at the time was that the violence was indeed justified. When asked why it was legitimate, the most popular answer was self-defence (22.7 per cent), followed by the personal, material gain to be made (16.4 per cent). However, this simply did not distinguish those who participated in the violence from those who did not. Both perpetrators (55.9 per cent) and non-perpetrators (54.1 per cent) were equally likely to report that most people believed the violence was legitimate, and also that it was self-defence (perpetrators – 21.3 per cent, non-perpetrators – 22.9 per cent).

Lastly, I looked at the threat's resonance. Rwanda's civil war had special cultural and historical resonance. As we saw in Chapter 4, Hutu shared a collective, historical memory of Tutsi oppression and favouritism during the Tutsi monarchy. The war had been framed as an attempt to reverse the outcome of the Hutu revolution that overthrew the monarchy, and to reinstate Tutsi rule. But once again, these memories were not unique to the perpetrators. Non-perpetrators were just as likely to hold them.

So, we have established that perpetrators and non-perpetrators *both*: (i) perceived the war as a threat; (ii) saw the threat as primarily existential; (iii) defined the threat in ethnic terms; (iv) attributed the threat to all Tutsi; (v) considered the Tutsi the 'threateners' and the Hutu the 'defenders' and (vi) felt the threat resonated historically. Threat, in short, mattered. Rwanda's civil war was an important background condition to the genocide. It did not, however, separate those who committed violence from those who did not.

Cluster V: Authority; Obedience; Peer Pressure; Coercion; Conformity

A fifth set of theories focus on what I collectively term 'influence'. I distinguish between (i) *vertical* influence: theories that emphasize

7.3 Comparing Perpetrators and Non-perpetrators Systematically 321

the importance of authority, obedience, and compliance; and (ii) *horizontal* influence: explanations that focus on peer pressure, coercion, and conformity.

'Vertical' explanations of civilian participation in Rwanda's genocide have pointed both to a culture of obedience and to Rwanda's unusually strong state. The two are related. Citizens are likely to obey when the state's authority is strong. Empirical studies of genocides have tended to emphasize cultures of obedience.[58] Yet we do not have strong cross-national evidence that measures how obedient-prone one culture is in comparison with another. Theoretical studies, in contrast, have privileged 'authority'. At the macro-level, political scientists look at the state's capacity and legitimacy.[59] At the micro-level, social psychologists have looked at individual authority. Stanley Milgram's experiments in the 1960s continue to be debated today. He demonstrated that the presence of a man in white coat, representing 'scientific authority', could influence participants to inflict harm on an actor in the form of electric shocks (Milgram, 1963).

I focused on measures of the Rwandan state's authority vis-à-vis Rwandans. Were perpetrators more likely to be deferential to or compliant with the Rwandan state's authority than non-perpetrators? The Rwandan government had considerable capacity in the eyes of ordinary Rwandans. When asked who provided eight, critical services in their community, respondents overwhelmingly replied the state, followed by themselves, the Church, and foreign NGOs. But perpetrators felt the same way as non-perpetrators in this respect. Both saw the state as the most influential actor in their lives. I then asked respondents whether they always participated in *umuganda*, the state's compulsory communal labour program. Again, equally large proportions of perpetrators (74.5 per cent) and non-perpetrators (71.3 per cent) said they did. Finally, I asked two questions to test Rwandans' perception of the legitimacy of state intervention in their lives. Were *umuganda* and the amount of taxes they had to pay fair? Approximately

---

[58] For Rwanda, see Prunier (1998, p. 248). For Germany, see Staub (1989, pp. 108–109).

[59] Valentino (2004, pp. 71–90) argues that certain types of mass killing are more likely, the greater the physical capabilities for mass killing possessed by the regime – a measure of state capacity. Rummel (1995) argues that regime type – authoritarian or democratic – is important for deciding whether the state will commit mass murder.

three-quarters felt that they were indeed fair but once again perpetrators were almost indistinguishable from non-perpetrators in their perceptions. In sum, vertical influence was important in Rwanda's genocide. The Rwandan state was very authoritative in the eyes of ordinary Rwandans. However, there is nothing to suggest that perpetrators had a different orientation to its authority from non-perpetrators. Table 7.8 summarizes these findings.

A second set of 'horizontal' explanations of participation in Rwanda's genocide emphasize peer pressure, coercion, and conformity. Previously, I found that coercion and peer pressure were effective tactics used to mobilize the population. They were a form of ingroup policing. A majority of Rwandans believed that you would face sanctions for helping Tutsi, and a smaller proportion believed that there would be reprisals for refusing to participate in the attack groups as well. These sanctions could be (i) social: individuals were stigmatized as enemy collaborators; (ii) monetary: individuals had to pay fines; or (iii) physical: individuals were the victims of either an attack or a threatened attack. But again, I did not find that perpetrators were any more likely to fear repercussions for resistance than non-perpetrators.

Perpetrator Heterogeneity

The overall picture that emerges then is that those in my sample who committed violence were not strongly distinguishable from those who did not. I did not find that Rwanda's killers were any more likely to be materially deprived, socially excluded, fearful for their security, deferential to authority, ethnically or racially prejudiced, ideologically nationalist, or susceptible to peer pressure. With the exception of being male and a little younger, they did not have characteristics, beliefs, or attitudes that strongly distinguished them. The distance between those who killed and those who did not appears small. The perpetrators I surveyed do appear to be ordinary.

This statement requires an important qualification, however. The perpetrators I sampled from the prisons were typically neither the leaders nor the hardened serial killers of Rwanda's genocide. As we saw previously, when I asked respondents to name the individuals who mobilized or led the violence in their communities and who killed with zeal, they identified 160 individuals. Two-thirds of these persons were not in prison. They were either still at large – usually over the border in

Table 7.8 Influence-related indicators for participation in violence

	All Hutu		Non-perpetrator			Perpetrator			Statistical Difference	
	%		N	%		N	%		Chi Square	Logit (s.e.)

Vertical Influence: Authority and Obedience

Before the genocide, who provided these 8 services in your community? (educ., health, agric. extension, roads, irrigation, justice, security, credit). (Scale 1–8: 8=most services provided) [mean (std dev)]	6.16 (0.35)		160	6.17 (0.37)		98	6.00 (0.21)		na	0.95 (0.13)
The State										
Church	0.84 (0.20)		160	0.85 (0.22)		98	0.68 (0.10)		na	0.85 (0.20)
Foreigners (usually NGOs)	0.46 (0.14)		160	0.45 (0.15)		98	0.59 (0.12)		na	1.15 (0.23)
Villagers themselves	2.33 (0.46)		160	2.32 (0.49)		98	2.52 (0.27)		na	1.04 (0.11)
Before the genocide, were there times when you chose *not* to do *umuganda* (state-imposed communal labour) other than when you were sick?	74.4		157	74.5		83	71.3		0.17	0.85 (0.34)
No, I always did *umuganda*										
Before the genocide, did you think *umuganda* (state-imposed communal labour) was fair?	76.7		169	76.1		104	87.4		2.90*	2.18 (1.02)
Yes, it was fair										

Table 7.8 (cont.)

	All Hutu %	Non-perpetrator N	Non-perpetrator %	Perpetrator N	Perpetrator %	Chi Square	Logit (s.e.)
Before the genocide, if you had to pay taxes, did you think the amount was fair? Yes, it was fair	83.5	125	83.2	79	89.6	1.07	1.73 (0.93)
Horizontal Influence: Peer Pressure and Coercion							
What happened to individuals who refused to join the attack groups? (open-ended) They faced sanctions (social, monetary, or physical)	34.8	164	34.4	98	41.8	0.49	1.37 (0.62)
What happened to individuals who were caught assisting Tutsi? (open-ended) They faced sanctions (social, monetary, or physical)	73.3	165	73.6	97	68.3	0.41	0.77 (0.31)

*** Significant at 1% level. ** 5% level. * 10% level.

7.3 Comparing Perpetrators and Non-perpetrators Systematically

Table 7.9 *Corroborated 'kill rates' for 69 sampled perpetrators*

No. of individuals in whose death the perpetrator was involved	Percentage of perpetrators who killed (%)
1	47.8
2	18.8
3	13.0
4	8.7
5	1.5
6	2.9
7	2.9
8	0
9	1.5
10+	2.9

the DRC – or dead. So, these perpetrators were under-represented in my sample. In fact, in January 2003 Rwanda's prison population totalled 101,469 *génocidaires*.[60] Yet I estimated that almost 423,000 Rwandans organized or committed violence during the genocide. So a very large number were missing from the prison population. Moreover, most of the perpetrators I sampled had been involved in the deaths of only one or two individuals. Table 7.9 indicates individual 'kill rates'. The vast majority killed only a few, while a small minority killed many. The differences reinforce earlier findings on the importance of small groups of radicals, typically comprising a leader supported by a core of committed killers, during the genocide.

The *gacaca* data, although crude in the categorization of crimes, also suggested important differences between perpetrators. As seen, a minority, 9.7 per cent, were highly committed to the genocide. They either organized the violence, executed it with zeal, or committed sexual torture. The majority, 63.3 per cent, however, did not display as deep a commitment to the violence. They joined an attack group and were involved in the commission of at least one act of violence. However, they were not the leaders, the serial killers, or the sadists of the genocide. The overwhelming majority of those in my sample fell into

---

[60] See International Committee for the Red Cross (2003). On file with author. The number excludes individuals imprisoned for non-genocide related crimes.

this category. These individuals participated either because they followed others in respecting the state's orders or else because they felt they had no option and were coerced by the state into doing so. Lastly, though likely a major underestimation, 26.9 per cent only looted. These individuals did not participate in the violence at all. They were simply material opportunists who sought to profit from the disorder created by the genocide.

I also asked my survey respondents about dispositional differences towards the violence in their communities. Their responses provide a clear finding. Important differences existed between the killers. Perpetrators varied in their commitment to the violence. To illustrate dispositional heterogeneity, I asked respondents first whether there were 'extremists', whom I defined as individuals who were especially enthusiastic about the violence in their community. Two-thirds confirmed the existence of highly committed killers. Just over half put their number at between one and ten individuals in their communities. Relatedly, I also asked whether there were individuals who enjoyed, that is took pleasure, in killing. Nearly four-fifths suggested the presence of sadists in their communities. Second, I asked whether there were individuals who joined the attack groups not to kill, but because they believed they would benefit materially in some way. More than half (53.1%) believed that some individuals participated to obtain material goods such as cows, mattresses, or zinc sheeting and 10 per cent indicated that land was a motivation.[61]

So, material opportunism was very powerful. Third, I asked whether Rwandans joined the attack groups because the authorities had ordered it. 17 per cent believed that individuals felt disposed to comply with the law. Conformism was a factor. Lastly, I asked whether there were individuals who actively tried to end the violence in their community. About a third said there were individuals who sought to stop the violence in their community and three-quarters said there were individuals who resisted joining the attack groups. Respondents then confirmed the presence of refuseniks or pacifists. Table 7.10 summarizes these findings. In short, perpetrators differed in their disposition or commitment toward the violence.

---

[61] 53.1% of Hutu respondents stated that they believed individuals joined attack groups for material reasons. See Table 7.11.

Table 7.10 Dispositional differences among perpetrators

	Ethnicity		Perpetrator Status		Region	
	Hutu	Tutsi	Non-perp.	Perp.	South	North

Extremists

Question: If groups were formed in your community, how many, if any, of those in the group were highly committed to killing Tutsis? (open-ended)

	(N=229)	(N=15)	(N=143)	(N=86)	(N=98)	(N=131)
None	32.7%	0	33.7%	12.6%	1.5%	57.8%
1–10	56.3%	93.5%	55.7%	68.4%	81.2%	36.2%
11–20	6.2%	6.5%	5.6%	17.0%	9.4%	3.6%
21+	4.8%	0	5.0%	2.1%	7.9%	2.4%

Material opportunists

Question: Were there people in your community who joined the groups because they believed they would get land?

	(N=268)	(N=21)	(N=167)	(N=101)	(N=128)	(N=140)
No one believed they would get land	67.6	42.9	67.3	74.7	49.2	84.6
I don't know	22.4	23.7	22.9	7	31.2	14.2
Yes	10.1	33.4	9.8	18.3	19.6	1.2

Table 7.10 (cont.)

	Ethnicity		Perpetrator Status			Region	
	Hutu	Tutsi	Non-perp.	Perp.		South	North
	(N=270)	(N=21)	(N=169)	(N=101)		(N=130)	(N=140)

Refuseniks/Pacifists

Question: Were there people in your community who tried to stop the genocide?

Yes, there were some who tried to stop it	31.2	31.8	30.1	51.7		50.2	13.9
No one tried to stop it	43.6	68.2	43.8	39.2		49.8	37.8
There were no attacks in my community	25.2	0	26.1	9.1		0	48.3

Sadists

Question: Were there people in your community who enjoyed, that is took pleasure in, killing?

	(N=229)	(N=20)	(N=147)	(N=82)		(N=125)	(N=104)
Yes, some people enjoyed killing	78.4%	85.1%	78.5%	75.5%		90.0%	63.4%

7.3 Comparing Perpetrators and Non-perpetrators Systematically

Putting the *gacaca* and survey data together, a rudimentary categorization of perpetrators becomes discernible: extremists, opportunists, and conformists all participated in the genocide, while pacifists resisted the violence. This classification, while crude, reflects the idea that individuals had different levels of commitment to the violence. Rwandans were heterogeneous in their disposition toward the killing. This four-fold categorization is evidently not definitive. In theory, as commitment is not discretely measured, an infinite number of commitment categories is possible. However, the data do not allow a more fine-grained typology. Extremists have the strongest commitment to the violence. I include here the leaders, the serial killers, and the sadists of the genocide. Opportunists have a lower level of commitment and view the violence instrumentally. In my four micro-case studies, I had identified *political* opportunists who saw the possibility for self-advancement and power in the fluidity and uncertainty created by the president's death. These political entrepreneurs, along with ethnic entrepreneurs who acted out of ideological or racist conviction, typically led the violence in their communities aided by a small group of committed supporters. Conformists have the weakest commitment to the violence. These individuals – who constituted a large proportion of my respondents – joined the attack groups not out of ideological conviction or a lust for killing. They were complying with what they perceived as a state-imposed obligation. Lastly, pacifists have no commitment to the violence. In fact, they oppose it. To be clear, not every person who did not participate in Rwanda's violence was a pacifist. As we shall see, disposition alone did not determine selection into the violence. Situational opportunities and relational ties would matter too.

Dispositional heterogeneity is an important finding. It qualifies the situationist perspective that has dominated and reinforces the minority position that traits exist that make individuals likely to conform or to defy.[62] It also reconciles the difference between two fundamentally different philosophical outlooks on human nature and violence. In the Hobbesian worldview, people are naturally violent and will kill when the constraints are removed if it is in their interest to do so.

---

[62] Baum (2008), for instance, distinguishes perpetrators, bystanders, and rescuers in genocides and argues that they differ in their emotional maturity. Rescuers are the most emotionally developed.

Hirshleifer's 'Machievellian theorem', adapted from Coases' theorem, articulates this perspective well: 'no one will ever pass up an opportunity to gain a one-sided advantage by exploiting another party' (Hirshleifer, 1994, p. 3). In the Lockean perspective, in contrast, people are naturally non-violent and require some exogenous influence to push them to kill. Yet both viewpoints may be true and their binary opposition false. Some people may be dispositionally inclined toward violence; others more committed to pacifism.

Some of the classic work often cited in support of the situationist and 'ordinary men' position may also be read as supportive of the dispositional heterogeneity thesis. Milgram (1963) found that twenty-six of forty (65 per cent) male subjects from New Haven, who responded to an advertisement soliciting paid participants for a memory experiment, were willing to administer increasingly powerful electric shocks when ordered by an individual clothed as a scientist, to the point that the 'victim', an actor who could be heard but not seen by the subject, ceased crying out in pain to simulate unconsciousness. But this still means that fourteen out of forty (35 per cent) refused to do so. Haney et al. (1973) found in a simulated prison experiment involving twenty-one American male college students, that of the eleven who played the role of guards, one third became increasingly physically aggressive towards the ten who played prisoners over the course of one week. But again, this means that two-thirds did not transform. Faced with the same opportunities and circumstances, individuals reacted differently.

Research on conflict and violence at aggregated levels of analysis all too often seeks out a single or dominant motivation. Scholarship on civil wars, for example, has been bifurcated between those who advocate greed or opportunity explanations and those who argue grievance matters more.[63] Similarly, in genocide studies, scholars often attempt to classify the killing according to what they deem its primary purpose to be: retributive, ideological, utilitarian, defensive, revolutionary, or purificatory, among others.[64] Yet the perpetrators may possess several or all of these motivations in the same genocide. And this is true for perpetrator elites as well as non-elites. We saw previously, for example,

[63] For greed or opportunity, see for example Collier & Hoeffler (2004). For grievance, see Buhaug et al. (2013).
[64] See for example Chalk & Jonassohn (1990); Chirot & McCauley (2010); (Fein, 1993); Gurr & Harff (1988). See Straus (2001) for an overview of such 'perpetrator-objective' approaches to classifying genocides.

that in the immediate aftermath of Habyarimana's assassination, his family and those close to it were motivated by the desire to avenge his death but others, such as Bagosora, were driven by a longstanding extreme ideological aversion to Tutsi.

Finally, although the survey failed to distinguish between perpetrators and non-perpetrators, it nonetheless highlighted potential background conditions for the genocide. Rwandans had internalised a set of historical, ideological beliefs regarding Hutu exploitation and Tutsi privilege; felt the threat of war strongly; showed a high tolerance for an intrusive and extractive state; and suffered deprivation and inequality acutely. Reliance on a single case study does not permit us to conclude that these facts were either necessary or sufficient conditions for the genocide. They are better described as facilitative or permissive background macro-level conditions to the genocide. However, when scaled down to the micro-foundational level, these factors do not explain differential participation in the violence.

7.4 Motives and Rationales

How do Rwandans explain the killing themselves? What motives do they give? There is, unsurprisingly, no single answer. Take this statement from Leopold, a young Hutu man, who was the vice-president of the *gacaca* committee in Mwendo cell. Leopold was unusually forthcoming and I returned to speak with him several times. In our last meeting, he volunteered his view on why people killed in his community.

After a few days it was evident that there were two groups – those being hunted and those who hunted. That is when people became greedy and started to kill and eat people's cows. After it was evident that there were some people who were the enemy, some people then said that 'We are used to this because of history.' Then those hiding people told these people to flee rather than dying where they hid them. There are people who participated in the genocide as a way of 'buying their lives.' They dodged at the beginning, but as time passed this became impossible. *Did some people participate because they wanted to get rich?* Because people had weak brains and some were hungry and poor, they started to harvest peoples' land and, in that way, they would not be so poor. That is when people started dividing the land, even those who did not participate, and so those at the bottom who had little land would get land. And those in the high authorities said if these people are not there, we would be better off than before. People fled and people said that they might have fled with nice clothes and property and that is when people went to attack them in the Parish and the other places. According to history, when people fled, others kept their property for them and returned it when they returned. But in 1994 it was different. It was like a time-bomb that exploded. It was different in 1994. It was a question of development. Today people used different weapons – grenades and *pangas* [machetes]. Also, the hate developed. This was because of the politicians who brought themselves close to the villagers. Before this, Tutsi and Hutu used to walk home together. I would say what caused this is people had big stomachs. There were those who were greedy, who were saying that we would be better off without these people. When villagers went to the places where the Tutsi fled, they said they could not leave them alive there and take their things, as they knew each other. And the community had been sensitized [*sensibilisé* in French] that one group was the enemy and this gave them energy to do what they did. It was evident in the *gacaca* that some people participated because of the sensitization and so most people killed to get rid of the enemy and those people who were being killed were the supporters of the enemy. *Do you think some people killed because they hated Tutsi?* I would say that in general there was a personal liking of each other and it was the authorities who are to blame, who turned people. Some of the villagers were saying that because the authorities told them to do this, they thought that they would not have to answer for anything. But now people see it was wrong. Now it is the villagers who are suffering and it is those in the prison who are in suffering, while those who organized the genocide are in Arusha where they get television and complain of not having enough to eat. (*Leopold, Hutu man, aged 32, April 2003, Mwendo cell, Butare Prefecture*)

Leopold's explanation is rich with diverse motives for why people killed. In this one piece of testimony he suggested material opportunism, poverty, coercion, impunity, historical memory, and ideological indoctrination all had something to do with why people killed in his community. In fact, I counted thirteen distinct motives in interviews with just a few hundred Rwandans alone: fear of an enemy threat; the desire to obey authority; upward political and social mobility; material gain – including land-grabs; physical coercion; avoidance of pecuniary losses; concepts of masculinity and self-esteem; ideological indoctrination – through radio or political parties; national pride; racism and ethnic bigotry; sadism; conformity and social stigma; and personal score-settling. The existence of multiple micro-motives is not itself contradictory. It simply reflects the fact that different individuals had

7.4 Motives and Rationales

different motivations during the genocide. Hinton (2004) reached the same conclusion for participants in Cambodia's killings fields and goes further to argue that individuals subjectively assign their own meaning to the killing.

Observing human motivation is complex for a number of reasons. First, individuals may have more than one motive. When multiple motives exist, it may not be clear even to the individuals themselves which is the most important. In fact, motivation may be altogether unconscious. Second, individuals' beliefs as to what motivated them may change following the action. *Ex post* motives may differ from those *ex ante*, especially if an individual is unhappy with his behaviour. Psychologists would describe this as an example of cognitive dissonance (Festinger 1957). Third, motivation may evolve with repeated behaviour. In the Rwandan context, as people committed violence over and over again, they may have adapted or learned, and their motivation may have changed as a result. Lastly, the motives that individuals present to third parties may differ from the motives they privately possess. The impulse to present socially acceptable reasons is strong. Given this complexity, it is perhaps more accurate to present what my interview techniques obtained as rationales rather than as motivations: the reasons that Rwandans gave to explain or to justify their actions to the world afterwards.

Quantifying the Many Rationales

So, the rationales that Rwandans provided were diverse, but were some more prevalent than others? I included four, standardized questions in the survey to gather and assess the various motives or rationales. I framed the questions both: (i) directly and indirectly; and (ii) explicitly and implicitly. I expected respondents to minimize their personal culpability when asked directly about their own involvement. Self-serving bias was inevitable. For this reason, I also asked questions indirectly. Why did others kill, for example? I also expected that Rwandans would be wary of questions in which killing was the explicit subject. So I also framed questions in terms of activities in which the violence was implicit.

The four questions were: (i) Why do you think people killed during the genocide? (indirect, explicit); (ii) Did you man a roadblock during the genocide, and if so why? (direct, explicit); (iii) Were groups organized to look for the enemy in your community, and if so why did people join them? (indirect, implicit); and (iv) Did you participate in night patrols in your community during the genocide, and if so why? (direct, implicit). Roadblocks in the Rwandan context were explicitly about violence. They were well-known as sites where many people were killed. The questions were open-ended and I coded the various answers into thirteen categories of responses. These were: physical coercion; material disincentive; material incentive; authority; conformity; enemy threat; patriotism; ethnic hatred; impunity; self-defence; ideological indoctrination; vengeance; and unwilling or unable to respond. I present the results in Table 7.11.

I then distilled these many responses into a simpler 2 × 2 table. Table 7.12 shows the two most popular answers for each of the four questions. Not all respondents answered all four questions. The Rwandan government interrupted this additional section of the survey stating that it was ethnically divisive. As a result, there is a northern bias in the indirect, explicit question and a southern bias in the direct, implicit question. Nonetheless, there are still several clear messages.

First, the rationales given are consistent with the book's three main themes. Threat, authority, and material opportunism broadly correspond to the civil war, Rwanda's unusually powerful state, and the breakdown in law and order caused by Habyarimana's assassination: security, authority, and opportunity. Coercion was the fourth rationale cited, and it corresponded to my finding in Chapter 5 of the importance of the micro-situational tactic used to mobilize the population: ingroup policing. The surprising fifth rationale was vengeance for Habyarimana's assassination, but this may be the result of the northern bias in one survey question. Habyarimana himself of course hailed from the north.

Second, the results predictably reflected self-serving bias. The two questions that asked respondents *directly* why they became involved received responses that minimized their personal agency and culpability: 'It was the law'; 'You could not disobey the high authorities'; 'I had no choice – they would kill me otherwise.' These answers emphasized authority and coercion: vertical and horizontal situational influences. The killers' actions were involuntary. In contrast, respondents attributed volition and self-interest to the behaviour of others: 'they were greedy'; 'they would profit from it'; 'they liked the power'. Social psychologists would term this an instance of 'fundamental attribution

7.4 Motives and Rationales

Table 7.11 *Quantifying rationales for violence (Hutu respondents only)*

	Indirect, explicit	Direct, explicit	Indirect, implicit	Direct, implicit
	Why did people kill	Why did you man a roadblock	Why did people join groups	Why did you do night patrols
	(N=144)	(N=61)	(N=186)	(N=50)
Physically threatened	0.4%	26.7%	3.2%	16.2%
Stood to lose financially or materially	0.0%	2.8%	0.2%	1.2%
Stood to gain financially or materially	12.3%	0.0%	53.1%	0%
It was the law/ordered by the authorities	2.4%	52.5%	16.9%	48.8%
Just did as everyone else did	0.0%	1.0%	1.1%	0%
Thought Tutsi were the enemy/collaborators	25.8%	0.1%	11.3%	0%
Believed they were fighting for their country	4.9%	1.7%	3.5%	5.5%
Hated the Tutsi	4.9%	0.0%	7.6%	0%
Believed the authorities would do nothing	5.2%	5.3%	9.4%	16.2%
Defending themselves	2.2%	1.0%	2.4%	12.2%
Been exposed to propaganda/ideology	10.9%	0.0%	13.9%	0%
Angered by Habyarimana's death	41.0%	0.0%	0.4%	0%
Unwilling/unable to answer	19.2%	0%	10.1%	0%

error' (Ross & Nisbett, 2011). Individuals tend to attribute their own behaviour to the situation and the behaviour of others to disposition.

Finally, the indirect, implicit question – why did people join the groups to look for the enemy – confirmed that participation in the genocide was not all involuntary. The opportunity to loot was a very powerful incentive. Material opportunism (53.1 per cent) was the most

Table 7.12 *Most common rationale for violence by type of question asked*

	Directly asked	Indirectly asked
Explicitly asked	Authority & Coercion	Vengeance & Threat
Implicitly asked	Authority & Coercion	Material Opportunism & Authority

popular motive. This does not necessarily contradict the importance of authority and coercion. As we shall see, motivation evolved: some said people were forced initially, but subsequently acted willingly when the potential for self-enrichment became apparent.

Delving Deeper into the Rationales

I probed several of the more commonly cited rationales more deeply to understand the logic that Rwandans provided for them. What follows are not definitive or representative statements on each of these rationales, but the reactions of a few Rwandans to provide some more depth on how these rationales worked.

The 'Opportunity' Rationale
How did the opportunity to profit – either from looting property or from seizing land – work in practice to motivate individuals to kill?

There is a link between the land and the genocide. Some young men hoped to get the land of those who were dead. There was also the historical precedent of Tutsi fleeing. People were afraid that they would ask for their land back that they lost in 1959 [Hutu revolution]. The RPF consisted of Tutsi – and some Hutu and even some Twa – and they intended to sort out these problems of land they had lost. *Did the authorities redistribute the land then?* After 1959 the state gave people who had no land the land that had been left. But there was no redistribution after the war of 1994. There was harvesting of the land but no redistribution. (*Jean-Claude, Hutu, aged 53, former teacher, focused group interview, Nyanza prison, July 2003*)

Jean-Claude tells us that land did matter, but in two different ways. Some young men did indeed hope to get the land of those killed – though as it turns out the state did not redistribute the land in his community, merely the crops on it. But people were also afraid that the rebels – who were mostly the descendants of the Hutu Revolution's refugees – would come to reclaim the land their ancestors had lost. For Jean-Claude then, there was the hope of land to gain and the fear of land to lose.

The burgomaster was saying he would sell the land to the villagers but he was saying that only after the genocide. No one was thinking that they would get the land during the genocide. I was close to the villagers and I never heard anyone say that. I think most people joined the attacks because they could get cows and other looted property. These things could be taken right away. (*Ernest Mulinda, Hutu, aged 44, cell responsable, Mwendo cell, Maraba commune, Butare prefecture, May 2003*)

Mulinda draws a distinction between land and moveable property. For him, land was not a motivation but cows, in contrast, were immediately consumable and thus a more powerful incentive.

Rwandans took advantage of the opportunity created by the genocide in more complex ways as well. Noel was sixteen at the time the genocide began. Several people from Mwendo cell mentioned his enthusiasm to kill to me.

He was a young adolescent. He lived still with his father. He came from a very poor family. To find food to eat he would have to be a shepherd for other people like my mother. He was a child who wanted to always be first, to want to be talked about. Even here in prison he is known as *ruharwa* [those who killed with zeal]. He boasted here of what he had done. He wanted to be a man, and to show others that he was a man. He killed many people on the hills. (*Oriel, Hutu accused of genocide-related crimes, aged 45, primary school teacher, Butare central prison, April 2003*)

For young Noel, the genocide was a means of social mobility and also the expression of his masculinity. He killed because he believed it brought him recognition within his community and earned him respect as a man. In the same community, I also heard the sad story of Aurelie who was killed by her two step-brothers early on in the genocide over a land dispute.

The first person to be killed was Aurelie. *What ethnicity was she?* She was Hutu. It was a misunderstanding between her and her brothers over land. Her father had two wives and when he died the two wives got equal shares. Aurelie's mother had only one daughter [Aurelie] while the other wife had two sons. The two sons were jealous that Aurelie got more. The father had died a long time ago and the sons used the chance of the war to get rid of her. Perhaps they were hoping people would say she died because of the war. The brothers perhaps paid someone to kill her. But she was killed early in the morning and the brothers brought the case to me at 10.00am. I asked why they took so long to report it to me. *What happened to them?* Nothing happened to them as the war [genocide] immediately started. We sent reports but nothing came of them. (*Ernest Mulinda again*)

Her two step-brothers then used the opportunity presented by the genocide to settle a score. They had long resented how much land their step-sister had received.

The 'Security' Rationale
The war featured heavily in perpetrator testimony. But what significance did it hold for Rwandans and how did it motivate them to kill?

This notion of an enemy is historical. During the colonial period the *Abahutu* were colonized and oppressed. Many fled overseas and so they had a little fear that the RPF would come and colonize them again – they were afraid that they would re-instate the monarchy. *But there were Hutu in the RPF.* The Hutu in the RPF fled the RPF – but it was after the war started – when they saw that they were not following the agenda. People also saw *Abahutu* being killed in Byumba. (*Geoffrey, Hutu, aged 38, former teacher, focused group interview, Nyanza prison, July 2003*)

For Geoffrey, the war had historical resonance. Like many of his compatriots, he had no memories – as he was too young – but rather historical beliefs about Rwanda's past. He believed that the Tutsi, as a group, had oppressed the Hutu, as a group. The current war threatened to bring back the Tutsi monarchy and to reinstate the socio-political order in which Tutsi ruled over Hutu.

People were very afraid that the Tutsi would come back to take their land they left in 1959. It was the air they were breathing. It was not all the land – just the land they had left behind. But the reasons why people participated are several. Most people were very poor and were hoping they would get things in an easy way when the war started. Cows, land, and foodstuffs. During the war there was also a rumour that the Tutsi were going to kill all the Hutu. And so, people felt they were only defending themselves. (*Williame, Hutu, aged 38, former teacher, focused group interview, Nyanza prison, July 2003.*)

For Williame, the war signified both an economic and existential threat. People feared that the Tutsi would take back the land they had lost in the Hutu revolution. But they also feared that the Tutsi would kill the Hutu. For him, the violence then was simply self-defence.

The 'Authority' Rationale
I had repeatedly heard responses along the lines of 'we obeyed what the authorities said'. How did Rwandans view state authority during the genocide?

Not everyone listened to what the authorities said about killing. There were those who followed not with the intention to kill, but out of fear. The respect for authority is very strong. But it was rather fear of the authorities. *Did the villagers like to do umuganda? Umuganda* would be liked depending on what the work was. If it was hard, they would not go there. But because this was also the time when they sorted out social problems people would be motivated to attend the *umuganda* meeting. (*Williame again*)

Williame feels that Rwandans complied with the orders from authority figures not out of a natural respect, but out of fear of the consequences otherwise. He also does not accept Rwandans are blindly obedient. As he points out, they are willing to defy authority if necessary.

At the beginning people were forced. But when people saw that people were not being arrested, then they gained confidence. *Was it like this before the genocide?* There was nothing like this before the genocide. If you harmed someone you would be punished for it – you would be put into prison. (*Jean-Claude again.*)

For Jean-Claude, the authorities did not need to order Rwandans to kill. Their failure to punish people for committing violence was encouragement enough. Impunity was a powerful incentive. He also tells us that Rwandans adapted or learned to kill. Having participated involuntarily at the outset, this came to change when they realized that they would not be held accountable.

At the beginning everyone was against any killing. But the radio convinced in seconds. The radio was 90 per cent responsible and the local authorities also re-taught what the high authorities said on the radio. But it was not the local authorities who did the killing. It was rather the military who started the killing and terrorized people to make them kill. In the areas where there were many Tutsi they sent the gendarmes in buses. Also, there were the GP [Presidential Guard] who came to the prefecture. Local authorities were first with the population but then the military would come to terrorize them. (*Geoffrey again*)

Geoffrey points to the state, but to the military rather than the civilian authorities. The local civilian authority figures – the sector councillor and cell *responsable* – played supporting roles in his community. They reinforced the message heard on the radio. As with Williame, the mechanism was coercion rather than blind obedience. Soldiers 'terrorized' Rwandans into action.

Motivations and the Passage of Time

It is not only that individual motives were diverse. Individual motivations also evolved and varied with time. The most obvious examples are the individuals who initially committed violence reluctantly or even against their will but who subsequently participated with increasing willingness. Psycho-social theory implicitly recognizes the distinction by suggesting differing mechanisms for initiating and sustaining participation in the violence.[65] Conformity, obedience, compliance, social pressure, and identification may all explain why an individual first engages in violence. Deindividuation, dehumanization, desensitization, and scapegoating may explain why he or she continues to engage in it. The evolution in an individual's motivation is likely to be more fluid and continuous than this binary distinction suggests. But the basic point is that motivation evolves with time.

I argued previously that Rwanda's radio broadcasts suggest that radicalization may not only have been a cause of violence but also a consequence of it. Individuals changed through the act of committing violence. Violence was itself transformative.[66] A common transformation in Rwanda, for instance, was from conformist to opportunist.

Why did people join the attack groups? If they were going to attack a rich person, more people would join. If they were going to attack a poor person, there would be less people. For example, in Eloise's case, her father had many cows and so many people – more than twenty – went... How often did these attacks happen? Ibitero [attack groups] was every day. They would go to several homes every day. But it depended on the level of resistance they encountered... How did they choose which place to attack? When they attacked a home, somebody would say so and so had cows. And they would

---

[65] See Lynch (2007) for an excellent exposition of this distinction.
[66] Luft (2015) makes a related argument that 'dehumanization' can follow the act of violence and that killers cognitively adapt to killing.

7.4 Motives and Rationales

plan to meet there. In the first days people went by force to go and rescue [*gutabara* in Kinyarwanda] and after that they went voluntarily because they could get property. *Who told them to go?* It was the extremists and the representatives of the political parties who would tell them where to go once they have reported that so and so had been completed. (*Same interview with Leopold*)

Leopold tells us that at the start people were *coerced* into participating but once they saw *ibitero* had material benefits, they began to participate voluntarily in the attack groups. Individuals adapted to the new opportunity. Adaptation and learning were central to the evolution in motivation.

Another transformation I encountered in Rwanda was from conformist to extremist, specifically to sadist. I asked survey respondents whether they felt there were individuals who enjoyed the killing – 78.4 percent said they knew someone in their community who did. The excessive cruelty, gratuitous pain and suffering, sexual torture, and general humiliation inflicted on victims observed in Rwanda ostensibly belie the argument that individuals were coerced into the violence. But unconscious, dark, and forbidden desires – more voluntarist behaviour – may become manifest through repeated opportunities to exercise the power of life and death over victims.[67]

How did he show his commitment to kill? He killed so many people. He also killed them in a hard way. *What do you mean?* At first, he used to hit the person on the head to kill them quickly. But then later he would chop them in other places so they didn't die immediately. (*Oriel again*)

It was difficult to find people willing to provide details of killings. Here Oriel is speaking again of Noel, the young orphaned shepherd who became one of the renowned killers in his community, and he hints that Noel changed and sought purposely to prolong the agony of his victims.

A final illustration of how motivation varied with time lies in the multiple, seemingly conflicting roles that Rwandans sometimes played in the genocide. The categories of killer, looter, rescuer, and bystander were not mutually exclusive. Individuals who joined attack groups at

[67] For a fascinating psycho-analytic explanation of how and why perpetrators enjoy the humiliation and suffering of their victims, see Weisband (2017). Fujii (2013) explains the phenomenon of extra-lethal violence as performative in character.

Table 7.13 *Samaritans in Rwanda's genocide*

	Hutu	Tutsi	Non-perpetrators.	Perpetrators
Question: Did you ever help any Tutsi, for example to escape or to hide, during the genocide? (If Tutsi, ask if s/he ever received any help)			
	N=266	N=13	N=164	N=102
Yes, I helped Tutsi (or if Tutsi, 'I received help')	34.9%	46.1%	33.4%	62.8%
Question: If you helped a Tutsi during the genocide, why did you so? (open-ended)			
I knew them personally	37.0%	0%	38.5%	21.4%
They were related to me	25.2%	83.8%	24.8%	29.3%
It was wrong to kill	25.6%	0%	24.6%	35.1%
Other reasons given	12.2%	16.2%	12.1%	14.2%

one time may also have helped Tutsi to hide or to escape at another time, for example. Nearly two in three of my surveyed perpetrators claimed that they helped Tutsi. While their answers cannot be taken at face value, tellingly almost half the Tutsi surveyed corroborated having received some help during the genocide. An individual could be both Samaritan and murderer, or rescuer and killer depending on the time and situation. I also asked these individuals why they helped. Over half replied it was because they had some family or other personal connection to that Tutsi individual. Table 7.13 presents these responses.

7.5 Why Some Killed and Others Not

This finding that there is nothing unusual about the perpetrators I sampled leaves unanswered the question of why they in particular came to kill and their neighbours not. My own and others' ethnographic evidence suggested that both physical geography and social connections may matter. Straus (2006, p. 137) found, for instance, that individuals in Rwanda were recruited sometimes simply by being located on the path on the way to a victim's home through what he termed 'accidental integration'. Fujii (2009, p. 19) found local ties 'served as mechanisms of recruitment and initiation into the violence'.

7.5 Why Some Killed and Others Not

But was it just geographic happenstance or were certain individuals systematically more likely to encounter other attackers? And to say that social ties matter offers little explanatory leverage as everyone is tied to someone, but did the social ties and networks of killers differ in some systematic way from those of non-killers? I returned to one of the four research sites I knew well, Tare sector in southern Rwanda, to investigate these two propositions more rigorously.

It's Where You Live

To reconstruct the pattern of ethnic settlement in Tare in April 1994, I returned to the micro-data produced through the *gacaca* pilot process. Importantly, this included (i) a census of every individual with their name, age, and gender resident in Tare on the eve of the genocide; and (ii) a list naming all the victims in the sector. Tare was home to 3,426 individuals in 647 households in April 1994 of whom 215 (6.3 per cent) were Tutsi. A total of 63 per cent of its Tutsi population were killed during the genocide and 24 per cent of its Hutu population were implicated in the killing.[68] Tellingly, the survivorship data showed that Tutsi girl children were much more likely to survive than Tutsi boys, strongly suggesting a genocidal or eliminationist intent as ethnicity was patrilineal in Rwanda. Table 7.14 profiles the community. I geo-coded the household residence of all 3,426 individuals to produce a map, Figure 7.2, distinguishing the location of perpetrators, bystanders, and victims.

I tested three micro-situational predictors of participation. First, I considered whether neighbourhood mattered. Specifically, I hypothesized that as the proportion of killers living in an individual's neighbourhood increased, the likelihood of that individual being drawn into the violence also increased.[69] I defined neighbourhoods as circles of increasing radii around each household (100 m, 200 m,

---

[68] The identification of perpetrators merited particular care. Reliance on the *gacaca* data could be problematic given the possibility of false accusations, false confessions, and witness intimidation. So, I considered both those *convicted* and those *suspected*. For suspects, I compared the names on the official *gacaca* suspect list against a list created by a less well-known informal, parallel *gacaca* process involving self-confessed killers within the prison system. Only if a name appeared on both suspect lists did I deem the individual likely to be a perpetrator.

[69] I construct neighbourhoods for Hutu aged fifteen and over. For more detail on the method followed and the results found, see McDoom (2013b).

Table 7.14 *Comparative profile of Tare sector, Rwanda*

	Sector Tare	Average sector in Butare prefecture	Average sector in Rwanda
Population (households)	3,426 (647)	3,862 (835)	5,192 (1090)
Ethnic Hutu & Twa	3,211 (93.7%)	82.7%	91.6%
Ethnic Tutsi	215 (6.3%)	17.3%	8.4%
Surface area (cultivable land)	5.62 km^2	8.49 km^2	12.58 km^2
Population density in 1994*	609 persons/km^2	455 persons/km^2	413 persons/km^2
All interethnic unions	38	na	na
All suspects (% Hutu men)	194 (24.2%)	26.5%	19.5%
Convicted suspects	94	na	na
All victims	136 (63.3%)	70%	73.7%
Killed inside Tare	10 (7.4%)	na	na
Killed outside Tare	126 (92.6%)	na	na
All survivors	79 (36.7%)	30.0%	26.3%
Male survivors	18 (22.8%)	na	na
Female survivors	61 (77.2%)	na	na

Sources: Government of Rwanda (1994); McDoom (2013b). *Projected from 1991 Census data.*

300 m, 400 m, 500 m) and then counted the number of killers relative to non-killers in each one. Second, I considered, using the same method, whether the proportion of *Tutsi* living in one's neighbourhood mattered. Inter-ethnic contact may encourage pro-Tutsi sentiment or, conversely, the proximity may make Tutsi seem more threatening or easier to target. Third, I hypothesized whether proximity to a mobilizing agent of the violence increased the chances of participation by measuring the distance between an individual's residence and the closest mobilizer's home.[70] I then conducted multivariate logistic regressions, using perpetrator status as the dependent variable, and controlled for individual socio-demographic and socioeconomic characteristics and the neighbourhood's population density. The results appear in Table 7.15.

[70] I identified local leaders through two separate focus group interviews with local *gacaca* officials and self-confessed perpetrators.

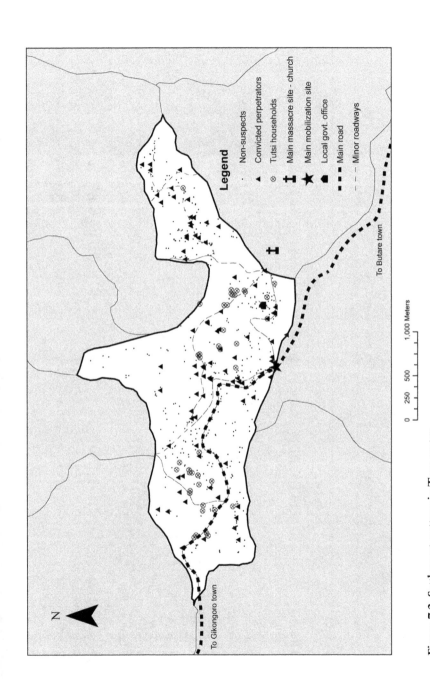

Figure 7.2 Settlement pattern in Tare sector

Table 7.15 *Neighbourhood as a predictor of participation in Rwanda's genocide*

	100 m neighbourhood		200 m neighbourhood		300 m neighbourhood	
	(1)	(2)	(3)	(4)	(5)	(6)
	Suspects	Convicts	Suspects	Convicts	Suspects	Convicts
Killers in neighbourhood (per cent)	1.03** (0.01)	1.04* (0.02)	1.11*** (0.02)	1.20*** (0.05)	1.10*** (0.03)	1.02 (0.07)
Tutsi in neighbourhood (per cent)	1.00 (0.01)	0.99 (0.02)	0.99 (0.02)	0.98 (0.02)	1.00 (0.02)	1.01 (0.02)
Killers in household (per cent)	1.23*** (0.05)	1.24*** (0.09)	1.22*** (0.05)	1.21*** (0.09)	1.22*** (0.05)	1.25*** (0.09)
Prox. to nearest mobilizer (km)	0.12*** (0.09)	0.30 (0.28)	0.28 (0.24)	0.85 (0.87)	0.29 (0.26)	0.30 (0.31)
Gender	46.38*** (25.29)	78.42*** (84.20)	50.66*** (28.14)	78.72*** (84.04)	48.79*** (26.61)	81.81*** (87.93)
Age in 1994	1.07 (0.04)	1.02 (0.06)	1.09** (0.05)	1.04 (0.06)	1.07 (0.04)	1.01 (0.06)
Age squared	0.88*** (0.04)	0.90 (0.06)	0.85*** (0.04)	0.88** (0.07)	0.87*** (0.04)	0.91 (0.06)
Household head	6.24** (1.78)	6.74*** (2.45)	5.91** (1.72)	6.47*** (2.39)	6.51*** (1.87)	7.54*** (2.73)
Inter-ethnic union	0.07 (0.13)	0.16 (0.29)	0.05 (0.10)	0.16 (0.28)	0.05 (0.10)	0.14 (0.25)
Household size	0.95 (0.05)	0.89* (0.06)	0.96 (0.05)	0.90 (0.06)	0.95 (0.05)	0.88* (0.06)

Pop density (100 persons/sq. km)	0.96** (0.02)	0.99 (0.02)	0.96 (0.04)	0.99 (0.05)	0.97 (0.05)	1.01 (0.06)
Prox. to community's centre (km)	1.21 (0.25)	1.14 (0.29)	0.96 (0.22)	1.01 (0.27)	1.03 (0.24)	1.15 (0.31)
Elevation of household (hectometres)	1.31 (0.41)	1.44 (0.56)	1.21 (0.40)	1.59 (0.66)	1.34 (0.43)	1.42 (0.56)
Slope of household (degrees)	0.99 (0.01)	0.99 (0.02)	0.98† (0.01)	0.98 (0.02)	0.98 (0.01)	0.99 (0.02)
N	1160	1142	1160	1142	1160	1142
Pseudo R^2	0.367	0.320	0.403	0.352	0.377	0.315

Logistic regression using binary dependent variable (participant/non-participant). Odds ratios reported. Values > 1 indicate a positive relationship and values < 1 indicate a negative relationship. Standard errors in parentheses; * indicates $p < 0.10$, ** $p < 0.05$, *** $p < 0.01$.

Source McDoom (2013b).

I found a significant neighbourhood effect. Living close to another killer made it more likely that an individual would join in the violence. Formally, the odds of an individual participating increase by 4 per cent for every single percentage point increase in the proportion of *convicted* perpetrators living within a 100 m radius. The odds increase by 3 per cent for *suspected* perpetrators in the same neighbourhood. This held for neighbourhoods also defined at 200 m.

The effect, however, faded at 300 m. The proportion of Tutsi neighbours, in contrast, made no difference to participation. Nor did the distance to a mobilizing agent.

As we shall see, I believe that the reason for this neighbourhood effect is social influence. As micro-spatial distances between individuals decrease, the likelihood of micro-social interaction increases. It is through this interaction that neighbours socially influence each other. The influence may operate through a number of psychological mechanisms: socialization, compliance, identification, conformity, social pressure, or internalization. Neighbourhoods are micro-spheres of influence and in Rwanda in 1994, where communication technologies were rudimentary, social interaction was overwhelmingly face-to-face.

But could it be instead that killers share unobserved characteristics that led them to live close to each other? If homophily – the tendency for similar individuals to associate with each other – were the reason, it would point to dispositional rather than situational or social forces. My research design did not permit *causal* inference so it remains possible that some factor other than neighbourhood explains the correlation. Yet it is not simply the presence of more killers in a neighbourhood that increases the chances of an individual participating in the violence. It is the *balance* between killers and non-killers; between pro- and anti-violence forces in the neighbourhood. Furthermore, the proportion of *household* members who were also killers was also a strong predictor. Both facts suggest the role of social influence. The influence of killers countervails the influence of non-killers. Moreover, in rural Rwanda in 1994, it was unlikely that individuals purchased land in the market to move close to preferred neighbours who might share similar dispositions to themselves. Land was overwhelmingly acquired through gift and inheritance. While homophily cannot be conclusively ruled out, it is at least an unlikely explanation of the neighbourhood effect.

It's Who You Know

Social influence suggests the role of social networks in the violence. Studies of terrorism, communal violence, civil wars, revolutions, and social movements have all found interpersonal connections a factor in participation.[71] Fujii (2009, p. 20), using excellent ethnographic data, has argued that social ties mattered in Rwanda's violence also, claiming that they served as '...propulsion mechanisms, pushing the violence forward by pulling in new participants, creating new targets, and engaging people in public, theatrical forms of killing'. But it's theoretically trivial to say that networks and connections matter. Everyone is part of a network and everyone has social ties. What is it about killers' networks and ties, if anything, that sets them apart? I considered this in Tare by taking a random sample of 116 individuals, stratified into 79 non-killers and 37 killers, and comparing their social networks.[72]

To identify an individual's social ties, I used both a roster and name generator. The roster technique comprised reading out a list of thirty names from the community, randomly selected and randomly ordered, of whom half were killers and the other half non-killers, and asking subjects to indicate whom they knew and, if applicable, to specify the nature of the connection. The name generator method worked in reverse by specifying a connection type and then asking respondents to name the individuals with whom they have such a connection. I identified thirty-four types of connections in Tare through a focus group interview which I distilled into kinship, economic, social, neighbourly, religious, and political ties.[73] Using logistic regressions again, with perpetrator status once more the dependent variable,

---

[71] For the role of social ties and networks in terrorism, see Sageman (2004); for communal violence, Varshney (2001); for civil wars, Humphreys & Weinstein (2008); for revolutions, Gould (1991); and for social movements, Snow et al. (1980).

[72] For non-perpetrators, I restricted the stratum to Hutu males aged fourteen and older to make it comparable with the perpetrator stratum. For more detail on the method followed and results found, see McDoom (2013a).

[73] To ensure that ties were formed *before* the genocide, respondents were asked to specify when they were established and prompted by using life-event markers such as school attendance, marriage, children, and parents' death.

I investigated whether the quantity and quality of ties distinguished the killers from the non-killers.[74]

I found, first, and counter-intuitively, that participants in the genocide were more socially connected within their community than non-participants. Their social networks were simply bigger. On average, perpetrators had twenty connections compared with thirteen for non-perpetrators. Each additional resident known on the roster increased the odds of participation by 9 per cent. Notwithstanding the anti-social nature of the behaviour, it was the socially gregarious rather than the social misanthropes who were more likely to join the violence. Second, perpetrators had more connections to other perpetrators than non-perpetrators. The average participant knew eleven other participants compared with only six for non-participants. Each additional perpetrator known in fact increased the odds of participation by 24 per cent. Third, kinship and neighbourly ties – more so than political, economic, or religious ties – were the strongest predictors of participation. Having a close family member participate in the violence increased the odds of participation by a remarkable 75 per cent. More generally, the stronger the tie to a perpetrator, the more likely an individual would be drawn into the violence. Degrees of consanguinity mattered, for instance, with parents, siblings, and children more likely than uncles, cousins, or grandparents to induce a family member to join in. Tables 7.16 and 7.17 present these results.

Social ties are also multivalent. Individuals typically have multiple, competing ties in their social network that can pull them in opposing directions. In studies of social movements, extra-movement ties constrain the structural availability of individuals to participate in movement activities (Snow et al., 1980). But did ties to Tutsi counteract ties to killers? I did not find this. Ties to perpetrators dominated. The data I collected do not explain why an individual might choose one set of ties over another. It is possible again that there is some unobserved characteristic killers share that explains why they choose to associate with each other. Similarity breeds connection. To help rule the homophily explanation out once more, I distinguished between voluntary and involuntary ties. Voluntary ties refer to relationships that individuals may freely enter and exit such as friendships, political party

---

[74] I controlled for individual-level characteristics, notably age, education, marital status, occupation, wealth, and political affiliation.

7.5 *Why Some Killed and Others Not* 351

Table 7.16 *Descriptive statistics of social connections of killers and non-killers*

		Non-convicts	Convicts only	All non-suspects	All Suspects
All ties		12.73	20.16***	12.24	19.17***
	To *non-participants*	6.30	9.03***	6.01	8.81***
	To *participants*	6.43	11.14***	6.22	10.35***
Voluntary ties	To all residents	1.73	2.16	1.59	2.25
	To *non-participants*	0.78	0.84	0.72	0.92
	To *participants*	0.95	1.30	0.87	1.33
Involuntary ties	To all residents	1.53	3.00**	1.46	2.77**
	To *non-participants*	0.73	0.86	0.68	0.92
	To *participants*	0.80	2.14***	0.78	1.85***
Kinship ties	To all residents	1.87	3.62***	1.72	3.44***
	To *non-participants*	0.94	1.22	0.87	1.25
	To *participants*	0.94	2.41***	0.85	2.19***
Economic ties	To all residents	0.70	1.24	0.57	1.29**
	To *non-participants*	0.41	0.41	0.32	0.52
	To *participants*	0.29	0.84**	0.25	0.77**
Social ties	To all residents	0.96	1.38	0.78	1.54*
	To *non-participants*	0.47	0.59	0.38	0.69
	To *participants*	0.49	0.78	0.40	0.85*
Political ties	To all residents	0.27	0.43	0.28	0.38
	To *non-participants*	0.09	0.05	0.09	0.06
	To *participants*	0.18	0.38	0.19	0.31
Religious ties	To all residents	0.48	0.30	0.50	0.31
	To *non-participants*	0.20	0.16	0.22	0.15
	To *participants*	0.28	0.14	0.28	0.17
Proximity ties	To all residents	8.57	13.46***	8.50	12.44**
	To *non-participants*	4.29	6.65***	4.22	6.21**
	To *participants*	4.28	6.81***	4.28	6.23**
Kinship 1st degree	To *non-perpetrators*	0.24	0.16	0.21	0.23
	To *perpetrators*	0.24	0.51**	0.24	0.46*
Kinship 2nd degree+	To *non-perpetrators*	0.70	1.05	0.66	1.02
	To *perpetrators*	0.70	1.89***	0.62	1.73***

*/**/*** difference statistically significance at 10%, 5%, and 1% levels using t-test.
Source: McDoom (2013a)

Table 7.17 Social connections as predictors of participation

	Model 1	Model 2	Model 3	Model 4
Age (years)	0.95(0.03)	0.96(0.03)	0.96(0.03)	0.99(0.03)
Marital status (married)	3.41(2.71)	3.54(2.88)	3.75*(3.00)	2.36(2.00)
Occupation status (non-farmer)	8.82***(6.43)	8.00***(6.04)	13.16***(10.73)	15.53***(13.84)
Education (years)	0.97(0.08)	0.98(0.08)	0.97(0.09)	0.99(0.10)
Wealth subjective (poor)	1.02(0.12)	1.02(0.13)	1.02(0.14)	0.90(0.14)
Wealth objective (cows owned)	0.89(0.43)	0.94(0.46)	0.80(0.42)	0.62(0.36)
Opposition support (yes)	1.23(0.62)	1.20(0.61)	1.58(0.88)	1.56(0.92)
All ties to residents	1.09***(0.03)			
To non-participants		0.96(0.07)		
To participants		1.24***(0.09)		
Kinship ties			1.36***(0.15)	
To non-participants				1.19(0.33)
To participants				1.75***(0.36)
Economic ties			1.07(0.20)	
To non-participants				0.70(0.37)
To participants				1.54*(0.40)
Social ties			0.95(0.11)	
To non-participants				0.83(0.37)
To participants				1.20(0.32)
Political ties			1.45(0.50)	
To non-participants				0.61(0.52)
To participants				2.63(1.63)

Neighbourhood ties			
To non-participants			1.20(0.15)
To participants			1.08(0.13)
Religious ties			
To non-participants		0.49(0.23)	1.17(0.92)
To participants			0.31(0.22)
		1.13***(0.04)	
Pseudo R^2	0.196	0.221	0.276	0.339

Logistic regressions. Dependent variable: convicted perpetrator=1, otherwise 0. Odds ratio reported with robust standard errors in parentheses. */**/*** statistical significance at 10%, 5%, and 1%. n=116.

Source McDoom (2013a)

membership, or marriage; involuntary ties refer to those over which they have no or little choice such as kinship or clientelist ties. I found involuntary ties a stronger predictor of participation suggesting it was not that killers seek out connections to other killers. Having said this, the evidence does not conclusively rule out homophily. Many involuntary ties are kinship-based and I am assuming that a proclivity to violence is socially learned rather than genetically inherited.

What is the mechanism explaining social networks' role in participation in genocide? I found at least two at work in Rwanda: social influence and information diffusion. Social influence refers to the inducement of one individual, by another individual, into doing something they otherwise would not have done (Cialdini & Goldstein, 2004). The relationship between the two individuals is key to how the influence operates. It may be long term and unconscious as in the socialization that takes place within families. In may also be short term and overt such as pressures exerted by peers or authority figures. The influence and relationship may not always be obvious unless explicitly sought out as this example of recruitment in Tare illustrates:

Who told you to man the roadblock? It was the *responsable* of the cellule, Sibomana. *How did Sibomana summon you to the roadblock?* It was before the *umuganda* [compulsory labour] that he came to my house and told me to work on the roadblock. He said no one must stay at home. *Do you have family ties to Sibomana?* No. We had an alliance founded on religion. Sibomana's mother was the godmother of my sister. *Do you have any economic links to Sibomana? Did you work for him?* I was not poor. I did not work for Sibomana. *Were you friends?* Yes.... *How did you first know Sibomana?* We grew up together on the same hill. And we kept cows together and we went to each other's house because Sibomana's mother was the godmother of my sister. (*Deogratias, Hutu participant, aged 48, Tare sector*)

In a community of over 1,000 individuals, it would have been impossible for the cell *responsable* to recruit everyone face-to-face and door-by-door as he did Deogratias. We learn, however, that the two also shared a personal, multiplex connection. They had been neighbours since childhood and the *responsable's* mother was the godmother of his sister. This may have been why he chose to call upon Deogratias.

Networks also diffuse information. In Tare, for instance, we saw previously that following Habyarimana's assassination, residents were initially uncertain how to react. Hutu and Tutsi in fact cooperated, manning roadblocks and conducting night patrols together to keep the community safe. But after two weeks, the situation changed when information entered the community that the Tutsi were to blame for the assassination and that Hutu had to defend themselves against the Tutsi enemy. In my survey, I asked respondents how they came to know this. The majority reported that they acquired the information locally. Only 6 per cent said they obtained it via the radio. In a joint interview, a perpetrator's wife described how a local politician, Rekeraho from Mwendo cell, obtained this information through his political networks that changed his attitude towards the Tutsi and then brought this information into the community.

When did he change? He attended meetings in Butare town and that is when he changed. *What kind of meetings?* They were secret meetings involving other politicians. *And when did it change here in Tare?* Rekeraho then began to hold secret security meetings at his house with members of the MDR here and his old soldier friends. That is how the genocide started here. (*Beatrice, perpetrator's wife aged 54, Tare sector*)

Rekeraho acted then as a 'bridging' connection between a central and a peripheral network. He brought information from the main town to the rural community and then circulated this information within the community through his network of party supporters and friends who had also served in the military.

Social networks and connections, along with situational opportunities and dispositional differences, then also mediated selection into the violence. They help resolve the 'macro-micro disjunction' (Kalyvas, 2006, pp. 390–391) that arises because macro-level concepts such as ethnicity, threat, and inequality used to explain ethnic violence often fail to account for choices and actions at the individual-level. The interdependence created by social bonds both constrains and enables an individual's freedom to act. Moreover, although the social capital that inheres in social networks is often thought of as a positive force to be promoted in societies, my findings here add to the growing evidence that it also has a dark side. Memberships of criminal gangs and terrorist cells have also been linked to the interpersonal ties that bring and bind individuals together, for instance.[75] So, participation in

---

[75] For the role of social ties in terrorism, see Perliger & Pedahzur (2011); for criminal gangs, see Ostrom & Ahn (2009).

Rwanda's genocide was another socially undesirable collective behaviour in which social capital produced anti-social outcomes.

Sociological or Ecological? Explaining the Scale and Speed of Mobilization

The remarkable scale and speed of civilian mobilization during the genocide may be traced to Rwanda's unusual socio-demography. Contrary to the neo-Malthusian claim, the country's exceptionally high population density is likely to have contributed to the exceptional violence more through a sociological than an ecological mechanism. Its population density and highly rural, traditional society strengthened the role of social networks and social influence in drawing individuals into the violence. Dense social networks are likely to arise in societies where individuals live in close proximity to each other. This is particularly the case in rural societies. Rural social networks are typically smaller and less diverse than in urban areas but the social connections between individuals are usually stronger (individuals know each other for longer) and more multiplex (individuals are tied in more than one way to each other). Urban society, in contrast, is quite different. Social ties in urban areas are frequently weaker, more transitory, more impersonal, and more segmented. Anonymity and social alienation are commonplace (Simmel, 1971).

These characteristics of rural ties are stronger still in traditional societies. Durkheim (1960) first distinguished societies based on mechanical rather than organic solidarity in his theory of social evolution where the former referred to social cohesion based on members' similar characteristics, such as the cultural beliefs, values, and norms shared by co-ethnics, and the latter to a social order based on individual differences and interdependence. Subsequent sociological theorists described the distinction in terms of level of modernity. The notions of *Gemeinschaft* and *Gessellschaft,* first employed by Tönnies (1940) and later adapted by Weber (1978), distinguished social ties based on affectivity and loyalty, common in traditional communities, to those based on rationality and mutual consent, found in more modern societies. Rwanda in 1994 was primarily a rural, traditional society whose solidarity was more mechanical than organic and more closely resembled *Gemeinschaft* than *Gessellschaft*. So, the strength and multiplexity of rural ties in densely populated Rwanda most likely amplified the forces of coercion, conformity, and co-optation observed during the genocide.

7.6 Modelling Participation

We know then that dispositional, situational, and relational forces all mattered for the initial selection into the violence. How do they interact? Formally, we can think of participation as a continuum along which individuals join in the violence at different points in time. Consider first the world in which these time-points are determined solely by individual disposition, by which I mean an individual's commitment toward the genocide. Extremists are fully committed to the violence; opportunists less so, conformists even less so, and pacifists are wholly opposed to violence. Participation also carries risk. I employ a simple definition of risk here to mean the probability that some adverse consequence will follow participation. In this case, joining in the violence risks injury or possibly punishment for the participant. An individual's decision to join in the violence, his 'payoff', then will be determined by both his (or occasionally her) commitment to the violence and the risk of participation in it. Logically, extremists will join first because they have the highest payoff (determined by multiplying their commitment by the risk). However, the risk has now also declined following the extremists' participation. There is safety in numbers. As more people participate, the chances of being harmed decrease. As a result, opportunists, who have a lower commitment to the violence, but for whom the likelihood of injury or punishment has decreased, now face a similarly attractive payoff. They also join in the violence, but after the extremists. The same logic applies for conformists. Each individual's decision to join induces another individual, who has a slightly lower commitment to the violence but also faces a slightly lower risk of harm, to join until only pacifists remain. Pacifists have zero commitment to the violence and will never join.

The top graph in Figure 7.3 illustrates this mobilization continuum using a hypothetical distribution of extremists, opportunists, conformists, and pacifists. The graph is an S-curve plotting participation against time with a tipping point set for the time when 50 per cent popular participation is achieved. Thus, a certain number of extremists participate at the start when the risk is very high because no one else has joined. Extremists are dispositionally highly committed to the

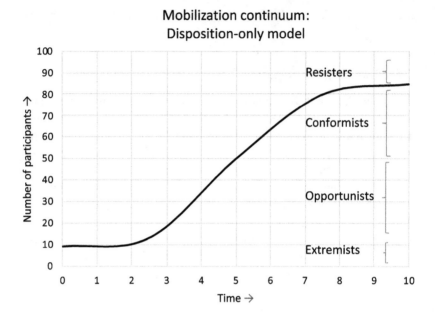
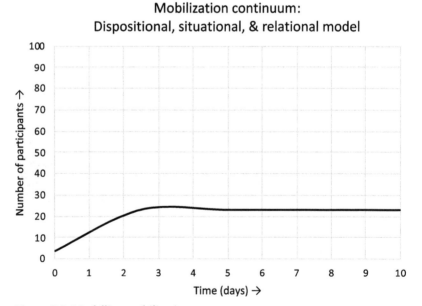

Figure 7.3 Modelling mobilization

7.6 Modelling Participation

violence. Opportunists join after the extremists but *before* the tipping point, that is, when there is still less than 50 per cent participation and the risk is less than for extremists. They believe an opportunity is to be gained only if it is still a minority who are participating. Conformists join in *after* the tipping point, that is, when participation is more than 50 per cent and the risk less than for opportunists. They only feel safe when a majority is participating. The S-curve lies below the forty-five-degree line before the tipping point and above it afterwards. This is to indicate that the rate of mobilization is slow in the early stages of the violence and increases in the later stages after the tipping point has been reached.[76] Importantly, for the mobilization to be self-sustaining there must be a critical mass of extremists who join the violence at the start to trigger the chain reaction. Too few extremists and the risk of participation will not be lowered sufficiently to induce opportunists to join. Similar interdependent 'critical mass' models have been developed to explain participation in other forms of collective action such as revolutions and social movements.[77]

What happens when we add situational and relational forces into the model? They either accelerate or decelerate an individual's integration into the violence. I had a crude sense of the distribution of extremists, conformists, material opportunists, and non-participants in Rwanda from the *gacaca* data.[78] When these data are plotted, the distribution more closely resembles what I depict in the second graph in Figure 7.3. As can be seen, the curve has a much lower tipping point and participation does not exceed 23 percent. The critical mass needed to jump-start the mobilization is small. It corroborates my findings in the four micro-case studies: small groups of highly committed individuals who move first and are willing to use coercion can mobilize a much larger

---

[76] The mobilization continuum presented here adapts the logic of Schelling's (2006) famous tipping point models.

[77] For a theoretical explanation of the role of social networks in critical mass models, see Marwell et al. (1988).

[78] For the purpose of plotting the distribution, I assume that the 3.6 per cent of persons in category I (the genocide's organizers and hardened killers) are extremists and the 19.5 per cent of persons in category II (individuals who committed at least one act of interpersonal violence) comprise both opportunists and conformists. I distinguish political and material opportunists. The latter only committed crimes against property and I do not include them in the mobilization continuum. I do not have data on *when* individuals joined the violence so no conclusion on the speed of mobilization should be inferred from the graph.

number of less committed persons. Moreover, these situational and social forces also appear to have imposed an upper limit on mobilization. Variation in individuals' situational opportunities and relational pressures resulted in participation levels that were lower than if disposition alone determined participation and if individuals faced identical opportunity sets and identical social forces. Thus, an opportunist who may have dispositionally been inclined to join the violence early in fact does so *after* a conformist – or perhaps not at all - because his situational opportunities and social ties are different. If we depended on dispositions or attitudes towards violence alone to predict participation, we would over-estimate the scale of mobilization in Rwanda. Opportunity sets then were an important mediator of selection into the killing.

***

'I wish I could say I would not have done this.' This comment in the Nyamata memorial visitors' log with which the book began invited us to ask ourselves how different we really are from those who committed the atrocities in that church. My findings here hopefully offer a brighter view on human nature than the dark, Hobbesian belief that we all would be capable of this violence if the constraints were removed and the opportunity presented itself. The findings, however, are also less sanguine than the Lockean view that people are all fundamentally good and require some exogenous push to commit such heinous acts. People are simply different. Some may kill willingly; some opportunistically, and some reluctantly. Some may never kill no matter what the circumstances. Differences in these proclivities should not be surprising. Cross-national evidence also suggests that the distribution of dispositions – here I distinguished extremists, opportunists, conformists, and pacifists – is likely to vary across societies and within them across time.[79] None of us, however, is likely to know our true disposition toward such violence until we are faced with the same circumstances and opportunities as Rwandans were in 1994. Moreover, Rwandans generally did not face a one-off choice to participate or

---

[79] Baum (2008) cogently argues that the distribution of 'perpetrator' characteristics differs across cultures. He points out that in Australia, in a replication of Milgram's authority experiment, only 28 per cent of subjects 'obeyed' compared with 88 per cent in South Africa.

7.6 Modelling Participation

not. The violence lasted over three months. Individuals confronted this choice over and over again. Their disposition toward violence evolved with each choice they made.

The question of why certain individuals participated in the violence and others did not is analytically distinct from the question of the genocide's onset. In the preceding chapters, I argued that the genocide was the product of the complex contestation created by the coincidence of a security threat with a break in the political opportunity structure. The civil war, political liberalization, and presidential assassination were important contextual conditions. However, it is not only the *macro*-political context that defines the circumstances individuals confront as they choose to participate in such violence or not. In this chapter, I have argued the *micro*-situational opportunities and relational pressures were also consequential. Where you lived and who you knew mediated individual selection into Rwanda's violence. So, initial disposition toward such violence did not alone determine our participation in it. Situational and relational factors were also part of the circumstances and opportunities Rwandans faced.

8 Conclusion: Rwanda in Retrospect

This book has offered answers to two major questions concerning the genocide. How and why did it occur? And how and why did many ordinary Rwandans participate in the violence but others not? In respect of the first question, I have argued that the genocide was the product of the extraordinary coincidence of three macro-political events: a civil war; democratization; and the assassination of a longstanding head of state. None of these is by itself such an unusual event on the continent. None inevitably leads to genocide. But their simultaneous occurrence had no precedent, bar Burundi, in Africa. In theoretical terms, they represented the conjunction of a security threat with a political opportunity.

Importantly, these three events also occurred against an unusual baseline. A set of highly distinctive demographic, geographic, and historical characteristics set Rwanda apart from other sub-Saharan states. I argued in Chapter 2 that these particularities accounted for the distinctive characteristics of Rwanda's violence. The remarkable scale, speed, and scope of the killing and civilian mobilization can all be traced to them. I also argued that Rwanda's unusual baseline characteristics accounted for its unusually powerful state. Although the regime was effectively an ethnocracy, the state itself enjoyed exceptional symbolic authority and material capacity for a sub-Saharan nation. It became a weapon of mass destruction *par excellence* for the extremists who would capture it.

In sum, these macro-factors point to the importance of security (the civil war and democratization), opportunity (democratization and the assassination), and authority (the Rwandan state) in the violence. To borrow a popular idiom from criminal law, they represent the motive (a war-time and democratic threat), the opportunity (democratization and the president's assassination), and the means (a powerful state) for genocide.

In respect of the second question, I have argued that the unusual scale of civilian mobilization may, in large part, be traced to one particular baseline characteristic. Rwanda's extraordinary population density implied dense social networks that amplified the pressures of coercion and co-optation. Contrary to neo-Malthusian arguments, the remarkable participation was more sociological than ecological in origin. I also argued that differential selection into the violence was the result of a mobilization continuum in which dispositional, situational, and relational factors each mattered for explaining why certain Rwandans would come to participate in the violence and others not.

8.1 Tracing the Causal Pathway to Genocide

Figure 8.1 models the path to genocide graphically and illustrates the causal flow of the overall argument. It distinguishes four principal stages in the genocide's trajectory. The process begins by recognizing Rwanda's unusual baseline vulnerability to division along ethnic boundaries in particular (stage one, before 1990). Rwanda had a ranked bi-ethnic demographic structure comprising an ascendant Tutsi minority and a subordinate Hutu majority who were governed together as one people, the Banyarwanda, in the precolonial era. Belgian colonial rule then magnified the disparity between Hutu and Tutsi by reinforcing the privilege of a Tutsi elite. As I argued in Chapter 2, while ethnic favouritism was not an unusual colonial strategy, the social revolution that followed and that ushered in Rwanda's postcolonial era was, in contrast, a highly unusual occurrence in Africa. The revolution marked a shift in the country's historical ethnic ranking. Such shifts are rare. The revolution replaced a Tutsi ruling elite with a Hutu political elite and inscribed ethnicity as a dominant force in Rwandan politics and society. This did not mean that ethnic violence or genocide were inevitable in Rwanda. But it did mean that the three macro-political events I believe mattered were more likely to be framed and understood in ethnic rather than in non-ethnic terms.

Against this unusual baseline, the first two macro-political events, the civil war and political liberalization, collided (stage two, starting in 1990). Their simultaneous occurrence was a historical accident. They represented the conjunction of an external military with an internal political threat in Rwanda. Initially, this threat was minor. In Chapter 3 we saw how war-time insecurity, through the operation of a set of psycho-social mechanisms, had a radicalizing effect on the population

364   Conclusion: Rwanda in Retrospect

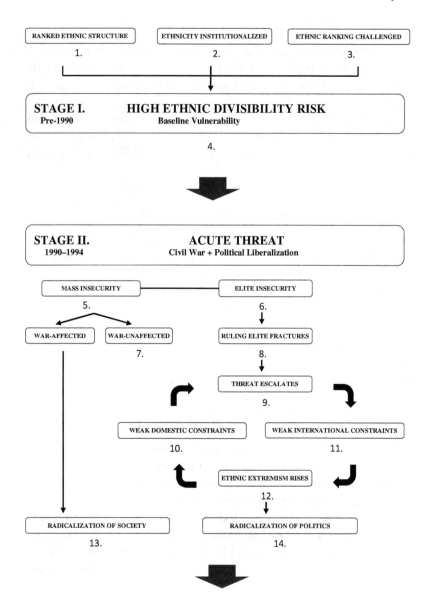

Figure 8.1 Tracing the causal pathway to genocide

8.1 *Tracing the Causal Pathway to Genocide*

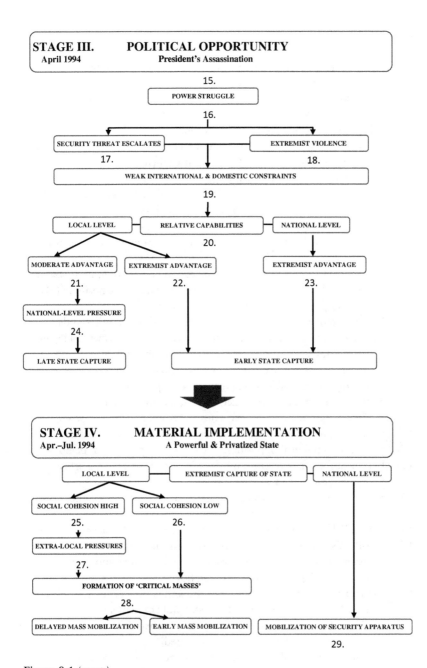

Figure 8.1 *(cont.)*

Key for Figure 8.1

1. In the precolonial era, unusual ethnic demography leads to emergence of an ethnically stratified social system in which Tutsi minority has high status and Hutu majority low status.
2. In the colonial era, the state reifies and accentuates the distinction between Hutu and Tutsi. Ethnicity becomes the basis for state-instituted discrimination and exclusion.
3. In the postcolonial era, social revolution (1959–1962) weakens the ethnic ranking as dominance of Tutsi elite is challenged by a Hutu elite with aspirations of political power.
4. Risk of fracture in Rwandan society and politics is highest along ethnic boundaries rather than class, clan, regional, party, ideological, or religious identities.
5. Civil war creates existential security fears in communities where ordinary Rwandans are directly affected.
6. (i) Political liberalization, through increased competition, participation, and pluralism, creates an internal threat to ruling elite position; (ii) civil war and peace process pose external threat.
7. No prior radicalization of communities, e.g. in southern Rwanda.
8. (i) Liberalization threat creates primary schism of reformers vs loyalists. (ii) War threat creates secondary schism of moderates vs extremists.
9. (i) Rebels (re-)act to strengthen their military position. (ii) Opposition parties strengthen political position with rebel alliance.
10. State institutions and civil society actors, including the media and the Church, fail to constrain extremists' rhetoric and violent actions.
11. International community (i) fails to enforce peace as war escalates and (ii) reinforces political opposition threat through pressure to democratize.
12. Extremist faction is reinforced by war's escalation. Primary schism becomes moderates vs. extremists.
13. Some ordinary Rwandans increasingly frame the threat in ethnic and existential terms e.g. in northern Rwanda.
14. Political elite increasingly frame threat in ethnic and existential terms.
15. President's assassination represents sudden rupture to the political opportunity structure. The power vacuum at centre and uncertainty at periphery trigger inter-elite contestation.
16. Extremists vie with moderates at centre and periphery for control of the state. Extremists make initial unsuccessful coup attempt at centre.
17. Civil war resumes as rebels re-engage government forces.
18. Tutsi civilians and Hutu moderates targeted.
19. Belated international diplomatic and military response to war's resumption and to extremist violence; domestic institutions fail to mediate the conflict over president's succession and fail to stop extremist violence.

20   Coordination, communication, and coercive capabilities of extremists and moderates.
21   Commune politically controlled by opposition burgomaster and/or weak militia presence.
22   Commune politically controlled by loyalist burgomaster and/or strong militia presence.
23   Evenly matched in terms of coordination and communication capabilities but extremists have stronger coercive capability.
24   Resistant burgomasters are co-opted, replaced, or killed once extremists capture the centre.
25   Inter-ethnic ties strong and/or population not previously radicalized by war.
26   Population already radicalized by war and/or inter-ethnic ties weak.
27   Contagion effects from neighbouring communes help jump-start the mobilization.
28   Emergence of local political and ethnic entrepreneurs. Social networks and ethnic settlement patterns mediate who joins the critical mass.
29   Government soldiers, gendarmes, and militia groups ordered to target Tutsi civilian population.

at the beginning, but primarily only in those communities that experienced the war's effects directly. In Chapter 4 we then saw that liberalization, through the mechanisms of increased political competition, pluralism, and participation, did not inflame ethnic politics but instead gave rise to predominantly *moderate* ideologies and encouraged *cross-ethnic* cooperation at the outset. The dominant schism in this early phase was between reformers and loyalists at both the national and local levels. Liberalization by itself did not push Rwanda closer to genocide. Nonetheless, the threat gradually escalated toward violence. It did so because, I argued, the war and liberalization processes interacted and drove each other forward. At the national level, the rebels and newly created political parties collaborated – principally through the peace process – to weaken the ruling party and to intensify the threat it faced. At the local level, liberalization also weakened the ruling party's authority, though its organizational *capacity* remained largely unaffected. Liberalization also provided instruction in the mobilization of local communities, the lessons of which would be repeated during the genocide. The threat also deepened, I argued, because there simply was no external constraint on its escalation.

Outside Rwanda, international actors did not intervene with force to contain the combat and in fact magnified the threat by pressuring the ruling party to democratize. Inside Rwanda, neither state institutions nor civil society actors stopped extremist actions and rhetoric. The outcome was the rise of ethnic extremism. Extremism continued to rise in a mutually reinforcing dynamic with the security threat as the external constraints remained weak. The principal elite schism in turn evolved into one between moderates and extremists. Rwandan politics radicalized.

So, at the moment when the threat created by the interaction of the war and liberalization was most acute, President Habyarimana was assassinated (stage three, April 1994). In Chapter 5, I argued that his death was the third macro-political event, causally distinct in its effect from the war and liberalization, leading to the genocide. Had Habyarimana remained alive, the genocide would likely not have occurred. Consider the two theories behind his assassination. If his removal as president had been the result of an internal coup but he had been kept alive, the coup's architects would not have had the command of the security forces, particularly the Presidential Guard, needed to implement the genocide if it was believed that they had betrayed Habyarimana. If the Rwandan Patriotic Front (RPF) had been responsible for his death, the security forces in Kigali would have lacked no motivation to follow extremist orders to kill Tutsi civilians and Hutu political moderates. Either way, his death was causally necessary.

Habyarimana's assassination marked a sudden rupture in the political opportunity structure. It created enormous political uncertainty and triggered power struggles between ethnic extremists and moderates for control of the state at both the national and local levels. As before, this intra-group contestation dynamically interacted with the inter-group contestation. Regime extremists targeted moderate Hutu politicians and Tutsi civilians at the same time as the rebels re-engaged the government forces and resumed the civil war. Yet, I argue, in the early moments of this third stage, it was still not certain that extremism would prevail and genocide would result. It was the weakness of external constraints again that allowed the contestation to escalate in favour of extremists. Domestically, Rwanda's state institutions failed to mediate the conflict over the president's succession; and internationally, belated intervention failed to stop the violence. In the absence of external constraints, I argued, the power struggle resolved according to

8.1 Tracing the Causal Pathway to Genocide

the relative material capabilities of the extremist and moderate factions. At the national level, the two sides were initially evenly matched in their coordination and communication capabilities. Each held strategically important positions in the civilian state apparatus. However, extremists held the advantage in coercive capability. They controlled superior security forces in the capital. As a result, the extremist faction ultimately triumphed and captured the state early on at the national level. The local level quickly followed. In communities where moderates held the advantage – because the burgomaster either opposed the extremists and/or a militia presence was weak – extremists exerted pressure from the national level to co-opt, replace, or eliminate them.

Once extremists had captured the state at both the national and local levels, they used its power – which was remarkable for a sub-Saharan polity – to implement the genocide (stage four, April to June 1994). In Chapter 6, I argued that the state's power comprised three dimensions and that it was the unusual combination of low autonomy, high legitimacy, and strong capacity that set the Rwandan state apart. However, I also argued that the top-down nature of the violence is often overstated. It did not simply radiate from the centre to the periphery. Violence began in multiple localities before the centre had even fallen. I showed that violence onset was a function not only of extremist control of the local state apparatus but also of inter-ethnic integration from below. In localities where extremist control was weak and social cohesion high, violence was delayed – though never avoided altogether – until extra-local forces intervened. However, where extremist control was strong and cross-ethnic ties frail – such as in places radicalized by the war – violence began early, even before the centre fell. The centre's capture would matter for the scaling-up of the violence as it became nationwide in scope.

The mass mobilization of the population, the final stage in the path to genocide, was also necessary for violence to achieve the scale that it did in Rwanda. In Chapter 5, I argued, contrary to the consensus that perpetrators were all ordinary, that important dispositional differences existed and mattered for the mobilization. The process began with the emergence of local ethnic and political entrepreneurs – extremists and opportunists highly committed in their disposition to violence – who built critical masses of supporters around them. Importantly, these first-movers were not all in the state's employ and not all local elites. They counted private citizens including ordinary farmers among them.

While often a small minority in their communities, these individuals drew on their social networks to coerce and co-opt others to join them. These others – I termed them conformists – were dispositionally less committed to the violence. They constituted the majority of those who joined the attack groups. In Chapter 7, I presented the results of a survey systematically comparing these mainly 'conformist' perpetrators against individuals from their communities who did not participate in the violence. I found no surprising differences in their socio-demographic profiles (other than gender and age) or in their attitudes and beliefs.

So, differential selection into the violence could not be explained as a matter of dispositional differences alone. I argued in Chapter 7 that non-dispositional factors also mattered. I found that perpetrators had different social ties to those of non-perpetrators. Their networks were larger. Additionally, I found that perpetrators tended to live in close proximity to each other. I concluded that dispositional, relational, and situational factors all mattered. Who you were, who you knew, and where you lived collectively predicted whether someone was likely to be drawn into the violence or not. However, I also argued that individual dispositions toward the violence changed over time. The act of violence was itself transformative. The attitudes and beliefs of some individuals radicalized as a consequence of killing. In this way, for instance, the sadistic cruelty and sexual torture observed in the violence becomes reconcilable with claims that individuals were coerced into the violence.

This was the sequence of events that marked Rwanda's path to genocide. It is possible that the genocide could have occurred through a different causal pathway or under a different set of conditions. However, I believe that this was the path followed in Rwanda in 1994 and that these were the conditions needed for the genocide to occur. The conjunction of the civil war, the political liberalization, and the president's assassination against Rwanda's unusual baseline all mattered. Each was causally necessary but none was individually a sufficient condition for the genocide. Having said this, the mere existence of these conditions did not make the genocide inevitable. The violence was not structurally determined. Individual agency also mattered. Agency was most consequential in the political opportunity created by the president's assassination. The choices of elite actors at this particular moment – at both the domestic and international levels – pushed Rwanda over the edge and into the abyss. I enumerated the most crucial choices in Chapter 5: the decision of regime extremists to eliminate moderate Hutu politicians and start killing Tutsi civilians in the capital; the decision by the RPF to move out of the Demilitarized Zone (DMZ) and to re-engage the civil war to a military finish; and the decision of international actors not to intervene initially. These decisions all strategically interacted with one another. Under the conditions I've highlighted, genocide was their outcome.

8.2 Toward a New Consensus on Rwanda's Genocide

It is perhaps expected that a book explaining a world historical event such as Rwanda's genocide would conclude by looking to the future and asking whether such violence could recur in Rwanda or elsewhere. I choose, however, to look back in time. At the time of writing, twenty-five years have passed since the genocide made its mark on world history. It is an opportune moment then to take stock and consider what we have learned cumulatively over the years. Which of the myriad explanations of the genocide's origins, and of Rwandans' participation in the violence, does this book reinforce? I believe that a broader scholarly consensus is now discernible and should be articulated. I begin with those of my findings for which I believe there is now a strong consensus, and then consider those for which the consensus is somewhat weaker because there remains some degree of scholarly disagreement.

First, the colonial legacy was consequential for the genocide. Scholars have levelled a number of distinct charges against the colonial state – and the Catholic Church – in respect of their management of the relations between native groups. The Belgians in particular stand variously accused of the institutionalization, politicization, racialization, and/or reification of the Hutu-Tutsi distinction (Des Forges, 1999, pp. 33–35; Kimonyo, 2016, pp. 19–29; Longman, 2010, pp. 59–66; Mamdani, 2001, pp. 76–102; Prunier, 1998, pp. 23–40; Straus, 2006, p. 22; Uvin, 1998, pp. 13–18). Colonial administrators propagated the idea of Tutsi *racial* superiority and alien origins; favoured Tutsi and discriminated against Hutu in political and administrative appointments and secondary educational places; and introduced mandatory identity cards denoting ethnicity. Some scholars have gone so far as to imply that these policies made conflict inevitable (Des Forges, 1999, p. 34; Mamdani, 2001, p. 14).

My findings support the general view that the colonial period elevated the status of ethnicity and that this contributed to its continued salience and ready instrumentalization in postcolonial society and politics. My specific claims regarding colonial responsibility and ethnicity's causal role are perhaps more modest, however. Ethnic stratification originated in the *precolonial* era; ethnic favouritism was not an unusual colonial policy; and both of Rwanda's postcolonial republics chose to keep ethnic identity cards even though they were abandoned by Belgium's two other colonies after independence. In my view, these colonial-era policies *contributed*, along with Rwanda's unusual precolonial demography, its social revolution challenging the ethnic hierarchy, and the postcolonial institutionalization of ethnicity, to making ethnicity a particularly important fault-line in Rwanda. Party, regional, clan, and class cleavages, as well of course as the citizen/refugee divide, also existed and mattered in postcolonial Rwanda. Ethnicity, however, was more *likely* to be the frame through which Rwanda's history and politics would be understood.

Second, it is now very evident that the civil war was a crucial factor. The consensus specifically has coalesced around a threat mechanism (Kaufman, 2015, pp. 129–130; Sémelin, 2005; Straus, 2006, pp. 224–226). Security fears had a radicalizing effect on Rwandan politics and society. These helped activate ethnicity as the frame through which the conflict would be understood. I've argued that the war was indeed a necessary condition for the genocide and highlighted the operation of several psycho-social mechanisms behind the threat that resonate with others' findings. For instance, Rwandans surveyed by another researcher also saw themselves as victims and framed the violence as self-defence to justify killing (Straus, 2006, p. 234). Similarly, my mechanism of 'outgroup homogenization' – equating Tutsi civilians with Tutsi rebels – is similar to Straus' (2006, p. 9) notion of 'collective ethnic categorization'. Yet the civil war was not a sufficient condition. Most wars do not end in genocide. Moreover, distinguishing elite from mass vulnerability, I found that many ordinary Rwandans were not deeply radicalized before the genocide began. The war alone does not explain the genocide or the massive participation of Rwandans.

Third, the unusual power of the Rwandan state is now widely recognized. It has been called a Leviathan and its ability to monitor and coerce the population highlighted (Straus, 2006, p. 201). Comparative studies of mass killings and genocide have also emphasized the material, coercive capacity of the state to kill its citizenry (Horowitz, 2002; Rummel, 2018; Valentino, 2004). I concur. While I emphasize different reasons for the state's extraordinary capacity, including the remarkable machinery of the ruling party, and argue that its low autonomy and high legitimacy mattered in addition to its strong capacity, I believe that the state represented an exceptionally powerful instrument with which to execute the genocide. The state did not 'cause' the genocide; but it did help to make violence on a massive scale possible. Relatedly, the failure of civil society to counter the state's power is also widely cited. Uvin (1998, p. 167) argues that although a plethora of civil society organizations existed in Rwanda, they generally lacked independence from the state and the foreign donors who financed them. Longman (2010) points to the Christian Churches, Rwanda's most influential non-state actors, and critiques in particular the close ties of the Catholic Church's leadership to the regime and its historical role in promoting ethnic politics. I also argue that civil society – in particular the Church and media – failed to react to constrain the rise of ethnic extremism in Rwanda and, in fact, in some instances, played an active role in promoting it.

Fourth, turning to the question of Rwandans' participation in the violence, there is now a consensus that individual motivation was heterogeneous (Fujii, 2009, p. 11; Straus, 2006, p. 39). Indeed, it seems unrealistic to claim that everyone was either racist, greedy, desperate, fearful, vengeful, coerced, obedient, or sadistic. Straus (2006, p. 39) also suggests, as my findings confirm, that motivation may have changed over time. The quest for a single motive then should be abandoned. It is also widely recognized that the violence was overwhelmingly collective. Groups – and the dynamics and pressures generated within them – mattered (Fujii, 2009, p. 154; Mironko, 2004). Straus (2006, p. 71) also found a small 'nucleus' of individuals, led by the rural elite and supported by local 'thugs', jump-started the violence. This is broadly similar to my finding of the emergence of 'ethnic and political entrepreneurs' and the formation of 'critical masses'. I did not find, however, that the leaders were all elites and the followers all thugs. Many entrepreneurs were ordinary farmers, and their supporters drawn from their social networks. Turning to the question of differential selection, Fujii (2009, p. 19) also finds that social ties mediated who was drawn into the killing. I sought to identify which specific ties mattered and to compare the networks of the killers against non-killers, but broadly I also concluded that social connections and influences mattered.

Several other of my findings also resonate with existing research but the consensus is weaker on these matters because scholarly disagreement persists. First, I have argued that the genocide was far from a certainty even several days after the president was assassinated. The political opportunity created by Habyarimana's death triggered a power struggle between extremist and moderate factions within the regime and it was not evident which side would prevail. Other research has pointed to the importance of this power struggle and the accompanying uncertainty of whether genocide would result (Guichaoua, 2015, p. 236; Straus, 2006, pp. 62–63). Yet this sits uncomfortably with, mainly early, claims that the genocide was planned in advance and executed meticulously following the president's assassination (Des Forges, 1999, pp. 10, 589; Kaufman, 2015, p. 119; Uvin, 1998, p. 1). I believe, however, that enough information has come to light of what transpired immediately after the plane went down – primarily through evidence submitted to the International Criminal Tribunal for Rwanda (ICTR) – that it is time to revise the original consensus of careful advance planning and meticulous execution.

Second, relatedly, is the feasibility of international action to prevent and stop the genocide after the plane went down. Much has been written claiming the international community knew much and could have done more. I've argued the absence of constraints at the international level meant that the power struggle between moderates and extremists at that moment would resolve ultimately according to the relative material capabilities of each side. The implication then is that international action could have tipped an otherwise precarious balance-of-power in favour of moderates. Specifically, I suggested that the diplomatic denunciation of the unlawful Interim Government (IG) and the resurrection and recognition of the rightful government may have made it more difficult for extremists to capture the state at the *local* level. Local control was crucial for the *nationwide* implementation of the genocide. Extremists' ability to issue legal commands to prefects and burgomasters – and to the sizeable security forces based outside of the capital – would have been compromised if an alternate authority existed and had exclusive international recognition and support. My proposal differs from the various other plans suggested but supports the general argument that international action was not a futile exercise.

The most credible objections have been that it was not known the violence was genocidal until too late and that it would have taken too long to deploy enough peacekeepers to protect the entire territory given the speed of the killing (Kuperman, 2001). My proposal, however, does not depend on recognizing that it was genocide. And while it may have taken more soldiers to protect the rightful government, this number was feasible. A total of 1,400 French and Belgian troops arrived as quickly as 9–10 April to evacuate foreigners.

Third, Rwanda's move to democratize mattered. It has been argued that multipartyism allowed the resurrection of the Mouvement Démocratique Répubicain (MDR) – Parmehutu, the party associated with Rwanda's social revolution, and that this party could not escape its historic roots as an ethnic Hutu party (Bertrand, 2000; Kimonyo, 2016). In effect, these studies are making the equation between democratization and ethnic politics in Rwanda. While I agree that political liberalization mattered for the genocide, I argue that this was due only to its conjunction with the civil war, and it mattered for a reason other than the return of the MDR. In fact, I found that multipartyism encouraged parties to seek *cross-ethnic* support at the outset. Only as the war escalated did Rwanda's politics ethnicize. This has led some to believe that, of these two macropolitical events, the war only was consequential for the genocide. Liberalization is conspicuous by its absence in Straus's (2006) explanation for instance. I disagree. Consider the counterfactual. If liberalization had not occurred, a coalition government would not have formed *before* the war ended. This coalition government, which incorporated the major opposition parties, gravely weakened the ruling party. Its weakness was to the rebels' advantage. The RPF secured major concessions in the peace process in large part because the government delegation, which included the ruling party's coalition partners, was divided. The delegation was also led by a foreign minister who belonged to the opposition and whom the ruling party suspected of sharing common cause with the RPF. It resulted in an unbalanced power-sharing arrangement that Mouvement Révolutionnaire National pour le Développement (et la Démocratie) (MRNDD) hardliners could not accept. It's even possible that the RPF knew the lopsided deal could never be enforced and that this led it to seek outright military victory. The peace process has been the target of other scholars' critiques (Clapham, 1998; Jones, 2001; Kuperman, 1996). Critics have pointed to both the *content* of the peace deal and to mediator misjudgement of how Habyarimana and extremists saw the stakes. I agree. However, I trace the flaw in the peace process – ultimately – to the unusual coincidence of the war with liberalization. Without liberalization, a coalition government – that is, power-sharing – would have properly been the *consequence* of the peace process, not also its antecedent.

Fourth, scholars have debated the role of the media and particularly the effect of the infamous Radio Télévision Libre des Mille Collines (RTLM) radio station. I argued that the radio's causal role may have been overstated. Having analysed its broadcasts over time, I found its language radicalized significantly only *after* much of the violence had already occurred. My survey of perpetrators and non-perpetrators also shows that both groups were equally likely to have listened to RTLM. I suggested that while the radio may have directly incited or mobilized relatively few people into violence, it may nonetheless have helped prime the population by the framing of the war in ethnic and historical terms *ex ante* as well as justify the violence *ex post*. This more qualified role of the radio is consistent with the findings of others (Li, 2004; Straus, 2007). However, we cannot yet write of a consensus given the challenge posed by a separate study that estimates 10 per cent of the overall participation in the violence can be causally attributed to the radio (Yanagizawa-Drott, 2014).

Finally, using new data, I have proposed estimates for the number of perpetrators and victims in the genocide. I estimated that about 423,000 Rwandans, or nearly one in four Hutu adult males aged 15–54 years old, organized or committed at least one act of violence during the genocide. There is, however, no clear scholarly consensus on the scale of participation. It has been suggested as few as 25,000 and as many as 1 million Rwandans may have been responsible for the killing. I also estimated somewhere between 491,000 and 522,000 Tutsi – or nearly two-thirds of the Tutsi population – were killed during the genocide. These numbers are broadly in line with the early estimate from Human Rights Watch of 507,000 (Des Forges, 1999) and the more recent finding by Belgian scholar, Verpoorten (2014), of between 512,000 and 662,000 Tutsi dead. While higher estimates exist, including the claim of over one million Tutsi dead by the Rwandan government, I believe a slightly clearer consensus is emerging for the death toll than for perpetration. It is centring around the lower figure of a half million Tutsi dead. The more sensitive figure, however, is the number of Hutu killed, particularly at the hands of the RPF. For those Hutu killed inside Rwanda and between April and July 1994, the consensus, albeit based on limited data, is clear that this figure is significantly lower than the number of Tutsi victims and in the low tens of thousands. However, for Hutu killed outside of Rwanda, mainly in the Democratic Republic of Congo (DRC) and after 1994, hard data are even scarcer. The claims here vary from the tens of thousands to over two hundred thousand. Consensus on this figure will remain elusive until these killings are widely recognized and further research and investigation are undertaken.

8.3 What More Have We Learned about Rwanda's Violence and Genocides Generally?

This book does not only reinforce and broaden the current consensus on Rwanda's genocide. It also contributes several more original insights that edge forward the frontier of our knowledge of Rwanda's violence specifically and, to a more modest degree, of our understanding of genocides and mass killings more generally. I do not claim a dramatic revision of what we already know and understand. But I do believe that the book offers several ideas hitherto under-explored. I highlight some of the more interesting ones here.

First, I have taken the time to explain how unusual a baseline Rwanda was. Rwanda possessed several extraordinary sociodemographic and physical geographic features whose significance for the genocide has not been fully understood. Some of these characteristics have been recognized and linked to the Rwandan state's power. Its capacity for surveillance and coercion of the population has been traced to the country's exceptionally high population density and hilly topography (Straus, 2006, p. 215). However, I believe its highly distinctive baseline characteristics mattered for much more than just the state's power. Rwanda's high rurality, small territorial size, intermixed ethnic settlement, numerical dominance of one ethnic group, and extraordinary population density mattered also for the remarkable scale, speed, and scope of the mobilization and the violence. So, I distinguish analytically the *characteristics* of the violence from its causes. And they mattered also because they amplified the effects of the three macro-political events – the war, liberalization, and assassination – whose conjunction led to the genocide. I explained in Chapter 2 how and why each of these characteristics mattered. But I reproduce two important examples here. Rwanda's extraordinary population density mattered for the extraordinary civilian mobilization because living in close proximity to one another amplified the social forces of conformity and coercion that led Rwandans to join the attack groups. Similarly, Rwanda's small territorial size and high road density amplified the effects of liberalization because the small, easily coverable distances between the centre and periphery meant that politicians could readily travel to rural localities to sensitize and mobilize the population.

The importance of Rwanda's baseline highlights the limits of comparison in the study of genocides. The events I argue that led to Rwanda's genocide – civil war, political liberalization, and the assassination of a Head of State – obviously can and will arise in other countries. However, I believe that it is improbable that we would see mobilization and violence on the scale of Rwanda elsewhere in Africa. The possible exception would be neighbouring Burundi, which shares many of the historical, geographic, and demographic characteristics that distinguish Rwanda. Nonetheless, Rwanda remains the high waterline for violence in Africa. While future outbreaks of violence elsewhere on the continent will likely draw comparisons, I suspect few – if any – will share the extraordinary characteristics of Rwanda's violence. I doubt if we will see nationwide killing, involving a similarly massive and rapid mobilization of the civilian population, and resulting in such a high proportion of the targeted group exterminated. Rwanda's genocide will remain an exceptional event in African and world history.

Second, I have suggested that the elite-centric, top-down, and state-driven perspective on the genocide implicit in almost all existing explanations of Rwanda's violence – and of genocides more generally – needs to be softened. I found pressure from below also existed. Violence did not begin in the centre and then radiate to the periphery in Rwanda. It began in various localities outside of Kigali even *before* the extremist faction prevailed in the national-level power struggle and captured the central state apparatus. In some localities, this early violence onset was attributable simply to existing extremist control of the local state apparatus. The incumbent burgomaster was pro-violence. However, independently of the burgomaster's orientation, I found inter-ethnic segregation from below also mattered. Where the

8.3 About Rwanda's Violence and Genocides Generally

distance between Hutu and Tutsi was small, violence was delayed. Conversely, where ethnic segregation was high, violence occurred early. It took very little time to break inter-ethnic bonds and divide these communities. Moreover, the individuals who mobilized the population at the local level were not all state employees and not all elites. My survey of 160 ethnic and political entrepreneurs – the grassroots leaders – found that the majority were in fact private citizens and almost half were ordinary farmers. Violence, then, resulted from the intersection of forces from below and above. The proposition of some societal pressure for the killing is perhaps uncomfortable to accept, but it is not an unprecedented claim in studies of mass violence (Gerlach, 2006). The reality is that some local actors acted independently of the state to organize violence in their communities. This is not to suggest, however, that the pressure from below was equivalent to the pressure from above. The pressure from the top was decisive. In no community where ethnic integration was high was violence ultimately avoided. Moreover, if extremists had not captured the state at the national-level, the violence would not have become *nationwide* in scope. Local racists and opportunists – ethnic and political entrepreneurs – had only minority support for violence in ethnically integrated communities initially. *Mass* mobilization occurred in these communities only once the authority of the state had been appropriated by an extremist.

Third, the book has highlighted the *interdependent* nature of the elite choices leading to the genocide. Existing explanations of genocides generally emphasize the agency of one particular actor over others. Often it is the regime, or a faction within the regime, that is the subject of scrutiny. In Rwanda, however, the opposition parties, the rebels, and the international community have each also come under investigation. The desire to identify one particular culprit perhaps results from the mistaken conflation of causal and moral responsibility for the genocide. However, I have sought to show how various elite decisions and actions strategically interacted and escalated toward genocide. For instance, I have argued that the intra-group power struggles – between hardliners and moderates – drove the inter-group contestation – between the government and rebels. This inter-group conflict in turn shaped the intra-group dynamics. I have also suggested that these strategic interactions operated at both the national and international levels. I argued, for example, that the absence of external constraints at the international level worked to the advantage of extremists and enabled the escalation of the dynamics toward confrontation and violence rather than toward moderation and peace. These strategic interactions were most consequential in the space of opportunity created by Habyarimana's assassination. Besides the massively momentous decision to eliminate the president (for which responsibility remains unclaimed) – the decisions of regime extremists to target Tutsi civilians and to restart the civil war, of the RPF to re-engage the war and to fight to the finish, and of the United Nations not to intervene initially – all collided. Each choice was *causally* responsible. However, this is not synonymous with *moral* responsibility. Primary moral culpability must remain with those who chose willingly to organize and to participate in the genocide.

Fourth, the book offers an explanation of how and why, in the context of ethnic conflict, one faction prevails over another in the inter-elite contests that so often arise between extremists and moderates. I have argued that at the outset, in 1990–1991, ethnic moderation was stronger in Rwandan politics than ethnic extremism but that support for extremism increased as the war and democratization processes unfolded. In fact, contrary to claims that democratization risks ethnic division, I found that it had an ethnically integrative effect in the Rwandan context at the outset. Rwanda's newly established political parties made ethnically unifying appeals and enjoyed cross-ethnic support initially. It was democratization's interaction with the war that led to ethnic radicalization. These findings corroborate the longstanding consensus that 'ancient tribal hatred' is a causally problematic explanation of the genocide. It mistakenly implies constancy in anti-Tutsi sentiment across time. This sentiment was variable in Rwanda. Threat/insecurity represented one important driver of this variability. These findings also confirm the notion of 'escalation' over time toward genocide (Straus, 2015). However, the principal contribution of the book on this question is its theoretical explanation of why such inter-elite contests sometimes escalate in favour of violence and at other times de-escalate in favour of peace. I argue that the outcome of power struggles between moderates and extremists will in the first instance be shaped by the *external* constraints operating on each actor: state institutions and civil society at the domestic level, for instance; and diplomatic support, military intervention, economic aid/sanctions, and criminal prosecutions at the international level, for example. If these constraints are weak or absent, then the power struggle will ultimately

8.3 About Rwanda's Violence and Genocides Generally 381

resolve according to the respective material capabilities *internal* to each actor. In Rwanda at the moment of the president's assassination, the external constraints were weak and extremists possessed superior coercive power.

Fifth, I have argued that we should re-think what we mean by perpetrator 'ordinariness', the current consensus in studies of genocide perpetrators. I have suggested that important dispositional differences existed between perpetrators that mattered for mobilization. My survey comparing those who participated with those who did not revealed few differences in either socio-demographic characteristics or in attitudes and beliefs between them. These surveyed perpetrators then did seem quite ordinary. However, the survey counted very few of the leaders, serial killers, and sadists of the genocide. Many of the individuals more committed to the killing remained outside of the prison system and at liberty in the DRC and elsewhere. Using other evidence, I suggested that extremist, opportunist, conformist, and pacifist dispositions existed in Rwanda and that most of the perpetrators I surveyed in the prison system belonged to the category of 'conformists'. These dispositional differences reflected different levels of commitment to the violence. I theorized that these different commitments also reflected different moments in a mobilization continuum that individuals were likely to join in the violence. Extremists, the most highly committed, were likely to be the first-movers; while conformists were likely to join only after a critical mass had already done so. Although the classification is crude and the reality is likely to be more complex, the basic point is that dispositional heterogeneity existed. This raises the question of what is meant by perpetrator ordinariness. The idea makes most sense if it means simply that perpetrators had similar, unremarkable *socio-demographic* profiles. Occupationally, many were farmers for instance. However, the notion breaks down if 'ordinariness' is intended to convey similarity in *attitudes* or *dispositions*. In this respect, discernible dispositional differences did exist among Rwanda's killers.

Sixth, relatedly, I have argued that individual radicalization was both a cause and consequence of the act of killing. I found that Rwandans were not widely radicalized – by which I mean that they had not developed intensely negative or extreme attitudes and beliefs about the outgroup – before the genocide began. To recall the indicators of radicalization highlighted in Chapter 3: they did not see all

Tutsi as the same; they did not all denigrate or resent Tutsi; and they did not all believe that the targeting of Tutsi was justified. In northern communities, close to the war's frontlines, prior radicalization was indeed widespread. However, in southern communities, for whom the war was distant, it was often only a small minority who held such radical or extreme views about the Tutsi. Yet Rwandans started killing extremely quickly after the plane went down. How was this possible if prior radicalization was limited? The explanation lies in recognizing that not only do attitudes shape behaviours; but behaviours may also shape attitudes. The proposition has been recognized in social psychology for some time (Newman & Erber, 2002, p. 52). Expressed crudely: some killed first; and hated later. The suggested psycho-social mechanism at work is a type of dissonance-reduction (Hinton, 2004). It is implicit in Staub's (1989) idea of a 'continuum of destruction' in which individuals 'learn by doing' and devalue their victims a little more with each anti-social act in order to justify their harm toward them. Some Rwandans killed Tutsi because they did indeed homogenize and denigrate them. However, others came to homogenize and denigrate Tutsi because they killed them. Individual disposition changed through the act of violence. The idea helps resolve the long-standing theoretical debate over whether situation or disposition better explains perpetrators' behaviours. Both mattered. Some Rwandans possessed a dispositional inclination toward violence *ex ante*. Others reacted to situational forces and developed dispositional inclinations *ex post*. Dispositions were heterogeneous and malleable. The idea also helps resolve the longstanding puzzle of non-instrumental violence in the genocide. How do we explain the cruelty, the gratuitous pain and suffering, the sexual torture, and the desire to humiliate victims if individuals were merely responding to situational pressures such as conformity and coercion? The answer I believe has to do with recognizing that some Rwandans developed such dispositions as a *consequence* of committing violence. Finally, the proposition also helps reconcile seemingly contradictory theoretical claims concerning the character and motivation of perpetrators. Theories emphasizing the prior dehumanization of the victims (Fein, 1993; Hagan & Rymond-Richmond, 2008), the internalization of exclusionary ideologies (Harff, 2003; Sémelin, 2005; Snyder, 2000), and the possession of deep-seated prejudices (Kaufman, 2015) sit uncomfortably with the idea that the perpetrators were ordinary individuals (Browning, 1992;

8.3 About Rwanda's Violence and Genocides Generally

Waller, 2002). These theories cohere better, however, if one recognizes that some individuals may also have come to dehumanize the victims, internalize extremist ideas, and develop animosities as a *consequence* of killing.

Seventh, I have addressed the analytically distinct question of differential selection into the violence: the enduring puzzle of why some killed and others not. I argued that participation was a function not only of dispositional variation between Rwandans, but also of *situational* and *relational* differences among them too. Having compared the household locations and social networks of participants and non-participants in one community, I found important differences between them. The killers tended to live in clusters closer to each other (a neighbourhood effect) and to have larger social networks than the non-killers. Who you were, where you lived, and who you knew all mattered for selection into the violence. The finding refines the situationalist consensus that has emerged in genocide studies following the pioneering work by social psychologists such as Milgram, Zimbardo, and Asch. It once more supports the proposition that both situation *and* disposition mattered and it corroborates (and quantifies) the importance of relational factors too (Fujii, 2009). It is also worth noting that although the survey found few systematic differences between participants and non-participants, certain questions generated such clear responses across *both* groups of respondents as to invite consideration of their relevance to the genocide. Very large percentages of those surveyed spoke of the fears created by the war, the omnipresence of the state, the collective historical memory of Tutsi oppression of Hutu, and the material deprivation in Rwanda. Evidently the responses relating to the war and the state reinforce two of the book's major themes: security and authority. We must, however, exercise caution in drawing inferences from these responses alone, given this is not a comparative study of genocide. At most, the survey evidence – taken alone – suggests possible *permissive* conditions for Rwanda's genocide but not causally necessary or sufficient ones.

Lastly, I have argued for a link between Rwanda's remarkable state power and remarkable popular mobilization. However, I suggest that the relationship is more complex than currently theorized. The state's strong monitoring and enforcement *capacity* has already been recognized. It has led to the claim that Rwandans were mainly *coerced* into participation because non-participation could be observed and sanctioned (Straus, 2006, p. 135). This idea represented a challenge to an earlier claim that Rwandans participated out of simple *obedience* to authority (Prunier, 1998). The coercion argument implied agency that was missing in the obedience explanation. I believe that both claims have merit. Their reconciliation lies in recognizing that the Rwandan state had multiple dimensions to its power and that perpetrators were heterogeneous in their reasons for participation. The Rwandan state was remarkable not only for its strong capacity, but also for its high legitimacy and low autonomy. Its high legitimacy, traceable to the continuity in its borders from the late precolonial to the postcolonial period and to its social revolution, meant that its symbolic authority was high. Some, but not all, Rwandans, were deferential to this authority. Its low autonomy, traceable in large measure to its privatization by the ruling parties of the first and second republics, meant that its authority could be readily appropriated and extremists succeeded in doing so. Some, but not all Rwandans, felt then that the state authorized them to participate. Lastly, some, but not all Rwandans, did indeed respond to the state's coercive capacity. They felt that they had little choice other than to participate.

8.4 Broader Implications for Theories of Genocide

The book also weighs in on two important theoretical debates that continue to be waged in the study of genocide, and ethnic conflict more broadly: the role of ideas; and the power of emotions.

Ideas, generally, have been eclipsed by structural, institutional, and other material factors in the theorization of genocide and mass killings (Besancon, 2005; Krain, 1997; Midlarsky, 2005; Valentino, 2004). In recent years, however, they have experienced a renaissance and have come to feature most evidently in explanations that highlight the role of *ideologies* (Leader Maynard, 2014): purity and contamination (Sémelin, 2005); race and utopias (Weitz, 2005); civilization and barbarism (Powell, 2011); and nationalism and nation-states (Levene, 2005). Each represent foundational ideas embedded in ideology-based theories of genocide. Ideas are central also to other constructs used to explain genocides: founding narratives (Straus, 2015, p. 10), myths (Kaufman, 2006), and symbolic predispositions (Kaufman, 2015, p. 31) each derive their explanatory value from ideas. Ideas fulfil a number of important theoretical functions. In framing theory, they

8.4 Broader Implications for Theories of Genocide 385

frame the problem (the diagnostic frame): the Tutsi are a threat; they frame the solution (the prognostic frame): the Tutsi must be eliminated; and they frame the justification (the motivational frame): the Tutsi will otherwise exterminate us (Benford & Snow, 2000). Scholars have looked to ideas principally to explain why genocide is chosen over other solutions to deal with groups considered problematic. Rulers generally face a choice between the accommodation or exclusion of problematic groups. If inclusive strategies are ruled out – integration, federalization/cantonization, and consociation for instance – then exclusionary solutions other than genocide remain available: population transfers; partition; and, perhaps most commonly, violence short of genocide are all possibilities. Rwanda's extremists could have engaged in limited retributive massacres against the Tutsi population. However, they opted for, or at the very least acquiesced in, their entire elimination. The choice of genocide then is distinctive. Unlike other forms of violence, whose purpose may be to control, punish, or otherwise manage a problematic group, genocide signifies the wish to end all communication and interaction with the group (Straus, 2015, p. 18). Genocide is a solution that embodies a highly distinct idea.

The key objection that I level against explanations that highlight the importance of ideas, however, is that ideas are rarely singular. More often than not, *multiple* ideas concerning inter-group relations compete for attention in the public sphere. Any explanation of genocide that emphasizes ideational factors must account for why one extreme idea – the desire to eliminate a group – prevails over the myriad, often more moderate, ideas in circulation. It is all too easy when studying genocide *ex post* to observe the existence of one extreme idea or ideology and to infer its causative role in the violence *ex ante*. Yet alternate ideas or ideologies likely existed. They may even have contradicted or conflicted with the genocidal idea. Kayibanda's revolutionary ideology recognized Rwanda as a Hutu nation and was exclusionary in nature. It contrasted with Habyarimana's more inclusive ideology that explicitly emphasized both Hutu and Tutsi as Rwandans. Framing theory acknowledges that contested frames are common. It suggests that the success of one frame may turn, principally, on its *credibility* (Benford & Snow, 2000, p. 619). Frames, and the ideas they enshrine, vary in their power. Implicitly, it is how the frame or idea resonates *below* that matters. Yet generally genocide scholars have emphasized that genocide is often the strategic choice of a particular elite faction from *above* (Chirot & McCauley, 2010; Valentino, 2004). Any theory then must explain how and why one elite faction prevails over another in propagating their ideas. In Rwanda, an extremist faction succeeded in capturing the state. This assured the triumph of its ideas over those of moderates. Importantly, extremists did not represent a plurality within the regime. Genocide was not simply the product of superior numbers. Instead, I argued that the extremists' success turned first on the strength of the external constraints acting on them, and second on their relative material capacity. The constraints were weak and their coercive capacity superior. Ultimately then, I conclude that *material* constraints and opportunities were decisive. To be clear: non-material factors – whether you term them an extremist ideology, hate narrative, or symbolic disposition – were a causally necessary condition. If extremists did not hold extremist ideas, genocide would not have occurred. These ideas alone were not, however, sufficient.

Emotions – in particular resentment, hostility, and fear – represent a second, non-material construct whose explanatory role in genocides and ethnic conflicts remains debated. Typically, emotion-based theories are contrasted against both *rationalist* approaches, and also, like ideas, against *materialist* explanations. The debate centres principally on their causal significance. Are emotions causes, consequences, or mechanisms of such violence? For rationalist and materialist proponents, emotions are epiphenomenal (Grigorian & Kaufman, 2007; Lake & Rothchild, 1998; Posen, 1993; Valentino, 2004): coincidental by-products of strategic choices and changes in structural and material opportunities. They have no independent causal significance. For others, however, emotions such as fear, resentment, and hostility are antecedent conditions or otherwise causally necessary for violence (Horowitz, 1985; Kaufman, 2015; Petersen, 2002; Ross, 2007). Violence cannot be explained solely as a rational choice.

I believe that the dichotomies between rationality and emotions, and between materiality and emotions, in fact represent false theoretical choices. There are two reasons to query the validity of these distinctions. First, over thirty years of research in social psychology has found that, instead of being opposing forces, reason and emotion in fact often *interact* to shape individual choices. The standard reference work for the discipline sums up these findings well: '[T]he study of emotion and reason reveals that almost every cognitive process – attention,

8.4 Broader Implications for Theories of Genocide

evaluative judgments, probability estimates, perceptions of risk, out-group biases, and moral judgment – is shaped by momentary emotions in systematic and profound ways' (Keltner & Lerner, 2010, p. 335). Yet extant theorization on conflict and violence rarely recognizes the conjunction of these two processes. Instead, a distinction is often made between elite decision-makers and the ordinary population. Leaders are frequently credited with higher rationality while their followers are instead thought to be driven by base emotions that are readily instrumentalized. Yet the assumption of elite rationality is difficult to reconcile with the extremist faction's decision to restart the civil war and to eliminate the Tutsi population in Rwanda. The rebels had already established their military superiority. The major offensive in February 1993, checked only by French reinforcements, brought the RPF within 20 km of the capital. It was clear to an objective observer that the Forces Armées Rwandaises (FAR) could not win on the battlefield and, indeed, this was the outcome. Why then would the extremist faction choose a course of action that would enable the RPF – which they saw as a Tutsi organization – to take control of the state outright? One answer is that they preferred death to life without power (Mamdani, 2001, p. 99). This is consistent with a rational, if unusual, ordering of preferences. Yet the government did not fight to the bitter end. It fled over the border into Zaire. A better answer is that the extremist calculus was influenced by emotions. It is not that they were perfectly rational. It is also not that they were entirely emotional either. It is that their judgement was affected by their *hostility* toward Tutsi and/or, if the RPF did kill Habyarimana, by their *anger* toward his assassins. Extremists 'gambled for resurrection' (de Figueiredo & Weingast, 1999) because emotion led them to over-estimate their chances of victory.

Second, while I believe that emotions were causally necessary, they nonetheless still required material factors to produce their effects. I showed in Chapter 3 that the war, a material threat, induced fear, a core emotion. It radicalized Rwandan politics: some elites feared the redistribution of political power. And it also radicalized Rwandan society: some ordinary Rwandans feared for their lives. As the security threat escalated, this fear broadened and deepened. Group emotions vary in their ambit and intensity; and material factors may drive this variation. So, in my theorization of their role, emotions are an essential, causally *intermediate* step between the material driver and the violence outcome (Costalli & Ruggeri, 2015). This does not make them epiphenomenal, however. As I have argued drawing on social psychology, emotions directly influence individual judgement and decision-making. Without them, Rwanda's extremist elite and ordinary Rwandans would likely have made different choices in respect of the genocide. Risk assessments, moral evaluations, and attention spans are all shaped by affect. Finally, it is worth noting that defining the causal role of emotions is complicated by the fact that they may also be endogenous to violence. As I have argued, radicalization was both a cause *and* consequence of the act of killing. Individuals may then also develop hostility and resentment *ex post* to justify their actions. This does not negate the independent causal significance of emotions. It simply means that there is more than one causal pathway to genocidal violence.

* * *

This book has attempted to synthesize social science theory and method with the best existing and new evidence known to me to explain what happened in Rwanda. Its objectives were scholarly. Genocide, however, is a highly politicized and emotionally charged subject. I fully anticipate strong reactions to the book that reflect the many sensitivities that Rwanda's genocide has created. Accusations of genocide denial, minimization, and trivialization are an occupational hazard for researchers in this field. Yet, more broadly, it is also right that the book's arguments should be subjected to careful scrutiny. Rwanda's genocide was a world-historical event whose repercussions continue to reverberate and whose significance merits the attention that claims concerning it continue to draw. Genocide more generally is also an enormously complex phenomenon. I do not pretend to have perfectly and fully explained Rwanda's genocide. The book should be seen as one more contribution to a continuing enterprise to understand and explain this exceptional and sad event. As we learn more, the violence will hopefully become less incomprehensible to non-Rwandans and the extraordinary, terrifying, and tragic circumstances through which Rwandans lived in 1994 will be better understood.

References

Adler, R. N., Globerman, J., Larson, E. B., and Loyle, C. E. (2008). Transforming Men into Killers: Attitudes Leading to Hands-on Violence during the 1994 Rwandan Genocide. *Global Public Health,* 3(3), 291–307.
African Rights (1994). *Rwanda: Death, Despair and Defiance.* London: African Rights.
Alesina, A., Devleeschauwer, A., Easterly, W., Kurlat, S., and Wacziarg, R. (2003). Fractionalization. *Journal of Economic Growth,* 8(2), 155–194.
Allport, G. W. (1958). *The Nature of Prejudice* (abridged ed.). Garden City, NY: Doubleday.
André, C., and Platteau, J. P. (1998). Land Relations under Unbearable Stress: Rwanda Caught in the Malthusian Trap. *Journal of Economic Behavior & Organization,* 34(1), 1–47.
Ansoms, A. (2009). Re-Engineering Rural Society: The Visions and Ambitions of the Rwandan Elite. *African Affairs,* 108(431), 289–309.
Arendt, H. (1963). *Eichmann in Jerusalem: A Report on the Banality of Evil.* NY: Viking.
Asch, S. E., and Guetzkow, H. (1951). Effects of Group Pressure upon the Modification and Distortion of Judgments. In H. Guetzkow (ed.), *Groups, Leadership, and Men.* Pittsburgh, PA: Carnegie, 222–236.
Avocats Sans Frontières. (2007). Monitoring des juridictions Gacaca: Phase de jugement, *Rapport Analytique 2, Octobre 2005–Septembre 2006.*
Barnett, M. N. (2002). *Eyewitness to a Genocide: The United Nations and Rwanda.* Ithaca, NY and London: Cornell University Press.
Bates, R. H. (1974). Ethnic Competition and Modernization in Contemporary Africa. *Comparative Political Studies,* 6(4), 457–484.
Baum, S. K. (2008). *The Psychology of Genocide: Perpetrators, Bystanders, and Rescuers.* New York, NY: Cambridge University Press.
Bauman, Z. (2000). *Modernity and the Holocaust.* Ithaca, NY: Cornell University Press.
Baumeister, R., and Campbell, K. (1999). The Intrinsic Appeal of Evil: Sadism, Sensational Thrills, and Threatened Egotism. *Personality and Social Psychology Review,* 3(3), 210–221.

Benford, R. D., and Snow, D. A. (2000). Framing Processes and Social Movements: An Overview and Assessment. *Annual Review of Sociology, 26*, 611–639.

Berkowitz, L. (1993). *Aggression: Its Causes, Consequences, and Control.* New York, NY: McGraw-Hill.

Bertrand, J. (2000). *Rwanda, le piège de l'histoire: L'Opposition démocratique avant le génocide (1990–1994).* Paris: Karthala.

Besançon, M. L. (2005). Relative Resources: Inequality in Ethnic Wars, Revolutions, and Genocides. *Journal of Peace Research, 42*(4), 393–415.

Beswick, D. (2011). Aiding State Building and Sacrificing Peace Building? The Rwanda–UK Relationship 1994–2011. *Third World Quarterly, 32* (10), 1911–1930.

Bhavnani, R., and Lavery, J. (2011). Transnational Ethnic Ties and the Incidence of Minority Rule in Rwanda and Burundi (1959–2003). *Nationalism and Ethnic Politics, 17*(3), 231–256.

Boersema, J. R. (2009). Genocide in een Rwandees dorp. In W. Berenschot and H. Schijf (eds.) *Etnisch Geweld: Groepsconflict in de schaduw van de staat.* Amsterdam: Amsterdam University Press.

Bonneux, L. (1994). Rwanda: A Case of Demographic Entrapment. *Lancet, 344*(8938), 1689–1690.

Booh-Booh, J.-R. (2005). *Le patron de Dallaire Parle: Révélations sur les dérives d'un général de L'ONU au Rwanda*: Paris: Éditions Duboiris.

Boone, C. (2003). *Political Topographies of the African State: Territorial Authority and Institutional Choice.* New York, NY; Cambridge, UK: Cambridge University Press.

Booth, D., and Golooba-Mutebi, F. (2012). Developmental Patrimonialism? The Case of Rwanda. *African Affairs, 111*(444), 379–403.

Bormann, N.-C., Cederman, L.-E, Girardin, L., Hunziker, P., Rüegger, S., and Vogt, M. (2015). Integrating Data on Ethnicity, Geography, and Conflict: The Ethnic Power Relations Data Set Family. *Journal of Conflict Resolution, 59*(7), 1327–1342.

Braeckmann, C. (1994). *Rwanda: Histoire d'un génocide.* Paris: Fayard.

Brass, P. R. (ed.) (1996). *Riots and Pogroms.* New York, NY: New York University Press.

Bratton, M., and van de Walle, N. (1997). *Democratic Experiments in Africa: Regime Transitions in Comparative Perspective.* Cambridge, UK; New York, NY: Cambridge University Press.

Brehm, H. N. (2017). Subnational Determinants of Killing in Rwanda. *Criminology: An Interdisciplinary Journal, 55*(1), 5–31.

Brewer, M. B. (1999). The Psychology of Prejudice: Ingroup Love or Outgroup Hate? *Journal of Social Issues, 55*(3), 429–444.

Browder, G. C. (2003). Perpetrator Character and Motivation: An Emerging Consensus? *Holocaust and Genocide Studies, 17*(3), 480–497.

Browning, C. R. (1992). *Ordinary Men: Reserve Police Battalion 101 and the Final Solution in Poland*. New York, NY: Harper Collins.

Brubaker, R., and Laitin, D. D. (1998). Ethnic and Nationalist Violence. *Annual Review of Sociology, 24*, 423–452.

Buckley-Zistel, S. (2006). Dividing and Uniting: The Use of Citizenship Discourses in Conflict and Reconciliation in Rwanda. *Global Society, 20*(1), 101–113.

Buhaug, H., Cederman, L.-E., and Gleditsch, K. S. (2013). *Inequality, Grievances, and Civil War*. Cambridge, UK: Cambridge University Press.

Burnet, J. E. (2012). *Genocide Lives in Us: Women, Memory, and Silence in Rwanda*. Madison, WI: University of Wisconsin Press.

Campioni, M., and Noack, P. (eds.) (2012). *Rwanda Fast Forward: Social, Economic, Military and Reconciliation Prospects*. London: Palgrave Macmillan.

Canetti, E. (2000). *Crowds and Power*. London: Phoenix.

Carlsmith, J. M., and Festinger, L. (1959). Cognitive Consequences of Forced Compliance. *Journal of Abnormal and Social Psychology, 58*(2), 203–210.

Chalk, F. R., and Jonassohn, K. (1990). *The History and Sociology of Genocide: Analyses and Case Studies*. New Haven: Yale University Press.

Chari, T. (2010). Representation or Misrepresentation? The *New York Times*'s Framing of the 1994 Rwanda Genocide. *African Identities, 8*(4), 333–349.

Chirot, D., and McCauley, C. (2010). *Why Not Kill Them All? The Logic and Prevention of Mass Political Murder*. Princeton, NJ: Princeton University Press.

Chossudovsky, M. (1996). Economic Genocide in Rwanda. *Economic and Political Weekly, 31*(15), 938–941.

Chrétien, J.-P. (ed.) (1995). *Rwanda: Les Médias Du Génocide*. Paris: Éditions Karthala.

Cialdini, R. B., and Goldstein, N. J. (2004). Social Influence: Compliance and Conformity. *Annual Review of Psychology, 55*, 591–621.

Cincotta, R. P., Engelman, R., Anastasion, D. (2003). *The Security Demographic: Population and Civil Conflict after the Cold War*. Washington, DC: Population Action International.

Clapham, C. (1998). Rwanda: The Perils of Peacemaking. *Journal of Peace Research, 35*(2), 193–210.

Clark, P. (2005). *Justice without Lawyers: The Gacaca Courts and Post-Genocide Justice and Reconciliation in Rwanda*. Oxford: University of Oxford (PhD thesis).

Clark, P., and Kaufman, Z. D. (eds.) (2009). *After Genocide: Transitional Justice, Post-Conflict Reconstruction and Reconciliation in Rwanda and Beyond*. New York, NY: Columbia University Press.

Cohen, J. (2007). *One-Hundred Days of Silence: America and the Rwanda Genocide*. Lanham: Rowman & Littlefield Publishers.

Collier, P., and Hoeffler, A. (2004). Greed and Grievance in Civil War. *Oxford Economic Papers*, 56(4).

Costalli, S., and Ruggeri, A. (2015). Indignation, Ideologies, and Armed Mobilization: Civil War in Italy, 1943–45. *International Security*, 40(2), 119–157.

Dallaire, R., and Beardsley, B. (2004). *Shake Hands with the Devil: The Failure of Humanity in Rwanda*. New York, NY: Carroll & Graf.

Des Forges, A. (1999). *Leave None to Tell the Story: Genocide in Rwanda*. New York, NY: Human Rights Watch.

Deutsch, K. (1966). *Nationalism and Social Communication: An Inquiry into the Foundations of Nationality* (2nd ed.). Cambridge, MA: MIT Press.

Diamond, J. (2005). *Collapse: How Societies Choose to Fail or Succeed*. Penguin.

Downes, A. B. (2007). Draining the Sea by Filling the Graves: Investigating the Effectiveness of Indiscriminate Violence as a Counterinsurgency Strategy. *Civil Wars*, 9(4), 420–444.

Durkheim, E. (1960). *The Division of Labor in Society* (2nd ed.). Glencoe, IL,: Free Press.

Easterly, W., and Levine, R. (1997). Africa's Growth Tragedy: Policies and Ethnic Divisions. *The Quarterly Journal of Economics*, 112(4), 1203–1250.

Emizet, K. N. F. (2000). The Massacre of Refugees in Congo: A Case of UN Peacekeeping Failure and International Law. *Journal of Modern African Studies*, 38(2), 163–202.

Englebert, P. (2009). *Africa: Unity, Sovereignty, and Sorrow*. Boulder, CO: Lynne Rienner Publishers.

(2000). *State Legitimacy and Development in Africa*. Boulder, CO: Lynne Rienner Publishers.

Faludi, S. (1999). *Stiffed: The Betrayal of the American Man*. New York, NY: W. Morrow and Co.

Fearon, J., and Laitin, D. (1996). Explaining Interethnic Cooperation. *The American Political Science Review*, 90(4), 715–735.

Fearon, J. D. (2003). Ethnic and Cultural Diversity by Country. *Journal of Economic Growth*, 8(2), 195–222.

Fein, H. (1993). *Genocide, a Sociological Perspective*. London; Newbury Park, CA: Sage Publications.

Festinger, L. (1957). *A Theory of Cognitive Dissonance*. Evanston, IL, Row.

Festinger, L., Newcomb, T., and Pepitone, A. (1952). Some Consequences of Deindividuation in a Group. *Journal of Abnormal and Social Psychology*, 47(2), 382–389.

de Figueiredo, R. J. P., and Weingast, B. R. (1999). The Rationality of Fear: Political Opportunism and Ethnic Conflict. In J. Snyder and B. F. Walter (eds.), *Civil Wars, Insecurity, and Intervention*. New York, NY: Columbia University Press, 261–302.

Ford, R. E. (1995). The Population-Environment Nexus and Vulnerability Assessment in Africa. *Geo-Journal*, 35(2), 207–216.

Fujii, L. A. (2006). *Killing Neighbours: Social Dimensions of Genocide in Rwanda*. Washington, DC: George Washington University (PhD thesis).

(2009). *Killing Neighbors: Webs of Violence in Rwanda*. Ithaca, NY: Cornell University Press.

(2013). The Puzzle of Extra-Lethal Violence. *Perspectives on Politics*, 11(2), 410–426.

Fukuyama, F. (2013). What Is Governance? *Governance*, 26(3), 347–368.

Galtung, J. (1969). Violence, Peace, and Peace Research. *Journal of Peace Research* 6(3), 167–191.

Gasana, J. K. (2002a). Remember Rwanda? *World Watch*, 15(5), 24–33.

(2002b). *Rwanda: Du parti-état à l'état-Garnison*. Paris: L'harmattan.

Geertz, C. (1975). *The Interpretation of Cultures: Selected Essays*. London: Hutchinson.

Gerlach, C. (2006). Extremely Violent Societies: An Alternative to the Concept of Genocide. *Journal of Genocide Research*, 8(4), 455–471.

Gerring, J. (1997). Ideology: A Definitional Analysis. *Political Research Quarterly*, 50(4), 957–994.

Goldhagen, D. J. (1997). *Hitler's Willing Executioners : Ordinary Germans and the Holocaust*. London: Abacus.

Goldstone, J. A. (1991). *Revolution and Rebellion in the Early Modern World*. Berkeley, CA: University of California Press.

Goldstone, J. A. (2002). Population and Security: How Demographic Change Can Lead to Violent Conflict. *Journal of International Affairs*, 56(1), 3–21.

Gould, R. V. (1991). Multiple Networks and Mobilization in the Paris Commune, 1871. *American Sociological Review*, 56(6), 716–729.

Gourevitch, P. (2004). *We Wish to Inform You That Tomorrow We Will Be Killed with Our Families: Stories from Rwanda*. New York, NY: Holtzbrinck Publishers.

Government of Rwanda (1994). *Recensement général de la population et de l'habitat au 15 Août 1991: Résultats définitifs*. Kigali: Commission Nationale De Récensement

(2001). *Dénombrement des victimes du génocide*. Kigali: Ministère de l'Administration Locale et des affaires sociales

(2005). *Final Report on Data Collection of the National Service of the Gacaca Jurisdictions*. Kigali:

(2008). *Récensement des rescapés du genocide de 1994: Rapport final*. Kigali: Institut National de la Statistique du Rwanda.

Gready, P. (2010). 'You're Either with Us or Against Us': Civil Society and Policy Making in Post-Genocide Rwanda. *African Affairs*, 109(437), 637–657.

Green, D. P., and Seher, R. L. (2003). What Role Does Prejudice Play in Ethnic Conflict? *Annual Review of Political Science*, 6, 509–531.

Grigorian, A., and Kaufman, S. J. (2007). Hate Narratives and Ethnic Conflict. *International Security*, 31(4), 180–191.

Guichaoua, A. (1992). *Le problème des réfugiés Rwandais et des populations Banyarwanda dans la région des Grands Lacs Africains*. Geneva: United Nations High Commission for Refugees.

(2005). *Rwanda 1994: Les politiques du génocide à Butare*. Paris: Karthala.

(2015). *From War to Genocide: Criminal Politics in Rwanda, 1990–1994*. Madison, WI: University of Wisconsin Press.

Gulseth, H. (2004). *The Use of Propaganda in the Rwandan Genocide: A Study of R.T.L.M.* Oslo: University of Oslo (Master's thesis).

Gurr, T. R. (1970). *Why Men Rebel*. Princeton, NJ: Princeton University Press.

Gurr, T. R., and Harff, B. (1988). Toward Empirical Theory of Genocides and Politicides: Identification and Measurement of Cases since 1945. *International Studies Quarterly*, 32(3), 359–371.

Habyarimana, J., Humphreys, M., Posner, D. N., and Weinstein, J. M. (2007). Why Does Ethnic Diversity Undermine Public Goods Provision? *American Political Science Review*, 101(4), 709–725.

Hagan, J., and Rymond-Richmond, W. (2008). The Collective Dynamics of Racial Dehumanization and Genocidal Victimization in Darfur. *American Sociological Review*, 73(6), 875–902.

Haney, C., Banks, C., and Zimbardo, P. (2001). Interpersonal Dynamics in a Simulated Prison. *International Journal of Criminology & Penology*, 1(1), 69–97.

Harff, B. (2003). No Lessons Learned from the Holocaust? Assessing Risks of Genocide and Political Mass Murder since 1955. *The American Political Science Review*, 97(1), 57–73.

Hatzfeld, J. (2005a). *Into the Quick of Life: The Rwandan Genocide: The Survivors Speak: A Report*. London: Serpent's Tail.

(2005b). *A Time for Machetes: The Rwandan Genocide: The Killers Speak: A Report*. London: Serpent's Tail.
Hayman, R. (2009). Going in the "Right" Direction? Promotion of Democracy in Rwanda since 1990. *Taiwan Journal of Democracy*, 5(1), 51–75.
Herbst, J. I. (2000). *States and Power in Africa: Comparative Lessons in Authority and Control*. Princeton, NJ: Princeton University Press.
Hewstone, M., and Swart, H. (2011). Fifty-Odd Years of Inter-Group Contact: From Hypothesis to Integrated Theory. *British Journal of Social Psychology*, 50(3), 374–386.
Hinton, A. L. (2004). *Why Did They Kill?: Cambodia in the Shadow of Genocide*: Berkeley, CA: University of California Press.
Hirshleifer, J. (1994). The Dark Side of the Force: Western Economic Association International 1993 Presidential Address. *Economic Inquiry*, 32(1), 1–10.
Homer-Dixon, T. F. (1999). *Environment, Scarcity, and Violence*. Princeton, NJ; Oxford: Princeton University Press.
Horowitz, D. L. (1985). *Ethnic Groups in Conflict*. Berkeley, CA: University of California Press.
(2002). *The Deadly Ethnic Riot*. New Delhi: Oxford University Press.
Horowitz, I. L. (2002). *Taking Lives: Genocide and State Power*: New Brunswick, NJ: Transaction Publishers.
Human Rights Watch (1996). *Shattered Lives: Sexual Violence during the Rwandan Genocide and Its Aftermath*. New York, NY: Human Rights Watch.
Humphreys, M., and Weinstein, J. M. (2008). Who Fights? The Determinants of Participation in Civil War. *American Journal of Political Science*, 52(2), 436–455.
Huntington, S. P. (2002). *The Clash of Civilizations and the Remaking of World Order*. London: Free Press.
Ingelaere, B. (2010). Peasants, Power and Ethnicity: A Bottom-up Perspective on Rwanda's Political Transition. *African Affairs*, 109(435), 273–292.
(2017). *Inside Rwanda's Gacaca Courts: Seeking Justice after Genocide*. Madison, WI: University of Wisconsin Press.
International Committee for the Red Cross. (2003). *Internal Document: Detained Population Registered by the I.C.R.C., January 15th 2003*. Kigali.
Ishiyama, J., and Pechenina, A. (2012). Environmental Degradation and Genocide, 1958–2007. *Ethnopolitics*, 11(2), 141–158.

Jackson, R. H., and Rosberg, C. G. (1982). Why Africa's Weak States Persist: The Empirical and the Juridical in Statehood. *World Politics*, 35(1), 1–24.

Jones, B. D. (2001). *Peacemaking in Rwanda: The Dynamics of Failure*. Boulder, CO: Lynne Rienner Publishers.

Kabagema, E. (2001). *Carnage d'une nation: Génocide et massacres au Rwanda 1994*. Paris: L'Harmattan.

Kagame, A. (1975). *Un abrégé de l'ethno-histoire du Rwanda (Vol. II)*. Butare: Éditions Universitaires du Rwanda.

Kahl, C. H. (1998). Population Growth, Environmental Degradation, and State-Sponsored Violence: The Case of Kenya, 1991–93. *International Security*, 23(2), 80–119.

Kalyvas, S. N. (2006). *The Logic of Violence in Civil War*. New York, NY: Cambridge University Press.

Kaplan, R. (1994, February). How Scarcity, Crime, Overpopulation, Tribalism, and Disease Are Rapidly Destroying the Social Fabric of Our Planet. *The Atlantic Monthly*.

Katz, J. (1988). *Seductions of Crime: Moral and Sensual Attractions in Doing Evil*. New York, NY: Basic Books.

Kaufman, S. J. (2001). *Modern Hatreds: The Symbolic Politics of Ethnic War*. Ithaca, NY: Cornell University Press.

(2006). Symbolic Politics or Rational Choice? Testing Theories of Extreme Ethnic Violence. *International Security*, 30(4), 45–86.

(2011). Symbols, Frames, and Violence: Studying Ethnic War in the Philippines. *International Studies Quarterly*, 55(4), 937–958.

(2015). *Nationalist Passions*. Ithaca, NY: Cornell University Press.

Keane, F. (1995). *Season of Blood: A Rwandan Journey*. London; New York, NY: Viking.

Keen, D. (2005). *Conflict & Collusion in Sierra Leone*. Oxford: James Currey; New York, NY; Palgrave Macmillan

Keltner, D., and Lerner, J. (2010). Emotion. In S. T. Fiske, D. T. Gilbert, and G. Lindzey (eds.), *Handbook of Social Psychology (5th ed.; Vol.I)*: Hoboken, NJ: John Wiley & Sons, 317–352.

Khan, S. M. (2000). *The Shallow Graves of Rwanda*. London; New York, NY: I.B. Tauris.

Kiernan, B. (2009). *Blood and Soil: A World History of Genocide and Extermination from Sparta to Darfur*: New Haven, CT: Yale University Press.

Kimonyo, J.-P. (2000). Revue critique des interprétations du conflit Rwandais (Cahiers 1). Butare: Université Nationale du Rwanda, Centre de gestion des conflits.

(2016). *Rwanda's Popular Genocide: A Perfect Storm*. Boulder, CO: Lynne Rienner Publishers.

Kotb, M., Mbonyingabo, C. D., and Scull, N. C. (2016). Transforming Ordinary People into Killers: A Psychosocial Examination of Hutu Participation in the Tutsi Genocide. *Peace and Conflict: Journal of Peace Psychology*, 22(4), 334–344.

Krain, M. (1997). State-Sponsored Mass Murder: The Onset and Severity of Genocides and Politicides. *The Journal of Conflict Resolution*, 41(3), 331–360.

Kuperman, A. J. (1996). The Other Lesson of Rwanda: Mediators Sometimes Do More Damage Than Good. *SAIS Review*, 16(1), 221–240.

(2001). *The Limits of Humanitarian Intervention: Genocide in Rwanda*. Washington, DC: Brookings Institute.

Lake, D. A., and Rothchild, D. S. (1998). *The International Spread of Ethnic Conflict: Fear, Diffusion, and Escalation*. Princeton, NJ: Princeton University Press.

Leader Maynard, J. (2014). Rethinking the Role of Ideology in Mass Atrocities. *Terrorism and Political Violence*, 26(5), 821–841.

Le Bon, G. (1896). *The Crowd: A Study of the Popular Mind*. London: T. F. Unwin.

Lemarchand, R. (1970). *Rwanda and Burundi*. London: Pall Mall Press.

(1972). Political Clientelism and Ethnicity in Tropical Africa: Competing Solidarities in Nation-Building. *American Political Science Review* 66(1), 68–90.

(2007). Rwanda: The State of Research. *Online Encyclopedia of Mass Violence*, www.massviolence.org

Levene, M. (2005). *Genocide in the Age of the Nation-State (Vol. I): The Meaning of Genocide*. London; New York, NY: I.B. Tauris.

Li, D. (2004). Echoes of Violence: Considerations on Radio and Genocide in Rwanda. *Journal of Genocide Research*, 6(1), 9–27.

Lieberson, S. (1981). An Asymmetrical Approach to Segregation. In C. Peach, V. Robinson, and S. Smith (eds.), *Ethnic Segregation in Cities*. London: Croom Helm, 61–82.

Longman, T. (1995). Genocide and Socio-Political Change: Massacres in Two Rwandan Villages. *African Issues*, 23(2), 18–21.

(2004). Placing Genocide in Context: Research Priorities for the Rwandan Genocide. *Journal of Genocide Research*, 6(1), 29–45.

(2010). *Christianity and Genocide in Rwanda*. Cambridge, UK; New York, NY: Cambridge University Press.

Luft, A. (2015). Toward a Dynamic Theory of Action at the Micro Level of Genocide: Killing, Desistance, and Saving in 1994 Rwanda. *Sociological Theory*, 33(2), 148–172.

Lynch, M. (2007). *The Social Psychology of Genocidal Violence*. Paper presented at the American Political Science Association Annual Convention, Chicago, IL.

Mamdani, M. (1996). *Citizen and Subject: Contemporary Africa and the Legacy of Late Colonialism*. Princeton, NJ: Princeton University Press.

  (2001). *When Victims Become Killers: Colonialism, Nativism and the Genocide in Rwanda*. Oxford: James Currey.

Mann, M. (2005). *The Dark Side of Democracy: Explaining Ethnic Cleansing*. Cambridge: Cambridge University Press.

Maquet, J. J. P. (1961). *The Premise of Inequality in Ruanda; a Study of Political Relations in a Central African Kingdom*. London: Published for the International African Institute by the Oxford University Press.

Marchal, L. (2001). *Rwanda: La descente aux enfers*. Brussels: Éditions Labor.

Marshall, M. G., Gurr, T. R., and Harff, B. (2017). *Political Instability Task Force State Failure Problem Set: Internal Wars and Failures of Governance, 1955–2016*.

Marshall, M. G., Gurr, T. R., and Jaggers, K. (2018). *Polity IV Project: Political Regime Characteristics and Transitions, 1800–2017*.

Marwell, G., Oliver, P. E., and Prahl, R. (1988). Social Networks and Collective Action: A Theory of the Critical Mass III. *American Journal of Sociology*, 94(3), 502–534.

McDoom, O. S. (2010). War and Genocide in Africa's Great Lakes since Independence. In D. B. A. D. Moses (ed.), *Oxford Handbook of Genocide Studies*. Oxford: Oxford University Press.

  (2011). Rwanda's Exit Pathway from Violence: A Strategic Assessment. *World Development Report 2011: Background Paper*. Washington, DC: World Bank.

  (2012). The Psychology of Threat in Intergroup Conflict: Emotions, Rationality, and Opportunity in the Rwandan Genocide. *International Security*, 37(2), 119–155.

  (2013a). Antisocial Capital: A Profile of Rwandan Genocide Perpetrators' Social Networks. *Journal of Conflict Resolution*, 58(5), 865–893.

  (2013b). Who Killed in Rwanda's Genocide? Micro-space, Social Influence and Individual Participation in Intergroup Violence. *Journal of Peace Research*, 50(4), 453–467.

  (2014). Predicting Violence within Genocide: A Model of Elite Competition and Ethnic Segregation from Rwanda. *Political Geography*, 42, 34–45.

Melson, R. (1992). *Revolution and Genocide: On the Origins of the Armenian Genocide and the Holocaust*. Chicago, IL; London: University of Chicago Press.

Melvern, L. (2006). *Conspiracy to Murder: The Rwandan Genocide* (rev. ed.). London; New York, NY: Verso.

Messick, D. M., and Mackie, D. M. (1989). Intergroup Relations. *Annual Review of Psychology, 40*(1), 45–81.

Michalopoulos, S. (2012). The Origins of Ethnolinguistic Diversity. *American Economic Review, 102*(4), 1508–1539.

Midlarsky, M. I. (2005). *The Killing Trap: Genocide in the Twentieth Century*: Cambridge, UK: Cambridge University Press.

Mildt, D. D. (1996). *In the Name of the People: Perpetrators of Genocide in the Reflection of Their Post-War Prosecution in West Germany: The 'Euthanasia' and 'Aktion Reinhard' Trial Cases*. The Hague; London: Martinus Nijhoff.

Milgram, S. (1963). Behavioral Study of Obedience. *Journal of Abnormal and Social Psychology, 67*(4), 371–378.

  (1964). Group Pressure and Action against a Person. *Journal of Abnormal and Social Psychology, 69*(2), 137–143.

  (1974). *Obedience to Authority; an Experimental View*. New York, NY: Harper & Row.

Mironko, C. (2004). *Social and Political Mechanisms of Mass Murder: An Analysis of the Perpetrators in the Rwandan Genocide*. New Haven, C.T.: Yale (PhD thesis).

Mitchell, N. J. (2004). *Agents of Atrocity: Leaders, Followers, and the Violation of Human Rights in Civil War*. New York, NY; Basingstoke: Palgrave Macmillan.

Mitchell, R. C., Morrison, D. G., and Paden, J. N. (1989). *Black Africa: A Comparative Handbook* (2nd ed.). London: Palgrave Macmillan.

Moller, H. (1968). Youth as a Force in the Modern World. *Comparative Studies in Society and History, 10*(3), 237–260.

Mukagasana, Y., and May, P. (1997). *La mort ne veut pas de moi*. Paris: Fixot.

Myrdal, G. (1967). The Soft State in Underdeveloped Countries. *UCLA Law Review, 15*(4), 1118–1134.

Nahimana, F. (1979). *Les principautés Hutus du Rwanda septentrional*. Paper presented at the Colloque de Bujumbura sur la Civilisation Ancienne des Peuples des Grands Lacs, Burundi.

Nduwayo, L. (2002). *Giti et le génocide Rwandais*. Paris: L'Harmattan.

Newbury, C. (1988). *The Cohesion of Oppression: Clientship and Ethnicity in Rwanda, 1860–1960*. New York, NY: Columbia University Press.

Newbury, D. (1994). Ecology and the Politics of Genocide: Rwanda 1994. *Cultural Survival Quarterly, 22*(4), 32–35.

  (1998). Ethnicity and the Politics of History in Rwanda. *Africa Today, 45*(1), 7–24.

Newman, L. S., and Erber, R. (2002). *Understanding Genocide: The Social Psychology of the Holocaust*. New York, NY: Oxford University Press.

Ohlsson, L. (1999). *Environment Scarcity and Conflict: A Study of Malthusian Concern* Gothenburg: University of Gothenburg (PhD thesis).

Olson, J. (1995). Behind the Recent Tragedy in Rwanda. *GeoJournal*, 35(2), 217–222.

Ostrom, E., and Ahn, T. K. (2009). The Meaning of Social Capital and Its Link to Collective Action. In G. T. Svendsen G. L. H. Svendsen (eds.), *Handbook of Social Capital: The Troika of Sociology, Political Science and Economics*. Northampton, MA: Edward Elgar Publishing, 17–35.

Paluck, E. L., Green, S. A., and Green, D. P. (2019). The Contact Hypothesis Re-Evaluated. *Behavioural Public Policy*, 3(2), 129–158.

Paris, R. (1997). Peacebuilding and the Limits of Liberal Internationalism. *International Security*, 22(2), 54–89.

Perliger, A., and Pedazhur, A. (2011). Social Network Analysis in the Study of Terrorism and Political Violence. *PS: Political Science & Politics*, 44(1), 45–50.

Penal Reform International (2005). *Integrated Report on Gacaca Research and Monitoring: Pilot Phase January 2002–December 2004*. London; Kigali: Penal Reform International.

Petersen, R. D. (2002). *Understanding Ethnic Violence: Fear, Hatred, and Resentment in Twentieth-Century Eastern Europe*. Cambridge, UK: Cambridge University Press.

Pfaffenberger, B. (1994). The Structure of Protracted Conflict: The Case of Sri Lanka. *Humboldt Journal of Social Relations*, 20(2), 121–147.

Posen, B. R. (1993). The Security Dilemma and Ethnic Conflict. *Survival*, 35(1), 27–47.

Pottier, J. (2002). *Re-Imagining Rwanda: Conflict, Survival and Disinformation in the Late Twentieth Century*. Cambridge, UK; New York, NY: Cambridge University Press.

Powell, C. J. (2011). *Barbaric Civilization: A Critical Sociology of Genocide*. Montreal: McGill-Queen's University Press.

Power, S. (2002). *A Problem from Hell: America and the Age of Genocide*. New York, NY: Basic Books.

Prunier, G. (1998). *The Rwanda Crisis: History of a Genocide* (rev. ed). London: Hurst.

 (2005). *From Genocide to Continental War: The Congo Conflict and the Crisis of Contemporary Africa*. London: Hurst.

Ramankutty, N., Foley, J. A., Norman, J., and McSweeney, K., (2002). The Global Distribution of Cultivable Lands: Current Patterns and

Sensitivity to Possible Climate Change. *Global Ecology and Biogeography*, 11(5), 377–392.
Rawls, J. (1993). The Law of Peoples. *Critical Inquiry*, 20(1), 36–68.
Rever, J. (2018). *In Praise of Blood*. Toronto: Penguin Random House Canada.
Reyntjens, F. (1985). *Pouvoir et droit au Rwanda: Droit public et évolution Politique, 1916–1973*. Butare: Institut National de Recherche Scientifique.
  (1994). *L'Afrique des grands lacs en crise: Rwanda, Burundi, 1988–1994*. Paris: Karthala.
  (1996). Rwanda: Genocide and Beyond. *Journal of Refugee Studies, 9(3)*, 240–251.
  (2004). Rwanda, Ten Years On: From Genocide to Dictatorship. *African Affairs*, 103(411), 177–210.
  (2009). *The Great African War: Congo and Regional Geopolitics, 1996–2006*. New York, NY: Cambridge University Press.
  (2013). *Political Governance in Post-Genocide Rwanda*. New York, NY: Cambridge University Press.
Richards, P. (1998). *Fighting for the Rain Forest: War, Youth & Resources in Sierra Leone*. Oxford; Portsmouth, N.H.: International African Institute in association with James Currey; Heinemann.
Roeder, P. (2003). *Ethnolinguistic Fractionalization (ELF) Indices, 1961 and 1985*. La Jolla, CA: University of California, San Diego.
Roessler, P. G. (2005). Donor-Induced Democratization and the Privatization of State Violence in Kenya and Rwanda. *Comparative Politics*, 37(2), 207–227.
Ross, M. H. (2007). *Cultural Contestation in Ethnic Conflict*. Cambridge, UK: Cambridge University Press.
Ross, L. and Nisbett, R. E. (2011). *The Person and the Situation: Perspectives of Social Psychology*. London: Pinter & Martin.
Rummel, R. J. (2018). *Death by Government: Genocide and Mass Murder since 1900*: New York, NY: Routledge.
Rusatira, L. (2005). *Rwanda, le droit à l'espoir*. Paris: L'harmattan.
Ruzibiza, A. J., and Vidal, C. (2005). *Rwanda, L'histoire Secrète*. Paris: Éditions du Panama.
Sageman, M. (2004). *Understanding Terror Networks*. Philadelphia, PA: University of Pennsylvania Press.
Scarritt, J. R., and Mozaffar, S. (1999). The Specification of Ethnic Cleavages and Ethnopolitical Groups for the Analysis of Democratic Competition in Contemporary Africa. *Nationalism and Ethnic Politics*, 5(1), 82–117.
Schelling, T. C. (2006). *Micromotives and Macrobehavior* (new ed.). New York, NY; London: W.W. Norton.

Scherrer, C. P. (2002). *Genocide and Crisis in Central Africa: Conflict Roots, Mass Violence, and Regional War*. Westport, CT: Praeger.

Scott, J. C. (1985). *Weapons of the Weak: Everyday Forms of Peasant Resistance*. New Haven, CT; London: Yale University Press.

Scull, N. C., Mbonyingabo, C. D., and Kotb, M. (2016) Transforming Ordinary People into Killers: A Psychosocial Examination of Hutu Participation in the Tutsi Genocide. *Peace and Conflict: Journal of Peace Psychology* 22(4), 334–344.

Sears, D. O., Huddy, L., and Jervis, R. (2003). *Oxford Handbook of Political Psychology*. Oxford; New York, NY: Oxford University Press.

Sémelin, J. (2005). *Purifier et détruire: Usages politiques des massacres et génocides*. Paris: Seuil.

Shaw, M. (2015). *War and Genocide: Organised Killing in Modern Society*. Hoboken, NJ: John Wiley & Sons.

Sherif, M. (1988). *The Robbers Cave Experiment: Intergroup Conflict and Cooperation* (1st Wesleyan ed.). Middletown, CT: Wesleyan University Press.

Shesterinina, A. (2016). Collective Threat Framing and Mobilization in Civil War. *American Political Science Review*, 110(3), 411–427.

Sibomana, A. (1999). *Hope for Rwanda: Conversations with Laure Guilbert and Hervé Deguine*. London; Sterling, V.A.: Pluto Press; Dar es Salaam: Mkuki na Nyota Publishers.

Silva-Leander, S. (2008). On the Danger and Necessity of Democratisation: Trade-Offs between Short-Term Stability and Long-Term Peace in Post-Genocide Rwanda. *Third World Quarterly*, 29(8), 1601–1620.

Simmel, G. (1971). Georg Simmel on Individuality and Social Forms. In D. N. Levine (ed.), *Heritage of Sociology*. Chicago, IL; London: University of Chicago Press.

Skocpol, T. (1979). *States and Social Revolutions: A Comparative Analysis of France, Russia and China*. Cambridge, UK: Cambridge University Press.

Smeulers, A. and Hoex, L. Studying the Microdynamics of the Rwandan Genocide. *British Journal of Criminology* 50(3), 435–454.

Snow, D., Zurcher, L., and Ekland-Olson, S. (1980). Social Networks and Social-Movements: A Microstructural Approach to Differential Recruitment. *American Sociological Review*, 45(5), 787–801.

Snyder, J. L. (2000). *From Voting to Violence: Democratization and Nationalist Conflict*. New York, NY; London: W.W. Norton.

Staub, E. (1989). *The Roots of Evil: The Origins of Genocide and Other Group Violence*. Cambridge, UK: Cambridge University Press.

(2003). *The Psychology of Good and Evil: Why Children, Adults, and Groups Help and Harm Others*. Cambridge, UK; New York, NY: Cambridge University Press.

Stewart, F. (2002). Horizontal Inequalities: A Neglected Dimension of Development. *Queen Elizabeth House Working Paper Series, (81)*.
Straus, S. (2001). Contested Meanings and Conflicting Imperatives: A Conceptual Analysis of Genocide. *Journal of Genocide Research, 3* (3), 349–375.
  (2004). How Many Perpetrators Were There in the Rwandan Genocide? An Estimate. *Journal of Genocide Research*, 6(1), 85–98.
  (2006). *The Order of Genocide: Race, Power, and War in Rwanda*. Ithaca, NY: Cornell University Press.
  (2007). What Is the Relationship between Hate Radio and Violence? Rethinking Rwanda's 'Radio Machete'. *Politics and Society*, 35(4), 609–637.
  (2012). Retreating from the Brink: Theorizing Mass Violence and the Dynamics of Restraint. *Perspectives on Politics*, 10(2), 343–362.
  (2015). *Making and Unmaking Nations: War, Leadership, and Genocide in Modern Africa*. Ithaca, NY: Cornell University Press.
  (2019). The Limits of a Genocide Lens: Violence against Rwandans in the 1990s. *Journal of Genocide Research, (21)*4, 1–21.
Straus, S., and Waldorf, L. (eds.) (2011). *Remaking Rwanda: State Building and Human Rights after Mass Violence*. Madison, WI: University of Wisconsin Press.
Sumner, W. G. (2007). *Folkways: A Study of Mores, Manners, Customs and Morals*. New York, NY: Cosimo.
Tajfel, H. (1982). Social-Psychology of Intergroup Relations. *Annual Review of Psychology, 33*, 1–39.
Tambiah, S. J. (1996). *Leveling Crowds: Ethnonationalist Conflicts and Collective Violence in South Asia*. Berkeley, CA: University of California Press.
Tanner, S. (2011). Towards a Pattern in Mass Violence Participation? An Analysis of Rwandan Perpetrators' Accounts from the 1994 Genocide. *Global Crime*, 12(4), 266–289.
Thompson, A. (2007). *The Media and the Rwanda Genocide*. London; Ann Arbour, M.I.: Pluto Press; Kampala: Foundation Publishers; Ottawa: International Development Research Centre.
Thomson, S. (2013). *Whispering Truth to Power: Everyday Resistance to Reconciliation in Postgenocide Rwanda*. Madison; WI: University of Wisconsin Press.
Tilly, C. (2003). *The Politics of Collective Violence*. Cambridge, UK; New York, NY: Cambridge University Press.
Tönnies, F. (1940). *Fundamental Concepts of Sociology (Gemeinschaft Und Gesellschaft)*. New York, NY: American Book Company.

Turner, T. (2007). *The Congo Wars: Conflict, Myth, and Reality*. New York, NY; London: Zed Books.

United Nations (2010). *Report of the Mapping Exercise Documenting the Most Serious Violations of Human Rights and International Humanitarian Law Committed within the Territory of the Democratic Republic of the Congo between March 1993 and June 2003*. Geneva: Office of the High Commissioner for Human Rights.

United Nations Security Council (1994a). *Resolution 912* New York, NY.

(1994b). *Resolution 918*. New York, NY.

(1994c). *Resolution 925*. New York, NY.

Urdal, H. (2006). A Clash of Generations? Youth Bulges and Political Violence. *International Studies Quarterly*, 50(3), 607–629.

Uvin, P. (1996). Tragedy in Rwanda: The Political Ecology of Conflict. *Environment: Science and Policy for Sustainable Development*, 38(3), 7–29.

(1998). *Aiding Violence: The Development Enterprise in Rwanda*. West Hartford, CT: Kumarian Press.

(2001). Reading the Rwandan Genocide. *International Studies Review*, 3(3), 75–99.

Valentino, B. (2004). *Final Solutions: Mass Killing and Genocide in the Twentieth Century*. Ithaca, NY: Cornell University Press.

Valentino, B., Huth, P., and Balch-Lindsay, D. (2004). 'Draining the Sea': Mass Killing and Guerrilla Warfare. *International Organization*, 58(2), 375–407.

Vansina, J. (2004). *Antecedents to Modern Rwanda: The Nyiginya Kingdom*. Madison, WI: University of Wisconsin Press.

Varshney, A. (2001). Ethnic Conflict and Civil Society: India and Beyond. *World Politics*, 53(3), 362–398.

Verpoorten, M. (2005). The Death Toll of the Rwandan Genocide: A Detailed Analysis for Gikongoro Province. *Population*, 4(60), 331–367.

(2012a). The Intensity of the Rwandan Genocide: Measures from the Gacaca Records. *Peace Economics, Peace Science and Public Policy* 18(1), 1–26.

(2012b). Leave None to Claim the Land: A Malthusian Catastrophe in Rwanda? *Journal of Peace Research*, 49(4), 547–563.

(2014). Why Claim That 200,000 Tutsi Died in the Genocide Is Wrong. *African Arguments:* www.africanarguments.org

Verschave, F.-X. (1994). *Complicité de génocide?: La politique de la France au Rwanda*. Paris: Éditions La Découverte.

Verwimp, P. (2003a). The Political Economy of Coffee, Dictatorship, and Genocide. *European Journal of Political Economy*, 19(2), 161–181.

(2003). Testing the Double-Genocide Thesis for Central and Southern Rwanda. *Journal of Conflict Resolution, 47*(4), 423–442.

(2004). Death and Survival During the 1994 Genocide in Rwanda. *Population Studies: A Journal of Demography, 58*(2), 233–245.

(2005). An Economic Profile of Peasant Perpetrators of Genocide: Micro-Level Evidence from Rwanda. *Journal of Development Economics, 77*(2), 297–323.

Vogt, M., Bormann, N.-C., Rüegger, S., Cederman, L.-E, Hunziker, P., and Girardin, L. (2015). Integrating Data on Ethnicity, Geography, and Conflict: The Ethnic Power Relations Data Set Family. *Journal of Conflict Resolution, 59*(7), 1327–1342.

Wagner, M. D. (1998). All the Bourgmestre's Men: Making Sense of Genocide in Rwanda. *Africa Today, 45*(1), 25–36.

Waldorf, L. (2006). Mass Justice for Mass Atrocities: Re-Thinking Local Justice as Transitional Justice. *Temple Law Review, 79*(1), 1–87.

Walker, I. and Smith, H. J. (2002). *Relative Deprivation: Specification, Development, and Integration.* Cambridge, UK; New York, NY: Cambridge University Press.

Waller, J. (2002). *Becoming Evil How Ordinary People Commit Genocide and Mass Killing.* Oxford; New York, NY: Oxford University Press

Walzer, M. (2006). *Just and Unjust Wars: A Moral Argument with Historical Illustrations* (4th ed.). New York, NY: Basic Books; London: Perseus.

Wayman, F. and Tago, A. (2010). Explaining the Onset of Mass Killing, 1949–87. *Journal of Peace Research, 47*(1), 3–13.

Weber, M. (ed.) (1978). *Economy and Society: An Outline of Interpretive Sociology.* Berkeley, CA: University of California Press.

Weisband, E. (2017). *The Macabresque: Human Violation and Hate in Genocide, Mass Atrocity and Enemy-Making.* New York, NY: Oxford University Press.

Weitz, E. D. (2005). *A Century of Genocide: Utopias of Race and Nation.* Princeton, NJ; Woodstock: Princeton University Press.

Williams, T. A. (2017). *The Complexity of Evil: Modelling Perpetration in Genocide.* Marburg: University of Marburg (PhD thesis).

Winter, J. (2003). Under Cover of War: The Armenian Genocide in the Context of Total War. In R. Gellately and B. Kiernan (eds.), *The Specter of Genocide: Mass Murder in Historical Perspective.* New York, NY: Cambridge University Press, 189–214.

Wood, E. J. (2008). The Social Processes of Civil War: The Wartime Transformation of Social Networks. *Annual Review of Political Science, 11*, 539–561.

World Bank. (2003). *African Development Indicators*. Washington, DC: World Bank.
Wucherpfennig, J., Weidmann, N. B., Girardin, L., Cederman, L.-E., and Wimmer, A. (2011). Politically Relevant Ethnic Groups across Space and Time: Introducing the GeoEPR Dataset. *Conflict Management and Peace Science* 28(5), 423–437.
Yanagizawa-Drott, D. (2014). Propaganda and Conflict: Evidence from the Rwandan Genocide. *The Quarterly Journal of Economics*, 129(4), 1947–1994.
Zakaria, F. (2001, October 15). Why Do They Hate Us? The Politics of Rage. *Newsweek*, 22–40.
Zartman, I. W. (1995). Introduction: Posing the Problem of State Collapse. In *Collapsed States: The Disintegration and Restoration of Legitimate Authority*. Boulder, CO: Lynne Rienner Publishers.
Zimbardo, P. G. (2007). *The Lucifer Effect: How Good People Turn Evil*. London: Rider.

Index

Abakiga 208, 254
Abakombozi 129
Abayanduga 254
Abyssinia 55, 160
Agency
 elite 24, 57, 183, 213–214
 individual 24, 250, 334, 384
Akayesu, Jean-Paul 209
Akazu 202
Alien, Tutsi as 19, 55, 98, 312, 371
APROSOMA (Association pour la Promotion Sociale de la Masse) 57
Arendt, Hannah 282
Arusha Accords 170–171, 173, 201
Asch, Solomon 25, 383
Assassination, Habyarimana's
 causal significance of 179
 effects of 184
 responsibility for 201
Authority
 as perpetrator rationale 339–340
 perpetrator perceptions of 320
 state symbolic 258–266

Bagogwe people 141, 170
Bagosora, Théoneste 148, 165, 185–187, 190–191, 202, 204, 331
Bahutu manifesto 57, 147
Baseline, Rwanda's extraordinary 45–72, 92–94, 126, 362–363, 377–378
Belgium 3, 53–57, 194
Bipolarity, ethnic 65–66
Bizimana, Augustin 135, 190
Booh-Booh, Jacques-Roger 185, 196–197
Boundaries, continuity of 51, 258, 263–264
Bruguière, Jean-Louis 201, 203
Burgomasters 208–214, 236, 263, 277, 369
Burnet, Jennie 6

Burundi 60, 102–104, 132, 378
Butare prefecture 118, 134–138, 213, 215–227, 234, 292
Bystander effect 26–27
Byumba prefecture 130, 170, 288

Catholic Church 152–155, 257–258
Causal mechanisms 13–28, 79, 306, 354, 372, 382
CDR (Coalition pour la Défense de la République) 128, 130, 133, 139–140
Chad 53
Chirot, Daniel 20, 24, 386
Chrétien, Jean-Pierre 87, 128, 146
Civil society, role of 127, 164, 172, 255–258, 373
Civil war
 limitations as explanation of genocide 116–117
 links with genocide 79–80
 radicalizing effect of 93–95
Clans 60, 76, 254–255
Cleavage, social 141, 202
Clientelism 64, 126, 253–256, 354
Coercion 250, 278, 320–322, 334
Colonial legacy 54, 371
Conformist perpetrator 340–341, 360, 370, 381
Conformity 322
Constraints, external
 examples of domestic and international 164–165
 to contain extremism 164
Contact theory 70, 114, 245
Contagion 33–35, 69, 215, 244–246
Contestation, political
 between moderates and extremists 165–167
 inter- and intra-group 171–172

407

Continuum, mobilization 357–361
Coup
  as motivation for Habyarimana's assassination 179, 202
  by Habyarimana in 1973 4, 150
Critical mass 183, 235, 359–360
Cultural homogeneity 66, 258, 265, 275
Cyangugu prefecture 213

Dallaire, Roméo 185, 191, 193, 196–197, 199
De-escalation *See* escalation
Dehumanization 19, 382
Democratization *See* liberalization, political
Demography 61–68
  role of 16, 114, 244–247, 265–266, 275, 356
Deprivation, role of 17–18, 305–310
Des Forges, Alison 7, 153, 196, 290, 296
Differential selection 357–360, 370, 373, 383
Disloyalty, ethnic 74, 106–111, 120
Disposition, for violence 25, 281–283, 326–330, 335, 357, 382
Distrust
  ethnic 139, 206
  role of 163, 284
Double genocide, claims of 295–297
DPKO (Department of Peacekeeping Operations) 193, 196, 199
DRC (Democratic Republic of Congo) 325, 377, 381

Ecological scarcity 16, 70, 305
Emotions, causal role of 386–388
Enemy, identification of 130
Englebert, Pierre 262, 264
Entrepreneur 34, 140, 183, 369
  ethnic 138, 174, 329
  political 125, 138, 142, 174, 329
Escalation
  during genocide period 188–189
  during pre-genocide period 167–173
Essentialism, ethnic 147–150
Ethnic diversity 28, 66, 266, 275
Ethnic dominance 67, 265
Ethnic settlement *See* settlement pattern, ethnic

Ethnicity
  causal role of 372
  theories of violence and 311–312
Ethnicization 95–104, 141, 149, 175
Ethnocracy 29, 59, 127, 252, 362
Extermination 112–113, 120
Extremism, ethnic
  definition of 163–164
  escalation of 167–169
Extremist, ethnic *See* extremism, ethnic

Fear
  as factor for participation 317
  theories of violence and 14–15
Feudalism 98, 102, 148–150, 157, 259
Framing theory 163–164, 197, 384–386
France 195, 198
Fujii, Lee-Ann 84, 282, 342, 349

Gacaca
  as a data source 41–42, 285–286
  as transitional justice 39, 285
Gasana, James 130, 132, 165
Gatsinzi, Marcel 185, 187, 191, 200
Gemeinschaft, concept of 356
Genocide
  definition of 13
  theories of 13–27
Geography, role of 61–71, 208, 230, 244–247, 262, 272–275, 342–348
Gersony report 296
Gikongoro prefecture 213, 215–216
Gitarama prefecture 118, 128, 207, 213
Goldhagen, Daniel 19
Guichaoua, André 170, 190, 222

Habineza, Jean-Marie 135, 137, 216–221, 236
Habyalimana, Jean-Baptiste 136, 216, 221, 236
Habyarimana, Juvénal 60
  assassination of 201
  ideology of 150
Hamitic hypothesis 55
Hardliners *See* extremism
Harelimana, Gervais 139, 174, 229
Harff, Barbara 73, 79
Hatzfeld, Jean 6
Hinton, Alex 333, 382

Index

Horowitz, Donald 23
Hutu *See* Tutsi

Ibitero [attack groups] 221, 341
Ibuka [survivors' organisation] 118
Ibyitso [accomplices] 109, 317
ICTR (International Criminal Tribunal for Rwanda) 295
Identity, theories of violence and 18–19
Ideology
  definition of 146
  role of 384–386
Impunity, effect of 26, 173, 180, 279, 339
Impuzamugambi 129, 139
Ingroup policing 241–244, 322, 334
Inkotanyi 92, 95
Institutional continuity 262–263
Institutions
  as conflict mediator 124
  as constraint on extremism 164
Integration, ethnic 183, 210–215
Interahamwe 16, 108, 129, 179, 206–207, 229
Interspersion, ethnic *See* settlement pattern
Intervention, international 170, 173, 193–201
Inyenzi 95, 98, 109, 120, 149, 156, 176

Kabegema, Ferdinand 185
Kajilijeli, Juvénal 206–207
Kambanda, Jean 166, 186, 209, 265
Kangura 21, 87, 139
Kanyamiheto sector 141, 232
Karamira, Froduald 100, 131–132, 166
Karemera, Édouard 166, 185
Karimunda, Emmanuel 137–138, 174, 227, 235, 240
Kavaruganda, Joseph 173, 188
Kayibanda, Grégoire 3, 58–59, 152, 257, 277
  ideology of 147–150
Kibungo prefecture 195
Kigali 68, 88, 170, 186, 191–196, 200, 262, 274
Kimonyo, Jean-Paul 7, 52
Kinigi commune 116, 140, 230, 235
Kinship ties 32, 60, 202, 251, 254, 350, 354
Kinyamateka 154, 257

Krain, Matthew 73, 79
Kubwimana, Silas 208–209
Kuperman, Alan 27, 198, 200, 375

Legitimacy
  of the state 67, 251–252, 258–266, 321
  of the violence 320
  of Tutsi status 160
Lemarchand, René 57, 263
Levene, Mark 384
Liberalization, political
  cross-ethnic support and 142
  effects of 127–134
  mechanisms behind 142–145
Longman, Timothy 257, 373
Loyalty *See* disloyalty, ethnic

Malthusian risk 16, 64, 305, 310, 356
Mamdani, Mahmood 54, 262
Mann, Michael 20, 281
Maraba commune 134, 215
Masculinity, role in violence 302–305, 337
Mbonampeka, Stanislas 131, 166
Mbonuyumutwa, Dominique 58
MDR (Mouvement Démocratique Républicain) 128, 135, 140, 155, 186, 208
  internal split 132, 162, 166
  support for 142
Melson, Robert 79
Melvern, Linda 6
Milgram, Stanley 25, 282, 321, 330, 360
Mironko, Charles 282
Mobilization
  amplifiers of 244–247
  micro-mechanics of 234–244
Moderate, ethnic *See* extremism, ethnic
Motivation *See* motives
Motives, perpetrator
  changing 340–342
  multiple 331–333
Mpiranya, Protais 179, 190
MRNDD (Mouvement Révolutionnaire National pour le Développement (et la Démocratie) 77, 139–140, 185, 213, 255
  internal split 128–133, 202
  support for 142

Mugaragu 54, 102
Mugenzi, Justin 133, 156, 166
Mugesera, Léon 130, 165
Mukamira sector 206, 227
Mukingo commune 205–207, 215
Multiplex ties *See* social ties
Murego, Donat 131, 166
Mutovu cell 97, 105, 138–140, 174, 227–230
Mutsinzi report 201, 203
Mwami 51–54, 157–160, 253, 259–262
Mwendo cell 134–137, 215–223, 240–241, 244
Myths, causal role of 20–21, 316–320

Narratives, causal role of 20–21, 68, 98, 260, 316
Nationalism 20–21, 108–111, 147, 311–316
Ndadaye, Melchior 102
  assassination of 102–104, 132, 166
Ndasginwa, Landoald 166
Ndindiliyimana, Augustin 185, 191
Neo-patrimonialism 59, 174, 179, 251, 254
Ngirumpatse, Matthieu 128, 132, 166, 185–186, 202
Ngulinzira, Boniface 78, 130–131
Nkuli commune 116, 138–139, 206–207, 227
Ntabakuze, Aloys 190
Ntaryamira, Cyprien 184
Nyabarongo river 165, 215
Nyiginya kingdom 51
Nyumbakumi 276, 292
Nyundo diocese 153
Nzirorera, Joseph 132, 166, 185, 202, 206
Nzuwonemeye, François-Xavier 190

Obedience, role of 24, 268, 279, 321, 384
Opportunist perpetrator 326–329, 336–338, 340, 360
Opportunity
  as a rationale for violence 335–338
  political created by assassination 31–34, 179–184
  political created by liberalization 123–125

Pacifists 147, 152, 326–329, 381
PARMEHUTU (Parti du Mouvement de l'Emancipation Hutu) 57–58, 142, 148, 155, 254
Patrimonial *See* neo-patrimonialism
PDC (Parti Démocrate Chrétien) 77, 145, 166
Peer pressure 64, 322
Perpetrator
  definition of 298–299
  estimate of 286–287
PL (Parti Libéral) 128, 131, 136, 155
  internal split 133, 162, 166
Pluralization, political 124, 145–162
Political culture 60, 125–126, 174, 251
Political opportunity structure 31
Politicide 73, 295
Population density 64, 214, 244, 356
Poux, Nathalie 201, 203
Power struggle 30–34, 180, 184–192, 211, 379–381
Power vacuum 138, 179, 184
Pre-disposition *See* disposition
Prejudice, ethnic 18–19, 70, 311–312
Prunier, Gérard 54, 166, 290–291, 384
PSD (Parti Social Démocrate) 128, 155
  internal split 133, 162, 166
  support for 142

Racialization of identities 371
Racism 19, 21, 175, 312–315
RADER (Rassemblement Démocratique Rwandais) 57
Radicalization
  as consequence of violence 118
  definition of 381
  indicators of 74
Radio Muhubura 88, 90, 156
Radio Rwanda 87, 156, 172, 256
Ranked system, ethnically 28, 52–61, 65–67, 72
RANU (Rwandese Alliance for National Unity) 75
Rationales, perpetrator 331–333
Rationality, role of 18, 356, 386
Reconciliation, inter-ethnic 39, 154, 284, 297
Refugees 231
Refusenik *See* pacifists

Index

Rekeraho, Emmanuel 134–137, 174, 216–222, 235, 240–241, 355
Relational forces, role of 357–360
Revolution, Hutu social 3, 29, 150, 257–261
   effects of 59–61, 75, 148, 258, 261, 263
   memory of 93, 260, 315, 336
   origins of 56–61, 148, 252
   role of 98–103
Reyntjens, Filip 127, 203, 296
RPF (Rwandan Patriotic Front)
   killings by 295–297
   military campaign 75–79
   political strategy 131
RTLM (Radio Télévision Libre des Mille Collines)
   causal role of 120–121
   listenership 88–90
Rudahigwa, *Mwami* 54, 261
Ruginga cell 97, 105, 140–141, 230–234
Ruhengeri prefecture 138–141, 170, 205, 227–234, 288, 292
Rusatira, Léon 191
Rusindana, Godefroid 195
Rutaremara, Tito 100
Ruzibiza, Abdul 203
Rwabugiri, *Mwami* 51–52
Rwigyema, Fred 76, 166

Sadism 341
Security
   as perpetrator rationales 338–339
   theories of participation and 316–317
   threat-based theories of genocide and 79–83
Security Council, United Nations 132–133, 196–200
Security dilemma 15, 300, 317
Security threat 74, 79–122, 149
Segregation, ethnic 213, 378
Sémelin, Jacques 384
Sendashonga, Seth 191
Settlement pattern, ethnic 34, 69–70, 245, 343–349
Sexual violence 5
Shiyarambere, Théophile 137, 223, 225, 236
Shyanda commune 137, 223, 236

Sibomana, André 154, 257, 354
Sindikubwabo, Théodore 187, 217–221, 225
Situational forces 25–26, 281–283, 334–335, 342–348, 357–360
Social capital 34, 355
Social cohesion 63, 213, 356, 369
Social connections *See* social networks
Social hierarchy 28
Social networks 63, 349–357, 360
Social stratification 53, 55, 299
Social ties *See* social networks
   multiplex 35, 63, 354, 356
Socialization 348, 354
South Africa 55, 360
State autonomy 253, 278
State capacity 321
Staub, Ervin 26, 306, 382
Straus, Scott 282, 299, 372–373, 375
Structural violence 305, 310
Surveillance, by state 64, 245, 273

Taba commune 207–209, 215
Tamba cell 137–138, 174, 223–227, 240, 245
Tanzania 39, 75, 112, 170
Tare sector 134, 343–356
Tipping point model 357–360
Trévidic, Marc 201, 203
Turquoise, Opération 195, 200
Tutsi
   origins of 51–53, 312
   significance of 52–53
Twagirumungu, Faustin 132

Ubuhake 54, 102, 157
Uganda 27, 30, 76, 78, 88, 169, 203
Ukubohoza 129
Umuganda 60, 216, 276, 321, 339
Umunyamuryango 257
UN (United Nations) 4, 56, 185–186, 188, 296, 380
UNAMIR (United Nations Assistance Mission for Rwanda) 132–133, 170, 173, 185–186, 193, 198–201
UNAR (Union Nationale Rwandaise) 57–58
Uvin, Peter 160, 373
Uwilingiyimana, Agathe 108, 132–133, 156, 166, 185–186

Valentino, Benjamin 248, 284, 385
Vansina, Jan 51–52, 268
Verpoorten, Marijke 17, 290–291, 376
Verwimp, Philip 296, 310
Victims, estimate of 293–295
Vidal, Claudine 6, 295

Waldorf, Lars 295
Weitz, Eric 384

Youth bulge 16, 303

Zaire *See* DRC
Zimbardo, Philip 25, 282, 330, 383

African Studies Series

1. *City Politics: A Study of Leopoldville, 1962–63*, J. S. La Fontaine
2. *Studies in Rural Capitalism in West Africa*, Polly Hill
3. *Land Policy in Buganda*, Henry W. West
4. *The Nigerian Military: A Sociological Analysis of Authority and Revolt, 1960–67*, Robin Luckham
5. *The Ghanaian Factory Worker: Industrial Man in Africa*, Margaret Peil
6. *Labour in the South African Gold Mines*, Francis Wilson
7. *The Price of Liberty: Personality and Politics in Colonial Nigeria*, Kenneth W. J. Post and George D. Jenkins
8. *Subsistence to Commercial Farming in Present-Day Buganda: An Economic and Anthropological Survey*, Audrey I. Richards, Fort Sturrock, and Jean M. Fortt (eds.)
9. *Dependence and Opportunity: Political Change in Ahafo*, John Dunn and A. F. Robertson
10. *African Railwaymen: Solidarity and Opposition in an East African Labour Force*, R. D. Grillo
11. *Islam and Tribal Art in West Africa*, René A. Bravmann
12. *Modern and Traditional Elites in the Politics of Lagos*, P. D. Cole
13. *Asante in the Nineteenth Century: The Structure and Evaluation of a Political Order*, Ivor Wilks
14. *Culture, Tradition and Society in the West African Novel*, Emmanuel Obiechina
15. *Saints and Politicians*, Donal B. Cruise O'Brien
16. *The Lions of Dagbon: Political Change in Northern Ghana*, Martin Staniland
17. *Politics of Decolonization: Kenya Europeans and the Land Issue 1960–1965*, Gary B. Wasserman
18. *Muslim Brotherhoods in the Nineteenth-Century Africa*, B. G. Martin
19. *Warfare in the Sokoto Caliphate: Historical and Sociological Perspectives*, Joseph P. Smaldone
20. *Liberia and Sierra Leone: An Essay in Comparative Politics*, Christopher Clapham
21. *Adam Kok's Griquas: A Study in the Development of Stratification in South Africa*, Robert Ross
22. *Class, Power and Ideology in Ghana: The Railwaymen of Sekondi*, Richard Jeffries
23. *West African States: Failure and Promise*, John Dunn (ed.)

24. *Afrikaaners of the Kalahari: White Minority in a Black State*, Margo Russell and Martin Russell
25. *A Modern History of Tanganyika*, John Iliffe
26. *A History of African Christianity 1950–1975*, Adrian Hastings
27. *Slaves, Peasants and Capitalists in Southern Angola, 1840–1926*, W. G. Clarence-Smith
28. *The Hidden Hippopotamus: Reappraised in African History: The Early Colonial Experience in Western Zambia*, Gywn Prins
29. *Families Divided: The Impact of Migrant Labour in Lesotho*, Colin Murray
30. *Slavery, Colonialism and Economic Growth in Dahomey, 1640–1960*, Patrick Manning
31. *Kings, Commoners and Concessionaries: The Evolution of Dissolution of the Nineteenth-Century Swazi State*, Philip Bonner
32. *Oral Poetry and Somali Nationalism: The Case of Sayid Mahammad 'Abdille Hasan*, Said S. Samatar
33. *The Political Economy of Pondoland 1860–1930*, William Beinart
34. *Volkskapitalisme: Class, Capitals and Ideology in the Development of Afrikaner Nationalism, 1934–1948*, Dan O'Meara
35. *The Settler Economies: Studies in the Economic History of Kenya and Rhodesia 1900–1963*, Paul Mosely
36. *Transformations in Slavery: A History of Slavery in Africa*, 1st edition, Paul Lovejoy
37. *Amilcar Cabral: Revolutionary Leadership and People's War*, Patrick Chabal
38. *Essays on the Political Economy of Rural Africa*, Robert H. Bates
39. *Ijeshas and Nigerians: The Incorporation of a Yoruba Kingdom, 1890s-1970s*, J. D. Y. Peel
40. *Black People and the South African War, 1899–1902*, Peter Warwick
41. *A History of Niger 1850–1960*, Finn Fuglestad
42. *Industrialisation and Trade Union Organization in South Africa, 1924–1955*, Stephen Ellis
43. *The Rising of the Red Shawls: A Revolt in Madagascar 1895–1899*, Stephen Ellis
44. *Slavery in Dutch South Africa*, Nigel Worden
45. *Law, Custom and Social Order: The Colonial Experience in Malawi and Zambia*, Martin Chanock
46. *Salt of the Desert Sun: A History of Salt Production and Trade in the Central Sudan*, Paul E. Lovejoy

47. *Marrying Well: Marriage, Status and Social Change among the Educated Elite in Colonial Lagos*, Kristin Mann
48. *Language and Colonial Power: The Appropriation of Swahili in the Former Belgian Congo, 1880–1938*, Johannes Fabian
49. *The Shell Money of the Slave Trade*, Jan Hogendorn and Marion Johnson
50. *Political Domination in Africa*, Patrick Chabal
51. *The Southern Marches of Imperial Ethiopia: Essays in History and Social Anthropology*, Donald Donham and Wendy James
52. *Islam and Urban Labor in Northern Nigeria: The Making of a Muslim Working Class*, Paul M. Lubeck
53. *Horn and Crescent: Cultural Change and Traditional Islam on the East African Coast, 800–1900*, Randall L. Pouwels
54. *Capital and Labour on the Kimberley Diamond Fields, 1871–1890*, Robert Vicat Turrell
55. *National and Class Conflict in the Horn of Africa*, John Markakis
56. *Democracy and Prebendal Politics in Nigeria: The Rise and Fall of the Second Republic*, Richard A. Joseph
57. *Entrepreneurs and Parasites: The Struggle for Indigenous Capitalism in Zaire*, Janet MacGaffey
58. *The African Poor: A History*, John Iliffe
59. *Palm Oil and Protest: An Economic History of the Ngwa Region, South-Eastern Nigeria, 1800–1980*, Susan M. Martin
60. *France and Islam in West Africa, 1860–1960*, Christopher Harrison
61. *Transformation and Continuity in Revolutionary Ethiopia*, Christopher Clapham
62. *Prelude to the Mahdiyya: Peasants and Traders in the Shendi Region, 1821–1885*, Anders Bjorkelo
63. *Wa and the Wala: Islam and Polity in Northwestern Ghana*, Ivor Wilks
64. *H.C. Bankole-Bright and Politics in Colonial Sierra Leone, 1919–1958*, Akintola Wyse
65. *Contemporary West African States*, Donal Cruise O'Brien, John Dunn, and Richard Rathbone (eds.)
66. *The Oromo of Ethiopia: A History, 1570–1860*, Mohammed Hassen
67. *Slavery and African Life: Occidental, Oriental, and African Slave Trades*, Patrick Manning
68. *Abraham Esau's War: A Black South African War in the Cape, 1899–1902*, Bill Nasson

69. *The Politics of Harmony: Land Dispute Strategies in Swaziland*, Laurel L. Rose
70. *Zimbabwe's Guerrilla War: Peasant Voices*, Norma J. Kriger
71. *Ethiopia: Power and Protest: Peasant Revolts in the Twentieth-Century*, Gebru Tareke
72. *White Supremacy and Black Resistance in Pre-Industrial South Africa: The Making of the Colonial Order in the Eastern Cape, 1770–1865*, Clifton C. Crais
73. *The Elusive Granary: Herder, Farmer, and State in Northern Kenya*, Peter D. Little
74. *The Kanyok of Zaire: An Institutional and Ideological History to 1895*, John C. Yoder
75. *Pragmatism in the Age of Jihad: The Precolonial State of Bundu*, Michael A. Gomez
76. *Slow Death for Slavery: The Course of Abolition in Northern Nigeria, 1897–1936*, Paul E. Lovejoy and Jan S. Hogendorn
77. *West African Slavery and Atlantic Commerce: The Senegal River Valley, 1700–1860*, James F. Searing
78. *A South African Kingdom: The Pursuit of Security in the Nineteenth-Century Lesotho*, Elizabeth A. Elredge
79. *State and Society in Pre-colonial Asante*, T. C. McCaskie
80. *Islamic Society and State Power in Senegal: Disciples and Citizens in Fatick*, Leonardo A. Villalon
81. *Ethnic Pride and Racial Prejudice in Victorian Cape Town: Group Identity and Social Practice*, Vivian Bickford-Smith
82. *The Eritrean Struggle for Independence: Domination, Resistance and Nationalism, 1941–1993*, RuthIyob
83. *Corruption and State Politics in Sierra Leone*, William Reno
84. *The Culture of Politics in Modern Kenya*, Angelique Haugerud
85. *Africans: The History of a Continent*, 1st edition, John Iliffe
86. *From Slave Trade to 'Legitimate' Commerce: The Commercial Transition in Nineteenth-Century West Africa*, Robin Law (ed.)
87. *Leisure and Society in Colonial Brazzaville*, Phyllis Martin
88. *Kingship and State: The Buganda Dynasty*, Christopher Wrigley
89. *Decolonialization and African Life: The Labour Question in French and British Africa*, Frederick Cooper
90. *Misreading the African Landscape: Society and Ecology in an African Forest-Savannah Mosaic*, James Fairhead, and Melissa Leach
91. *Peasant Revolution in Ethiopia: The Tigray People's Liberation Front, 1975–1991*, John Young
92. *Senegambia and the Atlantic Slave Trade*, Boubacar Barry

93. *Commerce and Economic Change in West Africa: The Oil Trade in the Nineteenth Century*, Martin Lynn
94. *Slavery and French Colonial Rule in West Africa: Senegal, Guinea and Mali*, Martin A. Klein
95. *East African Doctors: A History of the Modern Profession*, John Iliffe
96. *Middlemen of the Cameroons Rivers: The Duala and Their Hinterland, c.1600–1960*, Ralph Derrick, Ralph A. Austen, and Jonathan Derrick
97. *Masters and Servants on the Cape Eastern Frontier, 1760–1803*, Susan Newton-King
98. *Status and Respectability in the Cape Colony, 1750–1870: A Tragedy of Manners*, Robert Ross
99. *Slaves, Freedmen and Indentured Laborers in Colonial Mauritius*, Richard B. Allen
100. *Transformations in Slavery: A History of Slavery in Africa*, 2nd edition, Paul E. Lovejoy
101. *The Peasant Cotton Revolution in West Africa: Cote d'Ivoire, 1880–1995*, Thomas E. Basset
102. *Re-imagining Rwanda: Conflict, Survival and Disinformation in the Late Twentieth Century*, Johan Pottier
103. *The Politics of Evil: Magic, State Power and the Political Imagination in South Africa*, Clifton Crais
104. *Transforming Mozambique: The Politics of Privatization, 1975–2000*, M. Anne Pitcher
105. *Guerrilla Veterans in Post-War Zimbabwe: Symbolic and Violent Politics, 1980–1987*, Norma J. Kriger
106. *An Economic History of Imperial Madagascar, 1750–1895: The Rise and Fall of an Island Empire*, Gwyn Campbell
107. *Honour in African History*, John Iliffe
108. *Africans: A History of a Continent*, 2nd edition, John Iliffe
109. *Guns, Race, and Power in Colonial South Africa*, William Kelleher Storey
110. *Islam and Social Change in French West Africa: History of an Emancipatory Community*, Sean Hanretta
111. *Defeating Mau Mau, Creating Kenya: Counterinsurgency, Civil War and Decolonization*, Daniel Branch
112. *Christianity and Genocide in Rwanda*, Timothy Longman
113. *From Africa to Brazil: Culture, Identity, and an African Slave Trade, 1600–1830*, Walter Hawthorne
114. *Africa in the Time of Cholera: A History of Pandemics from 1817 to the Present*, Myron Echenberg

115. *A History of Race in Muslim West Africa, 1600–1960*, Bruce S. Hall
116. *Witchcraft and Colonial Rule in Kenya, 1900–1955*, Katherine Luongo
117. *Transformations in Slavery: A History of Slavery in Africa*, 3rd edition, Paul E. Lovejoy
118. *The Rise of the Trans-Atlantic Slave Trade in Western Africa, 1300–1589*, Toby Green
119. *Party Politics and Economic Reform in Africa's Democracies*, M. Anne Pitcher
120. *Smugglers and Saints of the Sahara: Regional Connectivity in the Twentieth Century*, Judith Scheele
121. *Cross-Cultural Exchange in the Atlantic World: Angola and Brazil during the Era of the Slave Trade*, Roquinaldo Ferreira
122. *Ethnic Patriotism and the East African Revival*, Derek Peterson
123. *Black Morocco: A History of Slavery and Islam*, Chouki El Hamel
124. *An African Slaving Port and the Atlantic World: Benguela and Its Hinterland*, Mariana Candido
125. *Making Citizens in Africa: Ethnicity, Gender, and National Identity in Ethiopia*, Lahra Smith
126. *Slavery and Emancipation in Islamic East Africa: From Honor to Respectability*, Elisabeth McMahon
127. *A History of African Motherhood: The Case of Uganda, 700–1900*, Rhiannon Stephens
128. *The Borders of Race in Colonial South Africa: The Kat River Settlement, 1829–1856*, Robert Ross
129. *From Empires to NGOs in the West African Sahel: The Road to Nongovernmentality*, Gregory Mann
130. *Dictators and Democracy in African Development: The Political Economy of Good Governance in Nigeria*, A. Carl LeVan
131. *Water, Civilization and Power in Sudan: The Political Economy of Military-Islamist State Building*, Harry Verhoeven
132. *The Fruits of Freedom in British Togoland: Literacy, Politics and Nationalism, 1914–2014*, Kate Skinner
133. *Political Thought and the Public Sphere in Tanzania: Freedom, Democracy and Citizenship in the Era of Decolonization*, Emma Hunter
134. *Political Identity and Conflict in Central Angola, 1975–2002*, Justin Pearce
135. *From Slavery to Aid: Politics, Labour, and Ecology in the Nigerian Sahel, 1800–2000*, Benedetta Rossi

136. *National Liberation in Postcolonial Southern Africa: A Historical Ethnography of SWAPO's Exile Camps*, Christian A. Williams
137. *Africans: A History of a Continent*, 3rd edition, John Iliffe
138. *Colonial Buganda and the End of Empire: Political Thought and Historical Imagination in Africa*, Jonathon L. Earle
139. *The Struggle over State Power in Zimbabwe: Law and Politics since 1950*, George Karekwaivanane
140. *Transforming Sudan: Decolonisation, Economic Development and State Formation*, Alden Young
141. *Colonizing Consent: Rape and Governance in South Africa's Eastern Cape*, Elizabeth Thornberry
142. *The Value of Disorder: Autonomy, Prosperity and Plunder in the Chadian Sahara*, Julien Brachet and Judith Scheele
143. *The Politics of Poverty: Policy-Making and Development in Rural Tanzania*, Felicitas Becker
144. *Boundaries, Communities, and State-Making in West Africa: The Centrality of the Margins*, Paul Nugent
145. *Politics and Violence in Burundi: The Language of Truth in an Emerging State*, Aidan Russell
146. *Power and the Presidency in Kenya: The Jomo Kenyatta Years*, Anaïs Angelo
147. *East Africa after Liberation: Conflict, Security and the State since the 1980s*, Jonathan Fisher
148. *Sultan, Caliph, and the Renewer of the Faith: Ahmad Lobbo, the Tārīkh al-fattāsh and the Making of an Islamic State in West Africa*, Mauro Nobili
149. *Shaping the African Savannah: From Capitalist Frontier to Arid Eden in Namibia*, Michael Bollig
150. *France's Wars in Chad: Military Intervention and Decolonization in Africa*, Nathaniel K. Powell
151. *Islam, Ethnicity, and Conflict in Ethiopia: The Bale Insurgency, 1963–1970*, Terje Østebø
152. *The Path to Genocide in Rwanda: Security, Opportunity, and Authority in an Ethnocratic State*, Omar Shahabudin McDoom

CPSIA information can be obtained
at www.ICGtesting.com
Printed in the USA
LVHW011609030821
694401LV00006B/366